MATHEMATICAL MODELING
AND DIGITAL SIMULATION
FOR ENGINEERS AND SCIENTISTS

MATHEMATICAL MODELING AND DIGITAL SIMULATION FOR ENGINEERS AND SCIENTISTS

SECOND EDITION

JON M. SMITH

NASA Headquarters
Washington, DC

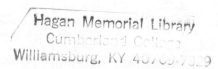
A Wiley-Interscience Publication
JOHN WILEY & SONS
NEW YORK CHICHESTER BRISBANE TORONTO SINGAPORE

Copyright © 1987 by John Wiley & Sons, Inc.

All rights reserved. Published simultaneously in Canada.

Library of Congress Cataloging in Publication Data

Smith, Jon M., 1938–
    Mathematical modeling and digital simulation for engineers and scientists.

    "A Wiley-Interscience publication."
    Bibliography: p.
    Includes index.
    1. Digital computer simulation.   2. Mathematical models.   3. Numerical analysis—Data processing.
    I. Title.
    QA76.9.C65S64   1987   001.4'24   86-24744
    ISBN 0-471-08599-5

Printed in the United States of America

10 9 8 7 6 5 4 3 2

To My Parents

MAURICE ALVIN SMITH
DOLORES ELIZABETH SMITH

And To My Sons

MICHAEL SMITH
CHRISTOPHER SMITH

PREFACE

It was gratifying to find the first edition well received here in the United States, as well as in other countries. My thanks to the many of you who wrote to me suggesting improvements on the book. I have included many of them in this, the second edition of *Mathematical Modeling and Digital Simulation for Engineers and Scientists*.

In this edition, you will find two new sections, Part IV, dedicated to the use of modern numerical methods for generating chaos and simulating random processes on a digital computer, and Part V, dealing with simulator verification.

Particular attention should be given to the new material on order in chaos. In 1975, M. J. Feigenbaum made a breakthrough in mathematically modeling transitions from purely ordered mathematical processes to chaotic mathematical processes. A part of his breakthrough was the discovery of new universal mathematical constants which were later found in physical, chemical, and biological phenomena. In the decade since Feigenbaum's discovery, considerable work has been done in advancing our understanding that some of what appears to be random phenomena is actually ordered phenomena in transition to a mathematically understandable state of chaos. What's covered in Part IV are the basics of these developments.

Since the first edition of this book, great strides have been made in the field of personal computers. Many have the capability of implementing the advanced numerical methods developed in this book. Interestingly, though these computers are state of the art in electronics, some of their software employs numerical methods developed in the 17th and 18th centuries. Many of these numerical methods are inefficient by 1987 standards. Much work needs to be done in improving the modern personal computers' scientific software, so I have added material for the math modelers and simulation engineers who use the personal computer. Hopefully this material will prove to be a stimulus for further developments in personal computer software for scientific analysis.

Additionally, new material has been added in various places throughout the text that serves to better explain the development and application of numerical methods developed in both the time and frequency domains.

The material in Part V is not a traditional view of simulator verification, and for that I ask your indulgence for letting me expound on a subject I feel is subtle, often difficult, and very important. The material is not easily quantified, so the presentation is more qualitative and thought provoking than mathematically crisp. The methods discussed in Part V have been used by the author at various times in various ways to solve simulator development problems when other methods failed. I have not seen them published or discussed before, and it is my hope that they will be helpful references when you encounter problems with traditional simulator verification methods.

A number of examples are developed in this book using the BASIC programming language. Certain reviewers of the manuscript recommended using more traditional simulation language, such as CSMP, ACSL, SLAM, and so forth. In my experience, these languages are fairly well known in the United States, but not abroad. For this reason, and because I want to reach the broadest technical audience in America, including controls and communications engineers, many of whom are unfamiliar with the simulation language, I have chosen to stay with BASIC, a simple computer language used and understood worldwide. Translations to any of the more sophisticated languages is straightforward and easy.

My thanks to Lorraine Walton, my friend and colleague, who managed the preparation of this, the second edition of *Mathematical Modeling and Digital Simulation for Engineers and Scientists*.

JON M. SMITH

Lake of the Woods, Virginia
March 1987

PREFACE TO THE FIRST EDITION

This book is about **fast** numerical methods for simulation.

Numerical methods, once discovered, do not change much with time. So, why should we have another book on this age-old subject? The answer is this. Shannon showed that there are limits to the information that can be gained about a continuous process from a finite number of samples of its motion. In the digital simulation of continuous systems we are particularly concerned with using numerical methods that give us high-fidelity information about the system being simulated. We shall discuss numerical methods that accurately simulate the motion of continuous systems or processes with the fewest sampled values and the least number of calculations. Interestingly, there are not many classical numerical methods that are both accurate and efficient. In fact the earliest numerical methods covered in this book (except for the classical methods discussed for completeness) date back only to 1959. Most of the methods for simulating nonlinear processes were developed in the early and mid 1970s. These modern numerical methods lead to efficient or **fast** algorithms for digital simulation that:

- Can cut batch processing simulation costs.
- Are excellent for high-fidelity real-time simulation or control.
- Are intrinsically stable; cannot be made to go unstable.
- Are highly accurate; exact for transient responses.
- Have global stability characteristics that match those of the system being simulated; ideal for design-type simulations.
- Lead to numerical integrators that can be "tuned" to the system of equations they are trying to solve.
- Lead to new numerical methods for which there are no classical counterparts.
- Are ideal for personal computers (PCs) when the objective is to get the greatest amount of information per line of code.

This book is also about techniques for the mathematical modeling of continuous and discrete systems. Based on numerous seminars and lectures about modern numerical methods given throughout the United States, I have found it useful (if not essential) to conduct an in-depth review of the concepts in continuous and discrete system mathematical modeling. The beginner will benefit by learning the highlights of mathematical modeling and the mathematical language of simulation. He or she can then pursue the details of mathematical modeling in other books. The experienced engineer will find the book to be a quick way to a common mathematical language for more advanced discussions. For all it will help bring into focus the need to maintain a tie between the physics of the process being studied and the equations being solved in the digital computer. Without the "physical feel" for the process being simulated and an understanding of how the physics of the process shows up in the mathematical model, it is difficult effectively to design and use a digital simulation.

This book is written for engineers and scientists involved in mathematically modeling a dynamic process and then simulating the process on a digital computer. The numerical methods covered here are based on sampled-data and discrete system technology. They are developed from both time-domain and frequency-domain viewpoints, the underlying idea being that mathematical models and computing algorithms based on both time-domain and frequency-domain considerations are better than those based on either one alone. Few classical methods are redeveloped here except when it is advantageous to show the relationship between the modern and classical viewpoints or when classical methods are useful for solving modern problems.

Each technique presented includes:

1. Consistent and thorough treatment of the modeling mathematics.
2. Discussion of each method's application on large digital computers, the minicomputer, and the microcomputer.
3. A description of the advantages and limitations of each method.
4. A tabulation of useful formulas for application to commonly encountered simulation problems.

The emphasis throughout is on applying these methods so as to be directly useful to engineers, scientists, and programmers involved in digital simulation.

The application of classical numerical methods (particularly useful in digital simulation) is also described in detail; their development, however, is left to the many other books where they are fully covered. Some classical methods are presented for a complete documentation of useful simulation techniques.

This book is based on the premise that a digital simulation is, in itself, a discrete dynamic system. It can be filtered, tuned, stabilized, controlled, analyzed, and synthesized in the same manner as any discrete system. This viewpoint broadens the scope of **allowed** numerical methods and mathematical modeling techniques for simulation to include not only the classically developed methods but also all of those developed from the sampled-data controls and discrete system viewpoints, on which there is an extensive (though scattered) literature. This viewpoint also leads to the development of new simulation methods that have no classical counterparts.

Because often different elements of a simulation software package are developed by different groups, occasionally at different locations and at different times, the simulation designer should not expect to develop complex simulation without some form of **adjustable software**. A common practice in complex control system design is to add trimming devices, such as trim-pots, to permit fine tuning and final adjustment of the control system's gains, **after** the system has been designed. This book emphasizes the development of numerical methods that can be adapted, adjusted, or tuned once the simulation is in operation.

More emphasis is placed on subjects of interest to the practitioner than those of interest to the theorist. Although the treatment of the material is mathematical, I have not striven for succinctness or rigor beyond that required for practical simulation design.

In part the intention is to interest the reader in mathematical modeling from the discrete system viewpoint. There is much work yet to be done in developing simulation methods from the sampled-data viewpoint. For this reason the book is largely pictorial, numerous simple examples are used in discussing each numerical method, and the practical considerations associated with implementing the methods on a computer are discussed in detail. The limitations of each method are also discussed. There is no universal method to solve every problem. A user must pick and choose based on the advantages and disadvantages of particular methods.

The book has nine chapters, some containing many sections. The intent in organizing the book by sections is to avoid overgeneralization in the treatment of mathematical modeling, which is as much an art as it is a science.

The book is divided into four parts. Part I acquaints (or reacquaints) the reader with mathematical modeling concepts, techniques, and notation used throughout the book. Part II deals with linear system simulation techniques. Part III covers nonlinear system simulation techniques. Part IV discusses a technique for fast function evaluation which, although well known to the experienced numerical analyst, may be new to the beginner if my seminar experience is an indicator. It is included for completeness and because it gives useful information (it is not a new development).

Part I, "Mathematical Modeling Preliminaries," includes two chapters that cover the mathematical properties of continuous and discrete processes. Those familiar with these topics may proceed directly to Part II.

Part II, "Numerical Methods for Simulating Linear Systems on a Digital Computer," includes three chapters describing methods for solving systems of equations that model continuous linear systems. Both real-time and scaled-time (batch processing) applications of each method are considered. Special methods for minicomputers and microcomputers are presented, and tables of commonly used difference equations to simulate discrete processes are provided.

Part III, "Numerical Methods for Simulating Nonlinear Systems on a Digital Computer," includes three chapters dealing with numerically integrating systems of nonlinear equations and difference equation methods for simulating nonlinear systems.

Part IV, "Fast Simulation Techniques," is a single chapter on the use of nested parenthetical forms, Chebyshev polynomials, and rational polynomial expansions as a means of quickly and accurately evaluating complicated mathematical expressions.

This book is the outgrowth of 10 years of research in simulating continuous systems on a digital computer, 15 years of system simulation on analog and digital computers, and 26 seminars on modern numerical methods based on sampled-data techniques. I am indebted to my associates at the Boeing Company, McDonnell Douglas Astronautics Company—Houston Operations, the Lockheed Space & Missiles Division of the Lockheed Company, M.I.T., the University of Florida, Bell Laboratories, and the Charles Sark Draper Laboratories. In particular, I express my thanks to two good friends, Dr. Richard Hamming and Dr. Jerrold Rosenbaum, for their help and improvements to the manuscript.

My special appreciation to "Hawkeye" Jack Van Wye who helped with the proofreading.

And finally my thanks go again to Florence Piaget who typed and managed the preparation of the manuscript for this book.

JON M. SMITH

St. Louis, Missouri
November 1976

CONTENTS

Mathematical models for digital simulation that are based on both time-domain and frequency-domain considerations are better than mathematical models based on either one alone.

PART I

MATHEMATICAL MODELING PRELIMINARIES

INTRODUCTION

A block diagram of the simulation design process is shown in Figure I-1, and the process is illustrated in Figure I-2. The inputs to the design process are the system to be simulated and the outputs are the system simulation. Although the four steps involved in simulation design are shown in series, they are actually interrelated tasks. The first step in the preparation of a simulation is the preparation of a **mathematical model of the system**. This involves the selection of the mathematical model format. In this book systems are usually modeled with block diagrams or systems of equations and other mathematical algorithms. The second step in the design process is to prepare a **mathematical model for the simulation**. The latter is usually in the form of a discrete system block diagram or a system of discrete equations. When properly completed this task results in two outputs, a simulation math flow and a complete discrete system block diagram. The discrete system block diagram will usually be identical to the continuous system block diagram from the standpoint of signal flow. The operators will be discrete versions of their continuous system counterparts. In general the discrete system block diagram will be analogous to the continuous system block diagram in some way. The methods presented in this book all deal with a synthesis of discrete systems that are analogous to the system being simulated, whether it be continuous, discrete, or both.

The third step is to **write the computer program** to implement the simulation math flow. This very crucial step involves strict adherence to the timing assumptions made in the synthesis of the simulation mathematical model. This is particularly true in real-time simulations where $\frac{1}{20}$-second sample periods are common and a one-sample-period delay in closing the feedback loop can result in as much as 16 degrees of phase shift for a 1-hertz system. Based on the author's consulting experience, the most common source of simulation problem occurs in going from task 2 to task 3.

An important step in task 2 is the preparation of the simulation requirements. These are usually based on an analysis of the system mathematical

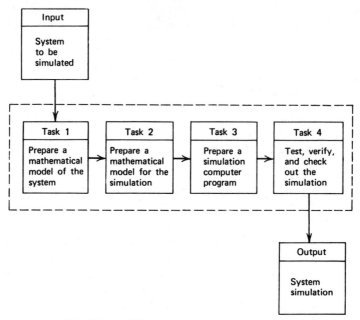

FIGURE I-1. The simulation design process.

model developed in task 1. Again, it is the author's experience that only infrequently are simulation requirements prepared and verification plans identified early in task 2. This step is essential for proceeding to step 4, **the verification and checkout of the simulation**. Only when the simulation designer has identified the simulation requirements and the test and verification plan for determining that these requirements are met will the simulation engineer be able to check out the simulation and proceed confidently with the operational phase. Simulator verification can be as much an art as a science. Searching for errors introduced in tasks 1 through 3 sounds easy—it is not. Gross errors in subsystem simulation are often easy to find, but the subtle interactions among error sources and the integrated simulation itself can often be difficult to detect and correct. For this reason, a chapter on simulator verification has been added to this edition of the book.

It is worth mentioning here that, while no one will argue the need for high-fidelity/high-confidence simulations, often the expedient development of a quick-look type of simulation is also required. This has led to an interesting trend to bypass tasks 1 and 2 and model the system to be simulated directly in computer program language. Confidence in a simulation developed in this manner is attributed to the confidence in the

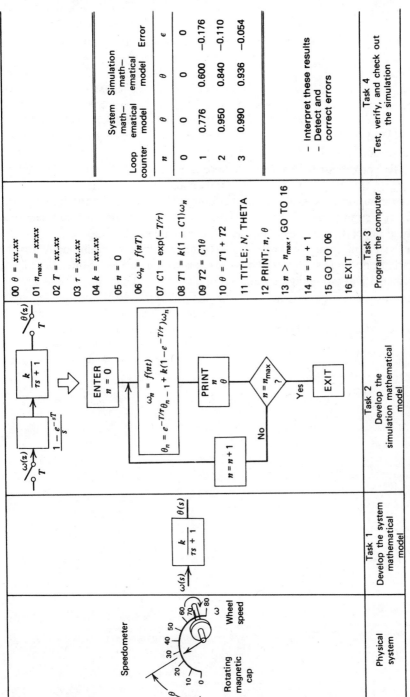

FIGURE I-2. Example of the simulation design process.

5

numerical methods embedded in the simulation language or in the numerical methods used in the computer program. For this reason and because all of the numerical methods presented in this book can be used explicitly in digital simulation design or implicitly through simulation language embedding, the advantages and limitations of each method discussed are examined in detail. Also for this reason the examples have been carefully selected to develop confidence in the proper application of each method. **Any method can be misused!** The author believes that whatever method is employed in simulation, the simulation designer should have some reason to feel that use of the method is justified.

This book deals primarily with steps 2, 3, and 4 of the simulation design process: the preparation of the mathematical model for the simulation, programming the simulation on the computer, and verifying and checking out the simulation. Since preparation of the simulation mathematical model depends so strongly on the system mathematical model and because the system mathematical model is used to identify the requirements for the simulation, the first part of the book deals with a survey of the methods for mathematical modeling and analyzing physical systems. The characteristics of continuous and discrete processes are examined from the standpoint of establishing simulation design requirements in both the time and frequency domains through analyzing both the system and its simulation.

CHAPTER 1

THE MATHEMATICAL MODELING OF CONTINUOUS PROCESSES

System simulation often results from the following:

1. The need to conduct a low-cost study or design of a system whose complex nature precludes development in a laboratory experiment or as a scale model.

2. The need to verify that a system of mathematical modeling equations which are to be used in a control system is valid.

3. The need to forecast the response of a system to complex controls or policies as a means of evaluating the consequences of control or policy alternatives.

It is assumed that the mathematical modeling equations used to represent a continuous process will simulate a system being studied in much the same way as in a laboratory model simulation. When properly derived the mathematical model will reflect (within certain limits) the characteristics of the physical process being analyzed. The limits of the mathematical model are determined completely by the assumptions used in its derivation. A poor set of assumptions can, and usually does, lead to erroneous conclusions being drawn from the simulation. It has long been recommended that the simulation designer prepare a complete and well-defined list of assumptions on which the simulation is to be built and then analytically determine that the assumptions are well founded. It is one thing to assume that a system has no *backlash, dead zones,* or *preloads,** but it is another thing to express this precisely and provide supporting documentation.

There are a great number of methods for developing systems of equations to describe continuous physical processes. In the field of mechanics, Newton's laws and force relationships in conjunction with free-body

*Nonlinearities that are found in many systems; they are defined later in this chapter.

7

diagrams lead to systems of simultaneous second-order differential equations to describe a system's dynamics. Similarly, Lagrange's equations and the Lagrangian energy concept result in systems of second-order simultaneous equations to describe the dynamics of mechanical systems. If the Newtonian and Lagrangian formulations use the same coordinates, the same equations result. A little-used technique in classical mechanics for deriving simulation equations of motion is Hamilton's method, where the Hamiltonian-defined energy relations and Hamilton's equations are used to derive a system of first-order differential equations in generalized coordinates and generalized momentums that also describe the dynamics of mechanical systems. Perhaps the reason that the Hamiltonian formulation of mechanics is not widely used to simulate mechanical systems is its use of generalized momentum, a concept that is often difficult to interpret in terms of the Newtonian formulation of dynamics of mechanical systems.

Schrödinger's method provides mathematical prescriptions for deriving a system of differential equations to describe quantum-mechanical dynamics and phenomena. In a sense, then, Newton's laws, Lagrange's equations, Hamilton's equations, and Schrödinger's method are all methods for deriving mathematical models of mechanical systems. Although it is true that physical laws result in equations that are mathematical models of the dynamics of the physical processes, it is not true that all mathematical models result directly from physical laws. Many systems today are modeled through laboratory experimentation. For example, this type of modeling can involve system identification through frequency- or time-domain experiments and measurements. In fact, many of today's systems are so complex (e.g., with cross-coupling, internal nonlinearities, unobserved states) that the technology of parameter (or system) identification has become important for precise large-scale system modeling and for empirical systems analysis.

This book begins, then, with the assumption that the differential equations describing the dynamics of the continuous process are already developed. This chapter covers the classification and properties of differential equations, their transformation among various domains, their properties in each domain, and the graphical and schematic representations of the systems that permit further visualization and insight into the dynamic systems they model. Both linear and nonlinear differential equations and their block diagrams will be discussed, as well as stationary and nonstationary linear systems. Fourier and Laplace transform analysis will be used to investigate the characteristics of continuous processes from both the forcing function and the system description viewpoints. Spectral, stability, and steady-state characteristics of linear stationary systems will be reviewed. Linear and nonlinear vector-matrix (state vector) *equations* and their block diagram representations of continuous processes are also covered.

In view of the condensed nature of the topics covered in Part I, emphasis is placed on reestablishing familiarity with the basic concepts, definitions, and notations. Care has been taken to address only the topics of interest to the simulation designer. The beginner should find the mathematical developments and concepts covered here immediately useful in the design and development of simulations as well as for understanding the dynamics of systems.

1.1   LINEAR SYSTEMS

Modeling linear systems is important primarily for four reasons:

1. Engineering systems and their simulations are often linear, at least within certain bounds.

2. Exact solutions of linear systems of equations can easily be found.

3. There are special high-fidelity methods for simulating linear systems.

4. Linear systems can often give a *feel* for perturbations in nonlinear systems.

Analytical methods for solving nonlinear systems of equations are the exception rather than the rule. Even when solutions can be determined, approximations are often necessary. The approximation methods are frequently peculiar to the situation being evaluated and require careful consideration to avoid overgeneralization.

In the first part of this chapter we direct our attention to the linear systems because their mathematical models are more analytically tractable than are those of the nonlinear systems.

Throughout this book we will be interested in determining the response of the system to a given forcing function. Suppose that a forcing function $f_1(t)$, which varies with time, produces a response $r_1(t)$ and that the second forcing function $f_2(t)$ produces a second response $r_2(t)$. Then we may write

$$f_1(t) \rightarrow r_1(t)$$

$$f_2(t) \rightarrow r_2(t)$$

For a linear system:

$$f_1(t) + f_2(t) \rightarrow r_1(t) + r_2(t) \tag{1-1}$$

Equation 1-1 describes the superposition principle: the superposition of individual forcing functions results in a response that is the superposition of the individual responses. A necessary condition for a system to be linear is that the principle of superposition apply to its motion.

Corollaries to the superposition principle are:

1. No forcing function affects the responses of other forcing functions.

2. There is no interaction among the responses caused by different forcing functions.

3. The combined effect of a number of forcing functions on a linear system can be determined by separately determining the response of the system to each individual forcing function and then combining or superimposing the responses to determine the overall system response to the combined forcing functions.

Another corollary of the superposition principle is that if n identical forcing functions drive a linear system at the same place, then

$$nf(t) \rightarrow nr(t) \qquad (1\text{-}2)$$

From (1-2) we see that linear systems preserve the forcing function scale factor (n) in the transition from input to output. This property of linear systems is referred to as the principle of homogeneity.

While it is true that these relations hold for linear systems, it is not true that either (1-1) or (1-2) specifies a linear system. **A system is linear if, and only if, both (1-1) and (1-2) are satisfied.** A well-known example of a nonlinear system where the principle of superposition holds but the property of homogeneity does not is shown in Figure 1-1.

A linear stationary system is further characterized by its response to a periodic forcing function. If a periodic forcing function with frequency F is applied to a stationary linear system, the steady-state response of the system will also be periodic with frequency F. In short, the response of a stationary linear system has the same *spectral components* as its forcing function. Thus a linear system is said to be stationary, if

$$f(t - T) \rightarrow r(t - T) \qquad (1\text{-}3)$$

where T is an arbitrary time delay.

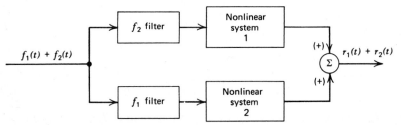

FIGURE 1-1. A simple nonlinear system that satisfies the superposition principle but not the homogeneity principle.

1.2   MODELING LINEAR SYSTEMS

Linear systems are those whose dynamics are modeled with linear equations. These may be linear algebraic equations, linear differential equations, linear difference equations, or a combination of them. Consider the differential equation

$$a_2 \frac{d^2r}{dt^2} + a_1 \frac{dr}{dt} + a_0 = f(t) \qquad (1\text{-}4)$$

where t is the independent variable, f is the forcing function, and r is the response function. The coefficients a_0, a_1, and a_2 are system parameters. The coefficients may or may not be time varying; they are usually determined entirely by the number and type of elements in the system. Equation 1-4 is an ordinary differential equation of the second order because it involves no partial derivatives and because the highest order of ordinary derivative is 2. Equation 1-4 is also a linear equation:

1. Neither the dependent variable r nor any of its derivatives are raised to a power other than 1.

2. None of its terms contains a product of two or more derivatives of the same dependent variable or a product of the dependent variable and one of its derivatives.

That the superposition principle applies can be seen as follows:

$$a_2 \frac{d^2r_1}{dt^2} + a_1 \frac{dr_1}{dt} + a_0 r_1 = f_1$$

$$a_2 \frac{d^2r_2}{dt^2} + a_1 \frac{dr_2}{dt} + a_0 r_2 = f_2$$

Adding, we see that the superposition principle holds:

$$a_2 \frac{d^2}{dt^2}(r_1 + r_2) + a_1 \frac{d}{dt}(r_1 + r_2) + a_0(r_1 + r_2) = (f_1 + f_2)$$

Furthermore, we see that the principle of superposition applies for either stationary or nonstationary forms of (1-4). In general superposition applies to both stationary and nonstationary linear equations.

An ordinary linear differential equation of order n may be written as

$$a_n(t) \frac{d^n}{dt^n}(r) + a_{n-1}(t) \frac{d^{n-1}}{dt^{n-1}}(r) + \cdots + a_0(t)r(t) = f(t) \quad (1\text{-}5)$$

where the coefficients and forcing functions are given functions of the independent variable t. This equation is said to be homogeneous if the forcing function equals zero and inhomogeneous if the forcing function is not zero. We can write (1-5) in the form

$$L(r) = f \qquad (1\text{-}6)$$

if we define

$$L = a_n(t) \frac{d^n}{dt^n} + a_{n-1}(t) \frac{d^{n-1}}{dt^{n-1}} + \cdots + a_0(t) \qquad (1\text{-}7)$$

where L can be regarded as an operator, operating on the dependent variable r. Using (1-6) we can derive the general properties of linear differential equations as follows:

1. Multiplying the dependent variable r by a constant multiplies each term of the equation by the same constant:

$$L(Kr) = KL(r) \qquad (1\text{-}8)$$

If $L(r) = 0$ (homogeneous case)

$$L(Kr) = 0 \qquad (1\text{-}9)$$

It follows then that if $r(t)$ is a solution of the homogeneous equation $L(r) = 0$, so is $Kr(t)$.

2. Replacing r by $r_1 + r_2$, where r_1 and r_2 are linearly independent, replaces each term by the sum of two similar terms, one in r_1 and the other in r_2. We see that

$$L(r_1 + r_2) = L(r_1) + L(r_2) \qquad (1\text{-}10)$$

and

$$L(r_1 + r_2) = 0 \qquad \text{only if} \quad L(r_1) = L(r_2) = 0. \qquad (1\text{-}11)$$

Relations (1-10) and (1-11) state that if r_1 and r_2 are solutions of the homogeneous equation $L(r) = 0$, then so also is $r_1 + r_2$.

From properties 1 and 2 above we can see that, if $r_1(t), r_2(t), \ldots, r_n(t)$ are linearly independent solutions of the homogeneous linear differential equation, $L(r) = 0$, then so also is the linear combination of them, $c_1 r_1 + c_2 r_2 + c_3 r_3 + \cdots + c_n r_n$, when the c's are arbitrary constants.

3. The solution $r_c = c_1 r_1 + c_2 r_2 + \cdots + c_n r_n$ with n arbitrary constants is a general solution of the homogeneous equation, provided that the n individual solutions $r_1, r_2, \ldots, r_n$ are linearly independent. Conversely a set of solutions is said to be linearly independent if none of them can be expressed as linear combinations of the others. The general solution of the homogeneous equation is usually called the complementary function.

4. If r_p is a particular solution of the inhomogeneous equation such that $L(r_p) = f(t)$, the sum of this particular solution and the complementary function is the complete solution of the inhomogeneous linear differential equation. In general any solution of (1-4) can be written as a combination of the complementary function and a particular solution (sometimes called particular integral) as

$$r(t) = r_c(t) + r_p(t) \tag{1-12}$$

This can be seen by noting that if $r(t)$ is a solution to (1-4), and if r_p is a particular solution to (1-4), then

$$L(r - r_p) = L(r) - L(r_p) = f(t) - f(t) = 0$$

Hence $r - r_p = r_c$ is a solution of the homogeneous equation which, by property c, must be expressible as

$$r - r_p = c_1 r_1 + c_2 r_2 + \cdots + c_n r_n$$

Taking the particular solution to the right side of this equation we obtain the desired solution.

5. The determination of the numerical values of the n arbitrary constants in the complete solution requires a knowledge of n values of the response or its derivatives. This will give n equations for determining the n unknown coefficients. Note that the values of the response or its derivatives need not be known at the same time.

1.3   SOLVING LINEAR DIFFERENTIAL EQUATIONS

It is essential to the numerical methods developed in this book that we be able to solve both stationary and nonstationary linear differential equations. This section reviews the more familiar classical methods for solving linear ordinary differential equations. These methods do not involve transformations of functions and operations. Although the equations are not in vector-matrix notation, the methods of solution are applicable to solving matrix differential equations. Also, while the Laplace transformation method for solving linear differential equations is simpler in many situations and more convenient than the classical methods, there are definite limitations to the applicability of the transform-type methods. The Laplace transformation method cannot, for example, conveniently solve linear differential equations with variable coefficients. In this case the classical approach can yield solutions to many nonstationary equations of practical importance.

It is important to refresh our understanding of classical methods for solving differential equations, as they are convenient methods for solving nonlinear differential equations. In real-world systems the Laplace transform method, even when applicable, becomes cumbersome where the known conditions of the problem are specified at times (or values of the independent variable) other than at zero. This is true even for linear differential equations with constant coefficients. The application of classical methods is not modified by the way in which the known conditions are specified.

We begin by examining a simple first-order process. A general linear differential equation of the first order can be written in the following form:

$$\frac{dr}{dt} + a(t)r = f(t) \tag{1-13}$$

This equation is solved by noting that the form of the two terms at the left side of (1-13) suggests that they are the derivative of a product containing r as a factor such as (ru), where u is an unknown function of t. That is,

$$\frac{d}{dt}(ru) = u\frac{dr}{dt} + r\frac{du}{dt} \tag{1-14}$$

Comparing (1-13) and (1-14), we see that by multiplying both sides of (1-13) by the unknown function $u(t)$ we get

$$u\frac{dr}{dt} + ua(t)r = uf(t) \tag{1-15}$$

For the left side of (1-15) to be an exact derivative of the product (ru) requires that

$$\frac{du}{dt} = ua(t)$$

$$\therefore \int \frac{du}{u} = \int a(t)\,dt$$

Integrating we find

$$\ln u = \int a(t)\,dt$$

Thus

$$u = e^{\int a(t)\,dt} \tag{1-16}$$

Since the coefficient a is a given function of time, u can be found from (1-16). Substituting u back into (1-4) we can write

$$\frac{d}{dt}\left(re^{\int a(t)\,dt}\right) = f(t)e^{\int a(t)\,dt}$$

Then

$$r = e^{-\int a(t)\,dt}\left[\int f(t)e^{\int a(t)\,dt}\,dt + C\right] \tag{1-17}$$

Notice the term in the brackets is a convolution-type term. We shall encounter the convolution integral again in the section on Laplace transformations.

The solution shown in (1-17) is the required solution for (1-13). Take note of the form of (1-17). It will appear again in a more generalized form for the solution of linear matrix differential equations. The solution to the general first-order linear differential equations is of particular importance because there are no general formulas available for the solution of such equations of an order other than 1. It is partly because of this that ordinary linear differential equations in vector-matrix notation are written in first-order form. Because of this lack of general solutions of high-order linear differential equations, the remainder of this chapter is devoted to certain useful methods for solving high-order stationary linear differential equations. Again the emphasis is on classical methods for solving differential equations because they are often more familiar and convenient to use than are the transform methods.

Examples of the classical methods for studying continuous systems are given below. Consider the linear process,

$$\dot{x} + kx = f(t)$$

We know from (1-17) that generally

$$x = e^{-\int_0^t k\,d\tau}\left(\int_0^t f(\tau)e^{\int_0^t k\,d\tau}\,d\tau + C\right)$$

Example 1

When k is constant and $f(t) = 0$

$$x = Ce^{-kt}$$

When $t = 0$, $x = x_0$

$$\therefore \quad x = x_0 e^{-kt}$$

Example 2

When k is positive constant and $f(t) = A$ (a constant)

$$x = Ce^{-kt} + Ae^{-kt} \int_0^t e^{k\tau} \, d\tau$$

$$= Ce^{-kt} + \frac{Ae^{-kt}}{k} (e^{k\tau}) \Big|_0^t$$

$$= Ce^{-kt} + \frac{Ae^{-kt}}{k} (e^{kt} - 1)$$

$$= Ce^{-kt} + \frac{A}{k} (1 - e^{-kt})$$

When $t = 0$, $x = x_0$

$$\therefore \qquad x_0 = C$$

And finally we have

$$x = x_0 e^{-kt} + \frac{A}{k} (1 - e^{-kt})$$

Note that

$$\lim_{t \to \infty} (x) = \frac{A}{k}, \qquad \text{for} \quad k > 0$$

This can also be seen from the differential equation itself:

$$\dot{x} + kx = A$$

In the steady state, $\dot{x} = 0$, by definition of steady state (an equilibrium state of x); thus

$$x = \frac{A}{k}$$

Example 3

When k is constant, $f(t) = t$ and $x_0 = 0$

$$x = e^{-kt} \int_0^t \tau e^{k\tau} \, d\tau$$

$$x = \frac{e^{-kt}}{k} \int_0^t k\tau e^{k\tau} \, d\tau$$

Integrating by parts we see that

$$x = \frac{e^{-kt}}{k} \left[\int_0^t d(\tau e^{k\tau}) - \frac{1}{k} \int_0^t k e^{k\tau} \, d\tau \right]$$

$$= \frac{e^{-kt}}{k} \left[(\tau e^{k\tau})\Big|_0^t - \left(\frac{e^{k\tau}}{k} \right)\Big|_0^t \right]$$

$$= \frac{e^{-kt}}{k} \left(t e^{kt} - \frac{1}{k} e^{kt} + \frac{1}{k} \right)$$

$$= \frac{t}{k} - \frac{1}{k^2} + \frac{e^{-kt}}{k^2}$$

For large t,

$$x \approx \frac{1}{k} \left(t - \frac{1}{k} \right), \qquad \text{when} \quad k > 0$$

Thus when a first-order stationary process is driven by a ramp, and after an exponentially decaying transient, the system's output x is also a ramp but delayed an amount $1/k$.

Example 4

When $k(t) = k_0 t$, where k_0 is a constant and $f(t) = 0$

$$x = Ce^{-\int_0^t k_0\tau \, d\tau}$$

$$x = Ce^{-k_0 t^2/2}$$

Note that when $t = 0$, $x = X_0$. Thus

$$x = X_0 e^{-k_0 t^2/2}$$

Example 5

When $k(t) = k_0 t$ and $f(t) = A_0 t$, where k_0 and A_0 are constants and k_0 is positive,

$$x = X_0 e^{-k_0 t^2/2} + e^{-k_0 t^2/2} \int_0^t A_0 \tau e^{k_0 \tau^2/2} \, d\tau$$

$$x = X_0 e^{-k_0 t^2/2} + \frac{e^{-k_0 t^2/2}}{k_0} \int_0^t A_0 \tau e^{k_0 \tau^2/2} k_0 \, d\tau$$

$$x = X_0 e^{-k_0 t^2/2} + \frac{A_0}{k_0} e^{-k_0 t^2/2} \left[\left(e^{k_0 \tau^2/2} \right) \Big|_0^t \right]$$

$$x = X_0 e^{-k_0 t^2/2} + \frac{A_0}{k_0} \left(1 - e^{-k_0 t^2/2} \right)$$

Note that

$$\lim_{t \to \infty} (x) = \frac{A_0}{k_0}, \qquad \text{for} \quad k_0 > 0$$

Example 6

When $k(t) = \omega \tan(\omega t)$ and $f(t) = 0$

$$x = C e^{-\int_0^t \omega \tan(\omega \tau) \, d\tau}$$

$$x = C e^{\ln \cos(\omega t)}$$

$$x = C \cos(\omega t)$$

When $t = 0$, $x = X_0$

$$\therefore \quad x = X_0 \cos(\omega t)$$

This interesting result shows that an oscillatory response need not necessarily be associated with second-order stationary linear systems. In fact first-order nonstationary differential equations can be developed whose solution would be any function it is desired to generate by simply noting that when $f(t) = 0$

$$k(t) = \frac{-\dot{x}(t)}{x(t)}$$

Here $k(t)$ is termed the generator. For example if we wish to generate

$$x = X_0 e^{-at}$$

where a is a constant, we let

$$k = a$$

If we want to generate the Gaussian distribution function

$$x = X_0 e^{-at^2}, \qquad \text{for} \quad a > 0$$

then we let

$$k(t) = 2at$$

Other generators are shown in Table 1-1.

Table 1-1. Generators for Certain Often-Used Functions, with $\dot{x} + k(t)x = 0$

$x(t)$	$k(t)$
$X_0 e^{\mp at}$	$\pm a$
$X_0 e^{\mp at^2}$	$\pm 2at$
$X_0 e^{\mp at^n}$	$\pm nat^{n-1}$
$X_0 \sin(\omega t)$	$-\omega \cotan(\omega t)$
$X_0 \cos(\omega t)$	$\omega \tan(\omega t)$
$X_0 t^{\pm n}$	$\mp nt^{-1}$
$X_0 t e^{\mp at}$	$(\pm a - t^{-1})$

Finally we can transform an input function $f(t)$ into another function $g(t)$ using the generator

$$k(t) = \frac{f(t) - \dot{g}(t)}{g(t)}$$

For example if we want $g(t) = \sin(\omega t)$ when $f(t) = \sin(\omega t)$ we require

$$k(t) = \frac{\sin(\omega t) - \cos(\omega t)}{\sin(\omega t)} = 1 - \cotan(\omega t)$$

Another example is to have $g(t) = U(t)^*$ when $f(t) = \sin(\omega t)$. Then we would require (for $t \geqslant 0$)

$$k(t) = \frac{\sin(\omega t) - \delta(t)}{u(t)} = \sin(\omega t)$$

There are of course practical difficulties with this type of function generation when the desired output is oscillatory because $k(t)$ has $g(t)$ in the denominator which results in $k(t)$ not being defined at the zeros of $g(t)$.

1.4 CLASSICAL METHODS FOR SOLVING HIGH-ORDER STATIONARY LINEAR DIFFERENTIAL EQUATIONS

Since there are no general formulas for the solution of linear differential equations (whether stationary or not) of order greater than 1, we are unable to extend the general method of the preceding section to equations of higher order. In this section we make maximum use of operational methods (other than the transformation methods) for solving linear differential equations. Thus let D denote the differentiation operation with respect to t (the independent variable). Then

$$D \stackrel{\Delta}{=} \frac{d}{dt}$$

It follows that

$$D^n(r) = \frac{d^n}{dt^n}(r) \tag{1-18}$$

The D operator satisfies the following laws:

$$(D^m + D^n)r(t) = D^m r(t) + D^n r(t) \tag{1-19}$$

$$\left[(D^m + D^n) + D^l\right]r(t) = \left[D^m + (D^n + D^l)\right]r(t) \tag{1-20}$$

$$(D^m \cdot D^n)r(t) = D^{m+n}r(t) = D^{n+m}r(t) = (D^n \cdot D^m)r(t) \tag{1-21}$$

$$D^m(D^n \cdot D^l)r(t) = (D^m \cdot D^n)D^l r(t) \tag{1-22}$$

$$D^l(D^m + D^n)r(t) = (D^{l+m} + D^{l+n})r(t) \tag{1-23}$$

$^*u(t)$ is the unit step function defined as

$$u(t) = \begin{cases} 0 & \text{for} \quad t < 0 \\ 1 & \text{for} \quad t \geqslant 0 \end{cases}$$

A first-order differential equation such as

$$\frac{dr}{dt} + ar = f(t) \tag{1-24}$$

can be rewritten in operator notation as

$$(D + a)r = f(t) \tag{1-25}$$

Thus

$$r(t) = \left(\frac{1}{D + a} \right) f(t) \tag{1-26}$$

From (1-17) we know that

$$r(t) = e^{-\int a(\tau)\, d\tau} \left\{ \int f(\tau) e^{\int a(\tau)\, d\tau}\, d\tau + C \right\}$$

which for this case where $a(t) = $ constant is

$$r(t) = e^{-at} \left\{ \int f(\tau) e^{a\tau}\, d\tau + C \right\} \tag{1-27}$$

Thus

$$\left(\frac{1}{D + a} \right) f(t) \rightarrow e^{-at} \left\{ \int f(\tau) e^{a\tau}\, d\tau + C \right\} \tag{1-28}$$

It is apparent that when $1/(D + a)$ operates on $f(t)$ it symbolizes the generation of the sum of the complementary and particular solutions.

Consider now the second-order stationary linear differential equation

$$a_2 \frac{d^2r}{dt^2} + a_1 \frac{dr}{dt} + a_0 r = f(t) \tag{1-29}$$

This can be rewritten in D notation as

$$(a_2 D^2 + a_1 D + a_0)r = f(t) \tag{1-30}$$

which can be written in factored form as

$$(D - s_1)(D - s_2)r = f(t) \tag{1-31}$$

where

$$s_1 = \frac{-a_1}{2a_2} + \frac{\left(a_1^2 - 4a_2a_0\right)^{1/2}}{2a_2} \tag{1-32}$$

$$s_2 = \frac{-a_1}{2a_2} - \frac{\left(a_1^2 - 4a_2a_0\right)^{1/2}}{2a_2} \tag{1-33}$$

Note that s_1 and s_2 may be complex. The complementary solution is developed from the equations

$$r_{1_{\text{comp}}} = \left(\frac{1}{D - s_1}\right) f(t)\bigg|_{f(t)=0} = C_1 e^{s_1 t} \tag{1-34}$$

and

$$r_{2_{\text{comp}}} = \left(\frac{1}{D - s_2}\right) f(t)\bigg|_{f(t)=0} = C_2 e^{s_2 t} \tag{1-35}$$

Thus the complementary solution of (1-30) takes the form

$$r_c = r_{1_{\text{comp}}} + r_{2_{\text{comp}}} = C_1 e^{s_1 t} + C_2 e^{s_2 t} \tag{1-36}$$

The particular solution is developed more interestingly. The inhomogeneous equation (1-31) takes the form

$$r_p = \left(\frac{1}{D - s_1}\right)\left(\frac{1}{D - s_2}\right) f(t)$$

or

$$r_p = \left\{\frac{1}{D - s_1}\left[\left(\frac{1}{D - s_2}\right) f(t)\right]\right\} \tag{1-37}$$

From (1-27) we can write

$$\left(\frac{1}{D - s_2}\right) f(t) \rightarrow e^{-s_2 t} \int f(\tau) e^{s_2 \tau} \, d\tau \tag{1-38}$$

Note that C in (1-28) is associated with the complementary solution and thus is zero here. Combining (1-37) and (1-38) we can write,

$$r_p = \frac{1}{D - s_1} \left\{ e^{-s_2 t} \int f(\tau_1) e^{s_2 \tau_1} \, d\tau_1 \right\}$$

$$= e^{s_1 t} \int e^{(s_2 - s_1)\tau_2} \int e^{-s_2 \tau} f(\tau) \, d\tau_1 \, d\tau_2 \qquad (1\text{-}39)$$

The complete solution is the sum of the complementary and particular solutions of (1-29). The complete solution takes the form

$$r = C_1 e^{s_1 t} + C_2 e^{s_2 t} + e^{s_1 t} \int e^{(s_2 - s_1)\tau_2} \int e^{-s_2 \tau} f(\tau) \, d\tau_1 \, d\tau_2 \qquad (1\text{-}40)$$

This procedure can be generalized for use in solving stationary linear differential equations of order n. Consider the general stationary linear system

$$a_n \frac{d^n r}{dt^n} + a_{n-1} \frac{d^{n-1}}{dt^{n-1}} r + \cdots + a_0 r = f(t) \qquad (1\text{-}41)$$

In operator notation (1-41) becomes

$$(a_n D^n + a_{n-1} D^{n-1} + \cdots + a_0) r = f(t) \qquad (1\text{-}42)$$

Then:

1. Write the characteristic equation for the system by replacing each D operator by s in the operator polynomial part of the differential equation and then setting the polynomial to zero.

2. Determine the n roots of this nth-order polynomial in s developed in step 1.

3. If the n roots are unequal, then the complementary solution of (1-41) takes the form

$$r_c = C_1 e^{s_1 t} + C_2 e^{s_2 t} + \cdots + C_n e^{s_n t} \qquad (1\text{-}43)$$

4. The particular solution of (1-41) can be found by the method of successive integrations. It takes the form

$$r_p = e^{s_1 t} \int e^{(s_2 - s_1)\tau} \int e^{(s_3 - s_2)\tau} \cdots \int e^{-s_n \tau} f(\tau) \, d\tau^{n*} \qquad (1\text{-}44)$$

* Symbolic form for $d\tau_1, d\tau_2, d\tau_3 \ldots, d\tau_n$.

5. The general solution of (1-41) is the sum of the complementary solution and the particular integral (solution).

6. The solution must be modified in accordance with Section 1.6 when the characteristic equation has multiple (repeated) roots.

7. If there are terms in the particular solution that duplicate any of the exponential terms in the complementary solution, the general solution must be modified in a manner similar to the modification for multiple roots.

Examples of the operator method of solving stationary linear differential equations follow.

Example 1

Consider the stationary linear process

$$\dot{x} + kx = f(t)$$

Rewriting in operator notation we get

$$(D + k)x = f(t)$$

Replacing D with s and by setting $f(t) = 0$, we can form the characteristic equation

$$s + k = 0$$

This equation has a single root at

$$s_1 = -k$$

Thus the complementary solution for this differential equation is

$$x_C = C_1 e^{s_1 t} = C_1 e^{-kt}$$

As before, when $t = 0$, $x = x_0$ then

$$x_C = x_0 e^{-kt}$$

The particular solution is given by the expression

$$x_p = e^{s_1 t} \int_0^t e^{-s_1 \tau} f(\tau) \, d\tau$$

when $f(t) = 0$, $x_p = 0$.

When $f(t) = A$ (a constant)

$$x_p = e^{-kt} \int_0^t A e^{k\tau} \, d\tau = \frac{A}{k} (1 - e^{-kt})$$

When $f(t) = A_0 t$ where A_0 is a constant,

$$x_p = A_0 e^{-kt} \int_0^t \tau e^{-k\tau} \, d\tau$$

$$x_p = \frac{A_0}{k} \left(t - \frac{1}{k} \right)$$

Example 2

Consider the stationary linear equation

$$\frac{d^2x}{dt^2} + k \frac{dx}{dt} = f(t)$$

In operator notation

$$(D^2 + kD)x = f(t)$$

or

$$[(D + 0)(D + k)]x = f(t)$$

As before the characteristic equation is formed by setting $f(t)$ to zero and D to s. Then

$$(s + 0)(s + k) = 0$$

Thus $s_1 = 0$ and $s_2 = -k$; so

$$x = x_C + x_p = C_1 e^{s_1 t} + C_2 e^{s_2 t} + e^{s_1 t} \int_0^t e^{(s_2 - s_1)\tau} \int_0^t e^{s_2\tau} f(\tau) \, d\tau^2$$

when $f(t) = 0$, $x = C_1 + Ce^{-kt}$. When $f(t) = A$ (a constant),

$$x = C_1 + C_2 e^{-kt} + \frac{A}{k} (1 - e^{-kt})$$

When $f(t) = A_0 t$ (A_0 is constant),

$$x = C_1 + C_2 e^{-kt} + \frac{A}{k^2}(e^{-kt} - 1) + \frac{A}{k}t$$

Example 3

The equation

$$\frac{d^3x}{dt^3} + 3\frac{d^2x}{dt^2} + 4\frac{dx}{dt} + 2x = 0$$

has the characteristic equation

$$s^3 + 3s^2 + 4s + 2 = 0$$

which has the roots

$$s_1 = -1$$

$$s_2 = -1 + j$$

$$s_3 = -1 - j$$

where $j = \sqrt{-1}$. Thus the complementary solution takes the form

$$x = C_1 e^{s_1 t} + C_2 e^{s_2 t} + C_3 e^{s_3 t}$$

$$= C_1 e^{-t} + e^{-t}(C_2 e^{jt} + C_3 e^{-jt})$$

$$= C_1 e^{-t} + e^{-t}\left[(C_2 + C_3)\cos(t) + j(C_2 - C_3)\sin(t)\right]$$

since

$$e^{jt} = \cos(t) + j\sin(t)$$

1.5 THE METHOD OF UNDETERMINED COEFFICIENTS

To develop particular solutions in Section 1.4, we used the method of successive integrations. Another method that is particularly easy and simple to apply is that of undetermined coefficients. It has the advantage that it involves only differentiation; no integrations are required. A limitation is that it does not apply to all types of forcing functions, but it is useful when the forcing function is of the types shown in Table 1-2. For our purposes, this is not as severe a limitation as it might appear at the outset. In deriving difference equations that simulate the response of linear systems to sampled and reconstructed forcing functions, most of the reconstruction processes examined will be made up of these simple functions.

Table 1-2. Particular Solutions to Known Forcing Functions

Form of Forcing Function	Form of Particular Solution
A constant, k	A constant, A
A power of the independent variable, t^n (n integer)	The series $\sum_0^n A_m t^m$
An exponential function, $e^{\gamma t}$	An exponential, $A e^{\gamma t}$
A cosine function, $\cos(\gamma t)$	$A_1 \cos(\gamma t) + A_2 \sin(\gamma t)$
A sine function, $\sin(\gamma t)$	$A_1 \cos(\gamma t) + A_2 \sin(\gamma t)$

The method of undetermined coefficients is simple to apply and leads to straightforward results. For a linear differential equation that has constant coefficients and a forcing function composed of the sum or the product of the functions in Table 1-2, the particular integral or particular solution is the sum or product, respectively, of the solution forms shown in the right-hand column. When this solution is substituted into the differential equation, coefficients on both sides of the equation can be equated to determine the coefficients of a particular solution in terms of the coefficients of the system. Only two modifications are necessary to this simple procedure: (1) when the characteristic equation has a zero root and (2) when the forcing function contains a term that also appears in the complementary solution. When the characteristic equation has a zero root, the assumed form of the particular integral should be *the integral* of the solution shown in Table 1-2. This modification can be extended to include cases where the characteristic equation possesses multiple zero roots. In the latter case, we would apply the method of undetermined coefficients as if a double root for the characteristic equation existed.

1.6 SOLVING SIMULTANEOUS STATIONARY LINEAR DIFFERENTIAL EQUATIONS WITH OPERATOR METHODS

Solutions of simultaneous linear differential equations with constant coefficients that contain one independent variable and several dependent variables are commonplace. The operator methods just discussed are convenient and useful for solving simultaneous equations. The most straightforward approach to solving simultaneous equations is to reduce the given system of equations to one with a single dependent variable. This equation can then be solved with the operator method discussed in Section 1.4. Consider the system of two stationary linear differential equations:

$$h_1(D)x + g_1(D)y = f_1(t)$$

$$h_2(D)x + g_2(D)y = f_2(t)$$

These can be written in terms of a single variable using the following method:

$$g_2(D)\left[h_1(D)x + g_1(D)y\right] = g_2(D)f_1(t)$$

and

$$g_1(D)\left[h_2(D)x + g_2(D)y\right] = g_1(D)f_2(t)$$

Substituting to eliminate y we find

$$\left[g_2(D)h_1(D) - g_1(D)h_2(D)\right]x = g_2(D)f_1(t) - g_1(D)f_2(t)$$

Similarly, had we multiplied both equations by $h_1(D)$ and $h_2(D)$, respectively, we would have found

$$\left[h_1(D)g_2(D) - h_2(D)g_1(D)\right]y = h_2(D)f_1(t) - h_1(D)f_2(t)$$

These equations can now be solved directly by the operator method.

1.7   FREQUENCY-DOMAIN METHODS FOR MODELING CONTINUOUS PROCESSES

Specifying a simulation begins with the determination of the characteristics in both the time and frequency domains of the system to be simulated. Since simulation requirements and simulation design from frequency-domain viewpoint are discussed extensively throughout this book, it is necessary that this section be understood before proceeding.

Fourier Series Expansion of Periodic Functions

Any periodic function $f(\theta)$ can be expanded into a Fourier series if it has a period of $2T$ and satisfies the Dirichlet conditions:

1. It has at most a finite number of discontinuities in one period.
2. It has at most a finite number of finite maxima and minima in one period.
3. The integral $\int_{-\pi}^{+\pi} |f(\theta)|\, d\theta$ is finite.

The Fourier series is

$$f(\theta) = \frac{a_0}{2} + \sum_{n=1}^{\infty} \left[a_n \cos(n\theta) + b_n \sin(n\theta) \right] \qquad (1\text{-}45)$$

where

$$a_n = \frac{1}{\pi} \int_{-\pi}^{\pi} f(\theta) \cos(n\theta)\, d\theta, \qquad \text{for} \quad n = 0, 1, 2, \ldots \qquad (1\text{-}46)$$

$$b_n = \frac{1}{\pi} \int_{-\pi}^{\pi} f(\theta) \sin(n\theta)\, d\theta, \qquad \text{for} \quad n = 1, 2, \ldots \qquad (1\text{-}47)$$

Most of the functions of concern in this book vary with time (if not explicitly at least implicitly). Equations (1-45), (1-46), and (1-47) are transformed to a time base by noting that, if the function is periodic with period T, then θ varies over the period according to the relation

$$\theta = 2\pi \left(\frac{t}{T} \right) = \omega t \qquad (1\text{-}48)$$

where $\omega = 2\pi/T$. Substituting (1-48) into (1-45), (1-46), and (1-47), we get

$$f(t) = \frac{a_0}{2} + \sum_{n=1}^{\infty} \left[a_n \cos(n\omega t) + b_n \sin(n\omega t) \right] \qquad (1\text{-}49)$$

$$a_n = \frac{2}{T} \int_{-T/2}^{T/2} f(t) \cos(n\omega t)\, dt, \qquad \text{for} \quad n = 0, 1, 2 \ldots \qquad (1\text{-}50)$$

$$b_n = \frac{2}{T} \int_{-T/2}^{T/2} f(t) \sin(n\omega t)\, dt, \qquad \text{for} \quad n = 1, 2 \ldots \qquad (1\text{-}51)$$

The $f(t)$ can be expressed in another form that is popular with systems analysts for data analysis:

$$f(t) = \frac{a_0}{2} + \sum_{n=1}^{\infty} c_n \cos(n\omega t - \Psi_n) \tag{1-52}$$

$$c_n = \left(a_n^2 + b_n^2\right)^{1/2} \tag{1-53}$$

$$\Psi_n = \tan^{-1}\left(\frac{b_n}{a_n}\right) \tag{1-54}$$

From (1-52) we see that a periodic function (that satisfies the Dirichlet conditions) is made up of the average value of $f(t)$ (over the period T)* at zero frequency and harmonically related sinusoid components whose frequencies are integral multiples of the fundamental frequency $(2\pi/T)$. The amplitude and relative phase of these components are given by (1-53) and (1-54).

A plot of the magnitude of c_n versus $n\omega$ is called the amplitude spectrum of the time function $f(t)$. The magnitude of the component at $\omega = 0$ is the average value of the given function. A plot of the phase Ψ_n versus $n\omega$ is called the phase spectrum of $f(t)$. Combinations of the amplitude spectrum and the phase spectrum can be used to determine the stability of dynamic processes. Plots of c_n and Ψ_n versus $n\omega$ are discrete and not continuous functions. These functions are often plotted with a line connecting the ordinate value with the abscissa value (see Figure 1-3). They are sometimes referred to as a line spectrum. Note that as T increases, ω decreases, and the lines are compressed. In the limit as T increases indefinitely, the discrete spectrum approaches a continuous spectrum and the Fourier series is said to become the Fourier integral. More will be said later about this.

When a function possesses symmetry properties, certain terms will be missing in its Fourier series expansion. In particular:

1. Even periodic functions satisfy the relation

$$f(t) = f(-t) \tag{1-55}$$

2. Odd periodic functions satisfy the relation

$$f(t) = -f(-t) \tag{1-56}$$

---

*This may be seen from (1-46) where $a_n = 2/2\pi \int_{-\pi}^{+\pi} f(\theta) \cos n\theta\, d\theta$. For $n = 0$, (1-46) becomes $a_0 = 2(1/2\pi \int_{-\pi}^{+\pi} f(\theta)\, d\theta) = 2$ (average of f over the interval 2π); thus $a_0/2 =$ average $f(\theta)$.

The series expansion of odd periodic functions contains only sine terms.

3. A periodic function with period T contains only even harmonics provided that it satisfies the conditions

$$f\left(t \pm \frac{T}{2}\right) = f(t) \tag{1-57}$$

4. A periodic function with period T contains only odd harmonics if it satisfies the condition

$$f\left(t \pm \frac{T}{2}\right) = -f(t) \tag{1-58}$$

5. Any function with no symmetry property can be decomposed into an even function and an odd function:

$$f(t) = \frac{f(t) + f(t)}{2} + \frac{f(t) - f(-t)}{2}$$

When analyzing a given periodic function, it is important to determine if simplifying symmetry conditions exist. When they do, the unused terms in the Fourier series are known and the others involve integration over only half a period for determination of the Fourier coefficients. These characteristics are summarized in Table 1-3.

Example 1

A well-known and often used example that is always highly informative (whether for the beginner in frequency-domain analysis or for review) is to determine the Fourier series expansion of the periodic rectangular function (rectangular wave) shown in Figure 1-2. The system of equations that describes this discontinuous* function is

$$f(t) = \begin{cases} 0; & -\dfrac{T}{2} < t < -\dfrac{T}{4} \\[2mm] f_0; & -\dfrac{T}{4} < t < \dfrac{T}{4} \\[2mm] 0; & \dfrac{T}{4} < t < \dfrac{T}{2} \end{cases} \tag{1-59}$$

*Continuous everywhere except at the points of discontinuity.

Table 1-3. Simplification in Fourier Series Evaluation Due to Symmetry Conditions

Symmetry Condition	Simplification	a_n	b_n
$f(t) = f(-t)$	cosine terms only	$\dfrac{4}{T}\displaystyle\int_0^{T/2}\left[f(t)\cos\left(\dfrac{2\pi n}{T}\right)t\right]dt$	0
$f(t) = -f(-t)$	sin terms only	0	$\dfrac{4}{T}\displaystyle\int_0^{T/2}\left[f(t)\sin\left(\dfrac{2\pi n}{T}\right)t\right]dt$
$f\left(t\pm\dfrac{T}{2}\right) = f(t)$	Even terms	$\dfrac{4}{T}\displaystyle\int_0^{T/2}\left[f(t)\cos\left(\dfrac{2\pi n}{T}\right)t\right]dt$	$\dfrac{4}{T}\displaystyle\int_0^{T/2}\left[f(t)\sin\left(\dfrac{2\pi n}{T}\right)t\right]dt$
	Odd terms	0	0
$f\left(t\pm\dfrac{T}{2}\right) = -f(t)$	Even terms	0	0
	Odd terms	$\dfrac{4}{T}\displaystyle\int_0^{T/2}\left[f(t)\cos\left(\dfrac{2\pi n}{T}\right)t\right]dt$	$\dfrac{4}{T}\displaystyle\int_0^{T/2}\left[f(t)\sin\left(\dfrac{2\pi n}{T}\right)t\right]dt$

FIGURE 1-2.   Periodic rectangular function.

Note that $f(t)$ is an even function. It is expected therefore that the Fourier series will contain only cosine terms. Let $\omega T = 2\pi$. Then the coefficients for the cosine terms can be developed as

$$a_n = \frac{4}{T} \int_0^{T/2} f_0 \cos(n\omega t) \, dt \qquad (1\text{-}60)$$

$$a_n = \frac{4f_0}{n\omega T} \left. \sin(n\omega t) \right|_0^{T/4} \qquad (1\text{-}61)$$

$$a_n = 2f_0 \left[\frac{\sin(n\pi/2)}{n\pi} \right], \qquad \text{for} \quad n = 1, 2, \ldots \qquad (1\text{-}62)$$

and

$$a_0 = \frac{f_0}{2} \qquad \text{for} \quad n = 0 \qquad (1\text{-}63)$$

That the coefficients for the sine terms are zero can be seen from

$$b_n = \frac{2}{T} \int_{-T/2}^{T/2} f_0 \sin(n\omega t) \, dt = \frac{2}{T} \int_{-T/4}^{T/4} f_0 \sin(n\omega t) \, dt$$

$$= \frac{-2f_0}{\omega n} \left. \cos(n\omega t) \right|_{-T/4}^{+T/4} = \frac{-2f_0}{\omega n} \left[\cos\left(\frac{n\omega T}{4} \right) - \cos\left(\frac{-n\omega T}{4} \right) \right] \equiv 0$$

With (1-62) and (1-63) we can now write

$$f(t) = \frac{f_0}{2} + \frac{2f_0}{\pi} \left[\cos(\omega t) - \tfrac{1}{3} \cos(3\omega t) \right.$$

$$\left. + \tfrac{1}{5} \cos(5\omega t) - \tfrac{1}{7} \cos(7\omega t) + \cdots \right] \qquad (1\text{-}64)$$

The amplitude spectrum of $f(t)$ is shown in Figure 1-3, and plots of partial sums of (1-64) are shown in Figure 1-4. The phase spectrum alternates between 0 and π for all values of n beginning at 0 for $n\omega = 0$.

Example 2

Determine the Fourier series expansion of the periodic triangular function shown in Figure 1-5. This function has the following symmetry conditions:

$$f(t) = -f(-t) \qquad \text{and} \qquad f\left(t \pm \frac{T}{2}\right) = -f(t) \qquad (1\text{-}65)$$

The first condition assures that the coefficients associated with the cosine terms will be zero. The second condition assures that the coefficients associated with the even harmonics will be zero. The Fourier series expansion of this function contains only b_n coefficients and, further, only

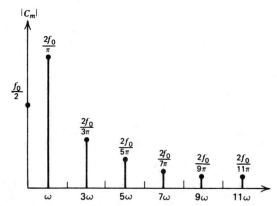

FIGURE 1-3. Amplitude spectrum of the periodic rectangular function shown in Figure 1-2.

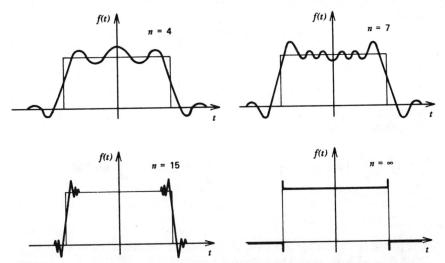

FIGURE 1-4. Partial sums of (1-64) illustrating the Gibbs phenomenon (over-shooting at the discontinuities) characteristic of Fourier series approximations of discontinuous functions.

those that are odd (i.e., b_{2n+1}). When two symmetry conditions exist, it is only necessary to integrate over one-fourth the period to determine the Fourier coefficients. The equation describing this function for $0 \leqslant t \leqslant T/4$ is

$$f(t) = \left(\frac{4f_0}{T} \right)t \tag{1-66}$$

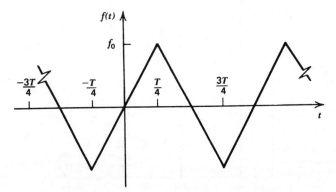

FIGURE 1-5. Periodic triangular function.

Then

$$b_n = \frac{8}{T} \int_0^{T/4} \left(\frac{4f_0}{T} \right) t \sin\left(\frac{n2\pi}{T} \right) t \, dt \tag{1-67}$$

$$b_n = \frac{8f_0}{n^2\pi^2} \sin\left(\frac{n\pi}{2} \right) \tag{1-68}$$

We can now write

$$f(t) = \frac{8f_0}{\pi^2} \left(\sin \omega t - \frac{1}{3^2} \sin 3\omega t + \frac{1}{5^2} \sin 5\omega t - \frac{1}{7^2} \sin 7\omega t + \cdots \right)$$

$$\tag{1-69}$$

The phase spectrum for this case also alternates between 0 and π for all $n\omega$ beginning with $\Psi_0 = 0$. The amplitude spectrum for the periodic triangular function is shown in Figure 1-6.

A number of important properties of the frequency-domain characterization of a system can be developed from these examples.

1. A parallel shift at the horizontal axis according to the equation

$$g(t) = f(t) + K$$

(where K is a constant) only changes the "average-value coefficient" a_0. It

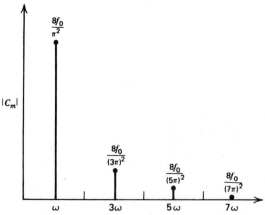

FIGURE 1-6.   Amplitude spectrum of the periodic triangular function.

may also uncover symmetry conditions. This is particularly true after the horizontal axis has been shifted to the average level of the given function $f(t)$. This procedure will not *generate* symmetries, however, but will expose those that already exist. In Example 1 only the odd harmonics were used in the Fourier series. But the given periodic rectangular function does not satisfy the test for the presence of only odd harmonics; it does, however, satisfy the odd harmonics test for $f(t) - f_0/2$.

2. A parallel shift in the position of the vertical axis (which amounts to a shift in time) does not change the harmonic content of a periodic function but it *will* change the sine and cosine structure of the Fourier series expansion. The power series defined by $p_n^2 = a_n^2 + b_n^2$ and plotted as a function of $n\omega$ (power spectrum) does not change with a time shift of periodic functions. This is a very important fact and one of the underlying reasons why spectrum analysis plays an important role from the frequency domain viewpoint in the design of numerical methods for high-fidelity simulation. The reader should develop a proof for this pivotal feature of frequency-domain modeling of continuous processes.

3. From Example 1 it was observed that the amplitude of the harmonic components of a periodic rectangular function, which has finite discontinuities, decreases at the rate $1/n$. From Example 2 it was observed that the amplitude of the harmonic components of the periodic triangular function, which is everywhere continuous but has discontinuous derivatives, decreases at the rate $1/n^2$. It is found in general that (*a*) the coefficients of the Fourier series expansion of periodic functions having one or more discontinuities decrease at the rate $1/n$ (when n is sufficiently large) and (*b*) the coefficients of the Fourier series expansion of periodic functions, which are everywhere continuous but have discontinuous first derivatives at one or more points, decrease at the rate $1/n^2$ (again when n is sufficiently large).

4. It is apparent that $f(t)$ *need not* be periodic if the Fourier series is to be used only to approximate $f(t)$ over the interval $-T/2 < t < T/2$. If the series is evaluated outside the interval, it will be found that $f(t)$ in the interval is being reproduced periodically with period T.

The Exponential Form of the Fourier Series

The Fourier series was previously written as a trigonometric series consisting of sine and cosine terms. The Fourier series can also be written in exponential form. This alternative form is easier to manipulate and also provides a convenient transition to the Fourier integral and Fourier transformations. The trigonometric form of the Fourier series expansion of a periodic function is copied here for convenience:

$$f(t) = \frac{a_0}{2} + \sum_{n=1}^{\infty} (a_n \cos n\omega t + b_n \sin n\omega t), \quad \text{for} \quad \omega = \frac{2\pi}{T} \quad (1\text{-}70)$$

$$a_n = \frac{2}{T} \int_{-T/2}^{T/2} f(t) \cos n\omega t \, dt, \quad \text{for} \quad n = 0, 1, 2, \ldots \quad (1\text{-}71)$$

$$b_n = \frac{2}{T} \int_{-T/2}^{T/2} f(t) \sin n\omega t \, dt, \quad \text{for} \quad n = 0, 1, 2, \ldots \quad (1\text{-}72)$$

By Euler's theorem

$$\sin n\omega t = \frac{1}{2j} \left(e^{jn\omega t} - e^{-jn\omega t} \right) \quad (1\text{-}73)$$

$$\cos n\omega t = \frac{1}{2} \left(e^{jn\omega t} + e^{-jn\omega t} \right) \quad (1\text{-}74)$$

Substituting (1-73) and (1-74) in (1-70), we find

$$f(t) = \frac{a_0}{2} + \sum_{n=1}^{\infty} \left[\left(\frac{a_n - jb_n}{2} \right) e^{jn\omega t} + \left(\frac{a_n + jb_n}{2} \right) e^{jn\omega t} \right] \quad (1\text{-}75)$$

$$f(t) = \alpha_0 + \sum_{n=1}^{\infty} \left(\alpha_n e^{j\omega nt} + \alpha_{-n} e^{jn\omega t} \right) \quad (1\text{-}76)$$

where

$$\alpha_n = \tfrac{1}{2}(a_n - jb_n), \quad \text{for} \quad n > 0 \quad (1\text{-}77)$$

$$\alpha_{-n} = \tfrac{1}{2}(a_n + jb_n), \quad \text{for} \quad n < 0 \quad (1\text{-}78)$$

$$\alpha_0 = \frac{a_0}{2}, \quad \text{for} \quad n = 0 \quad (1\text{-}79)$$

The second series in (1-76) can be written in a different form by substituting n for $-n$ and changing the limits of the summation as

$$\sum_{n=1}^{\infty} \alpha_{-n} e^{jn\omega t} = \sum_{n=-1}^{-\infty} \alpha_n e^{jn\omega t} \quad (1\text{-}80)$$

The right side of (1-76) can be simply combined in the single summation

$$f(t) = \sum_{n=-\infty}^{\infty} \alpha_n e^{jn\omega t} \qquad (1-81)$$

This is the exponential form of the Fourier series. Complex coefficients α_n are obtained by substituting (1-71) and (1-72) for a_n and b_n in (1-77):

$$\alpha_n = \frac{1}{T} \int_{-T/2}^{T/2} f(t) e^{jn\omega t} \, dt, \qquad \text{for all integer } n \qquad (1-82)$$

In (1-81) n takes on negative values. This gives rise to the so-called negative frequencies* that have no physical significance when analyzing real-valued functions such as those involved in the simulation of physical systems. They arise from the mathematical manipulation that converts sine and cosine functions into pairs of exponential functions. If there is a difficulty with the exponential Fourier series, it is that it uses complex functions and "negative frequencies" that often lead to interpretation difficulties. These issues can always be resolved by keeping *firmly* in mind that the numerical evaluation of the coefficients in the Fourier series will (must) be *real* when $f(t)$ is a *real* function of t. The reason for developing the exponential form of the Fourier series is that it leads directly to the Fourier integral and Fourier transformation concepts that are important for extending the frequency-domain concepts to nonperiodic functions and to the development of the Laplace transformation.

Fourier Integrals and Fourier Transformations

The amplitude spectra for the periodic functions we have been studying have been discrete (line spectra). As noted before, when T increases, the fundamental frequency $2\pi/T$ gets smaller and the amplitude and phase spectrum lines become denser. In the limit the discrete spectrum approaches a smooth curve called the *continuous amplitude spectrum*. Furthermore for $T \to \infty$, $f(t)$ need not be periodic. We now investigate the modifications to the Fourier series expansion of periodic functions so that it may represent nonperiodic functions with a continuous amplitude spectrum. Nonperiodic functions are of interest because virtually all transient response functions encountered in this book are nonperiodic.

---

*Those readers who are trained in electrical engineering would view the negative and positive frequencies as associated with a pair of counterrotating phasors in the complex plane whose sum is always on the real axis.

Table 1-4. Redefinition of Fourier Terms

Fourier Series	Definition	Fourier Integral
$n\omega$	Harmonic component	ω
ω	Fundamental frequency	$\Delta\omega$
T	Period of $f(t)$	$2\pi/\Delta\omega$

When $f(t)$ is a nonperiodic function, changes in notation must be made because the fundamental frequency $(2\pi/T)$ approaches 0 and n becomes meaningless as T gets very large. Also for a continuous spectrum angular frequency ω can assume any value, not just the value of n. For these reasons the Fourier terms are redefined in Table 1-4.

Then (1-81) and (1-82) become

$$f(t) = \sum_{-\infty}^{\infty} \alpha_\omega e^{j\omega t}, \qquad \text{for} \quad \omega = 0, \pm \Delta\omega, \pm 2\Delta\omega, \ldots \qquad (1\text{-}83)$$

$$\alpha_\omega = \frac{\Delta\omega}{2\pi} \int_{-T/2}^{T/2} f(t) e^{j\omega t}\, dt \qquad (1\text{-}84)$$

Substituting (1-84) into (1-74), we find

$$f(t) = \frac{1}{2\pi} \left[\sum_{-\infty}^{\infty} \int_{-T/2}^{T/2} f(t) e^{-j\omega t}\, dt \right] e^{j\omega t}\, dt \qquad (1\text{-}85)$$

Now, letting $T \to \infty$, we get

$$f(t) = \frac{1}{2\pi} \lim_{T\to\infty} \left[\left\{ \sum_{-\infty}^{\infty} \int_{-T/2}^{T/2} f(t) e^{-j\omega t}\, dt \right\} e^{j\omega t}\, \Delta\omega \right]$$

$$= \frac{1}{2\pi} \int_{-\infty}^{\infty} \left\{ \int_{-\infty}^{\infty} f(t) e^{-j\omega t}\, dt \right\} e^{j\omega t}\, d\omega \qquad (1\text{-}86)$$

Equation (1-86) is the Fourier integral representation of $f(t)$. We can now define the Fourier transformation and its inverse by letting

$$g(\omega) = \int_{-\infty}^{\infty} f(t) e^{-j\omega t}\, dt \qquad (1\text{-}87)$$

Then we see from (1-86) that

$$f(t) = \frac{1}{2\pi} \int_{-\infty}^{\infty} g(\omega) e^{j\omega t}\, d\omega \qquad (1\text{-}88)$$

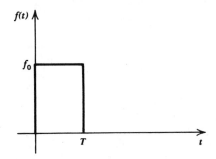

FIGURE 1-7.   A single rectangular pulse.

and

$$g(\omega) = \int_{-\infty}^{\infty} f(t)e^{-j\omega t} \, dt \qquad (1\text{-}89)$$

Equations (1-88) and (1-89) are called a Fourier transform pair, $g(\omega)$ is called the Fourier transform of $f(t)$, and $f(t)$ is called the inverse Fourier transform of $g(\omega)$. They are sometimes written as

$$g(\omega) = F\{f(t)\} \qquad (1\text{-}90)$$

$$f(t) = F^{-1}\{g(\omega)\} \qquad (1\text{-}91)$$

Example 3

Determine the amplitude spectrum of a single rectangular pulse of amplitude f_0 and duration T as shown in Figure 1-7, given that

$$f(t) = \begin{cases} f_0, & 0 < t < T \\ 0, & 0 \geqslant t \geqslant T \end{cases} \qquad (1\text{-}92)$$

Then

$$g(\omega) = \int_0^T f_0 e^{-j\omega t} \, dt = \frac{f_0}{j\omega}(1 - e^{-j\omega T}) \qquad (1\text{-}93)$$

$$g(\omega) = \frac{2f_0}{\omega} \sin\left(\frac{\omega T}{2}\right) e^{-j(\omega T/2)} \qquad (1\text{-}94)$$

$$|g(\omega)| = 2f_0 \left| \frac{\sin(\omega T/2)}{\omega} \right| = f_0 T \left| \frac{\sin(\omega T/2)}{\omega T/2} \right| \qquad (1\text{-}95)$$

The amplitude spectrum is graphed in Figure 1-8.

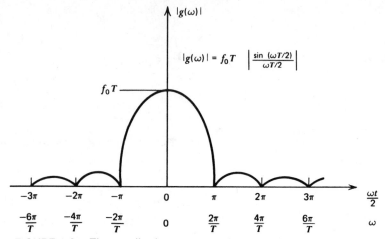

FIGURE 1-8.   The amplitude spectrum of a single rectangular pulse.

Example 4

Consider the function

$$f(t) = t - t^2$$

The Fourier expansion of $f(t)$ over the interval $0 < t < 1$ is developed as follows:

$b_n = 0$

$$a_0 = \tfrac{2}{1} \int_0^1 (t - t^2)\, dt = 2 \left[\frac{t^2}{2} - \frac{t^3}{3} \right]_0^1 = \tfrac{1}{3}$$

$$a_n = \tfrac{2}{1} \int_0^1 (t - t^2) \cos\left(\frac{n\pi t}{1} \right) dt$$

$$a_n = 2 \left[\left\{ \frac{\cos(n\pi t)}{n^2\pi^2} + \frac{t}{n\pi} \sin(n\pi t) \right\} \right.$$

$$\left. - \left\{ \frac{2t}{n^2\pi^2} \cos(n\pi t) - \frac{2}{n^3\pi^3} \sin(n\pi t) + \frac{t^2}{n\pi} \sin(n\pi t) \right\} \right]_0^1$$

$$a_n = 2 \left[\left(\frac{\cos(n\pi) - 1}{n^2\pi^2} \right) - \left(\frac{2 \cos n\pi}{n^2\pi^2} \right) \right]$$

$$a_n = \frac{-2(1 + \cos n\pi)}{n^2\pi^2}$$

Thus

$$t - t^2 = \frac{1}{6} - \frac{4}{\pi^2} \left[\tfrac{1}{4} \cos(2\pi t) + \tfrac{1}{16} \cos(4\pi t) + \tfrac{1}{36} \cos(6\pi t) + \cdots \right]$$

Example 5

The Fourier series of e^x on the interval $0 < x < 2$ is interesting because it involves both sine and cosine terms where the "oddness" of e^x is emphasized in the Fourier series expansion. In this case

$$a_0 = \int_0^2 e^x \, dx = e^2 - 1$$

$$a_n = \int_0^2 e^x \cos(n\pi x) \, dx = \frac{e^2 - 1}{n^2 + 1}$$

$$b_n = \int_0^2 e^x \sin(n\pi x) \, dx = \frac{-(e^2 - 1)n}{n^2 + 1}$$

Thus

$$e^x = (e^2 - 1)\left\{ 1 + \frac{1}{1^2 + 1} \cos(\pi x) + \frac{1}{2^2 + 1} \cos(2\pi x) + \cdots \right.$$

$$\left. - \left(\frac{1}{1^2 + 1} \right) \sin(\pi x) - \left(\frac{2}{2^2 + 1} \right) \sin(2\pi x) - \cdots \right\}$$

We see that for large n

$$a_n \rightarrow \frac{e^2 - 1}{n^2}$$

while

$$b_n \rightarrow \frac{e^2 - 1}{n}$$

For large n, the odd function component of e^x is emphasized on the interval $0 < x < 2$.

Fourier Series Expansion of Discrete Functions*

We now turn to the Fourier analysis of discrete functions. The periodic output of a numerical algorithm is an example of a discrete function. Periodic measurements taken from a sensor is an example of a discrete function. More precisely, a discrete function as used here is a single-valued relationship between a variable defined over the real number system and another variable defined over the integers. When the former is plotted against the latter, we see the function is not a continuous curve but a discrete set of points (see Figure 1-3). Discrete functions are often given in tabular form. The important relationships between the discrete spectrum of discrete functions and the discrete spectrum of continuous functions are discussed here. The aliasing concept is explained in detail to aid those not familiar with it in understanding this important peculiarity of the spectrum of sampled-data functions.

What's important in digital simulation, where the intent is to make a digital (discrete) process behave like a continuous process, is that we often want the frequency domain characteristics of the digital simulation to match those of the continuous process being simulated. To do so requires that the time step in simulation be $\frac{1}{7} - \frac{1}{10}$ the shortest time interval of interest in the process being simulated; said another way, the frequency at which the equations of motion are evaluated must be 7 to 10 times higher than the highest frequency of interest on the system being simulated. Under these conditions, the time and frequency domain characteristics of the discrete functions generated in the digital computer will be within a few percent of the time and frequency domain characteristics of the continuous process being simulated.

Let us reexamine the Fourier series of a continuous function; this time in a slightly different form.

The Fourier series of a continuous periodic function whose period is L can be given by

$$F(x) = \frac{a_0}{2} + \left[a_1\cos\left(\frac{2\pi x}{L}\right) + a_2\cos\left(\frac{4\pi x}{L}\right) + a_3\cos\left(\frac{6\pi x}{L}\right) + \cdots \right]$$

$$+ \left[b_1\sin\left(\frac{2\pi x}{L}\right) + b_2\sin\left(\frac{4\pi x}{L}\right) + b_3\sin\left(\frac{6\pi x}{L}\right) + \cdots \right] \quad (1\text{-}96)$$

---

*Adapted from J. M. Smith, *Scientific Analysis on the Pocket Calculator*, 2nd ed., Wiley, New York, 1977. Published with permission.

where the coefficients a_k and b_k are given by the discrete functions

$$a_k = \frac{2}{L}\int_0^L F(x)\cos\left(\frac{2k\pi x}{L}\right) dx, \quad (k = 0, 1, 2, \cdots) \quad (1\text{-}97)$$

$$b_k = \frac{2}{L}\int_0^L F(x)\sin\left(\frac{2k\pi x}{L}\right) dx, \quad (k = 1, 2, \cdots) \quad (1\text{-}98)$$

This series has an infinite number of terms. There are an infinite number of coefficients defined by (1-97) and (1-98). Physically, the fundamental and an infinity of its harmonics can determine an infinite sequence of coefficients for the sines and cosines in the series expansion of (1-96).

There are problems with the convergence of Fourier series, which are usually associated with special functions not frequently encountered in engineering analysis. Since the sines and cosines that make up the Fourier series are orthogonal functions, the coefficients of its components can be written in polar form. In this case, the modulus of the radius vector, as well as the phase angle of the resultant, can be plotted as a function of frequency. These form the amplitude and phase shift curves used, for example, by control systems analysts to examine the stability of feedback control processes.

Finally, the power spectrum of a function approximated with a Fourier series can be prepared by plotting the square of the modulus of the Fourier coefficients in polar form. Since this is equivalent to summing the squares of the coefficients for the sine and cosine functions at the same frequency, it is apparent that the phase information is lost when the power spectrum is presented.

Inspection of the Fourier series reveals that if the function $F(x)$ is moved vertically along the ordinate, only the value of a_0 is changed. This can readily be seen by noting in (1-97) that when $k = 0$ the coefficient becomes the average value of $F(x)$ on the interval zero to L. Note that if we were to set $F_1(x) = F(x) + a_0/2$ in equation (1-96), the Fourier series of $F_1(x)$ would have no average component (DC component). It is also apparent that if $F(x)$ is translated horizontally along the abscissa, the distribution of weight among the coefficients in the Fourier series changes. In particular, for any given frequency component, the distribution among the sine and cosine terms is different. However, the sum of their squares remains invariant. From this we see that the power spectrum of a Fourier series is invariant with respect to translation of the function $f(x)$ along the abscissa (assuming that $f(x)$ is periodic).

What should be kept in mind about the Fourier series approximation of a function is that the function being approximated with the Fourier series is assumed to be *periodic*. Though it can have discontinuities over the period, the function must be periodic. What might seem counterintuitive at first is that this function defined over a finite interval in the domain of the real numbers has an infinite number of lines in its discrete spectrum defined over the infinite domain of the discrete frequencies. The reason for this lies in the nature of the Fourier series. The fundamental frequency component for the finite length record is set by the length of the record itself. Then the harmonics that make up the rest of the series are determined by pairs of sines and cosines that fit with multiple oscillations over the period of the periodic function, and there are an infinity of these sines and cosines.

Now let us consider a discrete function defined by a set of equally spaced discrete values of the function Y defined at equally spaced values of the domain of the independent variable. Consider only an even number of points, $2N$. In what follows, the $2N$ sample points are

$$0, \frac{L}{2N}, \frac{2L}{2N}, \frac{3L}{2N}, \ldots, \frac{(2N-1)L}{2N} \tag{1-99}$$

which can be written as

$$x_n = \frac{nL}{2N}, \qquad (n = 0, 1, \ldots, 2N - 1) \tag{1-100}$$

The Fourier series expansion of an arbitrary function $F(x)$ defined on the set of points x_n can be written as

$$F(x) = \frac{A_0}{2} + \sum_{k=1}^{N-1} \left[A_k \cos\left(\frac{2k\pi x}{L}\right) + B_k \sin\left(\frac{2k\pi x}{L}\right) \right] + \frac{A_N}{2} \cos\left(\frac{2N\pi x}{L}\right) \tag{1-101}$$

where

$$A_k = \frac{1}{N} \sum_{n=0}^{2N-1} F(x_n) \cos\left(\frac{2k\pi x_n}{L}\right), \qquad (k = 0, 1, \ldots, N) \tag{1-102}$$

$$B_k = \frac{1}{N} \sum_{n=0}^{2N-1} F(x_n) \sin\left(\frac{2k\pi x_n}{L}\right), \qquad (k = 0, 1, \ldots, N - 1) \tag{1-103}$$

An interesting aspect of Fourier series is that the sine and cosine functions are not only defined and orthogonal over a continuous interval of the dependent variable but are also orthogonal on any set of equally spaced discrete points on the same interval. This is important for the numerical evaluation of the frequency components of the discrete functions in that we are usually only given samples of the function on the set of equally spaced points. One might expect that the coefficients for the continuous Fourier series could then be approximated using numerical integration. Although this, in fact, can be done, (1-102) and (1-103) show that the coefficients for the Fourier spectrum of a discrete function can be computed exactly without involving numerical integration approximation.

It is apparent from (1-102) and (1-103) that this expansion will have only $2N$ terms, rather than an infinity of terms, as is characteristic of the Fourier series approximation of continuous functions. Also, the frequency spectrum for the discrete Fourier transform will have only half as many lines as sampled values. Thus, if there are 10 sampled values, the power spectrum will have only five discrete lines. Clearly, a question that needs to be answered is, 'what happened to the rest of the infinity of components of the spectrum of the continuous function $F(x)$?' Another relevant and equally important question is, how can the discrete spectrum be constructed if we know the continuous spectrum and the number of sampled values? Conversely, given the discrete spectrum of the discrete function $f(n \Delta x)$, what can we tell about the discrete spectrum of the continuous function $f(x)$?

The Relations Between the Fourier Series Expansion of Discrete and Continuous Functions

Only a little analysis will show that the spectral components of a discrete function are related to the spectral components of its continuous function counterpart according to the relationship

$$A_k = a_k + \sum_{m=1}^{\infty} \left(a_{2Nm-k} + a_{2Nm+k} \right) \tag{1-104}$$

$$B_k = b_k + \sum_{m=1}^{\infty} \left(b_{2Nm+k} - b_{2Nm-k} \right) \tag{1-105}$$

The constant term A_0 is given by

$$A_0 = a_0 + 2 \sum_{m=1}^{\infty} a_{2Nm} \tag{1-106}$$

Let us examine (1-104). The first six terms of an even function discrete spectrum (say, for $2N = 10$ seconds) when written out take the following form:

Spectrum Component	Discrete Function Spectrum from Continuous Function Spectrum
$2\alpha_{\omega=0} =$	$A_0 = a_0 + 2(a_{10} + a_{20} + a_{30} + a_{40} + \cdots)$
$\alpha_{\omega=1\,Hz} =$	$A_1 = a_1 + (a_9 + a_{11}) + (a_{19} + a_{21}) + (a_{29} + a_{31}) + \cdots$
$\alpha_{\omega=2\,Hz} =$	$A_2 = a_2 + (a_8 + a_{12}) + (a_{18} + a_{22}) + (a_{28} + a_{32}) + \cdots$
$\alpha_{\omega=3\,Hz} =$	$A_3 = a_3 + (a_7 + a_{13}) + (a_{17} + a_{23}) + (a_{27} + a_{33}) + \cdots$
$\alpha_{\omega=4\,Hz} =$	$A_4 = a_4 + (a_6 + a_{14}) + (a_{16} + a_{24}) + (a_{26} + a_{34}) + \cdots$
$2\alpha_{\omega=5\,Hz} =$	$A_5 = a_5 + (a_5 + a_{15}) + (a_{15} + a_{25}) + (a_{25} + a_{35}) + \cdots$

Note: $B_k = 0 = b_k$ for even functions.

The factors of 2 at end points of the spectrum are due to the form of (1-101). Each of the discrete system coefficients when written out includes the effect of an infinite number of terms associated with the continuous spectrum. This somewhat stunning finding shows that any sizable power in the high-frequency components of the continuous-function spectrum will have the effect of those components appearing at low frequencies in the discrete-function spectrum. In the example chosen where the $2N$ is equal to 10 seconds, the lowest-frequency component in the discrete spectrum (besides the zero-frequency component) includes the amplitude of the 9- and 11-hertz frequency component in the Fourier series expansion of $F(x)$, as well as the 19th and 21st, the 29th and 31st, 39th and 41st, 49th and 51st, and so on.

Another *physical* way to think of this is this; had we been sampling an 11-hertz sine wave at 10 samples per second, the discrete function would have had spectral components at 1 hertz whose amplitude would be the *same* as that of the 11-Hz sine wave in the continuous spectrum. In general the frequencies present in the original continuous function $F(x)$ are summed together as a result of the sampling operation. In other words, the mere operation of sampling a continuous function (i.e., a discrete function defined only at integer multiples of the sampling period) results in the *folding* of the frequency spectrum around the information frequency (sampling frequency ω_s divided by 2), resulting in the folding of the high-frequency components of the continuous-function spectrum into the low-frequency components of the discrete-function spectrum. This effect is called "aliasing" (i.e., 1 hertz is the alias of 9 hertz when sampled at 10 hertz). Note that once the sampling process has taken place, its effect on the continuous-function spectrum cannot be undone. In our example, only when $a_k = 0$ for $k > 5$ will $A_k = a_k$. If $a_k \neq 0$ for $k > 5$, a_k cannot be determined by examining A_k! Finally, note that the highest-frequency component is $\omega_s/2$.

These formulas provide the means for computing the discrete-function spectrum directly from the continuous-function spectrum if it is known. The *CRC Standard Mathematical Tables* has a sizable table of Fourier series representations of commonly encountered functions and can be used to compute the discrete-function spectrum according to (1-104), (1-105), and (1-106).

The Numerical Evaluation of the Fourier Coefficients

The coefficients of the discrete-function Fourier series expansion, previously given by (1-102) and (1-103), are recopied here for convenience.

$$A_k = \frac{1}{N} \sum_{n=0}^{2N-1} F(x_n) \cos\left(\frac{2k\pi x_n}{L}\right), \qquad (k = 0, 1, \ldots, N) \quad (1\text{-}102)$$

$$B_k = \frac{1}{N} \sum_{n=0}^{2N-1} F(x_n) \sin\left(\frac{2k\pi x_n}{L}\right), \qquad (k = 0, 1, \ldots, N-1) \quad (1\text{-}103)$$

These coefficients may be numerically evaluated, using recursion formulas. The procedure is as follows:

Step 1. Prepare a table of values U_m using the recursion relations

$$U_m = \left(2\cos\frac{\pi k}{N}\right) U_{m-1} - U_{m-2} + F(2N - m) \quad \text{for } m = 2, 3, 4, \ldots, 2N - 1$$

where $U_0 = 0$ and $U_1 = F(2N - 1)$

Step 2. Evaluate the coefficients of the cosine terms in the series, using the equation

$$A_k = \frac{1}{N}\left\{\left(\cos\frac{\pi k}{N}\right) U_{2N-1} - U_{2N-2} + F(0)\right\}$$

Step 3. Compute the coefficients for the sine terms in the series expansion, using the recursion formula

$$B_k = \frac{1}{N}\left(\sin\frac{\pi k}{n}\right)U_{2N-1}$$

While evaluation according to these formulas takes longer than does the Cooley-Tukey fast Fourier transform algorithm, for the low-order Fourier series analysis this recursion formula method involves only slightly fewer operations than the Cooley-Tukey algorithm.

Hamming presents a convenient 12-point formula for Fourier analysis in his book *Numerical Methods for Scientists and Engineers*. First, the table of discrete values of the function F is written in an array ($A1$):

$$\left.\begin{array}{ccccccc} F(0) & F(1) & F(2) & F(3) & F(4) & F(5) & F(6) \\ & F(11) & F(10) & F(9) & F(8) & F(7) & \end{array}\right\} A1$$

From this array we can compute a sequence of S's and T's by adding and subtracting, respectively, the two lines in the array $A1$ to form an array ($A2$) of S's and T's:

$$\left.\begin{array}{lccccccc} \text{Sums} \rightarrow & S(0) & S(1) & S(2) & S(3) & S(4) & S(5) & S(6) \\ \text{Differences} \rightarrow & & T(1) & T(2) & T(3) & T(4) & T(5) & \end{array}\right\} A2$$

Then, rewriting array ($A2$) as

$$\left.\begin{array}{cccccccc} S(0) & S(1) & S(2) & S(3) & & T(1) & T(2) & T(3) \\ S(6) & S(5) & S(4) & & & & T(5) & T(4) \end{array}\right\} A3$$

we form array ($A4$) of U's, V's, P's, and Q's by adding and subtracting, respectively, the second line from the first line in array $A3$:

$$\left.\begin{array}{lcccccccc} \text{Sums} \rightarrow & U(0) & U(1) & U(2) & U(3) & P(1) & P(2) & P(3) \\ \text{Differences} \rightarrow & V(0) & V(1) & V(2) & & & Q(1) & Q(2) \end{array}\right\} A4$$

The coefficients associated with the six discrete frequencies that make up the Fourier series representation of the 12-point discrete function can now be developed. First compute

$$\alpha_1 = V(0) + \frac{V(2)}{2} \qquad \beta_1 = \frac{P(1)}{2} + P(3)$$

$$\alpha_2 = U(0) + U(3) \qquad \beta_2 = P(1) - P(3)$$

$$\alpha_3 = U(1) + U(2) \qquad \beta_3 = \frac{\sqrt{3}}{2}(Q(1) + Q(2))$$

$$\alpha_4 = \frac{\sqrt{3}}{2}V(1) \qquad \beta_4 = \frac{\sqrt{3}}{2}(Q(1) - Q(2))$$

$$\alpha_5 = U(0) - U(3) \qquad \beta_5 = \frac{\sqrt{3}}{2}P(2)$$

$$\alpha_6 = U(1) - U(2)$$

$$\alpha_7 = V(0) - V(2)$$

Then

$$A_0 = \tfrac{1}{6}(\alpha_2 + \alpha_3)$$

$$A_1 = \tfrac{1}{6}(\alpha_1 + \alpha_4) \qquad B_1 = \tfrac{1}{6}(\beta_1 + \beta_5)$$

$$A_2 = \tfrac{1}{6}\left(\alpha_5 + \frac{\alpha_6}{2}\right) \qquad B_2 = \tfrac{1}{6}\beta_3$$

$$A_3 = \tfrac{1}{6}\alpha_7 \qquad B_3 = \tfrac{1}{6}\beta_2$$

$$A_4 = \tfrac{1}{6}\left(\alpha_2 - \frac{\alpha_3}{2}\right) \qquad B_4 = \tfrac{1}{6}\beta_4$$

$$A_5 = \tfrac{1}{6}(\alpha_1 - \alpha_4) \qquad B_5 = \tfrac{1}{6}(\beta_1 - \beta_5)$$

$$A_6 = \tfrac{1}{6}(\alpha_5 - \alpha_6)$$

These coefficients are associated with the Fourier series

$$F(x) = \frac{A_0}{2} + \sum_{k=1}^{n-1}\left(A_k\cos\frac{2\pi kx}{L} + B_k\sin\frac{2\pi kx}{L}\right) + \frac{A_n}{2}\cos\frac{2\pi Nx}{L}$$

Example 6

Compute the coefficients in the Fourier series expansions of a continuous periodic triangular wave function. Then use these coefficients to compute the discrete function spectrum by way of (1-104) through (1-106).

The continuous periodic triangular wave form is shown below. It is apparent that

$$f(t) = -f(-t)$$

and

$$f\left(t \pm \frac{T}{2}\right) = -f(t)$$

The first equation shows that $f(t)$ is an odd function and thus only the sine components are involved in the Fourier series approximation of $f(t)$. The second equation shows that only the odd harmonics are involved in the series. Furthermore, when two symmetry conditions exist, it is necessary to integrate only over one-quarter of the period of the function to determine the Fourier coefficients (an interesting property for the reader to demonstrate to himself). It follows, that

$$b_n = \frac{8}{T}\int_0^{T/4} f(t)\sin n\left(\frac{2\pi}{T}\right) t\, dt, \qquad (n, \text{odd})$$

Since

$$f(t) = \frac{4At}{T}, \qquad 0 \le t \le \frac{T}{4}$$

$$b_n = \frac{8}{T}\int_0^{T/4}\left[\left(\frac{4A}{T}\right)t \sin\left\{n\left(\frac{2\pi}{T}\right)t\right\}\right] dt$$

$$b_n = \frac{8A}{n^2\pi^2}\sin\left(\frac{n\pi}{2}\right), \qquad (n, \text{odd})$$

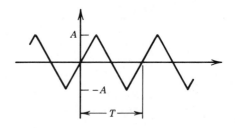

FIGURE 1-9.   Continuous periodic triangular waveform.

$$b_n = \begin{cases} \dfrac{8A}{n^2\pi^2}, & n = 1,5,9,\ldots \\[3mm] \dfrac{-8A}{n^2\pi^2}, & n = 3,7,11,\ldots \end{cases}$$

The first 15 continuous function spectrum components are tabulated below.

$$b_1 = \frac{8A}{\pi^2} \qquad\qquad b_6 = 0 \qquad\qquad b_{11} = \frac{-8A}{121\pi^2}$$

$$b_2 = 0 \qquad\qquad b_7 = \frac{-8A}{49\pi^2} \qquad\qquad b_{12} = 0$$

$$b_3 = \frac{-8A}{9\pi^2} \qquad\qquad b_8 = 0 \qquad\qquad b_{13} = \frac{8A}{169\pi^2}$$

$$b_4 = 0 \qquad\qquad b_9 = \frac{8A}{81\pi^2} \qquad\qquad b_{14} = 0$$

$$b_5 = \frac{8A}{25\pi^2} \qquad\qquad b_{10} = 0 \qquad\qquad b_{15} = \frac{-8A}{225\pi^2}$$

The discrete spectrum components are developed by using (1-105) for the case 2N = 10:

$$B_1 = b_1 + (b_{11} - b_9) + (b_{21} - b_{19}) + (b_{31} - b_{29}) + \cdots$$

$$B_2 = b_2 + (b_{12} - b_8) + (b_{22} - b_{18}) + (b_{32} - b_{28}) + \cdots$$

$$B_3 = b_3 + (b_{13} - b_7) + (b_{23} - b_{17}) + (b_{33} - b_{27}) + \cdots$$

$$B_4 = b_4 + (b_{14} - b_6) + (b_{24} - b_{16}) + (b_{34} - b_{26}) + \cdots$$

From the table of continuous function spectrum components we see that

$$B_1 \cong \frac{8A}{\pi^2}\left[\left(1 - \frac{1}{121}\right) - \left(\frac{1}{81}\right)\right] = 0.9793900\left(\frac{8A}{\pi^2}\right)$$

$$B_2 \cong \frac{8A}{\pi^2}\left[(0 + 0) - 0\right] = 0$$

$$B_3 \cong \frac{8A}{\pi^2}\left[\left(-\frac{1}{9} + \frac{1}{169}\right) - \left(\frac{-1}{49}\right)\right] = -0.0847859\left(\frac{8A}{\pi^2}\right)$$

$$B_4 \cong \frac{8A}{\pi^2}\left[(0 + 0) - (0)\right] = 0$$

The following table shows the discrete function spectrum elements and the continuous function spectrum elements side by side for easy comparison. The difference is the result of the alisasing phenomenon.

Continuous Function Spectrum Elements	Discrete Function Spectrum Elements
$b_1 = 1.0\left(\dfrac{8A}{\pi^2}\right)$	$B_1 = 0.9793900\left(\dfrac{8A}{\pi^2}\right)$
$b_2 = 0$	$B_2 = 0$
$b_3 = -0.1111111\left(\dfrac{8A}{\pi^2}\right)$	$B_3 = -0.08478659\left(\dfrac{8A}{\pi^2}\right)$
$b_4 = 0$	$B_4 = 0$

Example 7

Compute the Fourier coefficients for the Fourier series approximation of the discrete function

$$y_n = \sin(n\omega T)$$

where $\omega = 1$ Hz. This 12-point discrete function is tabulated below.

n	nT (seconds)	$n\omega T$ (degrees)	$\sin(n\omega T) = F(n)$
0	0	0	0.00
1	0.1	36	0.59
2	0.2	72	0.95
3	0.3	108	0.95
4	0.4	144	0.59
5	0.5	180	0.00
6	0.6	216	-0.59
7	0.7	252	-0.95
8	0.8	288	-0.95
9	0.9	324	-0.59
10	1.0	360	0.00
11	1.1	396	+0.59

A closer examination of the table reveals that the sine function is tabulated over the interval to 1.2 seconds, while the function is periodic on the interval 1 second. Clearly, the coefficients that we generate using the 12-point formulas apply to Fourier series approximations of the tabulated functions exactly as shown (with a period of 1.2 seconds, not 1 second), and not the coefficients for the Fourier series approximation of a pure 1-Hz since wave. The purpose for selecting this unusual problem is that it illustrates the effect of one of the practical problems associated with sampling periodic functions. The reality of sampling functions from experiments is that the functions are often not exactly periodic or, if they are, the period is not known precisely and some approximation of the period must be made. This example might be considered the result of an experiment where an estimate of the period of the function being sampled is made to be 1.2 seconds, where in reality the periodic function repeats on the interval 1 second. Following the 12-point Fourier analysis procedure, the discrete function 12-point Fourier coefficients are generated from the arrays as tabulated in Table 1-5. The array numbers in the table correspond to the array numbers in the text and are shown here for the sake of convenience. The numerical evaluation of the 12-point Fourier series coefficients are

Table 1-5. DiscreteFunction 12-point Fourier Series Coefficient Generation Arrays

$F(0) \rightarrow F(6)$	0.00	0.59	0.95	0.95	0.59	0.00	-0.59		$(A1)$
$F(12) \leftarrow F(7)$		0.59	0.00	-0.59	-0.95	-0.95			
Add	0.00	1.18	0.95	0.36	-0.36	-0.95	-0.59		$(A2)$
Subtract		0.00	0.95	1.54	1.54	0.95			
	$S(0)$	$S(1)$	$S(2)$	$S(3)$	$S(4)$	$S(5)$	$S(6)$		$(A2)$
		$T(1)$	$T(2)$	$T(3)$	$T(4)$	$T(5)$			
$S(0) \rightarrow S(3)$	0.00	1.18	0.95	0.36	0.00	0.95	1.54	$T(1) \rightarrow T(3)$	$(A3)$
$S(6) \leftarrow S(4)$	-0.59	-0.95	-0.36		0.95	1.54		$T(5) \leftarrow T(4)$	
Add	-0.59	0.23	0.59	0.36	0.95	2.49	1.54		$(A4)$
Subtract	0.59	2.13	1.31		-0.95	-0.59			
	$U(0)$	$U(1)$	$U(2)$	$U(3)$	$P(1)$	$P(2)$	$P(3)$		$(A4)$
	$V(0)$	$V(1)$	$V(2)$		$Q(1)$	$Q(2)$			

summarized in Table 1-6. The A-coefficients are associated with the cosine components and the B-coefficients are associated with the sine components. Also, the table shows a check of the initial conditions. At $t = 0$, the discrete function starts at 0. Therefore, the sum of the cosine amplitude coefficients should equal 0, as they do.

Though we could discuss the tail effects by examining the individual elements of the series expansion, it is more convenient to use the power spectrum or amplitude spectrum as a means of discussing this phenomenon. The 12-point spectrum calculations are tabulated in Table 1-7. First note that the DC component of the spectrum is given by P_0. This indicates that the average effect of the "tail" of our irregular periodic coefficient is to bias the otherwise 0-DC coefficient to the level 0.049. Second, the lowest-frequency component (the fundamental frequency equal to $1/1.2$ equal to $0.83333\ldots$) contains the greatest amount of power of all of the harmonics. Clearly, this is so because it is the closest frequency to the 1-Hz periodic

Table 1-6. 12-Point Fourier Series Coefficient Calculations

Cosine components

$$2A_0 = \frac{1}{6}(-0.59 + 0.36 + 0.23 + 0.59) = 0.098$$

$$A_1 = \frac{1}{6}(0.59 + 0.655 + 0.866 \times 2.13) = 0.5149$$

$$A_2 = \frac{1}{6}(-0.59 - 0.36 - 0.18) = -0.188$$

$$A_3 = \frac{1}{6}(-0.72) = -0.12$$

$$A_4 = \frac{1}{6}(0.59 + 0.36 - 0.41) = -0.107$$

$$A_5 = \frac{1}{6}(0.59 + 0.655 - 0.866 \times 2.13) = -0.0999$$

$$2A_6 = \frac{1}{6}(-0.59 - 0.36 - 0.23 + 0.59) = -0.098$$

Note that at $t = 0$, $\Sigma Ai \equiv 0$, as it should

Sine components

$$B_1 = \frac{1}{6}(0.475 + 1.54 + 0.866 \times 2.489) = 0.695$$

$$B_2 = \frac{0.866}{6}(-0.95 - 0.59) = -0.2223$$

$$B_3 = \frac{1}{6}(0.95 - 1.54) = 0.098$$

$$B_4 = \frac{0.866}{6}(-0.95 + 0.59) = -0.05196$$

$$B_5 = \frac{1}{6}(0.475 + 1.54 - 0.866 \times 2.49) = -0.0436$$

Table 1-7. 12-Point Spectrum Calculations

ω Hz	Power Spectrum (rounded)	Amplitude Spectrum
0	$P_0 = A_0^2/4 \quad = 0.00$	$\sqrt{P_0} = 0.049$
0.833	$P_1 = A_1^2 + B_1^2 = 0.75$	$\sqrt{P_1} = 0.865$
1.666	$P_2 = A_2^2 + B_2^2 = 0.08$	$\sqrt{P_2} = 0.291$
2.499	$P_3 = A_3^2 + B_3^2 = 0.02$	$\sqrt{P_3} = 0.155$
3.333	$P_4 = A_4^2 + B_4^2 = 0.01$	$\sqrt{P_4} = 0.119$
4.166	$P_5 = A_5^2 + B_5^2 = 0.01$	$\sqrt{P_5} = 0.109$
5.499	$P_6 = A_6^2/4 \quad = 0.00$	$\sqrt{P_6} = 0.049$

function that we have sampled. The power in the next-highest harmonic is approximately one-tenth that of the fundamental. Had we taken the 12 sample points equally distributed over the periodic sine wave function, we would have found a single harmonic component at 1 Hz and the rest of the components would have been zero or very small, depending only on truncation error as related to the number of terms carried in the pocket calculator analysis. Here we see the "tail" affect the DC level and spread the power in the 1-hertz sine function over higher-frequency harmonics. The reason for this is that the high-frequency components are required to take care of the discontinuous end effects associated with the "tail" in our sampled periodic discrete function. Specifically, this "tail" is associated with the jump discontinuity in going from $+0.59$ at $n = 11$ to 0 at $n = 12$ for the example function that we have chosen to analyze.

Summary

A number of important observations have been made on the Fourier expansion of discrete functions. Take, for example, the 12-point Fourier coefficient formulas. The 12 values of the discrete function result in a discrete spectrum with only six frequency components. In general, $2N$ values of a discrete function will result in a spectrum with only N spectral components. This generally holds true, reflecting the rule of thumb that data must be sampled at at least twice the highest frequency of interest for the coefficients of the spectral components to be determined at the frequency of interest.

The second observation deals with the physical characteristics of sampled data. Note that once a function is sampled the spectrum of the sequence of sampled functions has no frequency components greater than half the sampling frequency. What, then, happens to the high frequency components of a sampled continuous function? They are folded down into the low-frequency components of the discrete spectrum. They are summed with the low-frequency components. In this sense the high-frequency components are not actually rejected by the sampling process, but they are folded into the low-frequency components of the discrete function spectrum, resulting in distortion of the low-frequency components that made up the original continuous-function frequency spectrum. Thus, although the sampling operation does not result in high-frequency components in the sampled-functions spectrum, the true continuous-function spectrum can be much distorted by the sampling process in the low frequencies.

In this book, the practical application of *Fourier series* analysis results from the representation of an arbitrary periodic forcing function with series of sinusoidal periodic functions, each of which produces in linear systems a single response which is easily determined. The net effect of the periodic forcing function is then developed by the superposition of the individual responses to their harmonic components. Furthermore, since outputs associated with each harmonic component are sine waves of the same frequency, differing only in phase and amplitude, the characteristics of a system are completely determined by specifying the amplitude and phase shift *transfer functions*. Transfer functions are single-valued relations that relate the output of the system to its input. These transfer functions are only a function of the frequency of the input sinusoids. Our attention is thus directed from the time-domain characteristics of a system to its frequency-domain characteristics. In short since we know "sine wave in" produces "sine wave out" in the time domain, we are only left with the question of amplitude and phase shift, which are solely a function of the frequency of the input sine wave. In this sense, we have transformed the problem from a time-domain problem to a frequency-domain problem. Problems whose forcing functions are periodic and, where the interest is in the spectrum of the steady-state response of the system, are directly amenable to this type of Fourier analysis, whereas problems involving nonperiodic forcing functions and/or transient responses are not.

The practical application of the Fourier transform results from the fact that it can transform nonperiodic and transient functions from the time to the frequency domain. The response of a system to a given forcing function can be determined from the inverse Fourier transform of the product of the *spectrum function* of the forcing function and the spectrum function of the system transfer function. Although this is indeed important for dynamics analysis, two limitations of the Fourier transformation lead to the use of the more flexible Laplace transformation for this type of analysis. The first limitation is simply that the inverse Fourier transform involves improper integrals that are often difficult to derive. The second, and far more significant, difficulty is that the Fourier integrals do not converge for a number of the more commonly used engineering forcing functions, including the step function, sine, |sine|, and t^n (for $n = 1, 2, 3, \ldots$).

For example, the Fourier transform of the unit step

$$f(t) = \begin{cases} 0, & t < 0 \\ 1, & t \geqslant 0 \end{cases} \tag{1-107}$$

takes the form

$$g(\omega) = \int_0^\infty e^{-j\omega t}\, dt = \frac{e^{-j\omega t}}{-j\omega}\bigg|_0^\infty = \frac{\cos(\omega t) - j\sin(\omega t)}{-j\omega}\bigg|_0^\infty \tag{1-108}$$

which cannot be evaluated because both the sine and cosine oscillate without limit as their arguments become large without limit.

An approach to resolving this situation is to modify $f(t)$ so that the Fourier integral will converge. A "convergence factor" that works and leads to the Laplace transformation is $e^{-\sigma t}$. In this case

$$f'(t) = e^{-\sigma t} f(t) = \begin{cases} 0, & t < 0 \\ e^{-\sigma t}, & t \geqslant 0 \end{cases} \tag{1-109}$$

Then

$$g(\omega) = \int_0^\infty e^{-\sigma t} e^{-j\omega t}\, dt = \frac{e^{-(\sigma + j\omega)t}}{-(\sigma + j\omega)}\bigg|_0^\infty$$

$$= \frac{1}{\sigma + j\omega} \tag{1-110}$$

1.8 THE LAPLACE TRANSFORMATION

The alternative to modifying the function to be transformed is to modify the transformation kernel. The approach is to include the term $e^{-\sigma t}$ as a part of the transformation integral kernel $e^{j\omega t}$. The transformation becomes

$$g(\omega) = \int_0^\infty \left[e^{-\sigma t} f(t) \right] e^{-j\omega t} \, dt$$

$$g(\omega) = \int_0^\infty f(t) e^{-(\sigma + j\omega)t} \, dt$$

$$F(s) = \int_0^\infty f(t) e^{-st} \, dt \qquad\qquad (1\text{-}111)$$

The inverse transform becomes

$$e^{-\sigma t} f(t) = \frac{1}{2\pi} \int_{-\infty}^\infty g(\omega) e^{j\omega t} \, d\omega$$

Thus

$$f(t) = \frac{1}{2\pi} \int_{-\infty}^\infty g(\omega) e^{(\sigma + j\omega)t} \, d\omega$$

$$= \frac{1}{2\pi j} \int_{-j\infty}^{j\infty} g(\omega) e^{(\sigma + j\omega)t} \, d(j\omega)$$

$$= \frac{1}{2\pi j} \int_{\sigma - j\omega}^{\sigma + j\omega} g(\omega) e^{(\sigma + j\omega)t} \, d(\sigma + j\omega)$$

$$= \frac{1}{2\pi j} \int_{\sigma - j\infty}^{\sigma + j\infty} F(s) e^{st} \, ds \qquad\qquad (1\text{-}112)$$

Equations 1-111 and 1-112 define the Laplace transform pair. When the integral in (1-111) converges we say the function $f(t)$ is *Laplace transformable*.

Most engineering functions can be Laplace transformed. Examples of the types of functions that cannot be Laplace transformed are of the forms t^t and $e^{t^n}(n = 1, 2, 3, \ldots)$ and are not usually encountered in what will be studied here. Functions that are not Laplace transformable are often said to be *not* of exponential order. The meaning should now be obvious.

With regard to $f(t)$: (1) the real variable t need not represent time, (2) it must be a single-valued function in order to have a unique Laplace transform, (3) it may have a finite number of finite discontinuities, and (4) if there is a discontinuity at $t = 0$, the lower limit of the integral is to be approached from the positive side. Finally, in the Laplace transform, the evaluation of the inversion integral (1-112) is facilitated by the theory of residues.

The Laplace transformation is characterized by its use in simplifying functions and operations to the extent that only algebraic manipulation is necessary to perform otherwise fairly sophisticated analysis. The Laplace transform:

1. Transforms periodic functions with finite discontinuities (or discontinuous derivatives) into simple algebraic expressions.

2. Transforms differentiation and integration operations in the time domain into multiplication and division operations in the frequency domain.

3. Transforms integrodifferential equations into algebraic equations.

4. When used to solve differential equations, expediently determines the arbitrary constants in the solution to the differential equations.

5. Can conveniently handle impulse responses, an essential concept in linear system stability analysis.

There is extensive literature on fairly sophisticated analysis of linear systems using the Laplace transform. The basis of this literature is a small set of theorems that are presented here without proof, since the proofs are covered in many other books.

Theorem 1.   The Laplace transformation for the sum of two functions is equal to the sum of transformation of the individual functions:

$$\mathcal{L}(f_1 + f_2) = \mathcal{L}(f_1) + \mathcal{L}(f_2) \tag{1-113}$$

Theorem 2.   The Laplace transformation of a constant times a function is equal to the constant times the Laplace transformation of the function:

$$\mathcal{L}(cf) = c\mathcal{L}(f) \tag{1-114}$$

These two theorems express the linear nature of the Laplace transformation.

Theorem 3.   The shifting theorem. If the Laplace transform of $f(t) = F(s)$, then

$$\mathcal{L}\left[f(t - T)U(t - T)\right] = e^{-Ts}F(s) \tag{1-115}$$

Note that not only is the function shifted but the unit step function multiplier is also shifted in the time domain. Many mistakes are made in the application of the shifting theorem to the development of difference equations when this important qualification is overlooked.

Theorem 4.   The Laplace transform of a periodic function $f(t)$ is equal to $1/(1 - e^{-Ts})$ times the Laplace transformation of $f(t)$ over the first cycle.

$$\mathcal{L}f(t) = \frac{F(s, T)}{1 - e^{-Ts}} \tag{1-116}$$

Theorem 5.   The differentiation theorem. If a function $f(t)$ and its derivatives are both Laplace transformable, and if $\mathcal{L}[f(t)] = F(s)$, then

$$\mathcal{L}\left\{ \frac{d}{dt} f(t) \right\} = sF(s) - f(0+) \tag{1-117}$$

Theorem 6.   The integration theorem. If $\mathcal{L}f(t) = F(s)$, then

$$\mathcal{L}\left[\int_0^t f(\tau)\, d\tau \right] = \frac{F(s)}{s} \tag{1-118}$$

Theorem 7.   If $\mathcal{L}[f(t)] = F(s)$, and if the first derivative is Laplace transformable, then

$$f(0+) = \lim_{t \to 0+} f(t) = \lim_{s \to \infty} sF(s) \tag{1-119}$$

Theorem 8.   If $\mathcal{L}[f(t)] = F(s)$, and if the first derivative is Laplace transformable, then

$$\lim_{t \to \infty} f(t) = \lim_{s \to 0} sF(s) \tag{1-120}$$

Theorem 9.   The convolution theorem. If $\mathcal{L}[f_1(t)] = F_1(s)$ and $\mathcal{L}[f_2(t)] = F_2(s)$, then

$$\mathcal{L}\left[\int_0^t f_1(t - \tau) f_2(\tau)\, d\tau \right] = \mathcal{L}\left[\int_0^t f_1(t) f_2(t - \tau)\, d\tau \right] = F_1(s)F_2(s) \tag{1-121}$$

The convolution theorem is particularly important because it enables evaluation of the response of the linear system to a forcing function. The convolution integral generates the particular solution of any linear differential equation that is Laplace transformable and whose forcing function is Laplace transformable.

Theorem 10. If $\mathcal{L}(f) = F(s)$, then

$$\mathcal{L}\{e^{at}f(t)\} = F(s - a) \tag{1-122}$$

Theorem 11. The change of scale theorem. If $\mathcal{L}f(t) = F(s)$, then

$$\mathcal{L}f(at) = \frac{1}{a} F\left(\frac{s}{a}\right) \tag{1-123}$$

Theorem 12. If $\mathcal{L}f(t) = F(s)$, then

$$\mathcal{L}\{t^n f(t)\} = (-1)^n \frac{d^n}{ds^n} F(s) \tag{1-124}$$

Theorem 13. If $\mathcal{L}f(t) = F(s)$ and $\lim_{t \to 0} (f(t)/t)$ exists, then

$$\mathcal{L}\left\{\frac{f(t)}{t}\right\} = \int_s^\infty F(s)\, ds \tag{1-125}$$

There are a number of methods for deriving the Laplace transformation of functions other than the direct method of (1-111) and (1-112). Use of tables is the easiest method to avoid such derivations. E. C. Levy's book, *The Laplace Transformation* (McGraw-Hill) has a table of 1200 Laplace transforms in condensed form. The table is not often published outside of the McDonnell Douglas Corporation (the work was done by Levy while working at the former Douglas Aircraft Company in Santa Monica, California).

Another approach is to derive a differential equation of which the function to be transformed is a solution. Then the Laplace transform of the function is developed from the Laplace transform of the differential equation.

If the function to be Laplace transformed can be expanded in a power series, the Laplace transformation of the function will be the Laplace transform of the power series. Since the closed form of power series can sometimes be recognized, the closed form of the Laplace transform may be recognized and written. In general if

$$f(t) = \sum_{n=0}^\infty a_n t^n$$

Then

$$\mathcal{L}f(t) = \mathcal{L}\left\{\sum_{n=0}^\infty a_n t^n\right\} = \sum_{n=0}^\infty \frac{n! a_n}{s^{n+1}} \tag{1-126}$$

Of course the series of Laplace transforms of t^n must converge for this approach to work.

Example 1

If $f(t) = U(t)$, the unit step

$$\mathcal{L}U(t) = \int_0^\infty e^{-st}U(t)\, dt = \lim_{L\to\infty} \int_0^L e^{-st}U(t)\, dt$$

$$= \lim_{L\to\infty} \left(\frac{e^{-st}}{s} \right)\Bigg|_0^L = \lim_{L\to\infty} \left(\frac{1 - e^{-sL}}{s} \right) = \frac{1}{s}$$

In this simple example the result holds only when

$$\operatorname{Re}(s) > 0 \qquad \text{or} \qquad \sigma > 0$$

where $s = \sigma + j\omega$, a complex number.

Example 2

If $f(t) = t$, then

$$\mathcal{L}(t) = \lim_{L\to\infty} \int_0^L t e^{-st}\, dt$$

Integrating by parts we find

$$\mathcal{L}(t) = \lim_{L\to\infty} \left\{ \frac{t e^{-st}}{s} - \frac{e^{-st}}{s^2} \right\}\Bigg|_0^L = \frac{1}{s^2}, \qquad \text{for } s > 0$$

Example 3

If $f(t) = e^{at}$, then

$$\mathcal{L}e^{at} = \int_0^\infty e^{-(s-a)t}\, dt = \left(\frac{-1}{s-a} \right)\int_0^{-\infty} e^k\, dk$$

where $k = (s - a)t$, and

$$\mathcal{L}e^{at} = \left(\frac{-1}{s-a} \right)(0 - 1) = \frac{1}{s-a}$$

Example 4

If $f(t) = \sin(\omega t)$, then

$$\mathcal{L}\{\sin(\omega t)\} = \int_0^\infty e^{-st} \sin \omega t \, dt$$

$$= \frac{-e^{-st}\left[s \sin(\omega t) + \omega \cos(\omega t)\right]}{s^2 + \omega^2} \Bigg|_0^\infty$$

$$= \frac{\omega}{s^2 + \omega^2}$$

Example 5

If $f(t) = \cos(\omega t)$, since

$$\cos(\omega t) = \frac{1}{\omega} \frac{d}{dt} \sin(\omega t)$$

then

$$\mathcal{L} \cos(\omega t) = \frac{1}{\omega} \mathcal{L} \frac{d}{dt} \sin(\omega t) = \left(\frac{1}{\omega}\right)(s)\left(\frac{\omega}{s^2 + \omega^2}\right)$$

$$\mathcal{L} \cos(\omega t) = \frac{s}{s^2 + \omega^2}$$

Example 6

If $f(t) = \sinh(t)$, then

$$\mathcal{L}\{\sinh(\omega t)\} = \mathcal{L}\left\{ \frac{e^{+\omega t} - e^{-\omega t}}{2} \right\}$$

$$= \frac{1}{2} \int_0^\infty e^{-(s-\omega)t} \, dt - \frac{1}{2} \int_0^\infty e^{-(s+\omega)t} \, dt$$

$$\mathcal{L}\{\sinh(\omega t)\} = \frac{1}{2} \mathcal{L}\{e^{\omega t}\} + \frac{1}{2} \mathcal{L}\{e^{-\omega t}\}$$

$$\mathcal{L}\{\sinh(\omega t)\} = \frac{1}{2}\left\{ \frac{1}{s - \omega} - \frac{1}{s + \omega} \right\} = \frac{\omega}{s^2 - \omega^2}$$

Example 7

Reasoning as in Example 5, by inspection we can write

$$\mathcal{L}\{\cosh(\omega t)\} = \left(\frac{1}{\omega}\right)\left(\frac{\omega}{s^2 - \omega^2}\right)(s) = \frac{s}{s^2 - \omega^2}$$

Example 8

If $f(t) = te^{-t}$, and since

$$\mathcal{L}(t) = \frac{1}{s^2}$$

then

$$\mathcal{L}\{te^{-\omega t}\} = \frac{1}{(s + \omega)^2} = \frac{1}{s^2 + 2\omega s + \omega^2}$$

Example 9

If $f(t) = e^{-t/\tau} \sin(\omega t)$, then since

$$\mathcal{L}\{\sin(\omega t)\} = \frac{\omega}{s^2 + \omega^2}, \quad \mathcal{L}\{e^{-t/\tau} \sin(\omega t)\} = \frac{\omega}{(s + 1/\tau)^2 + \omega^2}$$

and

$$\mathcal{L}\{e^{-t/\tau} \sin(\omega t)\} = \frac{\omega}{s^2 + (2/\tau)s + (\omega^2 + 1/\tau^2)}$$

Example 10

If $f(t) = \sin(\omega t)$, the differential equation of which $f(t)$ is a solution is derived as

$$f'(t) = \omega \cos(\omega t)$$

$$f''(t) = -\omega^2 \sin(\omega t) = -\omega^2 f(t)$$

Then

$$\mathcal{L}\{\sin(\omega t)\} = \mathcal{L}\{f''(t) + \omega^2 f(t) = 0\}$$

$$= s^2 \mathcal{L}\{f(t)\} + \omega^2 \mathcal{L}\{f(t)\} - sf(0) - f'(0) = 0$$

and

$$(s^2 + \omega^2)\mathcal{L}\{f(t)\} = sf(0) + f'(0)$$

$$\mathcal{L}\{f(t)\} = \left(\frac{s}{s^2 + \omega^2} \right)f(0) + \left(\frac{1}{s^2 + \omega^2} \right)f'(0)$$

Now $f(0) = 0$ and $f'(0) = \omega$.

$$\therefore \mathcal{L}\{\sin(\omega t)\} = \frac{\omega}{s^2 + \omega^2}$$

Example 11

If $f(t) = t \sin(\omega t)$, then

$$\mathcal{L}f(t) = - \frac{d}{ds} \left(\frac{\omega}{s^2 + \omega^2} \right) = \frac{2\omega s}{\left(s^2 + \omega^2\right)^2}$$

The Inverse Laplace Transformation

The inverse Laplace transform is usually written in the complex integral form:

$$f(t) = \frac{1}{2\pi j} \int_{\sigma-j\infty}^{\sigma+j\infty} e^{st} f(s) \, ds$$

While easy to evaluate by residues for certain Laplace transforms, it is hardly the quickest method. Other more useful methods for deriving the inverse Laplace transform are the following:

1. Table look up.
2. The use of partial fraction expansions where $G(s) = N(s)/D(s)*$ can be written as the sum of rational functions,

$$\frac{A}{(as + b)}, \quad \frac{As + B}{(as^2 + bs + c)}, \quad \frac{As^2 + Bs + C}{(as^3 + bs^2 + cs + d)}$$

where the denominators match the terms of the denominator in $G(s)$.
3. The series expansion method, where the $G(s)$ to be inverted is expanded in an inverse power series of s and then inverted into a power series in t.

*For $D(s)$ of higher order than $N(s)$.

4. The differential equation method where $G(s)$ is inverted into a differential equation in t whose solution is the inverse Laplace transform of $G(s)$.

Example 12

$$\mathcal{L}^{-1}\left\{ \frac{s + \omega_1}{s^3} - \frac{s - \omega_2}{s^2 + \omega_n^2} \right\} = \mathcal{L}^{-1}\left\{ \frac{1}{s^2} + \frac{\omega_1}{s^3} - \frac{s}{s^2 + \omega_n^2} + \frac{\omega_2}{s^2 + \omega_n^2} \right\}$$

$$= t + \frac{\omega_1 t^2}{2} - \cos(\omega_n t) + \frac{\omega_2}{\omega_n} \sin(\omega_n t)$$

Example 13

$$\mathcal{L}^{-1}\left\{ \frac{s}{s^2 - 4s + 20} \right\} = \mathcal{L}^{-1}\left\{ \frac{(s - 2) + 2}{(s - 2)^2 + 16} \right\}$$

$$= \mathcal{L}^{-1}\left\{ \frac{s - 2}{(s - 2)^2 + 16} \right\} + \frac{1}{2} \mathcal{L}^{-1}\left\{ \frac{4}{(s - 2)^2 + 16} \right\}$$

$$= e^{2t} \cos(4t) + \tfrac{1}{2} e^{2t} \sin(4t)$$

$$= e^{2t} \left\{ \cos(4t) + \tfrac{1}{2} \sin(4t) \right\}$$

Example 14

$$\mathcal{L}^{-1} \frac{e^{-Ts}}{(s + 1/\tau)^4} = \mathcal{L}^{-1}\left[e^{-Ts} \left\{ \mathcal{L}f(t) \right\} \right]$$

where

$$f(t) = \mathcal{L}^{-1}\left\{ \frac{1}{(s + 1/\tau)^4} \right\} = \frac{t^3 e^{-t/\tau}}{6}$$

Then

$$\mathcal{L}^{-1} e^{-Ts}\left[\mathcal{L}\left\{ \frac{t^3 e^{-t/\tau}}{6} \right\} \right] = \frac{e^{-(t-T)/\tau}(t - T)^3}{6} U(t - T)$$

Another way of writing this function is

$$\mathcal{L}^{-1}\left\{ \frac{e^{-Ts}}{(s + 1/\tau)^4} \right\} = \begin{cases} \frac{1}{6}(t - T)^3 e^{-(t-T)/\tau} & t > T \\ 0 & t < T \end{cases}$$

Example 15

$$\mathcal{L}^{-1}\left\{ \frac{1}{s^2(s + 1)^2} \right\} = \mathcal{L}^{-1}\left\{ \frac{1}{(s + 1)^2} + \frac{2}{s + 1} + \frac{1}{s^2} + \frac{2}{s} \right\}$$

$$= te^{-t} + 2e^{-t} + t - 2$$

Example 16

$$\mathcal{L}^{-1}\left\{ \frac{3s + 7}{s^2 - 2s - 3} \right\} = \mathcal{L}^{-1}\left\{ \frac{3s + 7}{(s - 3)(s + 1)} \right\}$$

$$= \mathcal{L}^{-1}\left\{ \frac{A}{s - 3} + \frac{B}{s + 1} \right\}$$

by partial fraction expansion, where

$$\frac{3s + 7}{(s - 3)(s + 1)} = \frac{A}{s - 3} + \frac{B}{s + 1}$$

or

$$3s + 7 = A(s + 1) + B(s - 3)$$

$$= (A + B)s + (A - 3B)$$

Thus

$$A + B = 3$$

$$A - 3B = 7$$

Solving simultaneously, we find

$$A = 4 \quad \text{and} \quad B = -1$$

Thus

$$\mathcal{L}^{-1}\frac{3s+7}{(s-3)(s+1)} = \mathcal{L}\left\{\left(\frac{4}{s-3}\right) - \left(\frac{1}{s+1}\right)\right\} = 4e^{3t} - e^{-t}$$

Solving Differential Equations

The differential equation

$$\tau\dot{x} + x = f(t)$$

with the initial conditions

$$x(0) = 0$$

can be solved using Laplace transforms in the following way:

$$\mathcal{L}(\tau\dot{x} + x) = \mathcal{L}f(t)$$

$$\tau\mathcal{L}(\dot{x}) + \mathcal{L}(x) = \mathcal{L}f(t)$$

$$\tau[sx(s) - x(0)] + x(s) = f(s)$$

$$(\tau s + 1)x(s) = f(s) + \tau x(0)$$

$$x(s) = \frac{f(s)}{\tau s + 1} + \frac{\tau x(0)}{\tau s + 1}$$

$$\therefore x(t) = \mathcal{L}^{-1}\left(\frac{f(s)}{\tau s + 1}\right) + x(0)(1 - e^{-t/\tau})$$

The second term on the right side of this equation is the complementary solution of the differential equation. The first term is the particular solution of the differential equation. The particular solution is in general form so that we may examine a number of special cases:

1. If $f(t) = 0$, then $F(s) = 0$ and

$$\mathcal{L}^{-1}\left\{\frac{f(s)}{\tau s + 1}\right\} = 0$$

2. If $f(t) = U(t)$, then $F(s) = 1/s$ and

$$\mathcal{L}^{-1}\left\{ \frac{f(s)}{\tau s + 1} \right\} = \mathcal{L}^{-1}\left\{ \frac{1}{s(\tau s + 1)} \right\} = 1 - e^{-t/\tau}$$

3. If $f(t) = e^{-at}$, then $F(s) = a/(s + a)$ and

$$\mathcal{L}^{-1}\left\{ \frac{a/\tau}{(s + 1/\tau)(s + a)} \right\} = \left(\frac{1}{1 - \tau a} \right)(e^{-at} - e^{-t/\tau})$$

Stability Considerations

The stability of a linear stationary process is determined by examining the system's response to an impulse. In this case, the forcing function is a delta function applied at $t = 0$. Then

$$x(s) = \frac{\mathcal{L}\delta(0)}{\tau s + 1}$$

When developed carefully, it is found that

$$\mathcal{L}\delta(0) = 1$$

A heuristic argument to show this is that

$$\delta(0) \sim \frac{d}{dt}\{U(t)\}$$

$$\therefore \mathcal{L}\delta(0) \sim \mathcal{L}\frac{d}{dt}\{U(t)\} = s\mathcal{L}U(t) = s\left(\frac{1}{s} \right) = 1$$

The impulse response for this system is given by

$$x(s) = \frac{1}{\tau s + 1}$$

Thus

$$x(t) = \mathcal{L}^{-1}x(s) = 1 \cdot e^{-t/\tau} = 1 \cdot e^{s_{\text{pole}}t}$$

We can now make the following observations:

1. The stability of this process is determined by the location of the system's pole in the s plane. When $\text{Re}(s_{pole}) < 0$ this process is stable; that is, the exponent in the exponential is negative and thus the impulse response is bounded and decreasing in magnitude and is therefore said to be asymptotically stable. If, on the other hand, the exponent were positive, the impulse response would have been unbounded and is therefore said to be unstable. Finally, if the impulse response is bounded but not asymptotically stable, the system is said to be neutrally stable.

2. The system's impulse response is identical to the system's transfer function (as we shall see again in Section 1.9).

The application of the Laplace transform to solving higher-order stationary linear differential equations is identical to that shown for this first-order process.

The findings for higher-order system (polynomials in s) are identical to those found in this first-order example. For an nth order linear system to be stable, the n poles of the system must be less than, or equal to, zero.

1.9   BLOCK DIAGRAMS AND TRANSFER FUNCTIONS

Block diagram representations of systems were developed from the need to visualize the design of complex systems. Traceability between design parameters and system dynamics can be lost when a system of equations is used to mathematically model a system. An alternative is to diagram the cause-effect relationships between the inputs and outputs of each element in the system. The cause-effect relationships between the input and output of a system element are called the element's transfer functions. The transfer functions are enclosed with blocks. One-dimensional systems have a single input and a single output. Block diagrams of systems described with vector-matrix equations usually have high dimensionality and have more than one input and more than one output.

The simplest block diagram that can relate a system's input to its output is seen in Figure 1-10.

$$x \longrightarrow \boxed{f(\ )} \longrightarrow y \qquad \text{symbolizes } y = f(x)$$

FIGURE 1-10.   The simplest form of block diagram — the block symbol.

The chief characteristic of a block diagram of a process is that the signal flow is unidirectional and the symbol enclosed in the block is usually an operator that operates on the input to transform it into the output.

While a summation operator could be enclosed within a block, this operation is conventionally symbolized as seen in Figure 1-11.

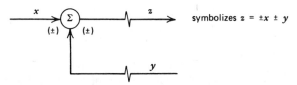

FIGURE 1-11.   The conventional symbol for summation.

This seemingly mundane set of symbols representing (*a*) system element transfer functions, (*b*) signal flow summation, and (*c*) signal flow branching (pickoff) can be used to develop a powerful block diagram algebra for manipulating system transfer functions, developing system equivalences, simplifying system transfer functions, and generally visualizing the system design and the interactions among the many elements of a complex system. The block diagram method of mathematically modeling a closed-loop process is particularly easy to visualize and understand. Block diagram algebra has been developed to a high art among engineers, perhaps because of the extensive interest in closed-loop processes. Most of the commonly used block diagram manipulations are shown in Table 1-8.

The symbol for *picking off* signal flow from a signal flow path is shown in Figure 1-12.

FIGURE 1-12.   The symbol for signal flow branching.

Examples of block diagram analysis appear below.

Example 1

Block diagram $y/x = 1/(\tau s + 1)$.

Note that

$$\tau s y(s) + y(s) = x(s)$$

$$\therefore y(s) = x(s) - \tau s y(s)$$

Table 1-8. Common Block Diagram Manipulations and Equivalence Relations Used in Block Diagram Analysis

Transformation	Original diagram	Equivalent diagram	Equation
Interchange of blocks			$b = aY_1Y_2$
Interchange of summing points			$d = a - b + c$
Rearrangement of summing points			$d = a - b - c$
Moving a summing point ahead of an element			$d = aY - c$
Moving a summing point beyond an element			$c = (a - b)Y$
Moving a takeoff point ahead of an element			$b = aY$
Moving a takeoff point beyond an element			$b = aY$ $a = b/Y$ $= a$
Moving a takeoff point ahead of a summing point			$c = a - b$
Moving a takeoff point beyond a summing point			$c = a - b$ $a = c + b$

Transformation	Equation
Combining cascade elements	$b = aY_1Y_2$
Removing an element from a forward loop	$d = a(Y_1 - Y_2)$
Inserting an element in a forward loop	$d = aY_1 - a$
Eliminating a forward loop	$d = a(Y_1 - Y_2)$
Removing an element from a feedback loop	$d = \dfrac{aY_1}{1 + Y_1Y_2}$
Inserting an element in a feedback loop	$d = \dfrac{aY_1}{1 + Y_1}$
Eliminating a feedback loop	$d = \dfrac{aY_1}{1 + Y_1Y_2}$
	$d = a\,\dfrac{1}{1 + Y_1}$
	$d = a\,\dfrac{Y_1}{1 + Y_2}$
Inserting a feedback loop	$d = aY_1$
	$d = aY_1$

75

The block diagram for this equation is

Also, since $\tau s y(s) + y(s) = x(s)$

$$y(s) = \frac{x(s) - y(s)}{\tau s}$$

Thus

These block diagrams are identical from a transfer function viewpoint as both reduce to

From a physical viewpoint each has a different interpretation. The first block diagram can be viewed as a positioning system with rate feedback to damp the motion of the process.

The second block diagram can be viewed as a positioning system that nulls the integral of the positioning error (i.e., the integral of the difference between the commanded position x and the system position y).

Example 2

Derive the transfer function for the system

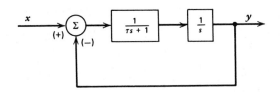

First the forward-loop elements are combined as

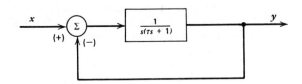

Then the transfer function for the closed-loop process is derived as

Thus

$$x \quad \boxed{\dfrac{1}{\tau s^2 + s + 1}} \quad y$$

The transfer function is

$$\frac{y(s)}{x(s)} = \frac{1}{\tau s^2 + s + 1}$$

Example 3

Without using free-body diagrams of Lagrange's equations per se, write the transfer function for the coupled spring system shown in Figure 1-13.

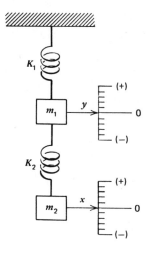

FIGURE 1-13. Coupled mass spring, damper system. K_1 = spring constant, first spring; K_2 = spring constant, second spring; m_1 = mass of first weight; m_2 = mass of second weight; y = displacement of m_1 from equilibrium condition; x = displacement of m_2 from equilibrium condition.

Step 1. If m_2 is displaced in the direction $+x$ and if there are no other instantaneous displacements, the forces on m_2 can be block diagrammed as follows:

Step 2. If m_1 is displaced in the direction of $+y$ and if there are no other instantaneous displacements, the forces on m_1 can be block diagrammed as:

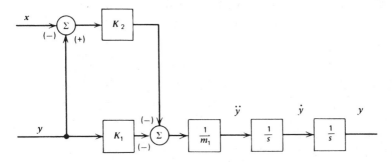

Step 3. Combining the results of steps 1 and 2, we find

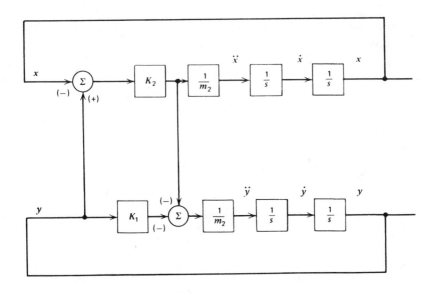

This example shows the "physical reasoning" that can quickly lead to block diagrams of relatively complex processes with only rudimentary concepts of force and motion. These block diagrams can be reduced to transfer functions quickly and easily by using block diagram algebra, and (if so desired) the equations of motion can be written after simple algebraic manipulation of the transfer function and inverse Laplace transformation. Perhaps the most important aspect of this use of block diagramming is that the engineer has good "physical feel" for the problem when developing the system block diagram in this manner. The payoff comes when interpreting, either analytically or on a computer, the information developed by the mathematical model. The interpretation is tied to the physics of the system, not the mathematical properties of the equations. This "physical" approach is quite different from using Newton's laws or Lagrange's equations where the analyst is fairly remote from the physics of the system.

Those who work with rotational motion should become familiar with the still as-yet not widely known work of LeCompte who developed a simple approach (which he calls "two-vector gyro mechanics") for analyzing the dynamics of rotational motion.* This is based on physical insights into the motions of gyro gained through block diagramming the motion of the angular velocity, angular momentum, and body coordinate unit vectors as rotational systems respond to torques. Unusually simple mathematical models of rotational motion were developed from two-vector gyro mechanics, and a number of interesting inventions have resulted, such as active nutation dampers, pointing control systems for spinning bodies, translation control systems for spinning bodies, and simple wobble sensors.

Deriving the equations of motion for most systems involves, for example, writing Newton's Second Law

$$\mathbb{F} = \frac{d}{dt}(m\mathbb{V}) = m\,\mathbb{A} \qquad \text{for constant } m^\dagger$$

then solving for $\mathbb{A}$ and double integrating to determine $\mathbb{V}$ and $\mathbb{X}$. For example, consider a mass-soring-damper system. Writing Newton's Second Law we have

$$m\ddot{x} + d\dot{x} + kx = f(t) \tag{1}$$

where,

m	System mass
k	Spring constant
d	Damper constant
x	Displacement
$f(t)$	External force

---

*"Simply Mechanized Attitude Control for Spinning Vehicles," G. W. LeCompte and J. G. Bland, *Journal of Spacecraft and Rockets*, November-December 1964. Old but good.
†Here $\mathbb{F}$ is force, $\mathbb{A}$ is acceleration, $\mathbb{V}$ is velocity and $\mathbb{X}$ is position.

Assuming $f(t) = 0$, (without the action of an external force) (1) becomes

$$m\ddot{x} = -kx - d\dot{x} \tag{2}$$

where x is the displacement (one dimension in this case), $\dot{x}$ is the time rate of change of the displacement (which is the velocity), and $\ddot{x}$ is the acceleration. Now solving for the highest derivative, which is the methodology for continuous simulation, we obtain (2). We can numerically integrate $\ddot{x}$ twice to obtain x. Of course, we need to know $\dot{x}(0)$ and $x(0)$, the two initial conditions to initiate the motion.

Another approach to developing a system's equations of motion that does not use Newton's force equations is available. Consider the following definitions:

$$F = m\ddot{x} \qquad \text{(Newton's Second Law)}$$

The space integral of Newton's Second Law is

$$\int F\,dx = \int m\ddot{x}\,dk = \int m\dot{x}\,d\dot{x} = \frac{m\dot{x}^2}{2} = K$$

Here the term K is recognized to be the kinetic energy of the moving mass m.

When only one spring is involved in the system

$$F = kx$$

$$\therefore \int F\,dx = \frac{kx^2}{2} = P$$

You will recognize the term P as the potential energy of the moving mass m. We see, then, that

$$\int (F - m\ddot{x})\,dx = \frac{m\dot{x}^2}{2} - \frac{kx^2}{2} = K - P = L = 0$$

Now let us examine the time-interval of Newton's Second Law:

$$\int F\,dt = \int m\ddot{x}\,dt = \int m\,d\dot{x} = m\dot{x} = M$$

The term M is, of course, the momentum of the moving mass.

Now note that

$$\frac{\partial K}{\partial \dot{x}} = M$$

and

$$\frac{\partial P}{\partial x} = F = \frac{d}{dt}(M) = \frac{d}{dt}\left(\frac{\partial K}{\partial \dot{x}}\right)$$

or

$$\frac{d}{dt}\left(\frac{\partial K}{\partial \dot{x}}\right) - \frac{\partial P}{\partial x} = 0$$

You may recall that this relationship is called Lagrange's equation for one-dimensional motion for this simple mass-spring conservative system.

Interestingly, we see that the relationship between kinetic and potential energy is given by Lagrange's equation, which does not involve the concept of force at all. In fact, knowing that

$$P = \frac{kx^2}{2}$$

$$K = \frac{m\dot{x}^2}{2}$$

we find that Newton's Law and Hooke's Law can be viewed as derivable from Lagrange's energy terms as follows:

$$\frac{\partial P}{\partial x} = kx \qquad \text{Hooke's Law}$$

and

$$\frac{d}{dt}\left(\frac{\partial K}{\partial \dot{x}}\right) = m\ddot{x} \qquad \text{Newton's Second Law}$$

Thus Lagrange's energy equations give the equation of motion

$$m\ddot{x} - kx = 0$$

It is an aesthetically pleasing meeting of the minds of Newton and Lagrange. It can be further shown that by defining the relation

$$L = K - P = \text{Lagrangian} = \text{Kinetic Energy} - \text{Potential Energy}$$

then it is *generally* true that

$$\frac{d}{dt}\left(\frac{\partial L}{\partial \dot{q}}\right) - \frac{\partial L}{\partial q} = 0 \qquad \text{(Generalized Lagrange's equations)}$$

defines the motion of a system. Note here that q symbolizes a "generalized" coordinate in that it is a variable which uniquely specifies the location of the object whose motion is being analyzed.

There is an elegant development of Lagrange's equation using the calculus of variations. Lagrange himself used the calculus of variations to develop his energy-based approach to classical mechanics. The approach used here to develop Lagrange's equations is simple, straightforward, and based on the definitions of energy and momentum. It requires only a little algebraic manipulation to proceed from Newton's Second Law to Lagrange's equations for a simple system, leaving the inference that the generalization is likely to hold true for more complex systems.

Example

Consider the system shown in Figure 1-14. The potential energy of the system is

$$P = -(m_1 g x - m_2 g x)$$

The kinetic energy of the system is

$$K = \tfrac{1}{2}m_1 \dot{x}^2 + \tfrac{1}{2}m_2(-\dot{x})^2$$

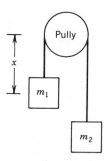

FIGURE 1-14.   Atwood's machine.

The Lagrangian is

$$L = K - P = \tfrac{1}{2}m_1\dot{x}^2 + \tfrac{1}{2}m_2\dot{x}^2 + m_1gx - m_2gx$$

Substituting the Lagrangian into (5) gives

$$\frac{d}{dt}\left((m_1 + m_2)\dot{x}\right) - g(m_1 - m_2) = 0$$

$$\therefore \ddot{x} = \left(\frac{m_1 - m_2}{m_1 + m_2}\right)g;$$

$$\dot{x} = \left(\frac{m_1 - m_2}{m_1 + m_2}\right)gt + \dot{x}_0;$$

$$x = \left(\frac{m_1 - m_2}{m_1 + m_2}\right)g_2t^2 + \dot{x}_0t + x_0$$

here t is time and the "0" subscripts indicate the "initial condition" of the position and velocity.

Now, suppose we examine a pendulum whose motion is damped by its passage through the air. By defining a *dissipation function D* whose partial derivative with respect to velocity will generate the proper force to velocity relationship, we can then write the equations of motion of a system as

$$\frac{d}{dt}\left(\frac{\partial L}{\partial \dot{q}}\right) - \frac{\partial L}{\partial q} + \frac{\partial D}{\partial \dot{q}} = 0 \tag{1}$$

The dissipation function for velocity-dependent frictional forces is

$$D = \frac{A}{2}\dot{q}^2$$

Now consider the application of this type of dissipation function to the motion of a pendulum where the friction of the air is significant (see Figure 1-15).

The kinetic energy is

$$K = \tfrac{1}{2}m(l\dot{\theta})^2 \tag{2}$$

The potential energy is

$$P = -mgl\cos\theta \tag{3}$$

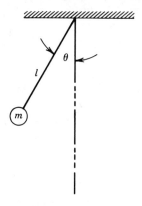

FIGURE 1-15.   A pendulum.

Thus

$$L = \frac{m}{2}(l\dot{\theta})^2 + mgl\cos\theta \tag{4}$$

The dissipation function is

$$D = \tfrac{1}{2}A(l\dot{\theta})^2 \tag{5}$$

Substituting (4) and (5) into (1) yields

$$ml^2\ddot{\theta} - 0 + mgl\sin\theta + Al^2\dot{\theta} = 0$$

$$\therefore \ddot{\theta} = -\frac{q}{l}\sin\theta - \frac{A}{m}\dot{\theta}$$

A system of n Simultaneous Lagrange's equations is used to describe the motion of a system with n degrees of freedom (n independent coordinates). Here, Lagrange's equations take the form

$$\frac{d}{dt}\left(\frac{\partial L}{\partial \dot{q}_n}\right) - \frac{\partial L}{\partial q_n} + \frac{\partial D}{\partial \dot{q}_n} = Q_n$$

where n is the number of degrees of freedom and Q_n are the "generalized" forces that drive the system (analogous to forcing functions in the study of one-dimensional differential equations).

Example

An elastic pendulum is shown in Figure 1-16. The mass of the bob is m; the length of the pendulum is r; the length of the pendulum at rest is r_0; the spring constant is k, and the coefficient of viscous friction is A. The objective is to derive the differential equations that describe the motion of this elastic pendulum.

The energy functions and the dissipation function of the entire system are

$$K = \tfrac{1}{2}m\dot{r}^2 + \tfrac{1}{2}m(r\dot{\theta})^2$$

$$P = \tfrac{1}{2}K(r - r_0)^2 + mg(r_0 - r\cos\theta)$$

$$D = \tfrac{1}{2}A\dot{r}^2 + \tfrac{1}{2}A(r\dot{\theta})^2$$

For this two degrees of freedom (two generalized coordinates, r and θ) problem, we have:

$$\frac{d}{dt}\left(\frac{\partial L}{\partial \dot{r}}\right) - \frac{\partial L}{\partial r} + \frac{\partial D}{\partial \dot{r}} = 0$$

which gives us the first differential equation of motion in the coordinate r

$$m\ddot{r} - mr\dot{\theta}^2 + A\dot{r} + K(r - r_0) - mg\cos\theta = 0$$

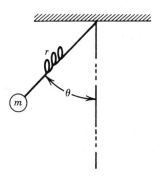

FIGURE 1-16.   Elastic pendulum simulation block diagram.

and

$$\frac{d}{dt}\left(\frac{\partial L}{\partial \dot{\theta}}\right) - \frac{\partial L}{\partial \theta} + \frac{\partial D}{\partial \dot{\theta}} = 0$$

which gives us the second differential equation of motion in the coordinate θ

$$mr^2\ddot{\theta} + 2m\dot{\theta}r\dot{r} + Ar^2\dot{\theta} + mgr \sin \theta = 0$$

The motion of the pendulum is then calculated by the simultaneous solution of these two differential equations and block diagrammed as shown in Figure 1-17.

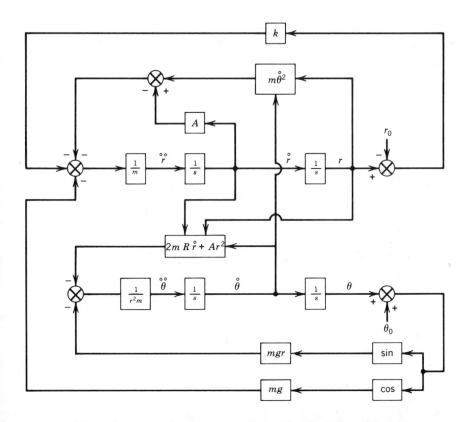

FIGURE 1-17. Elastic pendulum simulation blocked diagram.

1.10   SYSTEM REPRESENTATION IN STATE VARIABLE FORM

In general nth-order linear dynamic systems are described by nth-order linear differential equations which can be rewritten as n first-order linear differential equations:

$$\dot{x}_1(t) = a_{11}x_1 + a_{12}x_2 + \cdots + a_{1n}x_n + b_{11}u_1 + b_{12}u_2 + \cdots + b_{1m}u_m$$

$$\dot{x}_2(t) = a_{21}x_1 + a_{22}x_2 + \cdots + a_{2n}x_n + b_{21}u_1 + b_{22}u_2 + \cdots + b_{2m}u_m$$

$$\vdots$$

$$\dot{x}_n(t) = a_{n1}x_1 + a_{n2}x_2 + \cdots + a_{nn}x_n + b_{n1}u_1 + b_{n2}u_2 + \cdots + b_{nm}u_m$$

$$(1\text{-}127)$$

The n dependent variables in this system of differential equations are termed the state variables of the system. They can be written in matrix notation format as

$$\mathbf{X} = \begin{bmatrix} x_1 \\ x_2 \\ x_3 \\ \cdot \\ \cdot \\ \cdot \\ x_n \end{bmatrix} \qquad (1\text{-}128)$$

By defining an input vector as

$$\mathbf{U} = \begin{bmatrix} u_1 \\ u_2 \\ u_3 \\ \cdot \\ \cdot \\ \cdot \\ u_n \end{bmatrix} \qquad (1\text{-}129)$$

we can rewrite the system of (1-116) in the form:

$$
\begin{bmatrix} \dot{x}_1 \\ \dot{x}_2 \\ \cdot \\ \cdot \\ \cdot \\ \dot{x}_n \end{bmatrix} = \begin{bmatrix} a_{11} & a_{12} & \cdots & a_{1n} \\ a_{21} & a_{22} & \cdots & a_{2n} \\ \cdot & \cdot & & \cdot \\ \cdot & \cdot & & \cdot \\ \cdot & \cdot & & \cdot \\ a_{n1} & a_{n2} & \cdots & a_{nn} \end{bmatrix} \begin{bmatrix} x_1 \\ x_2 \\ \cdot \\ \cdot \\ \cdot \\ x_n \end{bmatrix} + \begin{bmatrix} b_{11} & b_{12} & \cdots & b_{1m} \\ b_{21} & b_{22} & \cdots & b_{2m} \\ \cdot & \cdot & & \cdot \\ \cdot & \cdot & & \cdot \\ \cdot & \cdot & & \cdot \\ b_{n1} & b_{n2} & \cdots & b_{nm} \end{bmatrix} \begin{bmatrix} u_1 \\ u_2 \\ \cdot \\ \cdot \\ \cdot \\ u_m \end{bmatrix}
$$

$$(1\text{-}130)$$

We have seen that a single output can be written in terms of a single input for systems that can be described by their transfer function. Having redefined the nth-order differential equation in the single-output variable in terms of n state vectors, we require another system of algebraic equations to relate the state variables and, more generally, the inputs to the outputs of the system. That is:

$$
y_1 = c_{11}x_1 + c_{12}x_2 + \cdots + c_{1n}x_n + d_{11}u_1 + d_{12}u_2 + \cdots + d_{1m}u_m
$$

$$
y_2 = c_{21}x_1 + c_{22}x_2 + \cdots + c_{2n}x_n + d'_{21}u_1 + d_{22}u_2 + \cdots + d_{2m}u_m
$$

$$
y_k = c_{k1}x_1 + c_{k2}x_2 + \cdots + c_{kn}x_n + d_{k1}u_1 + d_{k2}u_2 + \cdots + d_{km}u_m
$$

$$(1\text{-}131)$$

By writing the output variables in matrix form, we can rewrite (1-131) in the form:

$$
\begin{bmatrix} y_1 \\ y_2 \\ \cdot \\ \cdot \\ \cdot \\ y_k \end{bmatrix} = \begin{bmatrix} c_{11} & c_{12} & \cdots & c_{1n} \\ c_{21} & c_{22} & \cdots & c_{2n} \\ \cdot & \cdot & & \cdot \\ \cdot & \cdot & & \cdot \\ \cdot & \cdot & & \cdot \\ c_{k1} & c_{k2} & \cdots & c_{kn} \end{bmatrix} \begin{bmatrix} x_1 \\ x_2 \\ \cdot \\ \cdot \\ \cdot \\ x_n \end{bmatrix} + \begin{bmatrix} d_{11} & d_{12} & \cdots & d_{1m} \\ d_{21} & d_{22} & \cdots & d_{2m} \\ \cdot & \cdot & & \cdot \\ \cdot & \cdot & & \cdot \\ \cdot & \cdot & & \cdot \\ d_{k1} & d_{k2} & \cdots & d_{km} \end{bmatrix} \begin{bmatrix} u_1 \\ u_2 \\ \cdot \\ \cdot \\ \cdot \\ u_n \end{bmatrix}
$$

$$(1\text{-}132)$$

Both (1-130) and (1-132) can be more simply written in boldface notation as

$$\mathbf{X = AX + BU} \qquad (1\text{-}133)$$

$$\mathbf{Y = CX + DU} \qquad (1\text{-}134)$$

Usually there is no direct relationship between the inputs to the state vector system of equations and the output. Thus the matrix **D** is zero and the system of equations can be simplified to

$$\dot{X} = AX + BU \tag{1-135}$$

$$Y = CX \tag{1-136}$$

This system of equations is commonly termed the vector-matrix or state variable formulation of a system. The **A** is usually called the system matrix, **B** the input matrix, and **C** the output matrix. This type of mathematical model is both general and elegant in form. Its theoretical importance lies in its general treatment of all linear systems. The many theorems of *n*-dimensional vector spaces can be used to identify very broad properties of dynamic processes. For example the concept of *n*-dimensional vector spaces has been used in the field of control to develop optimal control systems by maximizing the vector-dot product of the control system output vector with the control command input vector. Similarly, some modern filtering techniques have been based on minimizing the dot product of the filter output vector with the input noise vector. Some optimally filtered control systems seek a combination of both.

The state vector formulation is important from a practical viewpoint, since methods for solving first-order linear differential equations are well known. This is not the case for the *n*th-order linear differential equation. For this reason the vector matrix formulation of an *n*th-order system carries over the general solution methods for first-order linear systems to *n*th-order linear systems. Although it appears that the vector-matrix formulation of a linear system is far removed from the physical system being modeled, the mathematical insights into the system's general characteristics add a wide dimension to an analyst's understanding of a system's characteristics and properties that block diagrams do not. This is usually important in complex systems of large dimensions where broad guiding principles are important in the synthesis of efficient systems.

The state equations (1-135) and (1-136) of stationary linear systems can be solved by either transform methods or by the convolution integral. By taking the Laplace transform of (1-135) we find

$$sX(s) - X(0+) = AX(s) + BU(s) \tag{1-137}$$

Thus

$$X(s) = (sI - A)^{-1}X(0+)$$
$$+ (sI - A)^{-1}BU(s)$$

(1-138)

which can be block diagrammed as shown in Figure 1-18. By using either block diagram reduction methods or solving for the state of the system, the solution to (1-135) can be written as

$$X(t) = \Phi(t)X(0+) + \int_0^t \Phi(t - \tau)BU(\tau)\, d\tau$$

(1-139)

where the transition matrix is defined by the relationship

$$\Phi = \mathcal{L}^{-1}(sI - A)^{-1}$$

(1-140)

The solution to the state equation (1-135) using the convolution integral takes the form

$$X(t) = \exp\left[A(t - t_0)\right]X(t_0) + \int_{t_0}^t \exp\left[A(t - \tau)\right]BU(\tau)\, d\tau$$

(1-141)

where the matrix exponential is defined to be

$$\exp\left[A(t)\right] = I + At + \frac{A^2 t^2}{2!} + \cdots$$

(1-142)

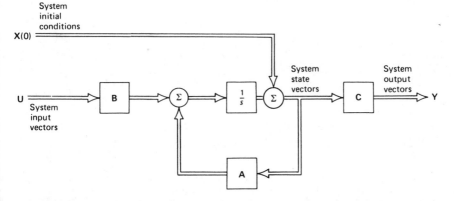

FIGURE 1-18. Vector-matrix block diagram of linear stationary processes.

The former of these two methods for solving state equations is more amenable to analytical investigation, since forming the transition matrix involves taking the inverse Laplace transform of the impulse response transfer function matrix, a process that a digital computer cannot do. The latter method is more useful in numerical analysis where the transition matrix is evaluated using the matrix infinite series. As a practical matter, the series usually converges for reasonable physical systems. Although the convolution integral solution method can be used for analytical investigation, writing the transition matrix in closed form can involve identifying closed forms for as many as n^2 infinite series (where n is the number of state vectors in the problem), a tedious process at best.

While on the subject of stationary linear systems, it is worth mentioning that the state equations are usually written either in phase-variable form or Jordan normal form.

The phase-variable representation of a transfer function

$$\frac{y(s)}{u(s)} = G(s)$$

$$= \frac{B\left(c_k s^{k-1} + c_{k-1} s^{k-2} + \cdots + c_2 s + c_1\right)}{s^n + a_n s^{n-1} + a_{n-1} s^{n-2} + \cdots + a_2 s + a_1} \tag{1-143}$$

when $k \leq n$, takes the form

$$
\begin{bmatrix} \dot{x}_1 \\ \dot{x}_2 \\ \vdots \\ \dot{x}_{n-1} \\ \dot{x}_n \end{bmatrix}
=
\begin{bmatrix}
0 & 1 & 0 & 0 & \cdots & 0 & 0 \\
0 & 0 & 1 & 0 & \cdots & 0 & 0 \\
\vdots & \vdots & \vdots & \vdots & & \vdots & \vdots \\
0 & 0 & 0 & 0 & \cdots & 0 & 1 \\
-a_1 & -a_2 & -a_3 & -a_4 & \cdots & -a_{n-1} & -a_n
\end{bmatrix}
\begin{bmatrix} x_1 \\ x_2 \\ \vdots \\ x_{n-1} \\ x_n \end{bmatrix}
+
\begin{bmatrix} 0 \\ 0 \\ \vdots \\ 0 \\ B \end{bmatrix}
u(s)
$$

$$\tag{1-144}$$

$$
y = \begin{bmatrix} c_1 & c_2 & \cdots & c_k & 0 & \cdots & 0 \end{bmatrix}
\begin{bmatrix} x_1 \\ x_2 \\ \vdots \\ x_{n-1} \\ x_n \end{bmatrix}
\tag{1-145}
$$

It is block diagrammed in Figure 1-19.

A block Diagram of the same system in Jordan normal form is shown in Figure 1-20. The Jordan form of (1-143) can be developed by noting that

$$\frac{y}{u} = G(s) = \frac{B\left(c_k s^{k-1} + c_{k-1} s^{k-2} + \cdots + c_2 s + c_1\right)}{(s - \lambda_1)(s - \lambda_2)(s - \lambda_3) \cdots (s - \lambda_n)} \qquad (1\text{-}146)$$

is the factored form of (1-143). The λ_i are the poles of the transfer function. Then by partial-fraction expansion we can write

$$\frac{y}{u} = \frac{d_1}{s - \lambda_1} + \frac{d_2}{s - \lambda_2} + \frac{d_3}{s - \lambda_3} + \cdots + \frac{d_n}{s - \lambda_n} \qquad (1\text{-}147)$$

Thus

$$\frac{y}{u} = d_1 \frac{z_1(s)}{u(s)} + d_2 \frac{z_2(s)}{u(s)} + d_3 \frac{z_3(s)}{u(s)} + \cdots + d_n \frac{z_n(s)}{u(s)} \qquad (1\text{-}148)$$

where

$$\frac{z_i}{u(s)} = \frac{1}{s - \lambda_i}, \qquad \text{for} \quad i = 1, 2, \ldots, n \qquad (1\text{-}149)$$

Then

$$y = d_1 z_1 + d_2 z_2 + \cdots + d_n z_n \qquad (1\text{-}150)$$

In the time domain, we can see that

$$\dot{z}_i = \lambda_i z_i + u, \qquad \text{for} \quad i = 1, 2, \ldots, n \qquad (1\text{-}151)$$

$$y = \sum_{i}^{n} d_i z_i \qquad (1\text{-}152)$$

In vector-matrix form

$$\dot{\mathbf{Z}} = \lambda \mathbf{Z} + \Gamma u \qquad (1\text{-}153)$$

$$y = \mathbf{CZ} \qquad (1\text{-}154)$$

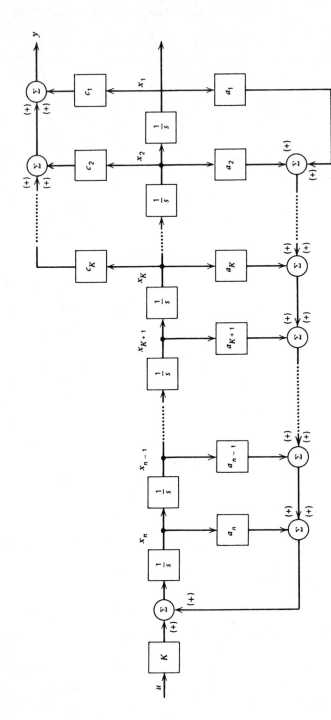

FIGURE 1-19. Block diagram of an nth order system in phase-variable form.

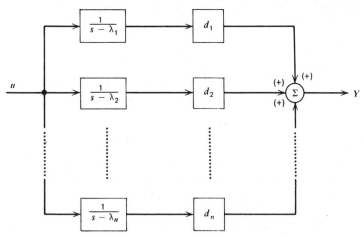

FIGURE 1-20.   Block diagram of an nth order system in Jordan normal form.

where

$$
\boldsymbol{\lambda} = \begin{bmatrix} \lambda_1 & & & 0 \\ & \lambda_2 & & \\ & & \ddots & \\ 0 & & & \lambda_n \end{bmatrix}, \quad \boldsymbol{\Gamma} = \begin{bmatrix} 1 \\ 1 \\ \cdot \\ \cdot \\ 1 \end{bmatrix}, \quad \text{and} \quad \mathbf{C} = \begin{bmatrix} d_1 \\ d_2 \\ \cdot \\ \cdot \\ d_n \end{bmatrix} \quad (1\text{-}155)
$$

In matrix terminology, the lambdas in the Jordan normal form are the eigenvalues of the matrix **A**, which are (again) the poles of the transfer function. Since the eigenvalues of the matrix $\boldsymbol{\lambda}$ are invariant under any linear transformation, there are linear transformation methods for numerically evaluating the lambdas in the Jordan normal form. Occasionally, systems of matrix equations will be submitted for use in system simulation with the transformation matrices buried in the state equations. When this happens care must be taken in developing check cases and conducting analysis to properly account for their presence and ensure that simulation eigenvalues match the system eigenvalues.

The solution to linear nonstationary systems [**A**, **B**, and **C** in (1-135) and (1-136) are nonstationary] in their vector-matrix form is given by

$$
\mathbf{X} = \boldsymbol{\Phi}(t, t_0)\mathbf{X}(t_0) + \int_{t_0}^{t} \boldsymbol{\Phi}(t, \tau)\mathbf{B}(\tau)\mathbf{U}(\tau)\, d\tau \quad (1\text{-}156)
$$

$$
\mathbf{Y} = \mathbf{C}(t)\mathbf{X}(t) \quad (1\text{-}157)
$$

where the transition matrix is defined by

$$\mathbf{\Phi}(t, t_0) = \exp\left[\int_{t_0}^{t} \mathbf{A}(t)\, dt\right] \tag{1-158}$$

That (1-156) is the solution to (1-135) when $\mathbf{A}$, $\mathbf{B}$, and $\mathbf{U}$ are not stationary can be shown by substitution.

A final word on solving linear vector-matrix differential equations. The methods that we have discussed have focused on determining the transition matrix from one solution point to another. Transition matrices have the very nice property that the transition involved in making n steps is equal to the product of n individual transitions, that is

$$\mathbf{\Phi}(t_2, t_0) = \mathbf{\Phi}(t_2, t_1)\mathbf{\Phi}(t_1, t_0) \tag{1-159}$$

This property holds for both stationary and nonstationary linear systems. Another important property of the transition matrix is that it will "step ahead" and the inverse of the transition matrix will "step back."

$$\mathbf{\Phi}^{-1}(t_1, t_0) = \mathbf{\Phi}(t_0, t_1) \tag{1-160}$$

In all these cases the transition matrix is used to solve the differential equation. Another approach is to integrate numerically the state vector differential equations, a subject covered later in this book.

1.11   NONLINEAR SYSTEMS

Nonlinear systems by definition encompass all systems that are not linear. Simulation is the commonly used tool for studying the dynamics of nonlinear systems, since there are no general methods for solving and analyzing such systems. In view of the broad scope of nonlinear systems, only those relevant to this book and the simulation of continuous systems will be discussed here, and then only briefly.

There are two common nonlinear processes encountered in simulation: processes with hard nonlinearities and soft nonlinear processes. The latter are characterized by the fact that the equations describing them are nonlinear differential equations. The hard nonlinear systems are characterized by being described (at least in part) by different equations under differing circumstances. Classical examples of soft nonlinear systems are pendulums with large angle motion and the van der Pol oscillator. Modern

Block Diagram	Equation

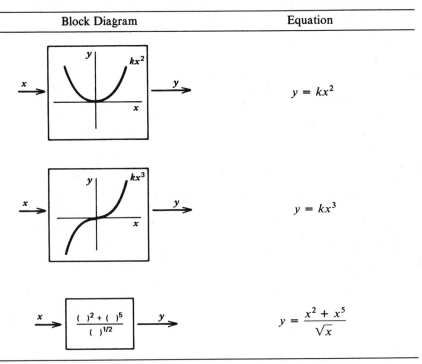

$$y = kx^2$$

$$y = kx^3$$

$$y = \frac{x^2 + x^5}{\sqrt{x}}$$

FIGURE 1-21. Examples of soft nonlinear elements.

nonlinear equations frequently encountered in simulation include the quaternion rotational equations of motion, nonlinear equations associated with modulation and demodulation dynamics in high-frequency transmitters and receivers and with the design of nonlinear filters associated with modern control systems, and the equations of motion of satellites. Examples of soft nonlinear elements are shown in Figure 1-21, and examples of hard nonlinear elements including relays, dead zones, and the absolute-value operator are shown in Figure 1-22.

Block diagramming of both soft and hard nonlinear processes is useful because the graphical visualization of a particular nonlinearity can often lead to practical approximation equations that hold fairly well over certain regions of nonlinear operations. As an example of simplifying assumptions that can be made for nonlinear systems, consider the relay of Figure 1-23 with a dead-zone nonlinearity. Such relays are typically used in on/off control systems. When excursions about $x = 0$ are small compared with the dead zone, the dynamics of the process are not influenced by y. On the other hand, if the excursions in x lie largely outside and to the right of the

Block Diagram	Common Name	Equation

Relay with dead zone

$$y = \begin{cases} y_0 & x \geqslant +D \\ 0 & -D < x < +D \\ -y_0 & x \leqslant -D \end{cases}$$

Dead zone

$$y = \begin{cases} kx & x > +D \\ 0 & -D < x < +D \\ kx & x < -D \end{cases}$$

Relay

$$y = \begin{cases} -y_0 & x < 0 \\ +y_0 & x > 0 \end{cases}$$

Limiter

$$y = \begin{cases} y_0 & x > x_0 \\ x & -x_0 \leqslant x \leqslant x_0 \\ -y_0 & x < -x_0 \end{cases}$$

FIGURE 1-22.   Examples of hard nonlinear elements.

dead zone, the dynamics of the system will be affected by $+y$. If excursions in x can be considered to reside equally to the right and to the left of the dead zone with a frequency that is high compared to the response time of the process, the stair-step nonlinearity can be replaced with (approximated by) a ramp whose slope is the output level divided by twice the extent of the dead zone. Similar approximations can be made for other hard nonlinearities and "qualitative" linear analysis conducted to anticipate the performance of such nonlinear systems.

Soft nonlinear systems can always be formulated as a set of first-order differential equations of the form

$$\dot{\mathbf{X}}(t) = \mathbf{f}(\mathbf{X}, \mathbf{U}, t) \tag{1-161}$$

where $\mathbf{X}$ is an n-vector, $\mathbf{U}$ is an n-vector of input variables, and t is the system-independent variable. As before, if t is not an explicit variable, the system is stationary and (1-161) reduces to

$$\dot{\mathbf{X}}(t) = \mathbf{f}(\mathbf{X}, \mathbf{U}) \qquad (1\text{-}162)$$

If $\mathbf{U}(t) = 0$, the system is called autonomous and is of the form

$$\dot{\mathbf{X}}(t) = \mathbf{f}(\mathbf{X}(t)) \qquad (1\text{-}163)$$

Although there are no general closed-form methods for solving nonlinear differential equations, particularly nonlinear vector-matrix equations, they can be solved on the digital computer by numerically integrating the differential equations of motion.

Block diagrams for soft nonlinear systems are developed in phase-variable form as follows:

1. By writing the nonlinear differential equation for the system.
2. By solving for the highest derivative.
3. By using multiple integration blocks to determine the system output.
4. By closing the feedback loops with the nonlinear operators.

Once the system block diagram is drawn, a general procedure for generating series solutions of either linear or nonlinear differential equations can be used.

Step 1. Prepare a phase-variable block diagram for the continuous process.

Step 2. Construct sequences of polynomial approximations of the solution to the differential equation by simply following the signal flow path and performing the indicated operations on the forcing function or initial conditions.

Example 1

Step 1. The nonlinear differential equation

$$\ddot{y} - ky^2 = f(t)$$

where

$$\dot{y}(0) = 0, \qquad y(0) = Y, \qquad f(t) = 0$$

can be block diagrammed in phase-variable form as shown in Figure 1-23.

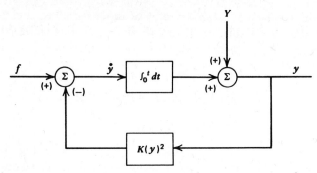

FIGURE 1-23.   Phase-variable block diagram of $\dot{y} - ky^2 = f$.

Step 2.   From the block diagram it can be seen that

$$y_0 = Y$$

$$y_1 = Y + \int_0^t (-kY^2)\,dt = Y - kY^2 t = Y(1 - kYt)$$

$$y_2 = Y\left[1 - kYt + k^2Y^2\left(t^2 - \frac{kt^3}{6}\right)\right]$$

$$\vdots \qquad\qquad \vdots \qquad \vdots$$

Example 2

Step 1.   The nonstationary linear differential equation

$$\dot{y} + kty = f(t)$$

where

$$\dot{y}(0) = 0, \qquad y(0) = Y, \qquad f(t) = 0$$

is block diagrammed in phase-variable form as shown in Figure 1-24.

Step 2.   From the block diagram it can be seen that

$$y_0 = Y$$

$$y_1 = Y - \frac{kYt^2}{2} = Y\left(1 - \frac{kt^2}{2}\right)$$

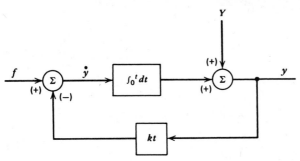

FIGURE 1-24. Phase-variable block diagram of $\dot{y} + kty = f(t)$.

$$y_2 = Y - \frac{kYt^2}{2} + \frac{k^2Yt^4}{8} = Y\left(1 - \frac{kt^2}{2} + \frac{k^2t^4}{8}\right)$$

$$\vdots \qquad \vdots \qquad \vdots \qquad \vdots$$

$$y_\infty = Y\left[1 + (-1)^n\sum_1^\infty \frac{k^n t^{2n}}{2^n n!}\right] = Ye^{-kt^2/2}$$

Example 3

Step 1. The equation

$$(1 - t^2)\ddot{y} - 2t\dot{y} + n(n + 1)y = f(t)$$

where

$$\ddot{y}(0) = 0, \qquad \dot{y}(0) = \dot{Y}, \qquad y(0) = Y, \qquad f(t) = 0$$

can be block diagrammed in phase-variable form as shown in Figure 1-25. Note that

$$\frac{O}{I} = \frac{1}{1 - t^2}$$

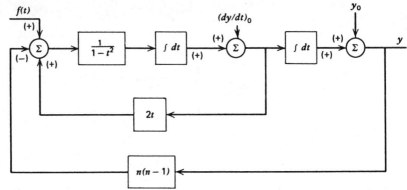

FIGURE 1-25.   Phase-variable block diagram of the equation $(1 - t^2)\ddot{y} - 2t\dot{y} + n(n + 1)y = f(t)$.

can be block diagrammed as

We can now simplify Figure 1-25 as shown in Figure 1-26.

FIGURE 1-26.   Simplified phase-variable block diagram of the equation $(1 - t^2)\ddot{y} - 2t\dot{y} + n(n + 1)y = f(t)$.

Step 2. By inspection of the block diagram of Figure 1-21, we can write

$$y = \left[Y - \int\int_0^t n(n + 1) Y \, dt^2 + \cdots \right]$$

$$+ \left[\int_0^t \dot{Y} \, dt - \int\int\int_0^t \dot{Y}n(n + 1) \, dt^3 + \int\int_0^t \dot{Y}t \, dt^2 + \cdots \right]$$

Thus

$$y = Y\left[1 - n(n + 1) \frac{t^2}{2!} + \cdots \right] + \dot{Y}\left[t - (n - 1)(n + 2) \frac{t^3}{3!} + \cdots \right]$$

Comparing Examples 1 and 2, we can make the following observations:

1. Soft nonlinear operations on polynomials lead to more complex combinations of terms and coefficients in the solution polynomial than linear operations. In this sense nonlinear systems can be said to be more complex than linear systems of the same order.

2. Although it is necessary to generate a sequence of approximating polynomials to solve a nonlinear equation, the terms of the infinite series solution of a linear differential equation can be written directly by inspecting the block diagram (without generating the intermediate polynomials). The first term in the series is the initial condition passing directly to the output of the block diagram. The second term in the series is the initial condition as it arrives at the output of the block diagram after passing once around the feedback loop, having been operated on by the appropriate mathematical operators. Similarly, the nth term in the infinite series is generated by processing the initial conditions around the loop $n - 1$ times before adding it to the output. This simplification holds for linear systems whether stationary or not.

Since this is a linear differential equation, the first term is simply the passage of the initial condition along the forward loop to the output. The second term comes from one complete circuit around the outer loop through the "multiply by $n(n + 1)$" operator and then through the two integration operators. Higher-order terms are generated in a similar way by passing around the other loops as well. For example, the next three terms come from:

1. $\dot{Y}$ passing directly to the output.
2. $\dot{Y}$ passing around the outer loop and then passing to the output.
3. $\dot{Y}$ passing around the inner loop through the operation of multiplying by $2t$, then passing to the output through the two integrators.

Very little practice is needed to see what sequence should be used to generate the terms in the series.

This procedure rather esthetically animates the otherwise pedantic classical method of obtaining series solutions of ordinary linear differential equations. It was developed by the author to generate simulation check cases and to investigate conditions under which a system's response would be a monotonically increasing series (i.e., the conditions under which the coefficients in the series solution of the differential equation are nonalternating). From a series viewpoint, it appears that one of the necessary conditions for stability is that the series solution of the differential equation be an alternating series. Of course this is not a sufficient test to determine the stability of the system.

The method just described is equivalent mathematically to Picard's method for solving ordinary differential equations, whether linear or nonlinear, stationary or nonstationary, autonomous or nonautonomous. Picard's method, you may remember, not only generates the series solution of ordinary differential equations but is also the basis for the theorems that guarantee the existence of a solution to the differential equation, that the solution is unique, and that the infinite series converges for all intervals where a solution to the differential equation exists.

Another method for solving first-order nonlinear differential equations that we will have occasion to use involves those systems that have solutions of the form $F(x, y) = C$. Then the solution of the first-order nonlinear differential equation

$$\frac{dy}{dx} = f(x, y) = - \frac{P(x, y)}{Q(x, y)} \tag{1-164}$$

That is,

$$P \, dx = Q \, dy \tag{1-165}$$

Then

$$\frac{\partial F}{\partial x} \, dx + \frac{\partial F}{\partial y} \, dy = 0 \tag{1-166}$$

Thus if

$$\frac{\partial F}{\partial x} = P(x, y) \quad \text{and} \quad \frac{\partial F}{\partial y} = Q(x, y) \tag{1-167}$$

and if, in addition,

$$\frac{\partial P}{\partial y} = \frac{\partial Q}{\partial x} \tag{1-168}$$

because of the relation between these two conditions, that is,

$$\frac{\partial^2 F}{\partial y\, \partial x} = \frac{\partial^2 F}{\partial x\, \partial y} \tag{1-169}$$

then (1-164) is said to be exact, and the solution $F(x, y) = C$ can be derived from (1-167). For example from the first equation in (1-167)

$$F(x, y) = \int P(x, y)\, dx + R(y) \tag{1-170}$$

where $R(y)$ is an arbitrary function of y. Using the second equation in (1-167)

$$\frac{dR(y)}{dy} = Q(x, y) - \frac{\partial}{\partial y} \int P(x, y)\, dx \tag{1-171}$$

Thus

$$R(y) = \int \left[Q(x, y) - \frac{\partial}{\partial y} \int P(x, y)\, dx \right] dy \tag{1-172}$$

If (1-164) is not exact, a function $h(x, y)$ which is to be determined from the condition

$$\frac{\partial (hP)}{\partial y} = \frac{\partial (hQ)}{\partial x} \tag{1-173}$$

may be used as an integrating factor.

Another technique that does not involve solving nonlinear differential equations per se is the use of transformation methods. These methods involve transformations in the dependent variable that transform nonlinear equations into linear equations. For example, Bernoulli's equation

$$\frac{dy}{dx} = yf(x) + y^n g(x) \tag{1-174}$$

is transformed into the linear differential equation

$$\frac{dz}{dx} = (1 - n)f(x)z + g(x)(1 - n) \tag{1-175}$$

using the transformation relationship $z = y^{1-n}$. Clearly a single integration will solve Bernoulli's equation.

Similarly the generalized form of Riccati's equation

$$\frac{dy}{dx} + a(x)y + b(x)y^2 = c(x) \tag{1-176}$$

can be transformed into a second-order linear differential equation by means of the transformation relation

$$y = \frac{dz}{dx}\left(\frac{1}{b(x)z}\right) \tag{1-177}$$

Conversely the second-order linear homogeneous differential equation

$$a'(x)\frac{d^2z}{dx^2} + b'(x)\frac{dz}{dx} + c'(x)z = 0 \tag{1-178}$$

can be transformed into Riccati's equation by means of the substitution $dz/dx = d(x)yz$. It should be noted that the general solution of this equation takes the form

$$y = \frac{A(x) + kB(x)}{C(x) + kD(x)} \tag{1-179}$$

where k is a constant.

CHAPTER 2

THE MATHEMATICAL MODELING OF DISCRETE PROCESSES

In digital simulation we are concerned with continuous functions [whose domain is the reals, $x(t)$], discrete functions [whose domain is the integers, $x(nT) = x_n$], and the *equivalence relationships* between them. We are particularly interested in continuous systems whose motion is characterized by continuous functions, in discrete systems whose motion is characterized by discrete functions (sequence of numbers), and the equivalence relationships between the two systems as well as between their dynamics. Additionally we are interested in *recursion formulas* which, strictly speaking, describe neither discrete nor continuous processes. Recursion formulas are simply *procedures* for computing a sequence of numbers (or deriving a sequence of formulas) where each new number (or formula) is based on current and past numbers (or formulas).

Difference Equations and Recursion Formulas and Their Interpretation

It is important to make the distinction between recursion formulas and difference equations. Difference equations describe discrete dynamic systems; they have solutions that are discrete functions whose domain is the real numbers. Recursion formulas are procedures for computing, say, the 100th number based on the 99th and previous numbers. It is common in numerical analysis literature to use notation that often makes it hard to recognize this distinction. For example, the equation

$$X(t) = X_0 e^{-(t + \gamma T)}$$

is the "time-shifted" response of a continuous first-order process ($\dot{X} + X = 0$) to an initial condition x_0. The discrete function that describes this system's response at times $(nT + \gamma T)$ is

$$X_n = X_0 e^{-(n+\gamma)T}$$

This function is the solution to the recursion formula

$$X_n - e^{-T}X_{n-1} = 0; \qquad X(0) = e^{-\gamma T}X_0$$

It is apparent in the *recursion formula* that the subscript on the independent variable is related to computing the nth of a sequence of n numbers $\{X_n\}$ based on previously computed numbers $\{X_{n-1}\}$. In this sense, this equation is a recursion formula. It is also a difference equation insofar as the sequence of numbers computed are related to each other in time; $X_n = X(nT + \gamma T)$. When $\gamma = 0$, the sequence of numbers computed with this equation relate both to the nth pass through the recursion formula and to the nth time interval nT. If $\gamma \neq 0$, the subscript n refers to the number of calculations made with the recursion formula, whereas the sequence of numbers $\{X_n\}$ are related to the system response at the time $t = (nT + \gamma T)$. **A number of phase-shifted difference equations are synthesized in the chapters that follow, and this distinction between recursion formulas and difference equations becomes important.**

In this book recursion formulas are written with equal signs and do not involve computing errors beyond roundoff error. Recursion formulas can be developed by substitution of differential equations into numerical integration formulas calculate sequences of X_n that approximate $X(t)|_{nT}$. The problem is in the interpretation of the approximation. The recursion formula

$$X_n = e^{-T}X_{n-1}$$

can be interpreted as calculating

$$X_1(t) = X_0 e^{-t}, \qquad \text{for} \quad t = nT$$

or

$$X_2(t) = X_0 e^{-(t+\varepsilon_1)}, \qquad \text{for} \quad t = nT, \quad \varepsilon_1 = \text{a constant}$$

or

$$X_3(t) = (X_0 + \varepsilon_2)e^{-t}, \qquad \text{for} \quad t = nT, \quad \varepsilon_2 = \text{a constant}$$

or, finally,

$$X_4(t) = (X_0 + \varepsilon_2)e^{-(t+\varepsilon_1)}, \qquad \text{for} \quad t = nT, \quad \varepsilon_1 \text{ and } \varepsilon_2 \text{ are constants}$$

Here ε_1 and ε_2 are assumed to be unknown errors in calculating time or X_0. These may be errors stemming from truncation or human errors in initializing the equations, or timing errors introduced by inadvertently holding data in memory too long because of, say, programming errors. Another source of timing error common in digital simulation (and in digital control) is a closed-loop calculation where it is necessary to calculate the forward loop before calculating the feedback loop. This introduces a time lag in closing the loop. This time lag would not be present in the signal flow of a continuous closed-loop system. Thus the problem is one of deciding what source of errors results in the difference between the recursion formula and (a) the continuous system being simulated or (b) a check case developed analytically.

The difficulty with interpreting the numbers generated with a difference equation of the form

$$X_n \cong e^{-T}X_{n-1}$$

is that when the sequences of X_n are compared with $X(t)|_{nT}$ and they do not agree by an amount ε, we can interpret the result three possible ways.

(1) X_n is in error due to an error in X_{n-1}.
(2) X_n is time-shifted relative to $X(t)|_{nT}$ ($\gamma \neq 0$).
(3) X_n is in error due to errors in both X_{n-1} and in timing.

Said another way: If you are given the equation

$$X_n \cong e^{-T}X_{n-1}$$

and the calculated values of X_n do not match a check case, the error can be interpreted as a timing error, a function evaluation error, or a combination of both. **We see later that what is often interpreted as function evaluation error (truncation and roundoff) is actually a timing error.** To reduce truncation error one usually takes smaller steps, since the error usually varies as a power of the step size, i.e., $\varepsilon \sim \Delta T^3$ means that for steps of size $(\Delta T/2)$,

$$\varepsilon\left(\frac{\Delta T}{2}\right)^3 = \frac{\varepsilon(\Delta T)^3}{8}$$

To eliminate timing errors one simply renames *print time* in the printout. The former is a costly way to reduce error, since more calculations are required to solve a given problem. The former has the seeming advantage that all state variables are printed at the same time.* The latter approach has the advantage that the calculations are done efficiently (large step size) but at the expense of the state vectors all being compared with the continuous system state vectors at slightly different times. In the latter case we simply acknowledge the obvious fact that **time is not invariant in the transformation of a differential equation into a simulating difference equation.**

This leads us to the concept of two kinds of time—real time and problem time—a concept we pursue in much more detail later in this book.

Difference Equations and Recursion Formulas

Typical examples of discrete system-describing equations are shown below:

Finite differ-
ence equation
$$\begin{cases} \dfrac{\Delta y}{\Delta t} + y = 0 \\ \Delta y + \Delta Ty = 0 \end{cases}$$

Difference
equation
$$\begin{cases} y(n + 1) + (\Delta T - 1)y(n) = 0 \\ y_{n+1} + (\Delta T - 1)y_n = 0 \end{cases}$$

Recursion
formula
$$\begin{cases} y_n = (1 - \Delta T)y_{n-1} + f_n \\ y_n = Ay_{n-1} + f_n \end{cases}$$

Nonlinear differ-
ence equation
$$y_n = A(y_{n-1})^2 + f_n$$

The term *difference equation* is often used to describe all of these equations and arises from the fact that classically they can be developed from finite difference equations.

Ordinary linear difference equations can be generated by substituting linear ordinary differential equations into numerical integration formulas and writing them in the difference equation form. Nonlinear difference equations can be generated in a similar manner by substituting nonlinear differential equations into numerical integration formulas and rewriting them in a nonlinear difference equation form. For example when the differential equation

$$\dot{x} - x = 0, \quad \text{where} \quad x_0 = 0$$

*In fact, they are not necessarily all printed at the same time, as we have just discussed and shall see again later.

is substituted into the rectangular integration formula*[†]

$$x_n \cong x_{n-1} + T\dot{x}_n^{\dagger}$$

we find

$$x_n \cong x_{n-1} + Tx_n$$

Thus

$$x_n \cong \left(\frac{1}{1-T}\right)x_{n-1}$$

Similarly for

$$\dot{x} - x^2 = 0, \qquad \text{where} \quad x_0 = 0$$

$$x_n \cong x_{n-1} + Tx_n^2$$

$$Tx_n^2 - x_n + x_{n-1} \cong 0$$

Thus

$$x_n \cong \frac{1}{2T} - \frac{1}{2T}\sqrt{1 - 4Tx_{n-1}}$$

A PROBLEM FOR THE STUDENT

The quadratic

$$Tx_n^2 - x_n + x_{n-1} \cong 0$$

has the solution

$$x_n = \frac{1}{2T} \pm \sqrt{1 - 4Tx_{n-1}}$$

Why was the negative second term chosen?

2.1 DIFFERENCE EQUATIONS

Difference equations generically arise when expressing the dynamics of a discrete process in terms of finite difference equations, such as

$$\Delta^m y = f\left(y_n, \Delta y_n, \Delta^2 y_n, \ldots, \Delta^{m-1} y_n, n\right)$$

---

*Generally, numerical integration only approximates analytic integration; therefore the "approximately equals" sign is used in the numerical integration formula.

[†]Note that if we treat these equations as recursion formulas the approximation signs are written as equal signs.

remembering that

$$\Delta y_n = y_n - y_{n-1}$$

$$\Delta^2 y_n = \Delta y_n - \Delta y_{n-1} = y_n - 2y_{n-1} + y_{n-2}$$

allows us to rewrite an mth-order difference equation in the form

$$y_n = g(y_n, y_{n-1}, y_{n-2}, y_{n-3}, \ldots, y_{n-m}, n)$$

When f (and therefore g) is known, the m initial conditions

$$y_0, y_1, y_2, \ldots, y_{m-1}$$

uniquely determine the solution of the difference equation.

Consider for example the second-order linear difference equation

$$y_n - 6y_{n-1} + 8y_{n-2} = n, \qquad \text{for} \quad y_0 = 3, y_1 = 2$$

Here the coefficients are assumed to be constant and the function y is defined only for $t = nT$ when $n = 0, 1, 2, \ldots$. We call this an equation of second order because it contains a value of the dependent variable when the independent variable is two periods away. We say that this equation is linear because it does not contain powers other than 1 or products of the dependent variable.

The classical methods for solving linear difference equations are quite similar to those for solving linear differential equations. The solution consists of two parts: a complementary solution and a particular solution. The total solution is the sum of both solutions.

The complementary solution is the general solution of the homogeneous equation with the forcing function set equal to zero;

$$y_n - 6y_{n-1} + 8y_{n-2} = 0$$

This equation is solved in a manner similar to that used for solving differential equations; that is, a trial solution of the form a^n is assumed. Then when

$$y_n = Ca^n$$

where a and C are constants, we find on substitution into the difference equation that

$$(a^2 - 6a + 8) = 0$$

This is the auxiliary equation; it has the roots

$$a_1 = 2$$

$$a_2 = 4$$

Then we can write the total complementary solution in the form

$$y_n = C_1 a_1^n + C_2 a_2^n = C_1 2^n + C_2 4^n$$

Using the initial conditions we find that when $n = 0$

$$3 = C_1 + C_2$$

and when $n = 1$

$$2 = 2C_1 + 4C_2$$

Solving this system of simultaneous equations we find $C_1 = 5$ and $C_2 = -2$. Thus

$$y_n = 5(2)^n - 2(4)^n$$

More generally if we have a linear difference equation of the form

$$a_0(nT)y_n + a_1(nT)y_{n-1} + \cdots + a_m(nT)y_{n-m} = f(nT)$$

it can be rewritten in the form

$$a_0 z^0 y_n + a_1 z^{-1} y_n + a_2 z^{-2} y_n + \cdots + a_m z^{-m} y_n = f(nT)$$

where $z^0 = 1$ and z^{-m} is a *shifting operator* (i.e., $z^{-m} y_n = y_{n-m}$). Then

$$\left(a_0 z^0 + a_1 z^{-1} + \cdots + a_m z^{-m} \right) y_n = f(nT)$$

$$\mathbf{L}(z)y_n = f_n$$

when $f_n = 0$ for all n, then we can assume a solution of the form

$$y_n = Cr^n$$

On substitution we will find the *auxiliary equation*

$$\left(a_0 r^n + a_1 r^{n-1} + \cdots + a_m r^{n-m} \right) = 0$$

- When the a_i are constants this polynomial has m roots. When the roots are real and distinct, the solution takes the form

$$y_n = C_1 r_1^n + C_2 r_2^n + \cdots + C_m r_m^n$$

- When the a_i are real and some roots are complex, the solution takes the form

$$y_n = \Gamma_1(\alpha_1 + i\beta_1)^n + \Gamma_2(\alpha_1 - i\beta_2)^n + \cdots \quad \text{(Cartesian)}$$

$$y_n = \rho^n(C_1 \cos n\theta + C_2 \sin n\theta) + \cdots \quad \text{(polar)}$$

- When the roots are real and equal, the solution takes the form

$$y_n = (C_1 + C_2 n + \cdots + C_k n^{k-1})r^n$$

When $f_n \neq 0$ then the task is to find a particular solution of the difference equation. When the particular solution is found it is summed with the complementary solution for the total or complete solution to the differential equation:

$$\text{total } y_n = \text{particular } y_n + \text{complementary } y_n$$

2.2   THE PARTICULAR SOLUTION

The particular solution of the inhomogeneous equation can be obtained by methods similar to those developed for differential equations. In particular, the method of undetermined coefficients can be used in a manner that is similar to that covered in Section 1.5. As before, the method of undetermined coefficients is used to find particular solutions when the forcing function $F(k)$ is made up of certain often encountered forms. The approach is to assume a form of the particular solution that is related to the form of the forcing function.

The method of undetermined coefficients is simple to apply and leads to straightforward results. For a linear difference equation with constant coefficients, whose excitation or forcing function is composed of the sum or the product of forcing functions shown in Table 2-1, the particular solution is the sum or product of the solution forms shown in the right-hand column. When this solution is substituted into the differential equation, coefficients on both sides of the equation can be equated to determine the coefficients of a particular solution in terms of the coefficients of the system. Only a slight modification is necessary to this simple procedure. When the forcing function contains a term that also appears in the complementary solution, the form of the solution shown in the table must be multiplied by a positive integer power of k, which must be large enough that no term in the modified solution will appear in the complementary function.

Table 2-1. Particular Solutions for Linear Difference Equations Using the Method of Undetermined Coefficients

Form of the Forcing Function	Form of Particular Solution
k	k
a	Aa
Polynomial $P(k)$ of degree m	$A_0 k^m + A_1 k^{m-1} + \cdots + A_m$
$\sin(ak)$	$A \cos(ak) + B \sin(ak)$
$\cos(ak)$	$A \cos(ak) + B \sin(ak)$
$a^k P(k)$	$a^k(A_0 k^m + A_1 k^{m-1} + \cdots + A_m)$
$a^k \sin(bk)$	$a^k[A \cos(bk) + B \sin(bk)]$
$a^k \cos(bk)$	$a^k[A \cos(bk) + B \sin(bk)]$

Example

Solve

$$X_n + TX_{n-1} = n^2$$

First solve the homogeneous equation

$$X_n + TX_{n-1} = 0$$

to get the complementary solution.

Step 1. Assume a solution of the form $X_c(n) = \alpha^n$. On substitution we find

$$\alpha^n(1 + T\alpha^{-1}) = 0$$

Thus

$$\alpha = -T$$

and

$$X_c(n) = C(-T)^n$$

Step 2. From Table 2-1 assume $X_p(n) = A_2 n^2 + A_1 n + A_0$, since the forcing function is of the form n^2. On substitution we find

$$A_2n^2 + A_1n + A_0 + TA_2(n-1)^2 + TA_1(n-1) + TA_0 = n^2$$

or

$$A_2n^2 + A_1n + A_0 + TA_2n^2 - 2TA_2n + TA_2$$

$$+ TA_1n - TA_1 + TA_0 = n^2$$

$$(1+T)A_2n^2 + (A_1 - 2TA_2 + TA_1)n$$

$$+ (A_0 + TA_2 - TA_1 + TA_0) = n^2$$

Since the left side must equal the right if X_p for all n is to be a solution of the difference equation, this allows us to equate powers to evaluate the three unknowns A_1, A_2, and A_3:

$$(1+T)A_2 = 1 \qquad\qquad (2\text{-}1)$$

$$A_1 - 2TA_2 + TA_1 = 0 \qquad\qquad (2\text{-}2)$$

$$A_0 + TA_0 + TA_2 - TA_1 = 0$$

$$\therefore A_2 = \frac{1}{(1+T)}$$

from (2-1),

$$A_1 = \frac{2TA_2}{1+T} = \frac{2T}{(1+T)^2}$$

from (2-2), and finally

$$A_0 = \frac{T(A_2 - A_1)}{1+T} = \frac{T\left[\dfrac{1}{1+T} - \dfrac{2T}{(1+T)^2}\right]}{1+T}$$

$$A_0 = \frac{T\left[1 - \dfrac{2T}{1+T}\right]}{(1+T)^2} = \frac{T(1-T)}{(1+T)^3}$$

Thus

$$X_p(n) = \frac{n^2}{1 + T} + \frac{2Tn}{(1 + T)^2} + \frac{T(1 - T)}{(1 + T)^3}$$

and

$$X_n = X_C(n) + X_p(n) = C_1(-T)^n + \frac{n^2}{1 + T} + \frac{2Tn}{(1 + T)^2} + \frac{T(1 - T)}{(1 + T)^3}$$

Discrete System Representation in State Variable Form

As with differential equations, difference equations can be written in state vector form. The approach is a straightforward transformation of an nth-order difference equation into n first-order difference equations. The solution of each separate difference equation is considered a vector. The ensemble of the n vectors is called the state vector. Because the vector of initial conditions and the vector of forcing functions result in vectors of responses for each first-order difference equation, we say the input state is transferred from one state to another. The transition from state to state is made with a transformation matrix called a *transition matrix*. This general system of vector-matrix equations takes the form

$$Y(n + 1) = B(n)Y(n) + X(n)$$

where $\{X(n)\}$ is a known sequence of vectors. If the initial conditions Y_0 are given, then the general solution takes the form

$$Y(n) = P_{n0}Y_0 + \sum_{j=1}^{n} P_{nj}X_{j-1}$$

where

$$P_{nj} = B_{n-1}B_{n-2} \cdots B_j$$

and

$$P_{nn} = I$$

When

$$B_{n-1} = B_{n-2} = \cdots = B_j = B$$

then the general solution takes the form

$$Y(n) = B^n Y(0) + \sum_{j=1}^{n} B^{n-j}X_{j-1} \qquad (2\text{-}3)$$

Example

Consider the one-dimensional first-order differential equation

$$\tau \frac{dy}{dt} + y = e^{-kt}, \quad \text{for} \quad \tau \text{ and } k = \text{positive constants}, y(0) = 1$$

This equation can be approximated by the difference equation

$$\tau(y_n - y_{n-1}) + \Delta T y_{n-1} = \Delta T e^{-kn\,\Delta T}, \quad \text{for} \quad \Delta T = \text{positive constant}$$

$$y_n - y_{n-1} + \frac{\Delta T}{\tau} y_{n-1} = \frac{\Delta T}{\tau} e^{-kn\,\Delta T}$$

$$y_n - \left(1 - \frac{\Delta T}{\tau}\right) y_{n-1} = \frac{\Delta T}{\tau} e^{-kn\,\Delta T} \quad \text{(note standard form)}$$

Using (2-3) we can now write the solution as

$$y_n = \left(1 - \frac{\Delta T}{\tau}\right)^n y_0 + \sum_{j=1}^{n} \left(1 - \frac{\Delta T}{\tau}\right)^{n-j} \left(\frac{\Delta T}{\tau}\right) e^{-k\,\Delta T(j-1)}$$

Thus

$$y_1 = \left(1 - \frac{\Delta T}{\tau}\right) y_0 + \frac{\Delta T}{\tau}$$

$$y_2 = \left(1 - \frac{\Delta T}{\tau}\right)^2 y_0 + \left(1 - \frac{\Delta T}{\tau}\right)\left(\frac{\Delta T}{\tau}\right) e^{-k\,\Delta T} + \left(\frac{\Delta T}{\tau}\right)$$

$$\vdots \qquad \vdots \qquad \vdots$$

As with differential equations, the constants in the solution to the difference equation are determined from known conditions. These conditions need not be the conditions at the beginning of the problem but can be any conditions where the sequence of solution values $\{X_n\}$ are known. Another approach to solving linear constant coefficient difference equations is to use the method of Z transforms. Let us briefly review the Z transformation and its important properties.

2.3   THE Z TRANSFORMATION

The Z transformation grew out of the need to define a sequence of numbers of sampled values in a form that was familiar to the control and communications engineers so that they could study sampled-data control and telemetry systems. The problem that engineers encountered was the interpretation of a sequence of sampled values of "pulsed" data in the frequency domain. The specific mathematical dilemma was that frequency-domain analysis was based on Fourier and Laplace transforms. Thus the control engineer's problem was to take the Laplace or Fourier transform of a sequence of sampled values or a sequence of numbers. Stated mathematically: if

$$\mathcal{L}f(t) = F(s)$$

then what is

$$\mathcal{L}\{f(nT)\}$$

The approach eventually used to resolve this dilemma was to note that the delta function is a well defined function that (a) is Laplace and Fourier transformable, (b) forms sequences of continuous well defined functions when a set of delta functions are modulated with a sequence of sampled values, and (c) leads to a transform pair that permits algebraic operations on difference equations in a manner similar to the algebraic operations on differential equations permitted by the Laplace transform. Additionally, and perhaps more importantly, the frequency-domain characteristics of this sequence of modulated impulses correspond closely to the frequency-domain characteristics of sampled data such as those found in telemetry and certain types of communications systems.

The approach to developing Laplace and Fourier transformable sequences of sampled values is sketched in Table 2-2. For integer multiples of the sample period T, there are corresponding values of $f(t)$ that form the sequence $\{f(nT)\}$. Although this discrete function in itself is neither Fourier nor Laplace transformable, the delta function (which is itself continuous, everywhere well defined, and is Laplace and Fourier transformable) can be modulated with the values of $f(t)$ at the sampling instant as shown in column 4. Each entry in column 4 is a continuous function, everywhere well defined, whose *strength* (area under the delta function) is $f(nT)$. By summing over column 4, a sequence of modulated impulses is formed, which itself is a continuous function everywhere well defined and is Laplace and Fourier transformable. Column 5 shows the Laplace transform of the sequence of modulated impulses. From Table 2-2 it is apparent that the Laplace-transformed sequence of modulated impulses and its inverse are defined by the relationships

$$\mathcal{L}(F^*(t)) = \sum_0^\infty f(nT)e^{-nsT} \triangleq F^*(s)$$

$$\mathcal{L}^{-1}(F^*(s)) = \sum_0^\infty f(nT)\,\delta(t - nT)$$

Table 2-2. Sequences of Numbers Considered as a Modulated Train of Modulated Delta Functions and Its Laplace Transform

1	2	3	4	5
t	$f(t)$	$\delta(t - \tau)$	$f(t)\,\delta(t - \tau)$	$\mathcal{L}\{f(t)\,\delta(t - \tau)\}$
0	$f(0)$	$\delta(0)$	$f(0)\,\delta(0)$	$f(0)$
T	$f(T)$	$\delta(t - T)$	$f(T)\,\delta(t - T)$	$f(T)e^{sT}$
$2T$	$f(2T)$	$\delta(t - 2T)$	$f(2T)\,\delta(t - 2T)$	$f(2T)e^{-2sT}$
$3T$	$f(3T)$	$\delta(t - 3T)$	$f(3T)\,\delta(t - 3T)$	$f(3T)e^{-3sT}$
$\vdots$	$\vdots$	$\vdots$	$\vdots$	$\vdots$
nT	$\{f(nT)\}$	$\delta(t - nT)$	$f(nT)\,\delta(t - nT)$	$f(nT)e^{-nsT}$
		$\downarrow$	$\downarrow$	$\downarrow$
		$\sum\limits_{0}^{\infty} \delta(t - nT)$	$f(t)^* = \sum\limits_{0}^{\infty} f(nT)\,\delta(t - nT)$	$\mathcal{L}\{f(t)^*\} = \sum\limits_{0}^{\infty} f(nT)e^{-nsT}$

$$\underbrace{\hspace{6cm}}$$
Modulated impulse
train

Defining $z = e^{st}$, this Laplace transform pair is rewritten in Z notation as

$$F(z) \overset{\Delta}{=} \sum_{0}^{\infty} f(nT)z^{-n} \overset{\Delta}{=} Z(f(t)^*)$$

$$f^*(t) \overset{\Delta}{=} \sum_{0}^{\infty} f(nT)\,\delta(t - nT) \overset{\Delta}{=} Z^{-1}(F(z))$$

At this point, as a means of review, we develop the Z transform for some important functions and operations.

Consider the function $f(t) = t$. The Z transform of $f(t)$ is developed as follows:

$$Z(t) \overset{\Delta}{=} Z\sum_{0}^{\infty} (nT)\,\delta(t - nT)$$

$$= (0T)z^{-0} + (T)z^{-1} + (2T)z^{-2} + \cdots + (nT)z^{-n} + \cdots$$

$$= T(z^{-1} + 2z^{-2} + 3z^{-3} + \cdots + nz^{-n} + \cdots)$$

$$= \frac{Tz}{(z - 1)^2}$$

Now consider the function $f(t) = e^{at}$. The Z transform of $f(t)$ is developed as follows:

$$\mathbf{Z}(e^{at}) = 1 + e^{aT}z^{-1} + e^{2aT}z^{-2} + e^{3aT}z^{-3} + \cdots$$

$$= \frac{1}{1 - e^{aT}z^{-1}} = \frac{z}{z - e^{aT}}$$

The Z transform of the unit step $U(t)$ can be obtained from the Z transform of the exponential function by setting a equal to zero. Thus

$$\mathbf{Z}(U(t)) = \lim_{a \to 0} \mathbf{Z}(e^{at}) = \lim_{a \to 0} \left(\frac{z}{z - e^{-aT}} \right) = \frac{z}{z - 1}$$

Also, the Z transformation of the sine and cosine functions can be developed from

$$\mathbf{Z}(e^{at})|_{a = j\omega}$$

and appropriate use is made of Euler's theorem

$$e^{j\omega t} = \cos(\omega t) - j \sin(\omega t)$$

It is found that

$$\mathbf{Z}(\sin(\omega t)) = \frac{z \sin(\omega T)}{z^2 - 2z \cos(\omega T) + 1}$$

and

$$\mathbf{Z}(\cos(\omega t)) = \frac{z[z - \cos(\omega T)]}{z^2 - 2z \cos(\omega T) + 1}$$

The Z-transform pairs that are used extensively throughout this book are summarized in Table 2-3. (See Appendix B for additional Z transforms.)

Table 2-3. Useful Transforms

$F(s)$	$f(t)$	$Z(F(s)) = Z(f(t)) = F(z)$
$\dfrac{1}{s}$	$u(t)$	$\dfrac{z}{z-1}$
$\dfrac{1}{s^2}$	t	$\dfrac{Tz}{(z-1)^2}$
$\dfrac{1}{s^3}$	$\dfrac{t^2}{2}$	$\dfrac{T^2 z(z+1)}{2(z-1)^3}$
$\dfrac{1}{s^4}$	$\dfrac{t^3}{3 \cdot 2}$	$\dfrac{T^3 z(z^2 + 4z + 1)}{6(z-1)^4}$
$\dfrac{1}{s+a}$	e^{-at}	$\dfrac{z}{z - e^{-aT}}$
$\dfrac{1}{(s+a)^2}$	te^{-at}	$\dfrac{Tze^{-aT}}{(z - e^{-aT})^2}$
$\dfrac{1}{(s+a)^3}$	$\dfrac{t^2}{2} e^{-at}$	$\dfrac{zT^2 e^{-aT}}{2(z - e^{-aT})^2} + \dfrac{zT^2 e^{-2aT}}{(z - e^{-aT})^3}$

$$\frac{a}{s(s+a)} \qquad 1 - e^{-at} \qquad \frac{z(1-e^{-aT})}{(z-1)(z-e^{-aT})}$$

$$\frac{a}{s^2(s+a)} \qquad \frac{at-(1-e^{-at})}{a} \qquad \frac{Tz}{(z-1)^2} - \frac{(1-e^{-aT})z}{a(z-1)(z-e^{-aT})}$$

$$\frac{a}{s^3(s+a)} \qquad \frac{1}{2}\left(t^2 - \frac{2}{a}t + \frac{2}{a^2} - \frac{2}{a^2}e^{-at}\right) \qquad \frac{T^2z}{(z-1)^3} + \frac{(aT-2)Tz}{2a(z-1)^2} + \frac{z}{a^2(z-1)} - \frac{z}{a^2(z-e^{-aT})}$$

$$\frac{\omega_0}{s^2+\omega_0^2} \qquad \sin\omega_0 t \qquad \frac{z\sin(\omega_0 T)}{z^2 - 2z\cos(\omega_0 T)+1}$$

$$\frac{s}{s^2+\omega_0^2} \qquad \cos\omega_0 t \qquad \frac{z[z-\cos(\omega_0 T)]}{z^2 - 2z\cos(\omega_0 T)+1}$$

$$\frac{\omega_0}{s^2-\omega_0^2} \qquad \sinh(\omega_0 t) \qquad \frac{z\sinh(\omega_0 T)}{z^2 - 2z\cosh(\omega_0 T)+1}$$

$$\frac{s}{s^2-\omega_0^2} \qquad \cosh(\omega_0 t) \qquad \frac{z[z-\cosh(\omega_0 T)]}{z^2 - 2z\cosh(\omega_0 T)+1}$$

Table 2-3. Useful Transforms *(Continued)*

$F(s)$	$f(t)$	$Z(F(s)) = Z(f(t)) = F(z)$
$\dfrac{b-a}{(s+a)(s+b)}$	$e^{-at} - e^{-bt}$	$\dfrac{z}{z-e^{-aT}} - \dfrac{z}{z-e^{-bT}}$
$\dfrac{(b-a)(s+c)}{(s+a)(s+b)}$	$(c-a)e^{-at} + (b-c)e^{-bt}$	$\dfrac{(c-a)z}{z-e^{-aT}} + \dfrac{(b-c)z}{z-e^{-bT}}$
$\dfrac{ab}{s(s+a)(s+b)}$	$1 + \dfrac{b}{a-b}e^{-at} - \dfrac{a}{a-b}e^{-bt}$	$\dfrac{z}{z-1} + \dfrac{bz}{(a-b)(z-e^{-aT})} - \dfrac{az}{(a-b)(z-e^{-bT})}$
$\dfrac{ab(s+c)}{s(s+a)(s+b)}$	$c + \dfrac{b(c-a)e^{-at}}{(a-b)} + \dfrac{a(b-c)e^{-bt}}{(a-b)}$	$\dfrac{cz}{z-1} + \dfrac{b(c-a)z}{(a-b)(z-e^{-aT})} + \dfrac{a(b-c)z}{(a-b)(z-e^{-bT})}$
$\dfrac{1}{(s+a)(s+b)(s+c)}$	$\dfrac{e^{-at}}{(b-a)(c-a)} + \dfrac{e^{-bt}}{(a-b)(c-b)} + \dfrac{e^{-ct}}{(a-c)(b-c)}$	$\dfrac{z}{(b-a)(c-a)(z-e^{-aT})} + \dfrac{z}{(a-b)(c-b)(z-e^{-bT})} + \dfrac{z}{(a-c)(b-c)(z-e^{-cT})}$
$\dfrac{\omega_0}{(s+a)^2 + \omega_0^2}$	$e^{-at}\sin(\omega_0 t)$	$\dfrac{ze^{-aT}\sin(\omega_0 T)}{z^2 - 2ze^{-aT}\cos(\omega_0 T) + e^{-2aT}}$
$\dfrac{s+a}{(s+a)^2 + \omega_0^2}$	$e^{-at}\cos(\omega_0 t)$	$\dfrac{z^2 - ze^{-aT}\cos(\omega_0 T)}{z^2 - 2ze^{-aT}\cos(\omega_0 T) + e^{-2aT}}$

Theorems that will be used are:

The Shifting Theorem. If $f(t)$ is **Z** transformable, $\mathbf{Z}f(t) = F(z)$, and if kT is a real positive number, and k is an integer, then

$$\mathbf{Z}\big[f(t - kT)\big] = z^{-k}F(z)$$

$$\mathbf{Z}\big[f(t + kT)\big] = z^{k}F(z)$$

The Initial Value Theorem. If $f(t)$ is **Z** transformable and if $\mathbf{Z}f(t) = F(z)$, then

$$\lim_{t \to 0} f(t) = \lim_{n \to 0} f(nT) = \lim_{z \to \infty} zF(z)$$

The Final Value Theorem. If $f(t)$ is **Z** transformable, $\mathbf{Z}f(t) = F(z)$, and if $F(z)$ contains no poles on or outside the unit circle, then

$$\lim_{t \to \infty} f(t) = \lim_{n \to \infty} f(nT) = \lim_{z \to 1} \left\{ \frac{z - 1}{z} F(z) \right\}$$

2.4 INVERSE Z TRANSFORMATION

The inverse Z transformation has special characteristics and properties. It is important to recognize that the Z transformation is defined by the relationship

$$\mathbf{Z}f(t) = \mathbf{Z}f^*(t) = \mathbf{Z}\sum f(nT)\,\delta(t - nT) = F(z)$$

Care should be taken to note that, though $f(t)$ is not equal to $f^*(t)$, the Z transform of $f(t)$ is identically equal to the Z transform of $f^*(t)$. While this is interesting, what is important is that this relationship does not hold true in the inverse Z transformation; that is,

$$\mathbf{Z}^{-1}F(z) \neq \sum f(nT)\,\delta(t - nT)$$

uniquely.
  For example,

$$\mathbf{Z}U(t) = \frac{z}{z - 1}$$

but

$$Z^{-1}\left(\frac{z}{z-1}\right) = \begin{cases} U(t) \\ \cos(\omega t) & \text{when} \quad \omega T = 0,\, 2\pi,\, 4\pi,\, \ldots \\ 1 + \sin(\omega\theta) & \text{when} \quad \omega T = 0,\, \pi,\, 2\pi,\, 3\pi,\, \ldots \\ \cosh(\omega t) & \text{when} \quad \omega = 0 \\ e^{-at} & \text{when} \quad a = 0 \\ \vdots \end{cases}$$

In other words, there is a unique Z transform for a given $f(t)$ but there are many $g(t)$'s whose sampled values pass through the $f(nT)$ for certain conditions on $g(t)$. This is visualized in Figure 2-1.

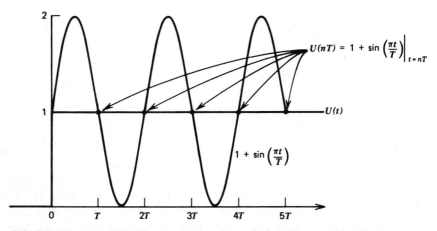

FIGURE 2-1.   Many functions can pass through the same set of points.

Two commonly used methods for performing inverse Z transformation are the power series expansion method and the partial fraction expansion method. We need only the power series expansion method for the material presented here. There is a third method, the "direct" method, that involves contour integration in the Z plane. This method is little used by engineers and thus is not discussed. It is mentioned for the sake of completeness.

The Power Series Expansion Method
of Inverse Z Transformation*

In this method a polynomial in z is expanded into a power series in z^{-1} by long division. The coefficients of each term in the power series correspond to the value of the time function $f(t)$ at the nth sampling instant.

$$\mathbf{Z}^{-1}F(z) = \mathbf{Z}^{-1}\left(\frac{z}{z - e^{-aT}} \right)$$

$$= \mathbf{Z}^{-1}\left(\frac{1}{1 - z^{-1}e^{-aT}} \right)$$

$$= \mathbf{Z}^{-1}(1 + z^{-1}e^{-aT} + z^{-2}e^{-2aT} + z^{-3}e^{-3aT} + \cdots)$$

$$\mathbf{Z}^{-1}\left(\frac{z}{z - e^{-aT}} \right) = 1\,\delta(0) + e^{-aT}\delta(t - T) + e^{-2aT}\,\delta(t - 2T)$$

$$+ e^{-3aT}\,\delta(t - 3T) + \cdots$$

Note that if we write

$$\frac{y(z)}{x(z)} = \frac{z}{z - e^{-aT}}$$

then we can derive the difference equation

$$y_{n+1} = e^{-aT}y_n + x_{n+1}$$

When $x_n = 0$, for all n and $y_0 = 1$, this difference equation generates the sequence of y_n

$$1, \quad e^{-aT}, \quad e^{-2aT}, \quad e^{-3aT}, \ldots$$

We see that these values correspond to the coefficients in the power series expansion of the Z-domain transfer function, $F(z)$.

Table 2-4 summarizes the highlights of the Z-transform operator method:

*One-sided Z transform.

Table 2-4. Summary of the Z-Transform Operator Method Transform, Time-Domain Functions, Differential Equations, and Difference Equations

Definitions

$$\mathcal{L}\{f^*(t)\} = \sum_{0}^{\infty} f(nT)e^{-nsT} = F^*(s)$$

$$\mathcal{L}^{-1}\{F^*(s)\} = f(0)\,\delta(t-0) + f(T)\,\delta(t-T) + f(2T)\,\delta(t-2T) + \cdots$$

Let

$$z \triangleq e^{sT}$$

Then

$$F(z) \triangleq \sum_{0}^{\infty} f(nT)z^{-n} = \mathbf{Z}\{f^*(t)\}$$

$$f^*(t) \triangleq \sum_{0}^{\infty} f(nT)\,\delta(t-nT) = \mathbf{Z}^{-1}\{F(z)\}$$

These equations are called the **Z-transform pair**. They are the logical extension of the Laplace transform.

This table should be read slowly top to bottom on first reading

Simple example of (a) Laplace transforms and (b) differential equations and

$$\dot{Y} = f(t);\; Y_0 = 0$$

$$\mathcal{L}(\dot{Y}(t)) = sy(s) \quad \text{and if } f(t) = U(t) \text{ then } \mathcal{L}f(t) = \frac{1}{s}$$

and $Y(s) = 1/s^2$. $\quad \therefore\; Y(t) = t$

so $Y(nT) = nT$

(c) Z transforms and (d) time-domain functions and (e) s-domain functions

$$\mathbf{Z}(t) \triangleq \mathbf{Z} \sum_0^\infty (nt)\, \delta(t - nT) = \mathbf{Z}(s^{-2})$$

$$= (0T)z^{-0} + (T)z^{-1} + (2T)z^{-2} + \cdots + (nT)z^{-nT}$$

$$= 0 + Tz^{-1} + 2Tz^{-2} + \cdots + (nT)z^{-n}$$

$$= T(z^{-1} + 2z^{-2} + 3z^{-3} + \cdots + nz^{-n} + \cdots)$$

$$F(z) = \frac{Tz}{(z-1)^2}$$

(Example continued)

Transforming $F(z)$ into a difference equation for computing the sequence $f(nT)$

(f) Z transforms and (g) difference equations that generate (h) sequences of numbers

we let

$$\frac{y(z)}{x(z)} = \frac{Tz}{(z-1)^2} = \frac{Tz^{-1}}{1 - 2z^{-1} + z^{-2}}$$

en

$$(1 - 2z^{-1} + z^{-2})y(z) = Tz^{-1}x(z)$$

$$y(s) - 2e^{-sT}y(s) + e^{-2sT}y(s) = Te^{-sT}x(s)$$

$$y(t) - 2y(t - T) + y(t - 2T) = Tx(t - T)$$

$$y(nT) = 2y((n-1)T) - y((n-2)T) + Tx((n-1)T)$$

$$y_n = 2y_{n-1} - y_n + Tx_{n-1}$$

1. For writing sequences of numbers in a form that permits them to be Laplace and Fourier transformable.

2. For transforming $f(t)$ into $F(z)$.

3. For transforming $F(s)$ into $F(z)$.

4. For deriving a difference equation from $F(z)$ that can be used to calculate the sequence $\{f(nT)\}$.

Clearly then, inverting the process we could proceed:

- From the difference equation to $F(z)$.
- From $F(z)$ to $f^*(t)$.
- From $F(z)$ to $f(t)$.
- From $F(z)$ to $F(s)$.
- From $F(s)$ to $F(z)$.
- And so on.

All that one must remember to use the Z-transform method is that one usually proceeds from a differential equation to a simulating difference equation in the sequence

$$\begin{matrix} \text{differential equation and} \\ \text{known type of forcing} \\ \text{function} \end{matrix} \to F(s) \to f(t) \to f^*(t) \to F(z) \to \begin{matrix} \text{difference} \\ \text{equation} \end{matrix}$$

Or one can proceed from the difference equation to a differential equation in the reverse sequence

$$\begin{matrix} \text{difference} \\ \text{equation} \end{matrix} \to F(z) \to f^*(t) \to f(t) \to F(s) \to \begin{matrix} \text{differential} \\ \text{equation} \end{matrix}$$

Of course one may stop or begin anywhere in the sequence. The only end-to-end sequences are in proceeding from a differential equation to a difference equation and vice versa.

2.5   SOLVING LINEAR CONSTANT COEFFICIENT DIFFERENCE EQUATIONS USING THE Z-TRANSFORM METHOD

Armed now with the Z-transform method, we can solve linear constant coefficient difference equations by (1) taking the Z transform of both sides of the difference equation and (2) using Z-transform algebra to write the discrete system's response to an arbitrary forcing function (the particular solution) and its initial conditions (the complementary solution). For example, consider the difference equation:

$$x_n = Ax_{n-1} + f_n, \quad \text{for} \quad x(0) = X_0$$

which, when Z transformed, takes the form

$$x(z) = Az^{-1}x(z) + f(z)$$

Solving for $x(z)$ we find

$$x(z) = \frac{zX_0}{z - A} + \frac{zf(z)}{z - A}$$

which, when inverse Z transformed, gives the discrete function solution* to the difference equation:

$$x(nT) = A^n x_0 + f(nT) + Af((n - 1)T) + A^2f((n - 2)T) + \cdots$$

The first term in the equation is the solution of the homogeneous equation or the complementary solution and the series of remaining terms is the particular solution. In passing we see that the transition coefficient A^n that propagates the initial conditions x_0 to $x(nT)$ can be developed directly from the difference equation as follows. If

$$f_n = 0 \text{ for all } n$$

then

$$x_n = Ax_{n-1}$$

Since

$$x_{n-1} = Ax_{n-2}$$

then

$$x_n = A^2 x_{n-2}$$

Similarly

$$x_n = A^3 x_{n-3}$$

$$\vdots \qquad \vdots$$

$$x_n = A^n x_0$$

*If $\mathbf{Z}[zf(z)]/(z - A)]$ has a closed form, the inverse of the particular solution can usually be found in a table of Z transforms.

This is carried forward in the vector-matrix notation (see Equation 2-3) as a means of propagating discrete states forward n equal time intervals through n repeated transitions.

Table 2-2 lists Z transforms that are useful for solving difference equations and relating time-domain, s-domain, and z-domain functions. Later it will also be found useful for simplified simulation difference equation derivations (Chapter 4).

2.6   FINITE AND INFINITE MEMORY FORMS OF DIFFERENCE EQUATIONS

A useful property of difference equations is that they can be written in finite or infinite memory forms. To this point we have dealt primarily with infinite memory forms, that is, equations of the form:

$$x_n = \sum a_i x_{n-i} + \sum b_j Q_{n-j}$$

A finite memory form difference equation has the form

$$x_n = \sum c_j Q_{n-j}$$

and computes the discrete function X_n only in terms of weighted sums of the discrete forcing function. As an example of the former, consider the differential equation

$$\tau \dot{x} + x = Q(t), \quad \text{for} \quad x(0) = 0$$

which is simulated with the difference equation

$$x_n = e^{-T/\tau} x_{n-1} + (1 - e^{-T/\tau}) Q_{n-1} \tag{2-4}$$

The *transfer function* for this discrete process is given by

$$\frac{x(z)}{Q(z)} = \frac{1 - e^{-T/\tau}}{z - e^{-T/\tau}}$$

whose power series expansion allows*

$$x(z) = (1 - e^{-T/\tau})(z^{-1} + e^{-T/\tau} z^{-2} + e^{-2T/\tau} z^{-3} + \cdots) Q(z)$$

*Infinite memory of past influence of Q.

which when inverted and *truncated* at the third term becomes*

$$x_n = (1 - e^{-T/\tau})(Q_{n-1} + e^{-T/\tau}Q_{n-2} + e^{-2T/\tau}Q_{n-3})$$

This is the finite memory form of (2-4). Finite memory form difference equations are useful for simulating systems when T is approximately equal to τ. They are also handy for estimating the noise propagation characteristics through discrete systems and through difference equations either by computer or by hand analysis. Finally, note that when $x(z)$ is written solely in terms of $Q(z)$ as shown at the bottom of page 109, the infinite series is the discrete form of the convolution integral

$$x(t) = \int_0^t h(t - \tau)Q(\tau)\, d\tau$$

The calculation of noise variance as propagated through systems described by finite memory difference equations is straightforward and easy to do. Since finite memory difference equations have the form

$$x_n = \Sigma a_i Q_{n-1}$$

when squared they become

$$x_n^2 = \Sigma\Sigma a_i a_j Q_{n-1} Q_{n-j}$$

Stationary, almost white and unbiased[†] random or pseudorandom forcing functions result in the variance transfer function developed as follows:

$$\sigma_x^2 \cong \Sigma E(a_i^2 Q_i^2) = (\Sigma a_i^2)\sigma_Q^2$$

$$\therefore \quad \frac{\sigma_x^2}{\sigma_Q^2} \cong \Sigma a_i^2$$

The variance transfer function is nothing more than the sum of the squares of the coefficients in the finite memory form difference equation.

Returning to our example of the first-order system, you will remember that the finite memory form difference equation

$$x_n \cong (1 - e^{-T/\tau})(Q_{n-1} + e^{-T/\tau}Q_{n-2} + e^{-2T/\tau}Q_{n-3} + \cdots)$$

---

*Finite memory of past influence of Q (three terms in this example).
[†]Stationary $\rightarrow E(X_n^2) = E(X_{n-1}^2)$; unbiased $\rightarrow E(X_n) = 0$; white $\rightarrow E(X_n X_m)_{m \neq n} = 0$.

when squared gives

$$x_n^2 \cong (1 - e^{-T/\tau})^2 (Q_{n-1}^2 + e^{-2T/\tau}Q_{n-2} + e^{-4T/\tau}Q_{n-3} + \cdots)$$

Under the unbiased $(EQ = 0)$, stationary $(EQ_n^2 = EQ_{n-1}^2 = EQ_{n-2}^2 = \cdots)$, and uncorrelated $(E(Q_{n-1}Q_{n-2}) = 0)$ assumptions, a random (or pseudorandom) Q_i results in the variance transfer function

$$\frac{\sigma_x^2}{\sigma_Q^2} \cong (1 - e^{-T/\tau})^2 (1 + e^{-2T/\tau} + e^{-4T/\tau} + \cdots)$$

Notice that this is the discrete form of Parseval's theorem

$$\sigma^2 = \int_0^\infty h^2(t)\Phi \, dt$$

where $h(t)$ is the system impulse response and Φ is the input noise power spectral density. In certain cases closed forms of the variance transfer function can be written. In this case

$$\frac{\sigma_x^2}{\sigma_Q^2} = \frac{(1 - e^{-T/\tau})^2}{(1 - e^{-2T/\tau})} = \frac{1 - e^{-T/\tau}}{1 + e^{-T/\tau}}$$

Furthermore, for a nonstationary noise the variance propagation characteristics of the equation would be described by the transfer function

$$\frac{\sigma_x^2}{\sigma_Q^2} = \frac{(1 - e^{-T/\tau})^2}{z - e^{-2T/\tau}}$$

which gives the variance propagating difference equation

$$\sigma_{x_n}^2 = e^{-2T/\tau}\sigma_{x_{n-1}}^2 + (1 - e^{-T/\tau})^2 \sigma_{Q_{n-1}}^2$$

2.7 MATHEMATICAL PROPERTIES OF SAMPLED DATA AND SAMPLED-DATA RECONSTRUCTION

It will become important for synthesizing discrete systems that can approximate continuous systems that the reader be able to *discretize* a continuous process. This is most easily accomplished by inserting samplers on the signal flow path and immediately following them with signal reconstruction processes to return the signal to an analog form. To complete the synthesis of difference equations to represent the discretized analog process, samplers are inserted at the outputs of interest and the transfer function is written from sampler to sampler, from which the simulating difference equation can be derived. If these output samplers disrupt the analog signal flow, they too must be followed by reconstruction processes. Much more will be said on this in Chapter 4.

It is imperative to understand the properties of the sampling process and its associated signal reconstruction. Two sources of error are introduced in discretizing continuous processes in this manner. First, the sampling process distorts the frequency spectrum of the continuous function being sampled. Second, the reconstruction process introduces further spectral distortion as well as phase shift (time lags) on the reconstructed signal as compared with its continuous counterpart. The spectral distortion associated with the sampling process can be determined by examining the spectral characteristics of a modulated train of impulses

$$f^*(t) = f(nT)\, \delta(t - nT)$$

Assuming that the Fourier transform of $f(t)$ is known and is of the form $f(j\omega)$, the Fourier transform of $f^*(t)$ is given by

$$f^*(j\omega) = \frac{1}{T} \sum_{-\infty}^{\infty} F(j(\omega + n\omega_s))$$

where ω_s is the sampling frequency. Comparisons of the original continuous system spectrum with the spectrum of the modulated impulse train can be made in Figure 2-2. Careful understanding of the equation for $f^*(j\omega)$ is essential before proceeding. Note that if $f(t)$ is a sine wave at 1 hertz and the sampling frequency is at 10 samples per second, the spectrum of the modulated train of impulses has *spectral lines* at 1, 11, 21, 31, 41, 51, and up to 1001 hertz and beyond. These high-frequency components in the spectrum of the modulated train of impulses come from the need for the high-frequency component of the Fourier series to form the train of delta functions. The modulating function determines precisely the shape of the distribution around each spectral line, whereas the delta functions are the functions that require the repeated high-frequency components for their formulation.

If the continuous function $f(t)$ is a sine wave at 11 hertz being sampled at 10 hertz, the high-frequency components are there at 21, 31, 41, and 51 hertz in real frequencies, but so too is 1 hertz. This arises from the fact that

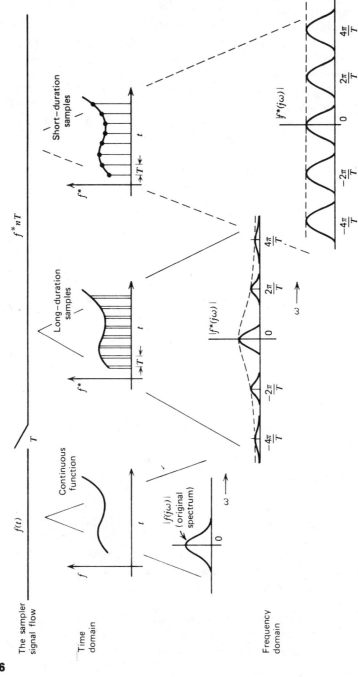

FIGURE 2-2. Effect of sampling on the spectrum of $f(t)$.

an 11-hertz sine wave sampled at 10 hertz will appear at the output of the sampler with precisely the same numerical values as would a 1-hertz signal sampled at 10 hertz. This type of spectral distortion is called frequency folding (11, 21, 31, 41 hertz, and so on, fold down to 1 hertz when sampled at 10 hertz) and is observed when a function is sampled at a rate slower than half the highest frequency components in its spectrum. This spectrum distortion and overlap are visualized in Figure 2-3. Thus sampling can lead to two types of spectrum distortion: (1) spectral overlap or frequency folding and (2) introduction of high-frequency components in the spectrum because of the delta function modulation.

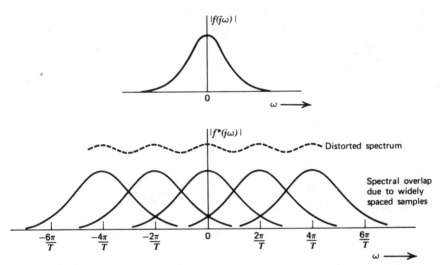

FIGURE 2-3.   Frequency folding signal distortion due to sampling at too low a frequency.

2.8   RECONSTRUCTION PROCESSES

Signal reconstruction is a term used in sampled-data and discrete system theory and refers to the reconstruction of a signal from its sampled values. It is apparent from Figure 2-2 that the spectrum of a *band-limited* continuous function could be restored if the sampled function were passed through an ideal filter whose transfer function is unity out to $\omega_s/2$ and zero thereafter. Practical considerations leave us with reconstruction processes that are substantially less than ideal but that are nonetheless sufficient for most engineering problems.

In this book we speak of the mathematical model of signal reconstruction rather than the physical reconstruction device itself. Data reconstruction processes are characterized in two ways: by the number of data points used to reconstruct the forcing function and by the way the sampled values are connected. The simplest type of reconstruction is the zero-order hold, so named because it uses a zero-order collating polynomial to reconstruct the sequence of sampled values into a sequence of stair-step functions. The zero-order hold is important to this book in two ways: first we use it as part of the process of synthesizing discrete systems that approximate continuous systems; second this hold is used extensively in hybrid simulations as a digital-to-analog conversion device. Figure 2-4 illustrates the

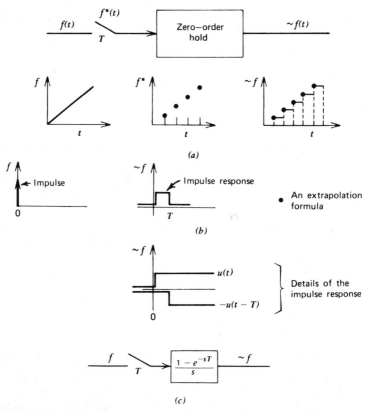

FIGURE 2-4. The zero-order hold. (*a*) Its time-domain characteristics. The stair step approximation is used in hybrid simulations to convert digital data to analog signals and to synthesize discrete system analogs of continuous systems. (*b*) Impulse response. (*c*) Transfer function derivation and block diagram. Impulse response $= uf = \sim f = u(t) - u(t - T)$; $L(\sim f) = 1/s - e^{-sT}/s = 1 - e^{-sT}/s = \sim f(s)$.

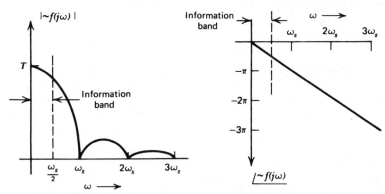

FIGURE 2-5. The zero-order hold frequency-domain characteristics. Advantages: easy to use and understand; reasonable trade-off between first-order hold disadvantages and triangular hold disadvantages (Figures 2-7 and 2-9). Disadvantages: about a half sample period delay; some attenuation in the information band; poor attenuation of signal outside the information band.

zero-order reconstruction process in the time domain, and Figure 2-5 shows the amplitude and phase characteristics of this hold.

The frequency-domain characteristics of the zero-order hold are determined by setting $s = j\omega$ in the transfer function as

$$f(j\omega) = \frac{1 - e^{-j\omega T}}{j\omega} = \frac{2}{\omega} e^{-j\omega T/2} \sin\left(\frac{\omega T}{2}\right)$$

from which we can develop the amplitude and phase shift as*

$$f(j\omega) = \frac{T \sin(\omega T/2)}{\omega T/2} \angle -\frac{\omega T}{2}$$

Note that the zero-order hold introduces significant phase lag on the high-frequency components of any signal that it passes. This is a key point to remember, as we will mention it repeatedly throughout the book. This is easy to interpret in the time domain if you consider a complex periodic signal driving the zero-order hold. Imagine that you are driving this hold with the Fourier series representation of the signal instead of the signal itself. The zero-order hold introduces a half sample period of time delay on each of the sine and cosine functions in the series. Obviously this can be a

---

* $\angle$ symbolizes the phase angle: phase angle = $-\omega T/2$.

significant effect when the sample period is on the order of the period of the highest frequency component of the signal.

First-order hold reconstruction is characterized by reconstructing a sequence of sampled values into a sequence of ramp functions (a sequence of linear functions that form a sawtooth approximation of the continuous function). This is seen in Figure 2-6. The first-order hold reconstructs the continuous signal with a sequence of first-order Newton-Gregory polynomials. The frequency-domain characteristics of the first-order hold are given by

$$f(j\omega) = T(1 + \omega^2 T^2)^{1/2}\left(\frac{\sin(\omega T/2)}{\omega T/2}\right) \angle \tan^{-1}\omega T - \omega T$$

and are shown in Figure 2-7. The dominant terms in the phase formulas indicate that these reconstruction processes introduce *lags* of $T/2$ for the zero-order hold and T for the first-order hold, out to the Shannon limit (i.e., $\omega_s/2$). In general an nth-order hold will involve fitting a curve through

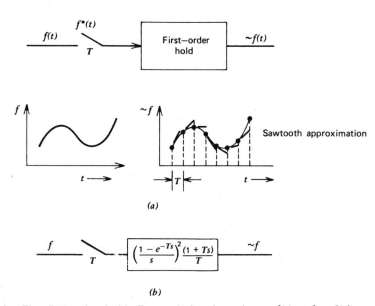

(a)

(b)

FIGURE 2-6. The first-order hold. Extrapolation formula: $\sim f(t) = f_n + [(f_n - f_{n-1})/T](t - nT)$ on the interval $nT \leqslant t \leqslant (n + 1)T$; $\sim f(s) = [(1 + Ts)/T][(1 - e^{-Ts})/s]^2$.

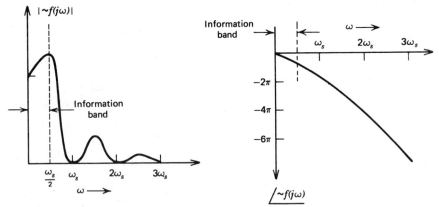

FIGURE 2-7.   First-order hold frequency-domain characteristics. Advantages: no attenuation in the information band (slight gain). Disadvantages: about a full sample period of delay, which is equal to twice the phase shift of zero-order hold.

n points and will introduce an effective delay of approximately $nT/2$ on the reconstructed signal* as compared with its continuous counterpart.

The triangular hold (see Figures 2-8 and 2-9) is not subject to these delays. In a true physical sense this hold is unrealizable because its transfer function has a sample period of lead (i.e., assumes f_{n+1} is known before it is calculated) and this is impossible to implement in a hardware system. Our concern however is only to use holds in mathematical models from which we can derive difference equations that can be used in the simulation of continuous systems. In mathematics the triangular hold leads to implicit equations that can *always* be solved for linear constant coefficient equations and often can be solved for nonlinear equations. Therefore we will admit the triangular hold as a reconstruction process for simulation purposes.

Signal reconstruction is an important concept in the synthesis of discrete systems because a number of modern simulation methods require the synthesis of a discrete system that approximates a continuous system. A difficulty arises when one tries to visualize digital computer information flow and its analogy with continuous system signal flow. For example the continuous process $G(s)$ has the block diagram

$$I(s) \rightarrow \boxed{G(s)} \rightarrow O(s)$$

*In the information band only.

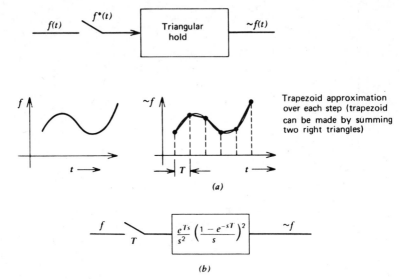

FIGURE 2-8. The triangular hold. Interpolation formula: $\sim f(t) = f_n + [(f_{n+1} - f_n)/T](t - nT)$ on the interval $nT \leqslant t \leqslant (n + 1)T$; $\sim f(s) = e^{Ts}/s^2[(1 - e^{-sT})/s]^2$.

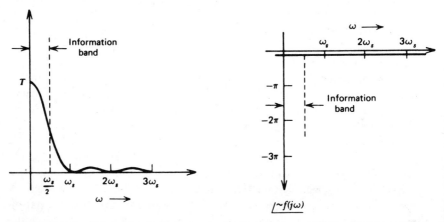

FIGURE 2-9. Triangular-hold frequency-domain characteristics. Advantages: no phase shift or signal delays; good attenuation outside the information band. Disadvantages: attenuation in the information band.

where O is the output and I is the input. When we know that there is a differential equation that relates the input and output we also know that there is a discrete (digital) process $H(z)$ that also relates O to I. $H(z)$ can be developed as follows:

1. Derive a difference equation* from finite difference approximations of the derivatives.
2. Z-transform the difference equations.
3. Write the transfer function $H(z)$ for the difference equation.

Then we can visualize the discrete system that approximates the continuous system as

$$\xrightarrow{I(z)}\boxed{H(z)}\xrightarrow{O(z)}$$

The difficulty here is that it is hard to relate $H(z)$ to $G(s)$ after all the algebra. Also consider this: $G(s)$ is intimately related to the physical system being simulated. If you have some physical feeling for the system it is easy to relate the mathematical model and computer results to the physical system represented by $G(s)$. For many it is virtually impossible to relate an $H(z)$ developed mathematically to $G(s)$ on the physical system. Those who have designed a continuous system on the digital computer know the frustration of starting with the design of a second-order system, being reassured it was modeled correctly, and then were startled to find the simulating difference equation had four extra poles and two new zeros: the result of simply substituting a fairly accurate third-order numerical integrator into the differential equation that described the second-order continuous system. For a simple example consider the system

$$\dot{x} + x = f, \qquad \text{for} \quad x_0 = 0$$

which has one real root at -1. This system has the transfer function

$$G(s) = \frac{x}{f}(s) = \frac{1}{s+1} \Rightarrow \xrightarrow{f}\boxed{\frac{1}{s+1}}\xrightarrow{x}$$

If we use the common numerical integration formula[†]

$$x_n = x_{n-1} + \frac{T}{2}(3\dot{x}_{n-1} - \dot{x}_{n-2})$$

---

*We can also numerically integrate or use other methods of proceeding from a differential equation to a difference equation.
[†]Especially in real-time simulations.

to integrate the differential equation, we find by direct substitution that

$$x_n = x_{n-1} + \frac{T}{2}\left[3(f_{n-1} - x_{n-1}) - (f_{n-2} - x_{n-2})\right]$$

or

$$x_n + \left(\frac{3T}{2} - 1\right)x_{n-1} - \frac{T}{2}x_{n-2} = \frac{T}{2}(3f_{n-1} - f_{n-2})$$

Taking the **Z**-transform of this difference equation we find

$$\left[z^2 + \left(\frac{3T}{2} - 1\right)z - \frac{T}{2}\right]x(z) = \frac{T}{2}(3z - 1)f(z)$$

which has the transfer function

$$\frac{x(z)}{f(z)} = \frac{(T/2)(3z - 1)}{z^2 + (3T/2 - 1)z - T/2} = H(z)$$

Thus we are led to conclude that

$$\xrightarrow{f(s)}\boxed{\frac{1}{s+1}}\xrightarrow{x(s)}$$

can be simulated (approximated) on the digital computer with

$$\xrightarrow{f(z)}\boxed{\frac{(T/2)(3z - 1)}{z^2 + (3T/2 - 1)z - T/2}}\xrightarrow{x(z)}$$

That is a big jump to make. The obvious questions are, "How does a system with two poles and one zero look like a system with one pole?" and "When is this discrete mathematical model system going to get my design of the continuous system in trouble?"

   A way out of this dilemma: The author believes that one way is to synthesize a discrete analog of the continuous process being simulated. Then *by analogy* one can relate $H(z)$ to $G(s)$. The process first developed independently by Jury, Tou, and Fowler (all at about the same time) and later found by a number of engineers "working the problem" was to synthesize hybrid systems of signal flow (not hybrid computer simulations) that could be described with difference equations. Then the difference equations were programmed on the digital computer. Thus what went on the computer was a discrete analog of the continuous process. The cornerstone is the signal reconstruction process.

Consider the following example. The discrete analog of the continuous system

$$f(s) \rightarrow \boxed{\frac{1}{\tau s + 1}} \rightarrow x(s)$$

Discretize the input signal

$$\begin{array}{c} f(s) \\ f(t) \end{array} \searrow \begin{array}{c} f(z); \\ f^*(nT); \end{array} \qquad \begin{array}{c} \text{frequency domain } (FD) \\ \text{time domain } (TD) \end{array}$$
$$\overline{T}$$

Reconstruct the input signal

$$\begin{array}{c} f(s) \\ f(t) \end{array} \searrow \begin{array}{c} f(z) \\ f^*(nT) \end{array} \boxed{\frac{1 - e^{-sT}}{s}} \begin{array}{c} \sim f(s); \ FD \\ \sim f(t); \ TD \end{array}$$
$$\overline{T}$$

Drive the continuous system with the continuous function $\sim f(t)$

$$\begin{array}{c} f(s) \\ f(t) \end{array} \searrow \begin{array}{c} f(z) \\ f^*(nT) \end{array} \boxed{\frac{1 - e^{-sT}}{s}} \begin{array}{c} \sim f(s) \\ \sim f(t) \end{array} \boxed{\frac{1}{\tau s + 1}} \begin{array}{c} \sim x(s); \ FD \\ \sim x(t); \ TD \end{array}$$
$$\overline{T}$$

Sample the output. This is the pickoff that allows us to write the difference equation from discrete input to discrete output

$$\searrow \begin{array}{c} f(z) \\ \overline{T} \end{array} \boxed{\frac{1 - e^{-sT}}{s}} \rightarrow \boxed{\frac{1}{\tau s + 1}} \begin{array}{c} \sim x(t) \\ \sim x(z) \end{array}$$
$$T$$

$$\frac{x(z)}{f(z)} = \mathbf{Z}\left(\frac{1 - e^{-sT}}{s} \right)\left(\frac{1}{s + 1} \right)$$

$$= \left(\frac{1 - e^{-T/\tau}}{z - e^{-T/\tau}} \right)$$

$$x_n = e^{-T/\tau} x_{n-1} + (1 - e^{-T/\tau}) f_{n-1}$$

We can now make the following observations:

• The discrete system transfer function

$$H(z) = \left(\frac{1 - e^{-T/\tau}}{z - e^{-T/\tau}} \right)$$

has one pole, as does $G(s)$.

- The pole of the discrete system is the s-plane pole mapped into the z plane using the relation

$$z \overset{\Delta}{=} e^{st}$$

$$z_{pole} = e^{s_{pole}T}$$

Now we know that

$$s_{pole} = -\frac{1}{\tau}$$

$$\therefore z_{pole} = e^{-T/\tau}$$

- The difference equation coefficient is the transition matrix for this one-dimensional problem.
- No numerical integration and its attendant approximation are used.

Somehow this approach is more satisfying and retains the ties to the physical system from the digital simulation better than does the pure algebra approach. This method is discussed further in Chapter 4.

2.9   DISCRETE SYSTEM STABILITY

The stability of linear constant coefficient discrete systems can be examined in both the s and z planes. In the s plane, the stability criterion would be that the poles of the system reside in the left half of the s plane. In discrete systems, a system is said to be stable provided that the magnitude of the z pole is less than or equal to 1. This z-plane criterion comes from the fact that the left half of the s plane maps into the interior of the unit circle in the z plane. This is sketched in Figure 2-10 and follows from the definition

$$z = e^{st}$$

In the same way that pole location in the s plane is related to the transient response in the time domain, pole location in the z plane is related to transient response in the time domain as sketched in Figure 2-11. It is interesting that real poles located on the left half of the imaginary axis do not have transient responses that have continuous system counterparts (except when the continuous systems are sampled more slowly than the sampling limit). Discrete systems whose poles reside on the left half of the real axis of the z plane are not useful for simulating continuous systems.

FIGURE 2-10. Discrete system stability criteria. (*a*) *S*-Plane stability; (*b*) *Z*-Plane stability.

FIGURE 2-11. Discrete system stability. Typical transient responses for (*a*) poles on the real axis and (*b*) pairs of complex conjugate poles.

2.10 DISCRETE SYSTEM STATE EQUATIONS

We saw before that the linear stationary systems could be described by the vector-matrix equations

$$\dot{\mathbf{X}} = \mathbf{AX} + \mathbf{BU}$$

$$\mathbf{Y} = \mathbf{CX}$$

where $\mathbf{X}$ is the state vector, $\mathbf{Y}$ is the output vector, $\mathbf{U}$ is the input vector, and $\mathbf{A, B, C}$ are constant matrices. It was also seen that the solution to this system of equations was given by

$$\mathbf{X} = e^{A(t-t_0)}\mathbf{X}(t_0) + \int_{t_0}^{t} e^{A(t-\tau)}\mathbf{BU}(\tau)\,d\tau$$

The discrete vector-matrix equations can be developed from the continuous vector-matrix equations as follows: Let

$$t = nT, \quad \text{for} \quad n = 0, 1, 2, \ldots$$

Since we will be solving a system of first-order differential equations we will seek a solution in the form of a first-order difference equation. Thus we require only the present and future values of the system's motion. These can be developed as:

$$\mathbf{X}_n = e^{A(nT-t_0)}\mathbf{X}(t_0) + \int_{t_0}^{nT} e^{A(nT-\tau)}\mathbf{BU}(\tau)\,d\tau$$

$$\mathbf{X}_{n+1} = e^{A(nT+T-t_0)}\mathbf{X}(t_0) + \int_{t_0}^{(n+1)T} e^{A(nT+T-\tau)}\mathbf{BU}(\tau)\,d\tau$$

Comparing these equations we see that

$$\mathbf{X}_{n+1} = e^{AT}\mathbf{X}_n + \int_{nT}^{(n+1)T} e^{A(nT+T-\tau)}\mathbf{BU}(\tau)\,d\tau$$

and

$$\mathbf{Y}_{n+1} = \mathbf{CX}_{n+1}$$

For constant coefficient systems

$$\mathbf{\Phi} = e^{AT}$$

B and **C** are calculated only once. If the integral is evaluated numerically, however (the usual approach for complex problems), the integrand must be calculated at each step. The alternative is to use a vector-matrix difference equation. If we synthesize a discrete approximation of this system of equations, we can use the techniques developed in Section 2.7 to derive the difference equation.

Consider now the continuous process shown in Figure 2-12. This can be simplified to the form of Figure 2-13. In this model it is clear that **X** is the response of the system to step inputs of $\mathbf{U}_n$. Over a step the value of $\mathbf{U}_n$ is

FIGURE 2-12. State vector form of the discrete approximation of the system $\mathbf{X} = \mathbf{AX} + \mathbf{BU}$.

FIGURE 2-13. Simplified form of the system shown in Figure 2-12.

constant as well as $\mathbf{A}$, $\mathbf{B}$, and $\mathbf{C}$. Thus the integral can be simplified to the form

$$\left(\int_0^T \mathbf{\Phi} \, d\tau \right) \mathbf{BU}_n$$

which is usually easy to derive. Then the simulating difference equations become

$$\mathbf{X}_{n+1} = \mathbf{\Phi X}_n + \mathbf{TU}_n, \quad \text{where} \quad \mathbf{\Phi} = e^{\mathbf{A}T} \quad \text{and} \quad \mathbf{T} = \left(\int_0^T e^{\mathbf{A}\tau} \, d\tau \right) \mathbf{B}$$

$$\mathbf{Y}_{n+1} = \mathbf{CX}_{n+1}$$

A similar development can be done for the nonstationary linear system. Because the coefficients are time varying, very little simplification occurs and the equations, although straightforward, are tedious to interpret and use. They are presented for the sake of completeness.

PART II

NUMERICAL METHODS FOR SIMULATING LINEAR SYSTEMS ON A DIGITAL COMPUTER

CHAPTER 3

AN INTRODUCTION TO LINEAR SYSTEM SIMULATION

The analysis of linear constant coefficient systems is important because they are frequently encountered in the design of continuous processes. The dynamic characteristics of a linear system's response to known types of forcing functions are usually studied when setting the parameters for a system design. In this chapter we discuss the synthesis of recursion formulas that can be used conveniently to compute the response of a dynamic process to sampled values of its forcing function.

The key concept introduced in this chapter is that of *matching the dynamics of a difference equation with the dynamics of a differential equation.* That is, the emphasis is on finding difference equations whose characteristic roots, poles, zeros, final value, and phasing are similar to those of the continuous differential equation. The difference equation is then used to simulate the continuous process described by the differential equation. Chapters 4 and 5 carry this approach to simulation to the state of the art.

Developing difference equations to simulate linear continuous processes on a digital computer leads to fast, highly efficient algorithms that are also accurate. These algorithms are particularly useful for scientific analysis on the personal computer (PC). In addition to being mathematically efficient, they are *sized* for efficient programming. Often, one difference equation can be programmed in one line of code while the numerical integration explicitly programmed to evaluate derivatives, rename past values, make the integration step, and then correct it can take 5 to 7 lines of code. In this instance, the difference equation approach is ideally suited to problem solving and simulation on PC's and other limited capability digital computers.

3.1   DIFFERENCE EQUATION DERIVATION BY NUMERICAL INTEGRATION SUBSTITUTION

In Chapters 7 and 8 we find examples of many classical integration formulas including Euler's integration formula, rectangular integration, trapezoidal integration, T integration, and a number of predict-correct formulas for numerical integration of a differential equation. The approach there is to use the differential equation to evaluate numerically the derivatives at the initial condition and, using starting values in the integration formulas, to predict the solution to the differential equation in the neighborhood of the initial conditions.

Another way to use the numerical integration formulas is to form a difference equation. Consider the first-order constant coefficient differential equation

$$\tau \dot{x} + x = Q \tag{3-1}$$

where

$$x = x(t)$$

$$Q = Q(t)$$

and τ is a constant. Now consider the Euler integration formula

$$x_n = x_{n-1} + T\dot{x}_{n-1} \tag{3-2}$$

We can solve for the rate in the integration formula using the differential equation

$$\dot{x}_{n-1} = \frac{1}{\tau}(Q_{n-1} - x_{n-1}) \tag{3-3}$$

which can be substituted into the numerical integration formula

$$x_n = x_{n-1} + \frac{T}{\tau}(Q_{n-1} - x_{n-1}) \tag{3-4}$$

When simplified, this gives the difference equation or recursion formula

$$x_n = \left(1 - \frac{T}{\tau}\right)x_{n-1} + \frac{T}{\tau}Q_{n-1} \tag{3-5}$$

This recursion formula computes, for example, the 100th step in the solution of the differential equation on the basis of data generation on the 99th step. The indices in the recursion formula keep track of the iteration that is being computed in solving the differential equation. They also indicate the approximate time at which the solution value will compare with $x(t)$, that is, $t = nT$ if the solution begins at $T \cong 0$. We see later that $t \neq nT$ but it is sufficiently close to label approximately the time in the sequence of solution values of the difference equation.

There are two advantages in using recursion formulas for solving differential equations. They reduce the number of calculations in simulating the difference equation, and in linear constant coefficient processes they permit the use of *implicit* integration formulas. It is in these formulas that the rates of a state variable are a function of the state itself. An example is the trapezoidal integration formula which has the form

$$x_n = x_{n-1} + \frac{T}{2}(\dot{x}_n + \dot{x}_{n-1}) \tag{3-6}$$

Trapezoidal integration computes the $n + 1$ value of x based on the $n + 1$ value of $\dot{x}$. However, evaluating $\dot{x}$ in this differential equation requires x_{n+1}. This results in an implicit equation whose solution is a function of itself. When implicit integration formulas are used to derive difference equations, the implicit equation can be solved *algebraically*. For example, consider the implicit Euler integration (rectangular integration), which takes the form

$$x_n = x_{n-1} + T\dot{x}_n \tag{3-7}$$

Using our first-order differential equation we see that

$$\dot{x}_n = \frac{1}{\tau}(Q_n - x_n) \tag{3-8}$$

which when substituted back into the implicit rectangular integration formula gives us the difference equation

$$x_n = x_{n-1} + \frac{T}{\tau}(Q_n - x_n) \tag{3-9}$$

Note that this equation is still in implicit form; that is, x_n is a function of itself. However, this equation can be solved algebraically as follows:

$$x_n + \frac{T}{\tau} x_n = x_{n-1} + \frac{T}{\tau} Q_n$$

$$\left(1 + \frac{T}{\tau}\right) x_n = x_{n-1} + \frac{T}{\tau} Q_n$$

$$\therefore \quad x_n = \left(\frac{1}{1 + T/\tau}\right) x_{n-1} + \left(\frac{T/\tau}{1 + T/\tau}\right) Q_n \qquad (3\text{-}10)$$

Let us now compare the Euler implicit and Euler explicit difference equations from the standpoint of numerical stability, numerical error, and the manner in which the differential equation seeks its final value.

The stability of these first-order difference equations is completely determined by the magnitude of the first coefficient in the difference equation. That is, if the term

$$\frac{1}{1 + T/\tau} \qquad\qquad 1 + \frac{T}{\tau}$$

Implicit integration   Explicit integration

exceeds ± 1 the difference equation becomes unstable. For example, if $a = 2$ in the difference equation $y_n = a y_{n-1}$, then the difference equation takes on the solution values shown in Table 3-1. Note however that if the value of $a = 0.9$, the difference equation is stable as shown in Table 3-2. The stability criterion in first-order difference equations generally is that the magnitude of a be less than or equal to 1. Now notice the first-order difference equation that is generated with explicit Euler integration.

Our aim here is to determine the conditions under which the integration step size and the system's time constant allow a stable difference equation,

Table 3-1.   Unstable Response of the Difference Equation $y_n = a y_{n-1} \ (a = 2)$

n	y_n
1	1
2	2
3	4
4	8
5	16
⋮	⋮

**Table 3-2.   Stable Response of the
Difference Equation** $y_n = ay_{n-1}$ $(a = 0.9)$

n	y_n
1	1
2	0.9
3	0.81
4	0.729
5	0.6561
.	.
.	.
.	.

rather than leading to numerical instability. We therefore first determine the conditions under which the magnitude of a is less than or equal to 1. That is

$$\left| 1 - \frac{T}{\tau} \right| \leqslant 1$$

Solving the inequality for T/τ, we see that the region of stability for the difference equations derived with explicit Euler integration is

$$0 \leqslant \frac{T}{\tau} \leqslant 2$$

On examining the difference equation derived with rectangular integration (implicit Euler integration), we see that the condition under which

$$\left| \frac{1}{1 + T/\tau} \right| \leqslant 1$$

is

$$0 \leqslant \frac{T}{\tau}$$

Clearly, the difference equation developed with rectangular integration is more stable than that generated by Euler explicit integration. This is a specific example of the more general result that implicit integration of constant coefficient linear differential equations leads to difference equations intrinsically more stable than those developed with explicit integration formulas. We therefore focus our attention on the use of implicit integration formulas in developing difference equations for simulating continuous processes.

Now let us examine the accuracy of these simulating difference equations. Table 3-3 shows the sequence of solution values for the explicit and implicit difference equation's response to a unit step. The greatest precision is achieved with the implicit formula. These difference equations were tested for the integration step size to time constant ratio of $\frac{3}{2}$, which challenges the stability of the Euler-derived difference equation. Both equations are stable. However, the implicit difference equation is obviously more accurate than is the explicit equation. This is another special case of a general property of difference equations derived with implicit integration to simulate linear constant coefficient systems. The implicitly derived difference equations are generally more accurate than those explicitly derived.

Finally, let us examine the steady state that all these difference equations achieve. To do so, we must examine the inhomogeneous equation (because in a homogeneous equation all the end conditions of the steady state approach zero, thus making comparison impossible). For the continuous and discrete equations, the step response has the forms shown below:

$$y = Q(1 - e^{-t/\tau}) \qquad y_n = \left(1 - \frac{T}{\tau}\right)y_{n-1} + \frac{T}{\tau}Q_{n-1}$$

Exact Explicit

$$y_n = \left(\frac{1}{1 + T/\tau}\right)y_{n-1} + \left(\frac{T/\tau}{1 + T/\tau}\right)Q_n$$

Implicit

In the steady state

$$x_n \overset{t \to \infty}{=} x_{n-1}$$

Table 3-3. Comparison of Implicit and Explicit Integration-Derived Difference Equations $(T/\tau = 1.5)$

Normalized Time	Exact	Implicit		Explicit	
	$x(nT)$	$x(nT)$	Error	$x(nT)$	Error
$\frac{T}{\tau} = 0$	0	0	0	0	0
$\frac{T}{\tau} = 1.5$	0.776	0.600	-0.176	1.500	$+0.724$
$\frac{T}{\tau} = 3.0$	0.950	0.840	-0.110	0.750	-0.200
$\frac{T}{\tau} = 4.5$	0.990	0.936	-0.054	1.125	$+0.135$

Thus we can write the final value as

$$\lim_{t \to \infty} y(t) = Q \quad y_n = Q_n = Q_{n-1} \quad y_n = Q_n$$

       Exact   Explicit   Implicit

Thus both the explicitly and implicitly derived difference equations achieve the same final value for the unit step forcing function which is the final value for the true continuous process. But the implicitly derived recursion formula is both more stable and more accurate than its explicitly derived counterpart.

These recursion formulas are particularly useful in evaluating the response of a system to an arbitrary forcing function. Provided that the integration step size is small compared with the largest period of interest in the oscillations of the forcing function, the recursion formulas can be used to evaluate the system's response to an arbitrary forcing function in an efficient manner.

A possible difficulty associated with the implicit integration formula for evaluating the response of a system to an arbitrary forcing function is its assumption that the forcing function is known at time n, in order to compute the response of the system at time n. If the forcing function is of the form

$$f = f(y, t)$$

the evaluation of f_n requires

$$f_n = f(y_n, nT)$$

but, since the difference equation is to compute y_n, it is not yet in the memory of solution values. Rather, we have only a tabulated value for y_{n-1}. In this case we can use an extrapolation formula to estimate y_n by way of the two past values, or we can use y_{n-1} merely as an approximation of y_n. This can be done when the forcing function's components are (from a Fourier analysis viewpoint) of lower frequency than is the natural frequency of the system described by the differential equation. To achieve this, we calculate a few values of the difference equation, assuming in the evaluation of the forcing function that $y_n \approx y_{n-1}$ and generating the first few terms of the forcing function f, and use a difference table to evaluate whether f is changing rapidly. If it is, we simply use an interpolation formula to make a first estimate of y_n based on y_{n-1} and y_{n-2}. The author finds that it is rarely necessary to use the extrapolation scheme in the practical evaluation of the solution to differential equations.

This technique of deriving difference equations to simulate continuous dynamic processes is very useful for simulating the dynamics of nonlinear processes. One problem, however, is that most implicit difference equations cannot be solved for nonlinear differential equations. That is, the implicit equation is a nonlinear equation, and usually only iterative techniques can be used to solve it. However the explicit difference equation is easily derived and easily put in a form that can be quickly evaluated as compared to numerically integrating (explicitly) the nonlinear equation.

3.2 STABLE DIFFERENCE EQUATIONS

Recursion formulas for simulating continuous dynamic processes can also be derived by assuming a difference equation of the same order as the differential equation to be simulated. Then match the roots of the difference equation with the roots of the differential equation and include an "adjustment factor" so as to match the final value of the difference equation with the final value of the differential equation. All that remains is to add another "adjustment" to match the phasing of the difference equation to the phasing of the solution to the differential equation. For example, again consider the simple first-order constant coefficient continuous process

$$\tau \dot{x} + x = Q$$

Assume that this equation has a solution of the homogeneous equation

$$x = e^{st} \tag{3-11}$$

On substitution, we can derive the indicial equation as

$$(\tau s + 1)e^{st} = 0 \tag{3-12}$$

which has the characteristic root

$$s = \frac{-1}{\tau} \tag{3-13}$$

Clearly, then, the solution to the homogeneous differential equation takes the form

$$x = c_1 e^{-t/\tau} \tag{3-14}$$

The solution to the nonhomogeneous equation can be derived with the convolution integral where the solution of the homogeneous equation is convolved with the forcing function

$$x = \int_0^t Q(k)e^{(k-t)/\tau} \, dk \qquad (3\text{-}15)$$

The complete solution to the differential equation then takes the form

$$x = e^{-t/\tau} \left\{ \int_0^t Q(k)e^{k/\tau} \, dk + c_1 \right\} \qquad (3\text{-}16)$$

Similar procedures can be followed for higher-order differential equations using either time-domain analysis, Laplace transform theory, or even Z-transform theory.

Let us assume we are going to simulate this continuous process with a difference equation whose roots and final value match those of the continuous process. We assume a difference equation of the form

$$x_n = ax_{n-1} + bQ_n \qquad (3\text{-}17)$$

and a solution to the homogeneous difference equation of the form

$$x_n = c_1 e^{-nT/\tau} \qquad (3\text{-}18)$$

Upon substitution, it leads to the indicial equation for the difference equation

$$c_1 e^{-nT/\tau} (1 - ae^{T/\tau}) = 0 \qquad (3\text{-}19)$$

Thus for the roots of the difference equation to match the roots of the differential equation we require that

$$a = e^{-T/\tau} \qquad (3\text{-}20)$$

This determines the coefficient in the difference equation that accomplishes the pole matching between the difference and differential equations. It is clear that the solution to the homogeneous difference equation is

$$x_n = e^{-T/\tau} x_{n-1} \qquad (3\text{-}21)$$

This procedure has now guaranteed that the dynamics of the difference equation will match the dynamics of the differential equation because their roots are equivalent and they will generate equivalent solution values as seen by the exponential decay of both. What remains now is to compute the final value of the difference equation and match it with the final value of the differential equation. The procedure here is more straightforward in that the inhomogeneous difference equation takes the form

$$x_n = e^{-T/\tau}x_{n-1} + bQ_n \qquad (3\text{-}22)$$

where the steady state of the root-matched difference equation is achieved when

$$Q_n = Q_{n-1}$$

$$x_n = x_{n-1}$$

Then

$$x_n = \frac{b}{1 - e^{-T/\tau}} Q_n \qquad (3\text{-}23)$$

By including the final value adjustment factor

$$b = 1 - e^{-T/\tau} \qquad (3\text{-}24)$$

we can make the difference equation achieve the same final value as the differential equation. Thus the simulating difference equation takes the form

$$x_n = e^{-T/\tau}x_{n-1} + (1 - e^{-T/\tau})Q_n \qquad (3\text{-}25)$$

Notice that the homogeneous solution of this difference equation matches the homogeneous solution of the differential equation EXACTLY. Also, it generates a sequence of solutions that are exact for the step response $Q(t) = U(t)$ and will generate solutions that are a good approximation of the differential equation's response to an arbitrary forcing function. Also notice that this difference equation is incapable of going unstable, regardless of the integration step size (because the term $e^{-T/\tau}$ is always less than one, no matter how big T gets provided $\tau > 0$).

From the tabulated values it may appear that there is significant error in a solution generated with the dynamics-matched difference equation and a solution generated with the continuous differential equation. However, (3-25) makes it clear that the difference equation solutions are lagging the continuous solutions. The dynamics are usually identical to the differential equation except for this effect of phase shift. Of course, we could reduce the step size to bring the two curves closer, but this is not an efficient or correct approach to reducing this kind of error. Or we can compensate for this phasing error (transport delay) by determining with interpolation at what time the sequence of solutions generated by the difference equation matches the differential equation and then including that transport time in the tabulation of the sequence of solutions generated in the difference equation. Suppose that we know that for the fourth entry in a table of solution values the true continuous solution lies somewhere between $T = 3T$ and $4T$. Using inverse interpolation, we can determine at what time the discrete solution matches the continuous solution and then arbitrarily select that time as the reference time from which we count nT intervals.

It is important to remember that the solution values generated with difference equations and even with numerical integration formulas are operating at a problem time that is different than the sequence of times nT. That is, problem time in a discrete approximation of a continuous time process is different from the sequence of values nT. Hence the indices in the recursion formulas represent the number of iterations, not time nT. The analyst must determine the actual timing of the sequence of solution values in order to compare them with a true continuous-time check case. It is the author's experience that many engineers and programmers on large digital computers overlook this problem of timing and try to compare continuous and discrete computing processes at times nT instead of recognizing that numerical integration is *an approximating process*. There is also a timing problem in the synthesis of simulating difference equations by dynamics matching. In fact, discrete systems are different in their operation on the flow of information in feedback loops, whether in numerical integrators or in difference equations. Thus the phasing of the two sequences of values between continuous and discrete dynamic processes must be taken into account by the analyst. The problem really only arises when large integration step sizes are being taken, but it is precisely then that efficiency is at a premium and the workload is substantially reduced from that for integration step sizes only half as long.

Some of the commonly encountered linear processes and their simulating difference equations using dynamics-matching methods are tabulated in Table 3-4. More difference equations are given in Chapters 4 and 5.

It is *imperative* that when the simulating difference equations are used the table of solution values be referenced to the number of iterations through the difference equations, not to time nT. The comparison of the discrete solution values with a continuous check case *involves timing considerations* that are the responsibility of the analyst to determine the proper comparison in a manner similar to that mentioned above.

The difference equations just developed by dynamics-matching methods have some very important general properties. These difference equations are intrinsically stable if the process under consideration is stable. That is, there is no sample period T to cause these equations to become unstable if

Table 3-4. Difference Equations for Commonly Encountered Linear Constant Coefficient Systems*

$G(s)$	$f(t)$	Difference Equations for Simulation
$\dfrac{I}{f} = \dfrac{1}{s}$	$I = \int f(t)\, dt$	$I_n = I_{n-1} + Tf_n$
$\dfrac{I}{f} = \dfrac{1}{s^2}$	$I = \int\int f(t)\, dt^2$	$I_n = 2I_{n-1} - I_{n-2} + \dfrac{T^2}{2}(f_n + f_{n-1})$
$\dfrac{y}{x} = \dfrac{1}{\tau s + 1}$	$e^{-t/\tau}$	$y_n = e^{-T/\tau} y_{n-1} + (1 - e^{-T/\tau}) x_n$
$\dfrac{y}{x} = \dfrac{\tau s}{\tau s + 1}$	$-e^{-t/\tau}$	$y_n = e^{-T/\tau} y_{n-1} + e^{-T/\tau}(x_n - x_{n-1})$
$\dfrac{y}{x} = \dfrac{w_n^2}{s^2 + 2\zeta w_n s + w_n^2}$		$y_n = Ay_{n-1} - By_{n-2} + (1 - A + B)x_n$

$$A = 2e^{-\zeta w_n T} \cos\left\{ w_n T (1 - \zeta^2)^{1/2} \right\}$$

$$B = e^{-2\zeta w_n T}$$

when $0 < \zeta < 1$

*See complementary filtering, Section 5.7, for extending these simple transfer functions to use in simulating high-order systems with both zeros and poles.

the continuous process that they are simulating is stable. This is because the roots of the differential equation are matched with the roots of the difference equation; hence if the continuous process is stable, the discrete process is stable independently of sample period. Showing that the magnitude of the roots of the discrete system is less than or equal to 1 will prove this; the very way in which they are formulated shows this to be so. For example, in the first-order case that we just developed, when the roots of the discrete system are matched to the roots of the continuous system, the discrete system root is given by

$$e^{-T/\tau}$$

which will be always less than or equal to 1 for all $T > 0$ and for $\tau > 0$. The only condition on using the difference equation is that the forcing function is sampled at a rate equal to twice the highest frequencies of interest in the forcing function. More detail is given in Chapter 1 where sampling rates are discussed.

Also the final value of the discrete difference equation will always match that of the continuous difference equation, independently of sampling period and without requiring the final value adjustment factor. That this is so can be established by the fact that in the steady state the present and past values of the response of the system are the same. When substituted into the difference equation the final value of the response can be computed in terms of the input forcing function, which is found to match the same final value of the continuous dynamic process being simulated.

There is a limitation in the use of these simulating difference equations. Clearly a second-order continuous system can have three completely different dynamic characteristics: when the two roots of the system are real and equal; when they are real and unequal; and when they are both complex. The dynamics of the second-order continuous system with complex roots is damped oscillatory in nature and the response of the system with real roots is nonoscillatory, being damped only. Each case requires separate types of difference equations. It is important, then, to know where the roots are in the complex plane to determine which difference equation is to be used. This is particularly true if the coefficients in the differential equation are changing with time and are not fixed, as in the case of linear variable coefficient systems. When the coefficients are time varying, these difference equations can be used for piecewise linear constant coefficient approximation, with the results matching closely the numerically integrated solution of the time-varying differential equation. However, if the time-varying roots jump on and off the real axis, switching from one difference equation to another is necessary. That is, one difference equation simulates the dynamics of the process when the roots are real but not equal; another difference equation simulates the dynamics when the roots are real and equal; and yet another difference equation serves when the roots are complex. The choice of the appropriate set of difference equations is fairly straightforward, but note that the implicit difference equation generated in Section 3.3 does not require this changing of difference equations and thus might be more applicable from the standpoint of quickly simulating continuous variable coefficient processes.

CHAPTER 4

DISCRETE ANALOG SIMULATION

In this chapter we cover a "discrete analog" method of simulating linear stationary systems. Although the method is applicable to nonstationary linear systems and nonlinear systems as well, the emphasis here is on *simulating the stationary linear system*. This is another method for deriving difference equations to simulate continuous processes.

Developing difference equations to simulate linear continuous processes on a digital computer leads to fast, highly efficient algorithms that are also accurate. These algorithms are particularly useful for scientific analysis on the personal computer (PC). In addition to being mathematically efficient, they are *sized* for efficient programming. Often, one difference equation can be programmed in one line of code while the numerical integration explicitly programmed to evaluate derivatives, rename past values, make the integration step, and then correct it can take 5 to 7 lines of code. In this instance, the difference equation approach is ideally suited to problem solving and simulation on PC's and other limited capability digital computers.

This method synthesizes a discrete system that is analogous to a continuous system; then the difference equations that describe the discrete system are derived and programmed on the digital computer. The sequence of solutions of the difference equations are of course sampled values of the motion of the **discrete system, not the continuous system**. Insofar as the discrete system is analogous to the continuous system we can attribute the sequence of solutions of the difference equations to sampled values of the motion of the continuous system **by analogy**.

In this method the discrete system is synthesized so that its signal flow is analogous to the continuous system signal flow. Then when the discrete system difference equation is solved on the digital computer, the signal flow (motion) of the continuous system is simulated by discrete system analogy. Simply stated, this method is a type of analog simulation, the analogy being between two types of systems, continuous and discrete.

166

An obvious advantage of this method (or of any analog simulation method) is that by synthesizing the discrete process that is analogous to a continuous process, the simulation designer becomes familiar with the continuous system and, perhaps more importantly, he knows that the difference equation on the digital computer calculates the motion of the discrete system, not the continuous system. This is a meaningful insight because the simulation designer will not attribute to the continuous system properties peculiar to the discrete system.

The sequence of numbers generated by the difference equation will only simulate the motion of the continuous system if the simulation designer correctly synthesizes the discrete analog of the continuous system. By proper synthesis of the discrete system, the simulation can also be made highly efficient as it will operate close to the Shannon information sampling limit.

4.1 DISCRETE ANALOG SYSTEM SYNTHESIS

Figure 4-1 shows a procedure for synthesizing a discrete system that can be used to simulate a continuous system.

Step 1. Draw a block diagram of the continuous system.

Step 2. Place samplers on the state vectors or signal flow paths of interest. If we were to operate this discrete process, the sampler would only be pulsing the system. Clearly that is not analogous to continuous signal flow. *To analogize the continuous signal flow in the continuous system, signal reconstruction processes $[H(s)]$ are inserted after each sampler.*

Step 3. Insert compensation $[C(s)]$ to control the distortion of the signal reconstruction process.

Step 4. Derive the difference equation that describes this discrete system.

Step 5. Program the difference equations to be solved on the digital computer and by analogy attribute their solution to the motion of the continuous system.

Note that this procedure leaves intact the linear dynamic elements of a process. Only the continuous signal flow is modified to form a discrete signal flow by introducing a sample and reconstruction process on the input signal. To synthesize the discrete system analogous to the continuous system, one merely breaks the continuous signal flow (information flow) into discrete information flow. The faster the discrete system is sampled,

$f(t)$	$x(t)$	Time domain
$f(s)$	$x(s)$	Frequency domain

(a)

$f(t)$	$f(nt)$	$\approx f(t)$	$\approx x(t)$	Time domain
$f(s)$	$f^*(s)$	$\approx f(s)$	$\approx x(s)$	Frequency domain

A "hold" process, such as a zero–order hold

(b)

$f(t)$	$f(nt)$	$\approx f(t)$	$\sim f(s)$	$\sim x(t)$	Time domain
$f(s)$	$f^*(s)$	$\approx f(s)$	$\sim f(s)$	$\sim x(s)$	Frequency domain

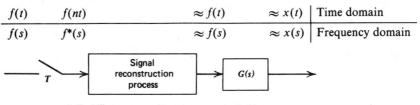

(c)

$$\frac{x^*(s)}{f^*(s)} = \frac{x(z)}{f(z)} = \mathbf{Z}(HCG) = \frac{N(z)}{D(z)} = \frac{a_0 + a_1 z^{-1} + a_2 z^{-2} + \cdots}{b_0 + b_1 z^{-1} + b_2 z^{-2} + \cdots}$$

$$\therefore x_n = -\frac{b_1}{b_0} x_{n-1} - \frac{b_2}{b_0} x_{n-2} - \cdots + \frac{a_0}{b_0} f_n + \frac{a_1}{b_0} f_{n-1} + \frac{a_2}{b_0} f_{n-2} + \cdots$$

(d)

FIGURE 4-1. Synthesizing a discrete system whose information flow is analogous to a continuous system. (a) Step 1. (b) Step 2. (c) Step 3. (d) Step 4. Dagger indicates that digital compensation can be applied directly on the signals at the output of the sampler instead of continuous compensation on the output of $H(s)$ if desired.

the closer will the discrete system approximate the continuous system. Furthermore, all the root locations are retained in their proper places in the s and z planes. In this method, the continuous process remains the same. Only the signal flow is different from the continuous system signal flow. The one concern then is the informational aspects of the signal sampling and reconstruction processes (we need not consider numerical instability at this point).

The signal reconstruction compensation is usually a linear process. There are two types of compensation that can be used: linear continuous compensation and linear discrete (digital) signal compensation. As discussed in Chapter 2, when a signal is sampled and reconstructed, these processes generally phase shift and attenuate the reconstructed signal relative to its sampled continuous signal counterpart. It is these undesirable side effects that we are trying to eliminate with compensation filtering. For example, when a zero-order hold is used for signal reconstruction it introduces a half sample period of lag on the discrete signal flow as compared to its continuous counterpart. Thus we would use a half sample period of lead compensation to cancel the effect of the lag introduced by the zero-order reconstruction process.

Figure 4-2 illustrates the discrete analog as applied to a second-order system. Note that the block diagram for the discrete analog is identical to the block diagram for the hybrid (analog computer plus digital computer) simulation of this second-order system. The forcing function would be passed from the digital computer through a D/A converter and reconstructed into an analog signal that would be used to drive the second-order continuous process on the analog computer. The output of the analog computer would then be sampled again through an A/D converter to digitize the measured output of the continuous system. Figure 4-3 shows a block diagram of this type of discrete analog to the continuous second-order system. In this example the sampler and zero-order hold on the input signal and the sampler output signal are approximately equivalent to D/A conversion and A/D conversion respectively associated with hybrid simulation. By writing the transfer function from sampler to sampler, we obtain the transfer function of a discrete process that is analogous to the continuous analog computer simulation of the second-order process. Inverting this transfer function into a difference equation is the process for generating a difference equation that can be used on the digital computer to simulate the second-order process.*

---

*In Chapter 5 we will find that this difference equation (except for a factor of z in the numerator) can also be derived by mapping the s-plane poles into the z plane so as to form a z-domain transfer function whose poles and final value match those of the continuous system.

- The system's equation of motion is

$$\ddot{y} + 2\zeta\omega_n\dot{y} + \omega_n^2 y = \omega_n^2 x, \quad \text{for} \quad x(0) = 0 = \dot{x}(0)$$

- The system's transfer function is

$$\frac{y}{x}(s) = \frac{\omega_n^2}{s^2 + 2\zeta\omega_n s + \omega_n^2}$$

- The system's block diagram is

- The discrete system that can simulate this second-order system is

To simplify this example we include one full sample period of lead compensation
- The discrete system's transfer function is developed as

$$\frac{y(z)}{x(z)} = Z\left(\frac{1 - e^{-sT}}{s} \right)(1)\left(\frac{\omega_n^2}{s^2 + 2\zeta\omega_n s + \omega_n^2} \right) = \frac{(1 - A + B)z^2}{Az^2 + Bz + C}$$

Here $A = 2e^{-\zeta\omega_n T} \cos\{\omega_n T(1 - \zeta^2)^{1/2}\}$; $B = e^{-2\zeta\omega_n T}$.
- The difference equation to use for simulation is

$$y_n = Ay_{n-1} - By_n + (1 - A + B)x_n$$

FIGURE 4-2. The discrete analog of a continuous second-order system.

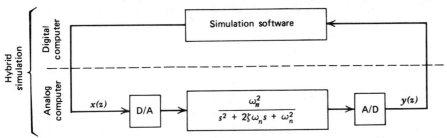

FIGURE 4-3. The discrete analog method for linear systems is analogous to the hybrid computer simulation of continuous systems.

The discrete analog block diagram of Figure 4-1 shows that the only difference between the discrete and continuous systems is the sample and reconstruction process. Significantly the accuracy considerations associated with this method deal solely with the fidelity of sampling and reconstructing the signal flow. This is important because "looking to the left" of the reconstruction process focuses attention on accuracy considerations, whereas "looking to the right" focuses attention on the stability of the process. **In the discrete analog method there is a separation of stability and accuracy considerations**.

4.2 DISCRETE ANALOG GENERALIZATION

Figure 4-4 shows the generalization of the discrete analogy. The process on the lower signal flow path is the discretizing of the continuous process on the upper signal flow path. The outputs of the samplers are the discrete values of the continuous process output and its discrete approximation output. Throughout this book when we refer to error we mean specifically the error shown as the output of the difference between sampled values of the continuous process and sampled values of its discrete approximation. Included in the discrete approximation is the hold $H(s)$, the compensation $C(s)$, and the continuous process itself $\dot{y} = f(x, t, y)$. The compensation $C(s)$ counteracts distortion introduced by $H(s)$ on the signal $x(t)$. Looking to the left of the compensation process, the concern is with the fidelity with which the forcing function $x(s)$ is reconstructed from a sequence of its sampled values. These considerations include:

- Sampling at a sufficiently high frequency to reconstruct the forcing function with $H(s)$.

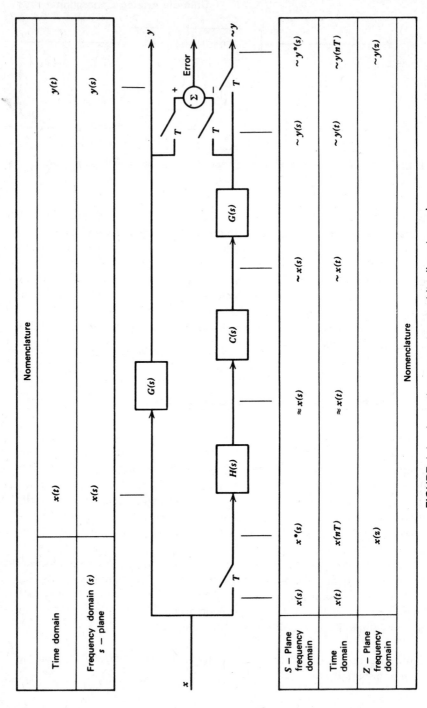

Nomenclature

	Time domain	$x(t)$	$y(t)$
	Frequency domain (s) s – plane	$x(s)$	$y(s)$

Nomenclature

S – Plane frequency domain	$x(s)$	$x^*(s)$	$\approx x(s)$	$\sim y(s)$	$\sim y^*(s)$
Time domain	$x(t)$	$x(nT)$	$\approx x(t)$	$\sim y(t)$	$\sim y(nT)$
Z – Plane frequency domain		$x(z)$			$\sim y(z)$

FIGURE 4-4. A continuous system and its discrete analog.

- Understanding the effect of the sampler on distorting the spectrum of $x(s)$.
- Understanding the distortion of the spectrum on $x(s)$ introduced by the hold circuit $H(s)$ both in phase and in amplitude.
- Determination of compensation to minimize the distortion of both $H(s)$ and the sampler on the spectrum of x.

Accuracy and information content of the forcing function $x(s)$ are the considerations between the first sampler and the compensation network. Between the output of the compensation network and the last sampler, the main consideration is the stability of the simulated process. Note that $y(s) = G(s) \cdot x(s)$. Thus by the convolution theorem $y(s)$ is the response of $G(s)$ to the forcing function $x(s)$. Since $x(s)$ over a sample period is known, $y(s)$ can be computed over that sample period by determining the system's $G(s)$ response to the known forcing function $x(s)$. Insofar as the sequence of functions $x(s)$ approximates the arbitrary function $x(s)$, the solution $y(s)$ is said to be the response of $G(s)$ to the arbitrary forcing function $x(s)$.

Note also that the response to initial conditions (the homogeneous solution to this system) of both the discrete approximation and the continuous process are identical. That is, the response to initial conditions of the discrete analog method is identical to that of the true continuous system because the initial conditions do not pass through the sample, hold, and compensation networks. In this regard it is worth noting that *Greene's theorem* (where initial conditions can be treated as forcing functions and vice versa for linear systems) *does not hold exactly for the discrete analog method.*

Figure 4-5 shows a vector-matrix generalization of the discrete analog method for linear and soft nonlinear processes. Again, the lower signal flow path is the discrete approximation of the continuous process described by the upper signal flow path. In this case the block diagram has been generalized to include both linear and nonlinear processes. The same principles apply as discussed for the strictly linear stationary systems. That is, the *considerations between the first sampler and the output of the compensation network are the reconstruction of the forcing function with sufficient fidelity to closely approximate the forcing function in both the time and frequency domains, and the considerations between the output of the compensation network and the last sampler are the solution of the system of equations for the known forcing function and the initial conditions.* In the discrete analog, the problem time is expected to be different from that in the true continuous problem. This is indicated by the parameters τ and t in the differential equation and in their sampled values. Even if the compensation

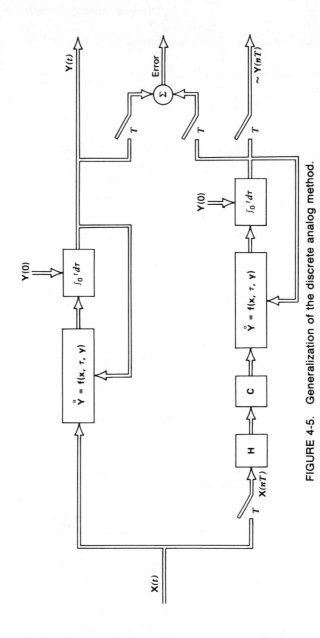

FIGURE 4-5. Generalization of the discrete analog method.

network were to compensate exactly for the delays introduced by the sample and reconstruction process, it is not necessarily true that time in the discrete analog process will be the same as that in the true continuous process, because there may be systematic delays associated with computing the vector integral in the discrete analog. That is, the forward loop must be computed before the feedback loop can be closed. In the discrete analog, if the nonlinear equations are actually integrated on the computer as opposed to being solved with manual analysis, this additional delay will change the problem time in the discrete system as compared with real time in the continuous system. Also, in the development of large-scale simulations it is often the practice to develop different simulation software packages by different groups and at different locations. In these cases it is difficult to control the timing of the information flow in each software package, and thus inadvertent delays can be introduced by design error that are unknown to the simulation designer until the simulation is being checked out. This can be seen in Figure 4-6 where the discretized integrator (numerical integrator) is shown with reconstruction and compensation processes, including the time delay in closing the feedback loop (the e^{-sT} in the feedback path).

An important feature of the difference equations generated using the discrete analog method is that they are intrinsically stable regardless of step size, provided that the simulated process is intrinsically stable. Even more generally, the difference equations will have the same global stability characteristics as the differential equations of the continuous system. As shown in Figure 4-5, if the sampling period is long compared with the response time of the process $G(s)$, the process will simply reach a steady-state condition. This is not true however for the numerically integrated system shown in Figure 4-6. When the ordinary differential equations are not analytically or manually solvable and must be solved through the numerical integration process, numerical instabilities can occur. In short, if the differential equation can be solved for the reconstruction function (particular solution) and for the initial condition (homogeneous solution), the difference equation that describes that solution from sample period to sample period will by definition have the global stability characteristics of the continuous process.

In this book the zero-, first-, second-, and triangular-hold reconstruction processes are emphasized, and the continuous compensation processes are usually simple lead, lag, lead-lag, or transport-lead compensation. Other types of reconstruction process that may be important in the development of a simulation but are not considered here are the Porter-Stoneman processes that are self-adaptive to the signal being reconstructed and the

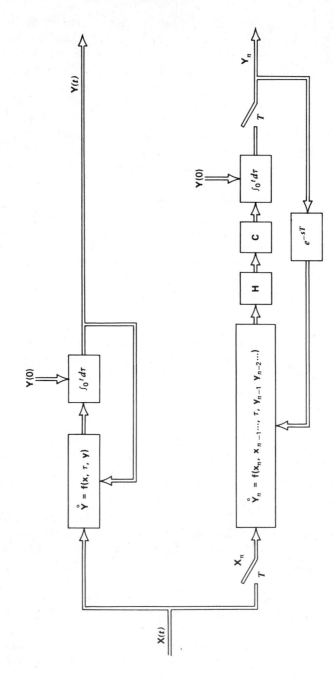

FIGURE 4-6. Generalization of the discrete analog method with numerical integration of the system of differential equations.

"Cardinal-hold" process that will exactly reconstruct band-limited functions. Nonlinear compensation filtering might also be considered. These processes are not discussed here because there is considerable groundwork still to be laid and research on the use of these techniques has not yet been carried out.

4.3   THE DISCRETE ANALOG METHOD AND HYBRID SIMULATION

In Section 4.2 we briefly mentioned that the discrete analog method is similar to hybrid computer simulation of a continuous system. This point needs to be further developed but from a different viewpoint. Figure 4-7 is a block diagram of the hybrid simulation of a linear stationary process $G(s)$ where discrete values of the forcing function (as computed by the digital computer) are reconstructed on the analog computer at the sample and hold process, which then drives the continuous process $G(s)$ (as implemented on the analog computer), the output of which is sampled and then fed back to the digital computer. It should now be apparent that the discrete analog method is analogous to hybrid simulation of $G(s)$. In this sense *the discrete analog method is sometimes referred to as the hybrid analogy*. The difference equations used to simulate $G(s)$ on the digital computer would generate the same results as those achieved on the analog computer except for the effect of the analog computer voltage quantizer (the function of a quantizer is to discretize the analog voltage levels and can be achieved by a hold circuit). **First** note that the difference equation generated by the discrete analog simulation process will be more accurate than the true hybrid counterpart which includes the effect of the quantizer. **Second**, since the accuracy limitations in the difference equation are set by the precision with which the coefficients in the difference equation on the digital computer can be set, implementing the difference equation on the digital computer can be far more accurate than on its analog counterpart. This is because the analog accuracy in setting potentiometers is usually limited to one part in 10^3 or 10^4, whereas setting the coefficients on the digital computer is limited to one part in 2^{nth} where n is the number of data bits in the digital computer's arithmetic register. It follows then that there is no need to tie up analog computer gear with fast analog processes when the difference equations can be written and implemented on the digital computer with greater precision than could be achieved with the hybrid computer. **Third**, in true hybrid computation, the hold process is generally

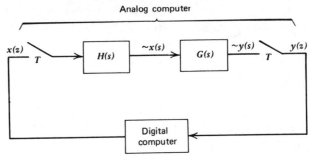

FIGURE 4-7. Hybrid computer simulation of $G(s)$. Key findings about the discrete-analog method based on its analogy with hybrid simulations: (1) If $G(s)$ is stable the difference equation that relates $y(z)$ to $x(z)$ will be stable no matter what the step size, T. (2) If $y(s)$ has frequency components out to ω_n hertz, the lowest sampling frequency should be on the order of $7\omega_n$. Thus $T_{min} \approx 1/7\omega_n$. Most simulations do not work well when $T = 1/2\omega_n$ (the Shannon lower limit) for a variety of reasons (i.e., y not band limited, large quantization error, etc.). A practical compromise is $T = 1/7\omega_n$. (3) If $y(s)$ has high-frequency components beyond $1/2T$, they will be folded back to lower frequencies as far as the digital computer software is concerned. If a simulation is designed to operate for various T, then it may be necessary to use anti-aliasing filters prior to the last sampler. The same technique can be used in the discrete analog method, although the author has never seen it done.

of zero order. This introduces half a sample period of delay on all of the frequency components of the forcing function, and the compensation for this effect is usually done in the digital computer with a digital filter. In the discrete analog method, compensation can conveniently be included on the signal flow path between the reconstruction hold and the continuous process $G(s)$, or the digital filter (or, equivalently, digital compensation) can be included as shown in Figure 4-8. Since the transfer functions in z are commutative for linear stationary processes, identical results can be achieved by placing the digital filter at the sampled output of $G(s)$. We can then conclude that the conditions that would normally justify having fast linear stationary processes on the analog part of a hybrid simulation would be for interfacing with hardware or other analog processes, not for doing analog computation.

FIGURE 4-8.   Digital compensation.

As mentioned in the preceding section, if the process is stable, the difference equations will also be stable, as seen heuristically in this hybrid analogy. In a true hybrid simulation, the stability of the continuous process on the analog computer is independent of the sample period at which the forcing function is brought into the reconstruction network. For this reason the discrete analog difference equations are intrinsically stable. It can also be inferred that the difference equations will have the right steady-state solution and the poles of the difference equation in the z plane will match the s-plane poles of the continuous system (when mapped into the z plane) because the reconstruction of the forcing function does not in any way influence the dynamic characteristics of the continuous process being simulated.

It is also apparent that the digital compensation process shown in Figure 4-8 can be generalized in vector-matrix notation as shown in Figure 4-9. In general the compensation used in the discrete analog method can be either discrete or continuous. Keeping in mind that a discrete filter transfer

FIGURE 4-9.   Vector-matrix digital compensation.

function $D(z)$ can be the transfer function associated with a sampler, a reconstruction process, and then a continuous compensation filter followed by another sampler, the discrete transfer function may be related to a continuous filter counterpart. The reason for retaining the continuous signal flow in the discretizing of an analog process is to maintain an understanding of the leads and lags in the discrete system that is simulating a continuous system. For this reason continuous compensation is used extensively in this text.

The Aliasing Problem

Finally, a very important consideration for both the discrete analog method and true hybrid simulation is the problem of **aliasing** or **frequency foldback**. Suppose that a pure oscillator is wired on the analog side of the hybrid computer. If a short pulse is input from the digital computer into this system, through the D/A converter, the system would oscillate as

$$y = \sin(\omega_n t + \Phi)$$

If the sampling frequency of the A/D converter is set at $\omega_s = 100\omega_n$, it will be easy to determine from the sampled values that the function being sampled is a sine wave of frequency ω_n. If $\omega_s = \omega_n$, the digital computer will see a constant out of the A/D converter (think about it). Obviously somewhere between $\omega_s = 100\omega_n$ and $\omega_s = \omega_n$ the digital computer loses its ability to track a simple sine wave. As you may have expected, the highest frequency that the digital computer is able to discern strictly from its sampled values is $\omega_s/2$. So if we simulate a system on the analog computer that has frequency-domain components greater than $\omega_s/2$, they will be seen in the digital computer as lower-frequency oscillations. This is called **frequency foldback** (see Section 1.7 under discrete Fourier transformation).

The point is that when using A/D conversion one either must be certain that there are no high-frequency components in the signal being sampled or must include **anti-aliasing filters** just ahead of the A/D converter. So it is with the discrete analog method. If the continuous process being simulated has high-frequency elements, writing a difference equation to calculate their motion will work and correctly calculate the high-frequency motion; but the systems driven with the outputs of the difference equations will interpret the forcing function to be at a lower frequency than the system driving them. In fact, if the *downstream* difference equations happen to resonate at low frequencies, the simulation results at large sample periods can be completely misleading and cause false conclusions. This phenomenon occurs no matter what method is used and must be dealt with correctly. Those interested in a quick-fix can simply set $\omega_s \gg \omega_H$, where ω_H is the highest frequency expected from the system's response.

4.4   THE UNIQUENESS PROBLEM

Consider the following process

$$\frac{x_1}{x_4} = \frac{s}{(s + a)(s + b)}$$

A digital approximation of this continuous system is shown in Figure 4-10. For simplicity of discussion, no compensation will be applied for the distortion due to the sample and reconstruction process. Writing the z-domain transfer function from sampler to sampler, for $H(s) = (1 - e^{-sT})/s$, we can form the equation

$$\sim x_{1_n} = (e^{-aT} + e^{-bT})x_{1_{n-1}} - e^{-(a+b)T}x_{1_{n-2}}$$

$$+ \frac{e^{-aT} - e^{-bT}}{b - a}(x_{4_{n-1}} - x_{4_{n-2}})$$

We see the differentiation process occurring in the difference between x_{4_n} and $x_{4_{n-1}}$ in the last term of the equation and in the smoothing process as the exponentials applied to $x_{1_{n-1}}$ and $x_{1_{n-2}}$. This difference equation would be used to simulate the band-limited differentiator.

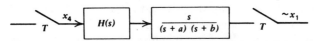

FIGURE 4-10.   The discrete analog of a band-limited differentiator.

Another discrete system that could be used to simulate this system is sketched in Figure 4-11. Here two difference equations are written to describe the discrete process between the first two samplers and that

FIGURE 4-11.   Another discrete analog of the band-limited differentiator. $H_1 = H_2 = (1 - e^{-sT})/s$ is the zero-order hold.

between the last two samplers. These equations, when solved simultaneously, generate the sequence of solutions approximating the sampled values of the continuous process. The difference equations are developed as follows:

$$\frac{\sim x_3}{x_4} = \mathbf{Z}\left(\frac{1 - e^{-sT}}{s}\right)\left(\frac{s}{s + a}\right) = \frac{z - 1}{z - e^{-aT}}$$

$$\therefore \sim x_{3_n} = e^{-aT}x_{3_{n-1}} + (x_{4_n} - x_{4_{n-1}})$$

and

$$\frac{\approx x_1}{\sim x_3} = \mathbf{Z}\left(\frac{1 - e^{-sT}}{s}\right)\left(\frac{1}{s + b}\right) = \frac{1}{b}\left(\frac{1 - e^{-bT}}{z - e^{-bT}}\right)$$

$$\therefore \approx x_{1_n} = e^{-bT}x_{1_{n-1}} + \frac{(1 - e^{-bT})}{b}x_{3_{n-1}}$$

In this case the first difference equation forms the differentiation function with some smoothing and the second difference equation forms the second smoothing operation. The low-pass filter in the first difference equation is the high-pass filter of the band-limited differentiator. The second low-pass filter filters out the low frequencies. Note that a zero-order hold reconstruction was used to derive the differentiator. Clearly the derivative of a stair-step alone is zero, and thus it might be expected that the transfer function for the high-pass filter would be zero. However the derivative is applied to the response of the low-pass filter $1/(s + a)$, resulting in differentiation by the simple finite difference on x_4.

In the difference equation derivation it was assumed that the difference equation for x_3 as a function of x_4 would be solved in parallel with the difference equation for x_1 as a function of x_3. Thus the first difference equation generates x_{3_n} and the second difference equation uses $x_{3_{n-1}}$. For this reason the z^{-1} is placed along the forward loop in the signal flow in Figure 4-12. If however we first compute x_3 on the basis of x_4 and then immediately use that result to drive the discrete approximation of the low-pass filter, the output of the first difference equation would be used immediately in computing the output of the second difference equation, thus eliminating the z^{-1} on the forward loop. The z^{-1} is a physical operator and is dependent on the way in which the difference equations are used in the computing process. It is not part of the discrete analog method. This fact is often omitted in the discussion of discrete approximations to continuous systems. *The signal flow diagram or block diagram of the discrete process that simulates a continuous process must include not only the mathematics of the process but also the mechanics of the data handling in the computing process.* It is the author's experience that this is the single most common source of error in difference equation derivation.

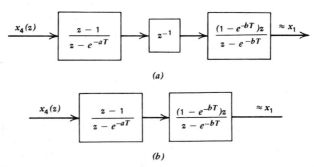

FIGURE 4-12. Parallel versus series difference equations. The simulating system when the simulating equations are solved (*a*) "in parallel" and (*b*) "in series."

A third approximation to this continuous system is sketched in Figure 4-13. Again the difference equations will be solved first in parallel and then in series. The derivation of the difference equation from sampler to sampler for the differentiator follows:

$$\frac{\sim x_3}{x_4} = \mathbf{Z}\left(\frac{1 + Ts}{s}\right)\left(\frac{1 - e^{-sT}}{s}\right)^2 (s) = \frac{z - 1}{T}$$

$$\therefore \sim x_{3_n} = \frac{1}{T}\left(x_{4_n} - x_{4_{n-1}}\right)$$

$$\frac{\approx x_2}{\sim x_3} = \mathbf{Z}\left(\frac{1 - e^{-Ts}}{s}\right)\left(\frac{1}{s + a}\right) = \frac{1}{a}\frac{(1 - e^{-aT})}{z - e^{-aT}}$$

$$\therefore \approx x_{2_n} = e^{-aT}x_{2_{n-1}} + \frac{(1 - e^{-aT})}{a}x_{3_{n-1}}$$

and

$$\approx x_{1_n} = e^{-bT}x_{1_{n-1}} + \frac{(1 - e^{-bT})}{b}x_{2_{n-1}}$$

In this case a triangular reconstruction process was used ahead of the differentiator so that a ramp function would be differentiated. Had a zero-order hold reconstruction been used, the transfer function would have been zero since the derivative of each stair-step would have been zero. Thus *the selection of the reconstruction process must include a consideration of the process that is being driven.*

The series solution to this process again results in x_{3_n} being computed with the first difference equation but not being used immediately in the second difference equation; similarly, the second difference equation output is not used immediately in the third difference equation. Of course no reasonable simulation designer would use these difference equations in this manner. If we adhere strictly to the notation of the difference equation,

FIGURE 4-13. Yet another discrete analog of a band-limited differentiator. Here $H_1 = [(1 + sT)/s][(1 - e^{sT})/s]^2$ and $H_2 = H_3 = (1 - e^{sT})/s$.

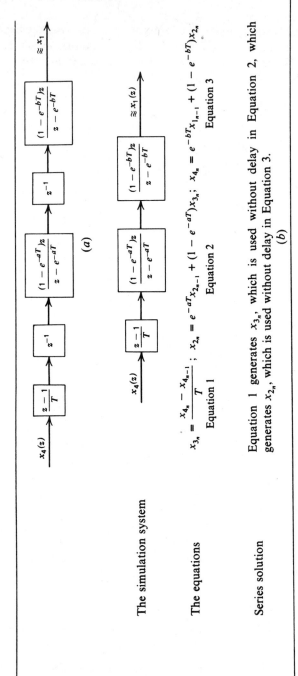

184

The simulation system

The equations

$$x_{3_n} = \frac{x_{4_n} - x_{4_{n-1}}}{T}; \quad x_{2_n} = e^{-aT}x_{2_{n-1}} + (1 - e^{-aT})x_{3_n}; \quad x_{4_n} = e^{-bT}x_{1_{n-1}} + (1 - e^{-bT})x_{2_n}$$

Equation 1   Equation 2   Equation 3

Series solution

Equation 1 generates x_{3_n}, which is used without delay in Equation 2, which generates x_{2_n}, which is used without delay in Equation 3.

(b)

FIGURE 4-14. The wrong *(a)* and right *(b)* way to simulate continuous signal flow.

however, the third difference equation calls for x_2 at $n - 1$, not at n, and the second difference equation calls for x_3 at $n - 1$, not at n, and we would introduce the z^{-1} in the forward loop of this process. At large step sizes, these two sample periods of delay would have devastating effects on the overall dynamics of any system, including this example of a band-limited differentiator. In Figure 4-14 we see the series formulation of this simulation where the first difference equation is used to feed the second, and the second to feed the third.

It is apparent from these examples, first, that there is *no unique system of difference equations to simulate any continuous process*; second, the question arises as to which system of equations is best for simulating the continuous system; third, the system of equations, when solved in parallel, can be solved in any order, but when solved in series must be solved precisely in the one-two-three order as written.

Certain high-level FORTRAN compilers can rearrange the difference equations in a computer program. This would negate all that the discrete analog method accomplishes from the standpoint of circumventing delays in the computing process.

With regard to the issue of accuracy, the following rule of thumb seems to apply best: *eliminate as many approximations as possible in the discrete analog method by introducing as few sample and reconstruction processes as possible*. In many cases the intermediate state vectors in a process are required for display or monitoring, and there is no recourse but to introduce a sample and reconstruct on all the state vectors of interest.

4.5 SIMPLIFIED DIFFERENCE EQUATION DERIVATION

The derivation of the difference equations in the discrete analog method for linear stationary systems involves taking the z transform of the product of the hold, compensation, and transfer functions of the continuous process. This is often difficult if $G(s)$, $C(s)$, and $H(s)$ are even slightly complex. For example when simpler reconstruction holds are used, the transfer function derivation takes the forms shown below.

$$\frac{O}{I}(z) = \mathbf{Z} H(s) C(s) G(s)$$

When the zero-order hold is used

$$H(s) = \frac{1 - e^{-sT}}{s} \; ; \qquad \frac{O}{I}(z) = \frac{z - 1}{z} \mathbf{Z} \left(\frac{CG}{s} \right) \qquad (4\text{-}1)$$

The first-order hold gives

$$\frac{O}{I}(z) = \left(\frac{z-1}{z}\right)^2 \mathbf{Z}\left[\frac{CG(1+Ts)}{Ts^2}\right],$$

$$\text{for} \quad H(s) = \frac{1+Ts}{T}\left(\frac{1-e^{-sT}}{s}\right)^2 \quad (4\text{-}2)$$

The triangular hold gives

$$\frac{O}{I}(z) = \frac{(z-1)^2}{z}\mathbf{Z}\left(\frac{CG}{Ts^2}\right), \quad \text{for} \quad H(s) = \frac{(1-e^{-sT})^2 e^{sT}}{Ts^2} \quad (4\text{-}3)$$

In all these cases, even when the simplest applicable compensation for these holds is used, the derivation does not simplify very much. When $C = e^{st}$, (4-1) becomes

$$\frac{O}{I} = (z-1)\mathbf{Z}\left(\frac{G}{s}\right)$$

When $C = e^{st}$, (4-2) becomes

$$\frac{O}{I} = \frac{(z-1)^2}{z}\mathbf{Z}\left[\frac{(1+Ts)G}{Ts^2}\right]$$

When $C = 1$, (4-3) becomes

$$\frac{O}{I} = \frac{(z-1)^2}{z}\mathbf{Z}\left(\frac{G}{Ts^2}\right)$$

The transfer functions in parentheses are sufficiently complex even in these simple forms to often require analysis other than simple z-transform table look-up to determine the z-domain transfer functions.

It is desirable to be able to modify this derivation process so that it simply requires z-transform table look-up. This can be done as follows. Each $G(s)$ in the parentheses can be block-diagrammed as shown in Figure 4-15. By sampling the output of each $G(s)$ and reconstructing the sampled values we form the discrete analog of these processes (Figure 4-16). In these forms the z transform between the first two samplers is a matter of table look-up of the transform of $G(s)$, and the discrete transfer

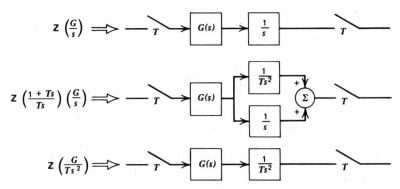

FIGURE 4-15. Block diagram of the difficult part of the transformation.

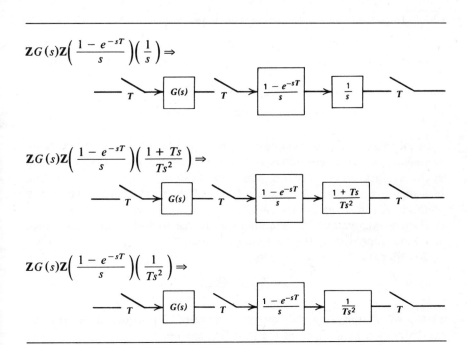

FIGURE 4-16. The discrete approximation boot-strapping itself.

function formed between the second two samplers is also a simple matter of z-transform table look-up. The simplified difference equation derivation formula for the discrete analog method using zero-order hold reconstruction is

$$\frac{O}{I} = T\mathbf{Z}G(s) \tag{4-4}$$

Similarly, the simplified derivation for the discrete analog method using the first-order hold reconstruction is given by the formula

$$\frac{O}{I} = \frac{T(3z - 1)}{2z} \mathbf{Z}G(s)$$

For triangular reconstruction:

$$\frac{O}{I} = \frac{T}{2}\left(\frac{z + 1}{z - 1}\right)\mathbf{Z}G(s)$$

Another useful compensation that we discuss later leads to the form*

$$\frac{O}{I} = \frac{\lambda T(\gamma z + (1 - \gamma))}{z} \mathbf{Z}G(s)$$

In all these cases the complex z transformation of the combined hold, compensation, and continuous system has been reduced to table look-up of the z transform of $G(s)$ and then multiplication by the transfer function of a digital filter that includes two levels of approximation in the overall method. For this reason the *resulting difference equations have a double level of approximation.* We examine the degree to which these difference equations approximate the continuous system.

Consider the first-order process

$$\frac{x}{f} = \frac{1}{\tau s + 1}$$

which, when approximated by the simplified zero-order hold discrete approximation method, gives the transfer function

---

*λ is a gain adjustment parameter and γ is a phase adjustment parameter. Both can be analytically or empirically adjusted to *tune* the simulating difference equation to the differential equation that is used to describe the system being simulated.

$$TZ\left(\frac{1}{\tau s + 1}\right) = \frac{(T/\tau)z}{z - e^{-T/\tau}} = \frac{x}{f}$$

which leads to the difference equation

$$x_n = e^{-T/\tau}x_{n-1} + \left(\frac{T}{\tau}\right)f_n$$

The discrete analog transfer function would have the form

$$\frac{x}{f} = \left(\frac{1 - e^{-T/\tau}}{z - e^{-T/\tau}}\right)$$

and a difference equation

$$x_n = e^{-T/\tau}x_{n-1} + (1 - e^{-T/\tau})f_n$$

It is apparent that the numerator in the simplified difference equation transfer function is the first-order expansion of the numerator of the desired transfer function. Thus the final value of the simplified difference equation will not equal the final value of the continuous process. For t/τ small as compared with 1, however, it is a reasonable approximation. All is not lost though, because a constant can be applied to this difference equation and empirically adjusted to give a correct final value or analytically adjusted by determining the final values of the discrete and continuous systems and adjusting the constant to match those final values. When this is done, it is found that (4-4) conveniently becomes

$$\frac{O}{I} = \frac{ZG(s)z^{(n-m)}}{ZG(s)\big|_{z=1}} \tag{4-5}$$

where n is the order of the denominator of $ZG(s)$ and m is the order of the numerator of $ZG(s)$.

Thus for our example

$$Z(G(s)) = \frac{z}{z - e^{-T/\tau}}, \qquad \text{for} \quad n = 1, m = 1$$

$$Z(G(s))\big|_{z=1} = \frac{1}{1 - e^{-T/\tau}}$$

the simulating difference equation transfer function is

$$\frac{x}{f} = \frac{(1 - e^{-T/\tau})z}{z - e^{-T/\tau}}$$

Similarly, the simulation of a damped oscillator becomes

$$\frac{O}{I} = \mathbf{Z}\frac{\omega_0}{(s + a)^2 + \omega_0^2} = \mathbf{Z}(e^{-at} \sin \omega_0 t)$$

$$= \frac{ze^{-aT} \sin(\omega_0 T)}{z^2 - 2ze^{-aT} \cos(\omega_0 T) + e^{-2aT}}$$

by table look-up. Now

$$\mathbf{Z}G(s)\Big|_{z=1} = \frac{e^{-aT} \sin(\omega_0 T)}{1 - 2e^{-aT} \cos(\omega_0 T) + e^{-2aT}}$$

and $n = 2$ while $m = 1$. Thus the simulating difference equation transfer function takes the form

$$\frac{\left[1 - e^{-aT} \cos(\omega_0 T) + e^{-2aT}\right]z^2}{z^2 - 2ze^{-aT} \cos(\omega_0 T) + e^{-2aT}}$$

which gives the simulating difference equation

$$\phi_n = 2e^{-aT} \cos(\omega_0 T)\phi_{n-1} - e^{-2aT}\phi_{n-2}$$

$$+ \left(1 - e^{-aT} \cos(\omega_0 T) + e^{-2aT}\right)I_n$$

Simple, *n'est-ce pas?*

Some $\mathbf{Z}G(s)$ have terms in the denominator of the form $(z - 1)$, which does not permit

$$\left[\mathbf{Z}G(s)\Big|_{z=1}\right]^{-1}$$

to be determined. In these cases we resort to the original simplified difference equation derivation or separation of the original $\mathbf{Z}G(s) = H(z)$ into two parts as

$$\frac{y}{x} = H(z) = F(z)S(z)$$

Then the process is treated as two different equations in series as

$$x \rightarrow \boxed{S(z)} \rightarrow \boxed{F(z)} \xrightarrow{y(z)}$$

For example, $1/s(s + a)$ has the z transform

$$\frac{z(1 - e^{-aT})}{(z - 1)(z - e^{-aT})}$$

This can be viewed as

$$x \rightarrow \boxed{\frac{1 - e^{-aT}}{z - e^{-aT}}} \xrightarrow{i(z)} \boxed{\frac{z}{z - 1}} \xrightarrow{y(z)}$$

Applying the simplified difference equation derivation technique (4-5) to the first part we find

$$\frac{i(z)}{x(z)} = \frac{(1 - e^{-aT})z}{z - e^{-aT}} \Rightarrow i_n = (e^{-aT})i_{n-1} + (1 - e^{-aT})\dot{x}_n$$

Then the second part is treated with the simplified difference equation derivation technique (4-4):

$$\frac{y}{i} = \frac{Tz}{z - 1} \Rightarrow y_n = y_{n-1} + Ti_n$$

Thus the combined system of equations

$$i_n = e^{-aT}i_{n-1} + (1 - e^{-aT})x_n$$

$$y_n = y_{n-1} + Ti_n$$

can be used to simulate the system $1/[s(s + a)]$.

Another way to see this is by noting that

$$\frac{1}{s(s + a)} \Rightarrow x \rightarrow \boxed{\frac{1}{s + a}} \rightarrow \boxed{\frac{1}{s}} \xrightarrow{y}$$

$$\Rightarrow \xrightarrow[T]{x(z)} \boxed{H} \rightarrow \boxed{C} \rightarrow \boxed{\frac{1}{s + a}} \xrightarrow[T]{i(z)} \boxed{H} \rightarrow \boxed{C} \rightarrow \boxed{\frac{1}{s}} \xrightarrow[T]{y(z)}$$

which uses two difference equations to simulate this process.

Returning to the other simplified methods for deriving difference equation transfer functions, we find that the simplified first-order hold reconstruction gives the transfer function for our first-order process

$$\frac{x}{f} = \frac{(3z - 1)T/2\tau}{(z - e^{-T/\tau})}$$

from which is obtained the difference equation

$$x_n = e^{-T/\tau}x_{n-1} + \frac{T}{2\tau}(3f_n - f_{n-1})$$

For the triangular hold, the transfer function takes the interesting form

$$\frac{x}{f} = \frac{(z^2 + z)T/2\tau}{z^2 - (1 + e^{-T/\tau})z + e^{-T/\tau}}$$

which inverts into the difference equation

$$x_n = (1 - e^{-T/\tau})x_{n-1} - e^{-T/\tau}x_{n-2} + \frac{T}{2\tau}(f_n + f_{n-1})$$

This transfer function is quadratic and has two poles at 1 and $e^{-t/\tau}$. Also the dynamic effect of the pole at 1 is compensated by the zero at -1.

Finally, the transfer function for the simplified discrete analog method with variable phase gain compensation is

$$\frac{x}{f} = \frac{\lambda(T/\tau)(\gamma z + (1 - \gamma))}{(z - e^{-T/\tau})}$$

which inverts into the difference equation

$$x_n = e^{-T/\tau}x_{n-1} + \lambda(T/\tau)(\gamma f_n + (1 - \gamma)f_{n-1})$$

Note that when $\gamma = 1$ and $\lambda = (1 - e^{-T/\tau})/(T/\tau)$ this difference equation becomes the desired difference equation. More is said on this later.

It is apparent that all of these approaches place the pole in the right location. Some include additional zeros that can introduce extraneous roots when used in closed-loop systems.

In summary, the simplified difference equation derivation methods lead to discrete approximations whose final value may differ from that of the

Table 4-1. Difference Equations for Digital Simulation

$\dfrac{y}{x} = G(s)$	Method of Derivation	$\dfrac{y}{x} = T(z)$	Recursion Formula (Subscript n Relates to the Number of Passes through the Equation)
$\dfrac{1}{s+a}$	E	$\dfrac{(1-e^{-aT})z}{z - e^{-aT}}$	$y_n = (e^{-aT})y_{n-1} + (1 - e^{-aT})x_n$
$\dfrac{1}{(s+a)^2}$	E	$\dfrac{(1-e^{-aT})^2 z^2}{(z - e^{-aT})^2}$	$y_n = (2e^{-aT})y_{n-1} - (e^{-2aT})y_{n-2} + (1 - e^{-aT})^2 x_n$
$\dfrac{\omega_0}{s^2 + \omega_0^2}$	E	$\dfrac{(2 - 2\cos\omega_0 T)z^2}{z^2 - 2z\cos\omega_0 T + 1}$	$y_n = (2\cos\omega_0 T)y_{n-1} - y_{n-2} + (2 - 2\cos\omega_0 T)x_n$
$\dfrac{s}{s^2 + \omega_0^2}$	E	$\dfrac{z(1-\cos\omega_0 T)^{-1}(z - \cos\omega_0 T)}{z^2 - 2z\cos\omega_0 T + 1}$	$y_n = (2\cos\omega_0 T)y_{n-1} - y_{n-2} + \left(\dfrac{1}{1 - \cos\omega_0 T}\right)x_n - \left(\dfrac{\cos\omega_0 T}{1 - \cos\omega_0 T}\right)x_{n-1}$
$\dfrac{\omega_0}{(s+a)^2 + \omega_0^2}$	E	$\dfrac{(1 - 2e^{-aT}\cos\omega_0 T + e^{-2aT})z^2}{z^2 - z2e^{-aT}\cos\omega_0 T + e^{-2aT}}$	$y_n = 2(e^{-aT}\cos\omega_0 T)y_{n-1} - (e^{-2aT})y_{n-2} + (1 - 2e^{-aT}\cos\omega_0 T + e^{-2aT})x_n$
$\dfrac{(s+a)}{(s+a)^2 + \omega_0}$	E	$\dfrac{(1 - e^{-aT}\cos\omega_0 T)^{-1}(z^2 - (e^{-aT}\cos\omega_0 T)z)}{z^2 - z2e^{-aT}\cos\omega_0 T + e^{-2aT}}$	$y_n = 2(e^{-aT}\cos\omega_0 T)y_{n-1} - (e^{-2aT})y_{n-2}$

Table 4-1. Difference Equations for Digital Simulation (cont.)

Continued recursion formula (from previous page):

$$+ \left(\frac{1}{1 - e^{-aT}\cos\omega_0 T}\right)x_n - \left(\frac{e^{-aT}\cos\omega_0 T}{1 - e^{-aT}\cos\omega_0 T}\right)x_{n-1}$$

$\dfrac{y}{x} = G(s)$	Method of Derivation	$\dfrac{y}{x} = T(z)$	Recursion Formula (Subscript n Relates to the Number of Passes through the Equation)
$\dfrac{1}{s}$	D	$\dfrac{Tz}{z-1}$	$y_n = y_{n-1} + Tx_n$
$\dfrac{1}{s^2}$	D	$\dfrac{T^2 z}{(z-1)^2}$	$y_n = 2y_{n-1} - y_{n-2} + T^2 x_n$
$\dfrac{(s+c)(b-a)}{(s+a)(s+b)}$	E	$\dfrac{(c-a)(1-e^{-aT})z}{z-e^{-aT}} + \dfrac{(b-c)(1-e^{-bT})z}{z-e^{-bT}}$	$\left\{\begin{array}{l} y_n = O_n + P_n \\ O_n = e^{-aT}O_{n-1} + (c-a)(1-e^{-aT})x_n \\ P_n = e^{-bT}P_{n-1} + (b-c)(1-e^{-bT})x_n \end{array}\right.$
$\dfrac{ab}{(s+a)(s+b)}$	D	$\dfrac{Tz}{z-1} + \dfrac{bTz}{(a-b)(z-e^{-aT})} - \dfrac{aTz}{(a-b)(z-e^{-bT})}$	$\left\{\begin{array}{l} y_n = O_n + P_n + S_n \\ O_n = O_{n-1} + Tx_n \\ P_n = e^{-aT}P_{n-1} + \left(\dfrac{bT}{a-b}\right)x_n \\ S_n = e^{-bT}S_{n-1} + \left(\dfrac{aT}{a-b}\right)x_n \end{array}\right.$

final value of the approximated continuous system. The exception to this rule is the compensated zero-order process as developed by (4-5). This simplified method always gives the desired difference equation that should be used whenever possible. The poles of the discrete system match the poles of the continuous system. Although the final value is not exactly right for small sample periods, it is close to a first-order approximation of the final value of the continuous system. Furthermore, if the final value of the continuous system can be determined, the addition of a constant in the numerator of the transfer function can be used to adjust the final value of the discrete system to match the final value of the continuous system.

Finally, and most importantly, the simplified difference equation derivation does lead to a simple z-transform table look-up method for determining difference equations for all transfer functions.

A number of difference equations developed using this method are shown in Table 4-1.

4.6 FOWLER'S METHOD*

When studying complex linear systems with nonlinearities such as dead zones and limiters, it is necessary to separate the linear elements of the system. For example, in the simple rate-limited first-order system in Figure 4-17 we see the need to write this system as a closed-loop process instead of a single transfer function $1/(s + 1)$. Simulation of this system requires a bit more care to develop the proper simulating difference equations.

Maurice E. Fowler studied this type of problem in considerable detail. His work is widely known by control systems designers and simulation engineers both for its utility and its controversial use of linear techniques to study nonlinear processes. Fowler's work is discussed here because his method does work and is useful to a broader class of continuous system simulation problems than control systems. The author's experience in using Fowler's method for eight years is that it leads to digital simulation of linear and certain nonlinear processes that is of exceptionally high fidelity. Fowler's explanation of how he arrived at the method is a mixture of insights gained from his years of work in four areas: linear continuous systems, linear discrete systems, nonlinear continuous systems, and nonlinear discrete systems. He has as much if not more hands-on experience in these areas than anyone in the United States. When he compresses all of

---

*"A New Numerical Method for Simulation," *Simulation*, Vol. 6, No. 2, pp. 90–92, February 1966; Vol. 6, pp. v and vi, June 1966; Vol. 8, pp. 308–310, June 1967 (although no longer new).

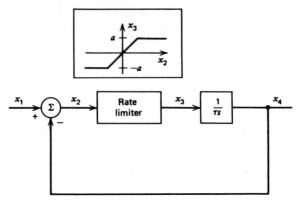

FIGURE 4-17.   A simple nonlinear continuous system.

this experience and insight into one paper or one lecture, it is sometimes hard for the inexperienced to follow his development. It is the author's opinion that this led to some of the early criticism of Fowler's work. Time has passed since the method was brought forward and it has withstood this test. Perhaps this section and the carefully selected simple example will illustrate the use of Fowler's method in a noncontroversial way. We shall see.

Fowler made the interesting observation that if one forms a discrete system whose linear elements all have the "proper" roots and if each $1/s$ is replaced with $Tz/(z - 1)$ (whenever it occurs alone), it is possible to close the loop around these linear elements and be assured that the closed-loop system:

- Has the right number of poles.
- Can be adjusted to achieve the proper final value.
- Can be adjusted to have the proper phasing (timing).
- Can be adjusted so as to have the closed-loop poles in their proper places.

From these observations Fowler developed the technique that now bears his name.

Again consider the simple nonlinear system shown in Figure 4-17. This system operates as a linear system until the magnitude of x_2 becomes sufficiently large that the limit on x_3 is reached. For $|x_2|$ beyond the zone of linearity permitted by the limiter, x_3 is limited to the value a or $-a$, depending on whether x_2 is positive or negative.

When the system is operating in the linear region it has the transfer function

$$\frac{x_4}{x_1} = \frac{1}{\tau s + 1}$$

which has a single pole at

$$s_{\text{pole}} = -\frac{1}{\tau}$$

Fowler's method can be summarized as follows.* Beginning with the continuous system block diagram, synthesize a discrete system to simulate the continuous system:

Step 1. Substitute $Tz/(z - 1)$ for each $1/s$.

Step 2. Substitute

$$H(z) = \frac{z - 1}{z} \, \mathbf{Z}\!\left(\frac{G(s)}{s} \right)$$

for each $G(s)$.

Step 3. Add a forward loop gain term k, the value of which will be set to locate the closed-loop poles.

Step 4. Add an input transfer function that will be used to make the closed-loop linear system respond like its transfer function.

Applying Fowler's method to the example problem, we would develop the discrete system block diagrammed in Figure 4-18. In this example, we do not use step 2. When x_3 is off the limit and this system is operating as a linear discrete system, it has the transfer function

$$\frac{x_4}{x_1} = \frac{kTz\,I(z)}{z - 1 + kT} = H(z)I(z)$$

which has a pole at

$$z_{\text{pole}} = 1 - kT$$

To match this discrete system pole with the continuous system pole we require that

$$z_{\text{pole}} = e^{s_{\text{pole}}T}$$

---

* This is the author's interpretation of Fowler's work.

FIGURE 4-18. The discrete system for simulating the system shown in Figure 4-17.

or that

$$1 - kT = e^{-T/\tau}$$

Thus if we set

$$k = \frac{1 - e^{-T/\tau}}{T}$$

we ensure that the closed-loop discrete system will behave like the closed-loop system when x_3 is off the limit. We can now draw the discrete simulation system block diagram as shown in Figure 4-19. This system has the closed-loop transfer function

$$\frac{x_4}{x_1} = I(z) \frac{(1 - e^{-T/\tau})z}{z - e^{-T/\tau}}$$

When x_3 is off the limit, it would be desirable if the discrete system of Figure 4-19 behaved like the discrete system shown in Figure 4-20, where the $C(s)$ compensated for the distortion introduced by $H(s)$. For this

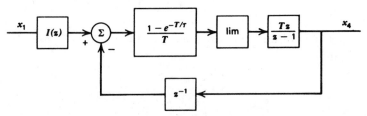

FIGURE 4-19. The discrete analog of the continuous nonlinear system.

FIGURE 4-20. The desirable discrete analog of the nonlinear system shown in Figure 4-19 when x_3 is off the limit.

example we will use the zero-order hold $(1 - e^{-sT})/s$ and a compensation of $e^{sT/2}$ to compensate for the half sample period of lag introduced by the hold. Thus the desirable transfer function for the discrete system we are trying to develop to simulate the nonlinear process is

$$\left(\frac{x_4}{x_1}\right)_D = Z\left(\frac{1 - e^{-sT}}{s}\right)(e^{sT/2})\left(\frac{1}{\tau s + 1}\right)$$

$$= \frac{(1 - e^{-T/2\tau})z + (e^{-T/2\tau} - e^{-T/\tau})}{z - e^{-T/\tau}}$$

To find $I(z)$ we equate the desired transfer function with the actual transfer of the discrete simulating system as

$$\frac{x_4}{x_1} = \left(\frac{x_4}{x_1}\right)_D$$

$$\therefore I(z) = \frac{\left[\dfrac{(1 - e^{-T/2\tau})z + (e^{-T/2\tau} - e^{-T/\tau})}{(z - e^{-T/\tau})}\right]}{\left[\dfrac{(1 - e^{-T/\tau})z}{(z - e^{-T/\tau})}\right]}$$

$$I(z) = \frac{(1 - e^{-T/2\tau})z + (e^{-T/2\tau} - e^{-T/\tau})}{(1 - e^{-T/\tau})z}$$

The final form of the discrete simulation of the nonlinear process would be as shown in Figure 4-21.

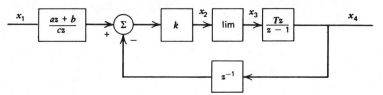

FIGURE 4-21. The final form of the discrete system for simulating the nonlinear system shown in Figure 4-17. Here $a = 1 - e^{-T/2\tau}$; $b = e^{-T/2\tau} - e^{-T/\tau}$; $c = 1 - e^{-T/\tau}$; $k = (1 - e^{-T/\tau})/T$.

A few comments are in order:

- This procedure is sufficiently complicated that for higher order systems analytical help will be required. Fowler foresaw this need and developed a computer program to do the work. The program is available commercially from IBM under the name CSAP or "Control Systems Analysis Program."
- $I(z)$ could have been set equal to 1 and the gain k could have been determined empirically by trial and error. This eliminates the need for CSAP and gives results that are sufficiently accurate for many engineering simulations.
- The author has refrained from discussing the behavior of the nonlinear process roots in the s plane. The entire procedure discussed here is to make the closed-loop linear discrete system behave like the desired linear discrete system transfer function. The idea is that when the nonlinear system is operating as a linear system it should behave like the system shown in Figure 4-20.
- It is interesting and now expected that since the discrete system information flow is analogous to the continuous system information flow, the discrete nonlinear system will behave in a manner similar to the continuous nonlinear system. And, of course, it does.

Figure 4-22 shows the simulation resulting from using Fowler's method to simulate the system shown in Figure 4-23. The object is to derive transfer functions such that the poles of the individual transfer functions are correct, the poles of the closed-loop transfer function are correct, and the zeros of the closed-loop input/output transfer function correspond to the desired input approximation. The procedure used by Fowler for synthesizing the simulating system was to first derive the correct poles for the individual z-transfer functions. For the first transfer function,

$$\frac{5}{s + 2}$$

FIGURE 4-22.   Simulation of the system of Figure 4-23. Courtesy of International Business Machines Corporation.

FIGURE 4-23.   A nonlinear continuous system used by Beisner to compare numerical methods for digital simulation. Courtesy of International Business Machines Corporation.

the correct pole in z notation is

$$z - e^{-2T}$$

For the case where $T = 0.5$, it is $z - 0.3679$.

The z-transfer function used for integration, $1/s$, is

$$\frac{Tz}{z - 1}$$

Note that the input approximations need not be used to compute internal transfer functions. Only those transfer functions that have sampled external inputs applied require this consideration. The numerator terms for the internal transfer functions are found very simply according to the following rule: **The steady-state gain of the z-domain transfer function is made equal to that of the s-domain transfer function.** For many linear systems the steady-state (final value) can be calculated by setting $s = 0$ and $z = 1$ in the $H(z)$. For the s-domain transfer function, the steady-state gain is the ratio of the constant term in the numerator to the constant term in the denominator. In the z-domain transfer function case the steady-state gain is the sum of the numerator coefficients divided by the sum of the denominator coefficients.

For the transfer function

$$\frac{5}{s + 2}$$

the steady-state gain is 2.5. As given above, the corresponding z pole when $T = 0.5$ is $z - 0.3679$. Thus 0.6325 is the sum of the denominator coefficients. The sum of the numerator coefficients should then be $K = 0.6325 \times 2.5 = 1.581$.

In case either the numerator or the denominator has no constant term, the appropriate power of s should be divided out to give a constant term. For example, the transfer function

$$\frac{5}{s^2 + 2s}$$

would be handled by dividing the denominator by s to give two functions multiplied

$$\left(\frac{1}{s}\right)\left(\frac{5}{s + 2}\right)$$

The corresponding z-transfer function can be in the form:

$$\left(\frac{A}{z - 1}\right)\left(\frac{B}{z - e^{-2T}}\right)$$

By always using the relationships $1/s \to Tz/(z - 1)$ and $s \to (z - 1)/Tz$, it can be shown that the steady-state gain of the remaining part of the transfer function can be found by the rule given above.

The numerator coefficients required to give the correct steady-state value are then lumped into one and applied as the coefficient to the highest numerator degree of z (the highest power is the degree of the denominator). The transfer functions shown in Figure 4-22 were derived by Fowler using the procedure just outlined. Figure 4-24 shows a root locus of the closed-loop portion of the system of Figure 4-22 as a function of K_L for the case where $K_A = 1$. Here K_L is a forward-loop gain inserted into the forward loop of the system in Figure 4-22. It is used as a means of plotting the root locus of the system when it is operating as a linear system. It can be seen that the root locus matches that for the continuous system except for the values of K_L (see Figure 4-25). By setting $K_A = 0.903$, the characteristic roots match exactly for $K_L = 1$. The match for $K_L < 1$ is not exact, but it is good. This insertion and adjustment of K_A is all that is necessary in this case to simulate the correct closed-loop transient response. In some cases it may be necessary to introduce a transportation lag into the loop. In higher-order systems the effect of lumping all coefficients into the highest order z terms can build up too much lead, thus rotating the root locus away from the imaginary axis. This can be corrected by introducing

FIGURE 4-24. Root-locus plot of the continuous nonlinear system when x_3 is off the limit and the system is operating as a linear system. Courtesy of International Business Machines Corporation.

FIGURE 4-25. Root-locus plot of simulation using Fowler's method. Courtesy of International Business Machines Corporation.

z transportation, lag which results in the addition of one or more terms of z in the numerator. The effect of the additional (lagging) terms in the numerator of the transfer functions is to rotate the root locus toward the imaginary axis.

The only thing left to compute is the input approximation. This is done as before. The desired transfer function for $T = 0.5$ is:

$$\mathbf{Z}\left(\frac{5H_0 e^{-0.25s}}{s^2 + 2s + 5} \right) = \frac{0.12985z^2 + 0.51604z + 0.06657}{z^2 + 0.65542z + 0.36788}$$

The correct input transfer function is found to be

$$\frac{0.1825z^2 + 0.7245z + 0.093}{z^2}$$

It can be verified that this input transfer function multiplied by the closed-loop transfer function x_5/x_1 of Figure 4-22 does give the desired transfer function.

The results for this simulation using a step input are shown in Figure

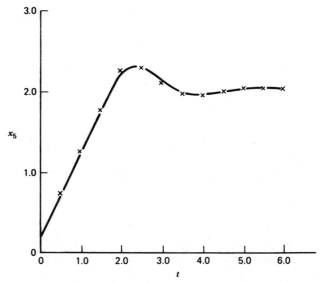

FIGURE 4-26. Response to step input at $t = -0.25$ (limiting). Courtesy of International Business Machines Corporation.

4-26. The difference equations that were used to get the results are:

$$x_1' = 0.1825x_1 + 0.7245x_1(-1) + 0.093x_1(-2)$$

$$x_2 = x_1' - x_5(-1)$$

$$x_3 = 0.3675x_3(-1) + 1.428x_2$$

$$x_4 = x_3 \quad \text{if} \quad x_3 \leqslant \text{limit value}$$

$$x_4 = \text{limit value with the sign of } x_3 \text{ if } x_3 > \text{limit value}$$

$$x_5 = x_5(-1) + 0.5x_4$$

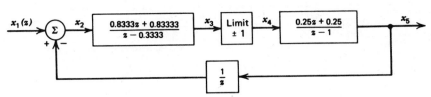

FIGURE 4-27. Simulation using Tustin's substitution method. Courtesy of International Business Machines Corporation.

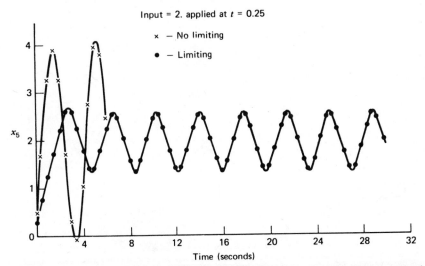

FIGURE 4-28. Response of simulation to a step input, using Tustin's method. Courtesy of International Business Machines Corporation.

It should be noted that x_2 is calculated using the past value of x_5. This is the latest available value of x_5, since the present value is computed last in this set of equations.

To compare his method with other often-used methods, Fowler developed a similar simulation using Tustin's method* (see Figure 4-27). The simulation results for a step of magnitude 2 into the Tustin simulation gave the results shown in Figure 4-28. This example is included here because it also illustrates the important point that even a method as good as Tustin's can lead to trouble when used improperly. Perhaps the most important reason for using the discrete analog method or Fowler's method is that the method itself forces the user to understand his system. The substitution methods of Tustin, Truxal, and others do not. They are procedures for arriving at a system of equations without really thinking through the implications of similarities or dissimilarities to the discrete system they represent and the system being simulated.

---

* See Appendix A.

CHAPTER 5

ROOT-MATCHING METHODS

Root-matching methods are yet another way to develop difference equations which are useful for simulating continuous processes on a digital computer.

Remember:

Developing difference equations to simulate linear continuous processes on a digital computer leads to fast, highly efficient algorithms that are also accurate. These algorithms are particularly useful for scientific analysis on the personal computer (PC). In addition to being mathematically efficient, they are sized for efficient programming.* Often, one difference equation can be programmed in one line of code while the numerical integration explicitly programmed to evaluate derivatives, rename past values, make the integration step, and then correct it can take 5 to 7 lines of code. In this instance, the difference equation approach is ideally suited to problem solving and simulation on PCs and other limited capability digital computer.

In Chapter 4 we discussed Fowler's method for simulating linear systems with embedded nonlinearities whose closed-loop transfer function matched the transfer function of the difference equation developed by the discrete analog method. In the course of that development and in the discussion of simulation in Chapter 3 we talked about matching the roots of a continuous differential equation with the roots of a simulating difference equation as a means of simulating continuous processes. The subject is addressed here because some of the details of root matching are subtle and deserve special explanation. Furthermore, the concept of matching the roots of a difference equation with those of a differential equation can be better understood when Laplace transforms are used and the equations of motion are thought of as transfer functions.

In conducting seminars on modern numerical methods since the publication of Fowler's work,* the author has often heard criticism of root-match-

---

*"A New Numerical Method for Simulation," *Simulation*, Vol. 6, No. 2, pp. 90–92, February 1966; Vol. 6, pp. v and vi, June 1966; Vol. 8, pp. 308–310, June 1967.

ing methods in the same breath with criticism of Fowler's method. While his work did cover as a special case the methods to be discussed here, the main criticism was for his extension to nonlinear systems of methods for synthesizing and analyzing linear continuous systems. Also, Fowler's method is somewhat difficult for the beginning simulation design engineer to use, because it assumes an in-depth familiarity with the properties of both continuous and discrete systems.

Fowler's work might be summarized as a method for matching the **root locus** of a system of **difference** equations with the root locus of a system of **differential** equations. In this sense, matching a specific set of difference equation roots with a specific set of differential equation roots is a special case of Fowler's method.

Root-matching methods for discretizing continuous systems were studied by a number of sampled-data communications and control systems analysts, among them Tou, Jury, Ragazini, Korn, Franklin, and Kalman. In fact, in the state transition recursive formulas developed by many of the innovators of that time, the roots of the recursion formulas match the roots of the differential equations that describe the continuous process, *by definition*. All this is to point out that root-matched difference equations are not necessarily subject to the same criticism as Fowler's method.

The idea of using root-matched difference equations occurred not only to noted academicians but also to the working engineers involved in simulation throughout the world. Dan Rosamond of McDonnell Douglas Corporation, Bill Edwards of Lockheed, Dave Lang and Roland Bowles of NASA, Steineman of Boeing, together with Elliott Pyron, Brian Schoonmaker, the author, and other members of the Apollo crew-training simulator design staff, were among the engineers using root matching or its equivalent to simulate continuous systems. They turned to these methods because the problems in the information sciences (e.g., communications, controls, and computer design) being simulated were forcing classical numerical methods to their limits and leading to numerical instabilities of such drastic extent that very small step sizes were required to stabilize the digital simulation. This led to costly simulation at best and inaccurate simulation (due to the propagation of roundoff error) at worst. Many classical methods were not useful for real-time simulations, such as required for man-in-the-loop training simulators, because:

- The time required to execute one pass through the simulation computer program was larger than the largest step size required for the numerical method to remain stable.
- The numerical method would not remain both stable and accurate over the entire dynamic range of the simulated motion.

It seemed natural at the time to attack the problem of numerical instability by controlling the roots of the simulation system by root-matching methods. Whereas the classical numerical methods focus primarily on numerical accuracy, the modern methods, based on the work of Norbert Weiner in 1943, have addressed both numerical accuracy and numerical stability, the underlying idea being that methods designed from both the stability (frequency-domain) and accuracy (time-domain) viewpoints should be better than methods designed from either viewpoint alone.

5.1 ROOT-MATCHING METHODS

Numerical instability in simulation is usually considered to be the unbounded compounding of numerical error resulting from either truncation or roundoff error or a combination of the two. One approach to resolving truncation error is to reduce the simulation problem's step size until the simulation difference equations or numerical integration process is stable. Then tests are made to determine if, at the small step size, roundoff error introduces a significant error in the simulation. This is generally no problem when using large computing machines. With personal computers and minicomputers, however, the roundoff error in the least significant digits can occasionally be transformed into errors in significant digits through differencing of large numbers, for example. Algorithms for simulating systems can usually be found that eliminate instabilities due to truncation and roundoff errors.

Root-matching methods are quite unlike the discrete analog approach or the substitution method.* These methods are particularly useful for simulating linear stationary systems whether continuous or discrete and are based on the concept that any simulation method eventually results in a difference equation, or system of difference equations, that must be solved on the digital computer. The system of difference equations will have a set of characteristic roots, final values, and some phase relation to the continuous system they are trying to simulate. Furthermore, in any valid system of discrete simulating equations: (1) the difference equations will approach the differential equations in the limit as the discrete step size approaches zero, and (2) the discrete system's poles, zeros, and final value will approach the continuous system's poles, zeros, and final value. Heuristically, it seems reasonable to expect that if we were to synthesize a system of difference equations whose poles, zeros, and final value match those of the continuous system at the outset, we would obtain a useful system of

*See Appendix A.

simulating difference equations for simulating the continuous system.

Not surprisingly, this is the case. The root-matching objective in simulation is to form a system of difference equations whose dynamics are similar to the dynamics of the continuous system to be simulated. Since the *dynamics* of the continuous system are completely characterized by its roots and final value, it seems appropriate to make the roots and final value of the simulating difference equation match those of the system being simulated.

The root-matching method is similar to the discrete analog method to the extent that both focus on the dynamics of the process being simulated, and neither involves numerical integration. The root-matching method is unlike the discrete analog method because the former is an analytical method for synthesizing a difference equation to simulate a continuous process as opposed to a method for synthesizing a discrete system analogous to a continuous system and then using that system of difference equations to simulate the continuous system.

5.2   MATCHING THE DYNAMICS OF A DIFFERENCE EQUATION TRANSFER FUNCTION WITH A DIFFERENTIAL EQUATION TRANSFER FUNCTION

The objective of the dynamics matching is to synthesize a difference equation that:

- Has the same number of poles and zeros as the differential equation that describes the continuous process.
- Has poles and zeros matching the poles and zeros in the differential equation.
- Has a final value matching the final value of the differential equation.
- Is phase adjusted to best match the response of the discrete system with the response of the continuous system.

This objective can be met for transfer functions by the following 9-step algorithm:

1. Determine the transfer function of the system to be simulated using the Laplace transform.

2. Compute the poles and zeros of the transfer function given in step 1.

3. Map the s-plane poles and zeros into the z plane using the relationship

$$z_{pole} = e^{s_{pole}T}; \qquad z_{zero} = e^{s_{zero}T}$$

4. Form a transfer function polynomial in z with the poles and zeros determined in step 3.

5. Determine the final value of the continuous system's unit step response.

6. Determine the final value of the discrete system's unit step response.

7. Match the discrete system's final value to the continuous system's final value by introducing a constant in the transfer function generated in step 4.

8. Add additional zeros to the discrete system's transfer function until the order of the discrete system's denominator matches the order of the discrete system's numerator.

9. Inverse z-transform the z-transfer function developed in step 8 to form the simulating difference equation.

To develop difference equations using this algorithm, the following conditions must be met:

- The system must be linear.
- The system must possess a Laplace transformation.
- The system must be asymptotically stable and satisfy the final value theorem. Furthermore, the final value must be nonzero.

The difference equation generated in this manner is not only stable, but is also accurate. That is, the solution to the homogeneous difference equation exactly matches the homogeneous solution to the differential equation. The difference equation will exactly compute the sequence of sampled values of the homogeneous solution of the continuous process and will exactly compute the sequence of solutions of the continuous system to unit step forcing functions. It follows then that, insofar as the sequence of values of the functions are sampled at least twice as fast (nominally five to seven times as fast) as the highest frequency in the forcing function, the difference equation can be used to simulate the continuous system's response to an arbitrary forcing function.

Example

Develop the difference equation to simulate the simple system $\tau\dot{x} + x = f$.

Step 1

$$\tau\dot{x} + x = f, \quad \text{for} \quad x(0) = 0$$

$$\mathcal{L}(\tau\dot{x} + x = f) = (\tau s + 1)x = f$$

$$\frac{x}{f} = \frac{1}{\tau s + 1}$$

Step 2

$$s_{\text{pole}} = -\frac{1}{\tau}$$

Step 3

$$z_{\text{pole}} = e^{s_{\text{pole}}T} = e^{-T/\tau}$$

Step 4

$$\frac{1}{z - e^{-T/\tau}} = \frac{p}{q}$$

Step 5 $\underbrace{s \text{ for the final value theorem}}$ $\overbrace{\begin{array}{c}\text{Laplace transform } (LT) \\ \text{of the unit step}\end{array}}$

$$\lim_{s \to 0} \left\{ s \left(\frac{1}{\tau s + 1} \right) \left(\frac{1}{s} \right) \right\} = 1$$

$$\underbrace{\qquad\qquad\qquad\qquad\qquad\qquad}_{LT \text{ of the system transfer function}}$$

Step 6 $\underbrace{\dfrac{z-1}{z}} \begin{array}{c}\text{for the final} \\ \text{value theorem}\end{array}$ $\overbrace{\begin{array}{c}Z \text{ transform } (ZT) \\ \text{of the unit step}\end{array}}$

$$\lim_{z \to 1} \left\{ \frac{z-1}{z} \left(\frac{1}{z - e^{-T/\tau}} \right) \left(\frac{z}{z-1} \right) \right\} = \frac{1}{1 - e^{-T/\tau}}$$

$$\underbrace{\qquad\qquad\qquad\qquad\qquad\qquad}_{ZT \text{ of the simulation transfer function}}$$

Step 7

$$\frac{x}{f} \approx k \frac{p}{q} = \frac{k}{z - e^{-T/\tau}}$$

$$\begin{array}{c}\text{Final value} \\ \text{match}\end{array} \Rightarrow \frac{k}{1 - e^{-T/\tau}} = 1$$

$$\therefore k = 1 - e^{-T/\tau}$$

thus

$$\frac{x}{f} \approx \frac{k}{z - e^{-T/\tau}} = \frac{1 - e^{-T/\tau}}{z - e^{-t/\tau}}$$

Step 8

$$\frac{x}{f} \cong \frac{(1 - e^{-T/\tau})z}{z - e^{-T/\tau}}$$

Step 9

$$xz - e^{-T/\tau}x = (1 - e^{-T/\tau})zf$$

$$x - z^{-1}e^{-T/\tau}x = (1 - e^{-T/\tau})f$$

Taking the inverse **Z** transform (by inspection),

$$x_n - e^{-T/\tau}x_{n-1} = (1 - e^{-T/\tau})f_n$$

$$\therefore \boxed{x_n = e^{-T/\tau}x_{n-1} + (1 - e^{-T/\tau})f_n}$$

5.3 OBSERVATIONS ABOUT THE ROOT-MATCHING METHOD

A few subtle points about the root-matching method are:

1. The final value theorem must lead to a nonzero result; otherwise the value of the final value matching constant cannot be determined. It so happens that there are a large number of systems that respond to the derivative of the input signal and have step responses whose final value is zero. In these cases there are two alternatives:

(*a*) Calculate the steady-state response to a unit ramp ($f = t$).
(*b*) Rewrite the system's transfer function so that the differentiator is developed as the complement to a low-pass filter. Complementary filtering is covered later in this chapter.

2. Had the continuous system been of second order, the roots could have been:

(*a*) Real and equal (critically damped response).

(*b*) Real and unequal (damped response).

(*c*) Complex and conjugate (oscillatory response).

A unique difference equation would have been required for each of these cases. The point is this: each difference equation holds only for a certain region in the *s* or *z* plane and one must be alert to use the proper equation for the proper system. This situation holds, obviously, for systems of higher order than second.

3. Difference equations generated in this manner are intrinsically stable if the system they are simulating is stable, NO MATTER WHAT THE STEP SIZE! To see this in our example, note that

$$z_{\text{pole}} = e^{-T/\tau} \leqslant 1, \quad \text{for} \quad T/\tau \geqslant 0$$

The significance of this is that the difference equation

$$x_n = e^{-T/\tau}x_{n-1} + (1 - e^{-T/\tau})f_n, \quad \text{for} \quad \tau > 0$$

cannot be made to go unstable. Simulating with this difference equation eliminates the problem of numerical instability! This is true for all difference equations generated in the manner just described. Since the simulating difference equation will not go unstable, what sets the rate at which we sample *f*? The answer is determined by Shannon's theorem.

5.4   SHANNON'S THEOREM AND ITS RELATION TO SIMULATION

Shannon's Theorem.   If a function $f(t)$ contains no frequencies higher than ω hertz, it is completely determined by giving its ordinates at a series of points spaced $1/\omega$ seconds apart.* In modern terms we would say that if $f(t)$ is band limited at ω_L, the minimum rate at which we must sample $f(t)$ is $2\omega_L$. Since most functions encountered in simulation are not band limited, the minimum rate at which we must sample $f(t)$ is 5 to 10 times the highest frequency *of interest* in $f(t)$. The question of precisely what

*"Communications in the Presence of Noise," Claude E. Shannon, *Proceedings of the IRE*, January 1949. The manuscript was received by the IRE on July 23, 1940—a story in itself, which the curious reader will enjoy uncovering on his own.

does "the highest frequency of interest" mean has no crisp answer. The author uses the following technique to determine the "HFI":

1. Select a segment of the known response of the system being simulated where rapid changes in the state of the system are taking place.
2. "Window" the segment with a Hann function.
3. Calculate the coefficients (frequency components) for a 12-point Fourier series of the "windowed" segment.
4. Adjust the coefficients for the window effect.
5. Square the coefficients (calculate the power spectrum components).
6. Plot the cumulative percentage of total power contributed by the components of the power spectrum.
7. The highest frequency of interest is the frequency at which the cumulative percentage power curve intersects the 90% power line.

This process is visualized in Figure 5-1.

$$8.4/T \overset{\sim}{<} \omega_{sampling} \overset{\sim}{<} 42/T$$

Nominally, $\omega_{sampling} \approx 30/T$

FIGURE 5-1. Determining the frequency of interest in $f(t)$. Those not familiar with window carpentry should refer to a book on harmonic analysis, such as R. W. Hamming, *Numerical Analysis for Engineers and Scientists*, McGraw-Hill, 1972.

5.5 SIMULATING A SECOND-ORDER SYSTEM

Another slightly more difficult example of root matching should make the method clear and illustrate some of the subtleties just discussed.

Example

The system

$$\frac{x}{f} = \frac{\omega_n^2}{s^2 + 2\zeta\omega_n s + \omega_n^2}$$

is the math model for a second-order continuous process with damping ζ and undamped natural frequency ω_n. The equations of motion of ships, automobiles, aircraft, sensors, and the like, and certain economic phenomena, can be characterized by this simple system or they at least have elements in their overall mathematical model that are second-order systems such as this.

When $\zeta = 1$ this system has two real roots

$$s_1 = s_2 = -\omega_n$$

When $\zeta = 0$ this system is a pure oscillator with a pair of complex conjugate roots

$$s = \pm\sqrt{-\omega_n^2} = \pm j\omega_n$$

When $\zeta > 1$ the roots are real and unequal and the system is overdamped. Finally, when $\zeta < 1$ the roots are complex conjugate of the form

$$s_1 = -\zeta\omega_n + j\omega_n\sqrt{1 - \zeta^2}$$

$$s_2 = -\zeta\omega_n - j\omega_n\sqrt{1 - \zeta^2}$$

Following the root-matching rules (we will leap-frog to the proper form of the difference equation transfer function, however) we seek to find a transfer function of the form

$$\frac{x(z)}{f(z)} = \frac{kz^2}{(z - z_p)(z - z_{pc})}$$

where

$$z_p = e^{S_{pole}T} = e^{-\zeta\omega_n T}e^{\left(j\omega_n T\sqrt{1-\zeta^2}\right)}$$

$$z_{pC} = e^{S_{pole}^{conj}T} = e^{-\zeta\omega_n T}e^{\left(-j\omega_n T\sqrt{1-\zeta^2}\right)}$$

On substitution and after a little algebra we find

$$\frac{x}{f} = \frac{kz^2}{z^2 - z\left\{2e^{-\zeta\omega_n T}\cos\left(\omega_n T\sqrt{1-\zeta^2}\right)\right\} + e^{-2\zeta\omega_n T}}$$

Let

$$A = 2e^{-\zeta\omega_n T}\cos\left(\omega_n T\sqrt{1-\zeta^2}\right)$$

$$B = e^{-2\zeta\omega_n T}$$

Then

$$\frac{x}{f} = \frac{kz^2}{z^2 - Az + B}$$

Applying the final value theorem and equating the final value of the discrete transfer function with the continuous system transfer function, we find

$$\frac{k}{1 - A + B} = 1$$

$$\therefore k = 1 - A + B$$

Thus the simulation difference equation transfer function takes the form

$$\frac{x}{f} = \frac{(1 - A + B)z^2}{z^2 - Az + B}$$

and the simulating difference equation is developed as

$$z^2 x - Azx + Bx = (1 - A + B)z^2 f$$

To get the difference equation in terms of its present and past values we divide both sides by z^2:

$$x - Az^{-1}x + Bz^{-2}x = (1 - A + B)f$$

Inverting we find

$$x_n - Ax_{n-1} + Bx_{n-2} = (1 - A + B)f_n$$

Thus the simulating difference equation is

$$x_n = Ax_{n-1} - Bx_{n-2} + (1 - A + B)f_n$$

In this case note that this system resonates at

$$\omega_R = \omega_n\sqrt{1 - \zeta^2}$$

If we do not know anything about the forcing function, we might reason that it would be prudent to sample the forcing function at least often enough so that we can excite the resonant frequency of the system being simulated. In this case we would set

$$7\omega_n\sqrt{1 - \zeta^2} \leqslant \omega_{\text{sampling}}$$

An example of the transient response of this system is shown in Figure 5-2. Note that this equation is not only accurate but is also stable for large intervals. In fact it can easily be shown that

$$|z_{\text{poles}}| \leqslant 1 \in \zeta, \omega_n \geqslant 1$$

for this second-order system.

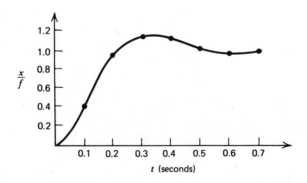

FIGURE 5-2. Response of the system $\omega_n^2/(s^2 + 2\zeta\omega_n s + \omega_n^2)$ to a unit step. $\zeta = 0.3$, $\omega_n = 13$ radians per second, $\omega_s = 10$ samples per second, and $\omega_s/(\omega_n\sqrt{1 - \zeta^2}) = 5.07$.

5.6   THE ROOT-MATCHING METHOD APPLIED TO DISCRETE SYSTEM SIMULATION

It is not unusual to encounter the problem of simulating a digital system operating at one frequency with a digital simulation operating at a different frequency (a process sometimes referred to as emulation). The author faced this situation in the Apollo program where it was necessary to simulate (at 10 samples per second) a digital autopilot (DAP) that operated at a 40-millisecond sample interval (25 samples per second). The DAP had a filter of the form

$$\frac{\phi}{I} = 2.62\left(\frac{z - 0.98}{z - 0.64}\right) = D(z)$$

which was implemented with the difference equation

$$\phi_n = 0.64\phi_{n-1} + 2.62(I_n - 0.98I_{n-1})$$

The aim was to maintain the stability characteristics of $D(z)$. We maintained the location of the poles and zeros in the s plane and adjusted the pole and zero in the z plane to account for the difference in the sample period. We see that the DAP filter pole and zero in the s plane occur at

$$\frac{1}{T}\ln(z_{pole}) = s_{pole} = \sigma_p$$

$$\frac{1}{T}\ln(z_{zero}) = s_{zero} = \sigma_s$$

In the case of $T = 4 \times 10^{-2}$ seconds (the real DAP sample interval)

$$\sigma_p = 25\ln(0.64) = 25 \times -0.4463 = -11.16$$

$$\sigma_z = 25\ln(0.98) = 25 \times -0.0202 = -0.505$$

The z-plane pole and zero, when $T = 0.1$ second, were

$$z_{zero} = e^{-0.0505} = 0.9508$$

$$z_{pole} = e^{-1.116} = 0.3277$$

Thus the new DAP filter equation transfer function would take the form

$$D_s(z) = k\left(\frac{z - 0.9508}{z - 0.3277}\right)$$

where k is determined by matching the step response of the real DAP filter with the simulation filter.

The real DAP filter had a step response of the form

$$\text{output}(z) = 2.62\left(\frac{z - 0.98}{z - 0.64}\right)\left(\frac{z}{z - 1}\right)$$

which had a final value

$$\frac{(2.62)(0.02)}{(0.36)} = FV$$

The simulation filter had the final value

$$k\frac{0.0492}{0.6723} = FV_s$$

Since we wanted $FV_s = FV$ we determined k as

$$k = \frac{(0.6723)(2.62)(0.02)}{(0.0492)(0.36)} = 1.9889$$

The final

$$D_s(z) = 1.9889\left(\frac{z - 0.9508}{z - 0.3277}\right)$$

Finally, the simulating difference equation took the form

$$\phi_n = 0.3277\phi_{n-1} + 1.9823(I_n - 0.9508 I_{n-1})$$

This equation gave quite satisfactory results.

The extension of the root matching to other discrete systems is straightforward. The same reservations discussed in Section 5.3 carry over to discrete system simulation.

5.7 COMPLEMENTARY FILTERING AND ITS USE IN DIGITAL SIMULATION

A commonly used filtering technique in the field of controls and communications is complementary filtering which very quickly leads to many useful and seemingly surprising results. For example, by using complementary low-pass filters one can differentiate with high fidelity. Also one can strip out parts of a forcing function frequency spectrum and operate on it in some unique manner and then recombine the forcing function components, being assured it is appropriately reconstructed in the frequency domain as well as in the time domain. Finally, the concept of complementary filtering takes the guesswork and mysteries out of filter design and makes it easily understandable.

Consider the filter $G(s)$, the block diagram for which is shown in Figure 5-3. If $G(s)$ is a simple low-pass filter of the form

$$G(s) = \frac{1}{\tau s + 1}$$

we say that the output of the filter is $x_{\text{low frequency}}$, the low-frequency components of $x(s)$. Now consider the filter

$$G_c(s) = 1 - G(s) = \frac{\tau s}{\tau s + 1}$$

This is a simple high-pass filter that passes all of the frequencies rejected by the low-pass filter $1/(\tau s + 1)$ and rejects the frequencies passed by the low-pass filter. It follows, then, that if we were to sum the outputs of these two filters we would simply get $x(s)$ again (see Figure 5-4).

To see that this is so, note that

$$\frac{\tau s}{\tau s + 1} + \frac{1}{\tau s + 1} = 1$$

Now, how can we use the concepts of complementary filtering in simulation and/or design? The answer is that complementary filtering provides alternative ways to simulate or implement a given filter form. Suppose we

FIGURE 5-3. Block diagram of $G(s)$.

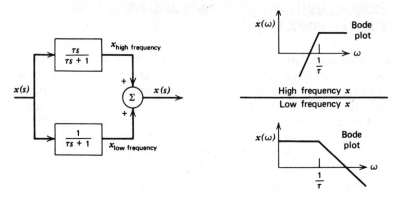

FIGURE 5-4.   Block diagram of a pair of complementary filters.

are given a filter of the form $G(s)$ and the task is to simulate this filter on either an analog or digital computer. Typically, the simulation engineer inverts the transfer function into a differential equation and numerically integrates the DEQ to simulate the filter. Another approach is to substitute (s) with $((z - 1)/Tz)$(or other substitution transfer function), and invert the resulting transfer function in z into a difference equation that simulates the filter. Of course there are other methods, all of which work to varying degrees. If the results lead to numerical instabilities or inaccuracies, however, it is often possible to apply the derivative substitution or numerical integration method to the filter in its *complementary form* and avoid the difficulty.

Example

Suppose the task is to simulate the filter $\pi s/(\pi s + 1)$ using the substitution method where

$$\frac{1}{s} \approx \frac{Tz}{z - 1}, \qquad \text{Rectangular integration}$$

Here

$$G(s) = \frac{\tau s}{\tau s + 1} = \frac{x_f}{x}(s)$$

$$G(z) = \frac{(\tau/T)(z - 1/z)}{(\tau/T)(z - 1/z) - 1} = \frac{(\tau/T)(z - 1)}{(\tau/T)z + (1 - (\tau/T))} = \frac{x_f}{x}(z)$$

which inverts into the simulating difference equation

$$x_{f_n} = \left[\frac{((\tau/T) - 1)}{(\tau/T)}\right] x_{f_{n-1}} + \frac{\tau}{T}(x_n - x_{n-1}).$$

Note that $G(z)$ has a pole at

$$z_{\text{pole}} = \frac{(\tau/T) - 1}{\tau/T} = 1 - T/\tau$$

and is stable when

$$|z_{\text{pole}}| \leq 1$$

which occurs for

$$2 \geq \frac{T}{\tau} \geq 0.$$

If, however, we apply this substitution technique to $G(s)$ in its complementary form, we would implement the filter as shown in Figures 5-5 and 5-6.

Here we only need to apply the substitution method to the low-pass filter

$$1 - G(s) = \frac{1}{\tau s + 1}$$

FIGURE 5-5.   The complementary filter equivalent of a filter G.

FIGURE 5-6.   High-pass filtering using only low-pass filters.

with the result that

$$1 - G(z) = \frac{1}{(\tau/T)((z-1)/z) + 1}$$

$$= \frac{z}{(1 + (\tau/T))z - (\tau/T)} = \frac{x_c}{x}(z)$$

which is implemented with the difference equation

$$x_{G_n} = \left(\frac{(\tau/T)}{1 + (\tau/T)}\right) x_{c_{n-1}} + \left(\frac{1}{1 + (\tau/T)}\right) x_n$$

Note that $1 - G(z)$ has a pole at

$$z_{\text{pole}} = \frac{(\tau/T)}{1 + (\tau/T)} = \frac{1}{(T/\tau) + 1}$$

which is stable for

$$\frac{T}{\tau} \geq 0$$

We see, then, that the filter developed in its complementary form is stable over a greater interval of the parameter (T/τ).

Complementary filtering has other unique applications in the design of high performance numerical integrators. In classical numerical analysis, certain types of highly accurate numerical integrators are developed using predict-correct algorithms. (See Predict-Correct in the index). Other series expansion techniques are used to develop accurate, high-order numerical integrators by combining a series of low-order integrations (see Runga–Kutta numerical integration in the index). Complementary filtering can be used to develop the frequency domain counterpart of these time domain methods by simply separating an integrand into its high and low frequency components and integrating the low-frequency components with a high-order (accurate) numerical and the high-frequency components with a low-order numerical integrator (stable). The result is numerical integration that is:

- Both accurate and stable.
- Better than either integrator alone.

Example

Using complementary filtering, separate the high- and low-frequency components of an integrand and (1) integrate the high-frequency components with a low-order numerical integrator and (2) integrate the low-frequency components with a high-order integrator. Keep in mind that the low-frequency components of the integrand are slowly varying and can be thought of as a running average of the integrand. Being slow to vary, it can be accurately integrated with a high-order numerical integrator (many terms in the numerical integration formula). Conversely, the high-frequency components of the integrand are quickly varying departures from the average and can be integrated quickly with a low-order numerical integrator (few terms in the numerical integration formula).

The power spectrum of integrands differ from application to application of course, so the low-pass filter time constant must be tuned to the particular application in a manner similar to the selection of integration step-size in Predict-Correct (P-C) algorithms. In a sense, then, complementary integration is a frequency domain counterpart to P-C, which also uses a combination of high- and low-order numerical integrators. The difference is that the P-C classical time domain approach uses them in series while the complementary integration approach uses them in parallel.

The transfer function for the complementary integration process is shown here

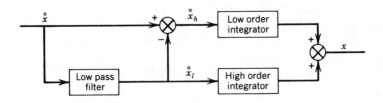

In analog form, the simplest complementary integrator takes the form

in digital form, complementary integration takes the more meaningful form

When low-order hold (LOH) is a zero-order hold and the high-order hold (HOH) is a first-order hold and when both are compensated with a sample period of lead (e^{sT}) complementary integration takes the form

which is implemented with the recursion formulas

$$\dot{x}_{1_n} = e^{-T/\tau} x_{1_{n-1}} + (1 - e^{-T/\tau}) \mathring{x}_n \qquad \text{Low-Frequency Integrand}$$

$$\mathring{x}_{2_n} = \mathring{x}_n - \mathring{x}_{1_n} \qquad\qquad\qquad \text{High-Frequency Integrand}$$

$$x_{3_n} = x_{3_{n-1}} + T\mathring{x}_{2_n} \qquad\qquad \text{Low-Order Integrator}$$

$$x_{4_n} = x_{4_{n-1}} + \frac{T}{2}(3\mathring{x}_{1_n} - \mathring{x}_{1_{n-1}}) \qquad \text{High-Order Integrator}$$

$$x_n = x_{3_n} + x_{4_n} \qquad\qquad\qquad \text{Complementary Combination of Integrals}$$

Note carefully that to tune this integration process to the problem being solving requires the selection of T/τ, the integration step size and the filter time constant. For fixed interval integration, T can be set at one seventh the shortest period of interest in the integrand and then τ can be set at approximately $2T$ and fine tuned by trial and error. Specifically, if the highest frequency of interest in the integrand is 1 hertz, then $T = \frac{1}{7}$ second, and a τ of $\frac{2}{7}$ second will reasonably initiate the integrator.

Let us further develop complementary filtering from a somewhat different point of view, namely that of the filter designer. Typically, when one develops a filter, little or no thought is given to that part of the signal *that is removed* by the filter. Usually, the designer only cares about what is passed by the filter. Suppose instead we were to keep track of all components of a signal as we filter it; doing so can often help make further spectrum manipulation or signal conditioning easy. Even if this process of keeping track of the *entire signal* is only done mentally, it leads to creative ideas for filter design that otherwise might not occur. Let us look at the problems of differentiation using low-pass filters, only now from the total signal conditioning point of view.

Typically, low-pass filters of the form $1/\tau s + 1$ are associated with the process of integration or averaging. The rationale is as follows for $\tau s \gg 1$,

$$\left(\frac{1}{\tau s + 1}\right) \to \frac{1}{\tau s}$$

and

$$\mathcal{L}^{-1}\left\{\frac{G(s)}{\tau(s)}\right\} = \frac{1}{\tau}\int G(t)\,dt \approx \overline{G(t)}$$

the average value of $G(t)$ over the interval τ. Note, however, that when a low-pass filter is used in the feedback of a high-gain feedback loop, the filter operates IMPLICITLY as a forward loop differentiator. The argument proceeds as follows: The transfer function for the system

is

$$\frac{\phi}{i} = \frac{G}{1 + GF}$$

If G is a constant and $\gg 1$, then

$$\lim_{G \to \infty}\left(\frac{\phi}{i}\right) = \frac{1}{F(s)}$$

If

$$F(s) = \frac{1}{\tau s + 1}$$

then

$$\frac{\phi}{i} \to \tau s + 1 \text{ as } G \to \infty$$

For $\tau s \gg 1$

$$\phi \simeq \tau \frac{di}{dt}$$

Thus, we see that one way to differentiate using low-pass filters is to put the filter in the feedback loop of a high-gain network. The practical problem is that as $G \to \infty$ this type of differentiator gets very noisy.

The complementary filter approach, which is both mathematically precise and far more practical, is to develop the differentiator as follows: Every $G(s)$ has a COMPLEMENT. Its complement is

$$C(s) = 1 - G(s)$$

For the filter:

$$i \longrightarrow \boxed{G(s)} \xrightarrow{\phi_T}$$

where ϕ_T is the signal passed by the filter $G(s)$. There is a complement:

$$i \longrightarrow \boxed{1 - G(s)} \xrightarrow{\phi_r}$$

where ϕ_r is the signal rejected by the filter $G(s)$. Another way to visualize this is:
If

Then its complement is

Now note that if $G = 1/\tau s + 1$ then, $C(s) = 1 - 1/\tau s + 1 = \tau s/\tau s + 1$. Thus,

In other words, the derivative of the input i, is the part of i rejected by the low-pass filter and then scaled up by the inverse of the filter time constant. Often the design of complex filters is more easily understood when viewed from the "total signal" point of view. This type of differentiator is smooth running and introduces no noise into the filter that is not already present in the input. In this sense, the complementary filtering approach is superior to the approach of low-pass filtering the feedback of a high-gain feedback loop.

Now notice that repeated application of complementary differentiation leads to higher order derivatives of the input as

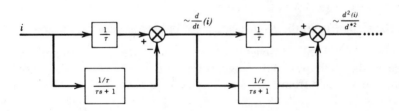

and as such can be used in the development of an extrapolator. This can be seen by noting that

$$f(t + T) = f(t) + Tf'(t) + \frac{T^2}{2}f''(t) + \cdots$$

which can be implemented with complementary filtering as follows:

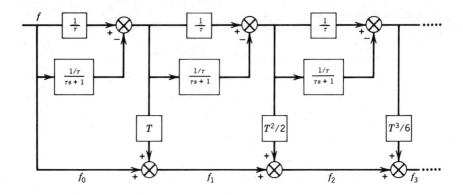

It is clear that the higher n, the better the approximation to $f(t + T)$.

The design of simple band pass type filters is particularly easy. Suppose you are asked to build a filter with the following Bode plot properties,

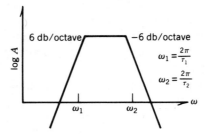

The design from the *total signal* point of view proceeds as follows:

Step 1.   Using only low-pass (6 db per octave) filters, we start with the left side of the Bode plot and recognize that the desired rise in the amplitude can be developed from the rejected signal (complement) of a low pass filter that rejects all frequencies higher than ω_1. This is seen as follows:

Step 2.   Now we low-pass filter this high-frequency signal with a filter of

the form $[1/(2\Pi/\omega_2)s + 1]$ to suppress the band pass beyond ω_2. This is seen as

Another way to visualize a simple band pass filter design is as follows:

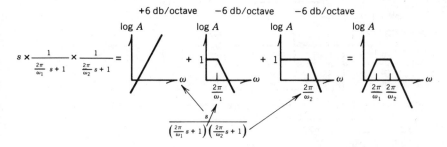

Note that a notch filter is just the rejected spectrum of a band pass filter and can be developed as shown in Figure 5-7. Other important points worth remembering are that:

High-pass filters can be developed entirely with low-pass filters and summers, thus eliminating the generation of more noise than is already present in the signal.

Given any order linear transfer function, it can be developed completely from a combination of first- and second-order filters and their complements. Said slightly differently, complementary filtering permits transfer functions with poles. Thus, the simple first- and second-order low-pass systems developed in Sections 5.3 and 5.5 are all that are required to simulate even the most complicated transfer functions.

The concept and applications of complementary filtering carries over into digital filtering without modification.

Higher order complex filters are often more easily developed using the "intuitive" complementary filtering concepts than some mathematically abstract filter design concepts.

It gives the simulation designer the insight necessary to design special filters for such purposes as frequency foldback filtering.

It gives the simulation designer the flexibility to implement his or her simulation of a filter in many different ways.

FIGURE 5-7. Band-pass filters, notch filters, and differentiators using low-pass filters. $\dot{x} \cong \{x - [s/(\tau s + 1)]x\}(1/\tau)$. Therefore, $\dot{x} \cong [s/(\tau s + 1)]x$.

Example

Simulate $(s + a)/(s + b)$, using only the difference equations for a low-pass filter.

Step 1

$$\frac{\phi}{I} = \frac{s + a}{s + b} = \frac{s}{s + b} + \frac{a}{s + b}$$

Step 2

$$\frac{s}{s + b} = \frac{s}{s + b} - 1 + 1 = \frac{s}{s + b} - \frac{s + b}{s + b} + 1$$

$$= \frac{-b}{s + b} + 1$$

Step 3

$$\frac{s + a}{s + b} = \frac{-b}{s + b} + 1 + \frac{a}{s + b} = \frac{\phi}{I}$$

which can be simulated with

$$\frac{\phi}{I} = \frac{-(1 - e^{-bT})z}{(z - e^{-bT})} + 1 + \frac{a/b(1 - e^{-bT})z}{(z - e^{-bT})}$$

The block diagram of this system is seen in Figure 5-8.

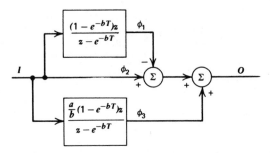

FIGURE 5-8.   The simulation of $(s + a)/(s + b)$ with low-pass filters. Note the series formulations and use of the different equations. $(\phi_1)_n = e^{-bT}(\phi_1)_{n-1} + (1 - e^{-bT})I_n$; $(\phi_2)_n = I_n$; $(\phi_3)_n = e^{-bT}(\phi_3)_{n-1} + (a/b)(1 - e^{-bT})I_n$; $(\phi)_n = (\phi_1)_n + (\phi_2)_n + (\phi_3)_n$.

The system of equations for this simulation is:

$$\phi_{1_n} = e^{-bT}\phi_{1_{n-1}} + (1 - e^{-bT})I_n$$

$$\phi_{2_n} = I_n$$

$$\phi_{3_n} = e^{-bT}\phi_{3_{n-1}} + (a/b)(1 - e^{-bT})I_n$$

$$\phi = \phi_1 + \phi_2 + \phi_3$$

PART III

NUMERICAL METHODS FOR SIMULATING NONLINEAR SYSTEMS ON A DIGITAL COMPUTER

CHAPTER 6

NONLINEAR SYSTEM SIMULATION

Though this chapter does present difference equation methods for simulating nonlinear systems, the tone is soft because no general methods seem to exist for synthesizing fast nonlinear difference equations to simulate nonlinear systems that can be described by nonlinear differential equations. Some inroads have been made for certain problems, and a few of the more recent findings are presented here.

This chapter deals with the digital simulation of continuous systems described by nonlinear differential equations of the form

$$\dot{x} = F(x, t)$$

A number of investigators have dealt with this problem from the modern numerical method viewpoint. Fowler examined it from the root-locus matching viewpoint. Among his more interesting findings was an empirical observation about simulating nonlinear systems described by the equation

$$\dot{x} - kx^2 = f(t); \quad x(0) = x_0, \text{ a constant, and } f(t) = 0$$

This system can be block diagrammed as shown in Figure 6-1. It might be thought that this system could be treated as a piecewise constant coefficient linear process where kx is held constant over the period of a digital simulation step. Fowler developed a system of difference equations based on his method and demonstrated that the response of this simple system to an initial condition (or a step input from an equilibrium) was too slow compared to the true continuous system's response. He found that the proper response time was achieved, however, when the feedback gain was increased by a factor of 2 (see Figure 6-2).

The problem, of course, is that in reaching its equilibrium condition the system arrived at the wrong steady-state value. This is easy to see; in the

237

FIGURE 6-1. Block diagram of the system $\dot{x} - kx^2 = f(t)$—the system to be simulated.

FIGURE 6-2. Block diagram of the system $\dot{x} - (2kx)x = f(t)$.

steady state $\dot{x} = 0$ and thus

$$x_{\text{steady state}} = \sqrt{\frac{-f}{k}}, \qquad \text{for} \quad f = \text{constant}, k < 0$$

for the system to be simulated; whereas

$$x_{\text{steady state}} = \sqrt{\frac{-f}{2k}}, \qquad \text{for} \quad f = \text{constant}, k < 0$$

for the system that, when developed into a piecewise linear difference equation, gave the correct simulated response time. The obvious solution was to add a forward loop gain to the input f. The extension to other more complex nonlinear differential equations was not so straightforward.

At that point Fowler made the interesting observation that $2kx$ is the Jacobian of this nonlinear system:

$$\dot{x} = kx^2 + f(t)$$

$$\frac{\partial \dot{x}}{\partial x} = 2kx = \mathbf{J}, \text{ the Jacobian}$$

Others had noted similar findings from different approaches, but all seemed to focus on the fact that the Jacobian was not only the way to study the local stability of nonlinear processes but also a key parameter to

FIGURE 6-3.   Ways to improve the simulation of nonlinear systems.

fast simulation. The difficulty was to develop a method to transform the nonlinear differential equation into a piecewise linear differential equation whose

1. Constant coefficient was the same as the Jacobian of the nonlinear differential equation.

2. Final value matched the final value of the nonlinear differential equation.

In the early 1970s a number of attempts were made without general success. Particular techniques were developed for particular systems but no general methods seemed forthcoming. At that point the author took a somewhat different approach that proved unusually simple and easy to use and is reported here for the first time. This approach reverts to improving the efficiency of numerically integrating nonlinear differential equations through improving the estimate of the integrand (see Figure 6-3). Interestingly, this led to an approach for developing piecewise linear differential equations satisfying one of the two properties mentioned before. As it turned out, the difference equations were identical to those developed by Roland Bowles using a completely different approach: an esthetically pleasing meeting of the minds. Both methods are covered in this chapter.

6.1 IMPROVED INTEGRAND ESTIMATION

The emphasis on developing an improved approach to the numerical integration of nonlinear differential equations stems from the author's experience and conviction that numerical integration is a concept that is easier to employ in the digital simulation of continuous processes than difference equation methods. Also it seems easier to understand and is more useful to simulation engineers of limited experience. For this reason it is covered first.

This method, in hindsight, is deceptively simple but took three years to find. The objective is to transform the nonlinear differential equation into a piecewise linear constant coefficient differential equation, whose coefficients are the Jacobian of the nonlinear system and whose final value is the final value of the nonlinear system. Then when this linear differential equation's coefficients are calculated and held constant over the integration step, they are by definition holding the Jacobian fixed over the period of the integration step.

The piecewise linear differential equation is developed using the following 3-step algorithm:

Step 1. Differentiate the nonlinear differential equation (this results in coefficients that are the Jacobian of the nonlinear process).

Step 2. Substitute the original differential equation into the results of step 1 (this ensures that the final value of the piecewise linear differential equation will match the final value of the nonlinear differential equation).

Step 3. Numerically integrate the differential equation developed in step 2 holding the Jacobian fixed over the integration step.

One-Dimensional Example

$$\dot{x} = kx^2 + f(t) \tag{6-1}$$

Step 1.

$$\ddot{x} = (2kx)\dot{x} + \dot{f}(t)$$

Step 2.

$$\ddot{x} = (2kx)\big(kx^2 + f(t)\big) + \dot{f}(t) \tag{6-2}$$

$$\ddot{x} = \mathbf{J}\big(kx^2 + f(t)\big) + \dot{f}(t) \tag{6-3}$$

Step 3. Double integrate (numerically)

$$\ddot{x} = \mathbf{J}\big(kx^2 + f(t)\big) + \dot{f}(t)$$

holding **J** fixed over the interval of integration.

In the applications studied to date, it has been found that the double integration of (6-3) proceeds much faster than the single integration of (6-1) because the integration step size for solving (6-3) can be made substantially larger than for two single steps (two integrations) of (6-1).

This method can be stated more generally as follows. Given

$$\dot{\mathbf{X}} = \mathbf{f}(\mathbf{X}, t) \tag{6-4}$$

this system can be numerically integrated quickly using the piecewise linear differential equation developed below.

Step 1.

$$\ddot{\mathbf{X}} = \mathbf{J}\dot{\mathbf{X}} + \frac{\partial \mathbf{f}(\mathbf{X}, t)}{\partial t} \tag{6-5}$$

Step 2.

$$\ddot{\mathbf{X}} = \mathbf{Jf}(\mathbf{X}, t) + \frac{\partial \mathbf{f}(\mathbf{X}, t)}{\partial t} \tag{6-6}$$

Step 3.   Numerically integrate

$$\ddot{\mathbf{X}} = \mathbf{Jf}(\mathbf{X}, t) + \frac{\partial \mathbf{f}(\mathbf{X}, t)}{\partial t}$$

holding **J** fixed over the interval of integration.

The difference between the classical methods and the Jacobian matching method can be visualized by comparing their block diagrams. The classical approach is shown in Figure 6-4. Figure 6-5 shows the piecewise linear approach that holds the Jacobian fixed at each integration step.

Another way to implement the numerical integration of the piecewise linear differential equation is shown in Figure 6-6. This approach illustrates the numerical integration of (6-3).

FIGURE 6-4.   Block diagram of the numerical integration of the nonlinear differential equation (6-4).

FIGURE 6-5. Block diagram of the numerical integration of the piecewise linear differential equation (6-5).

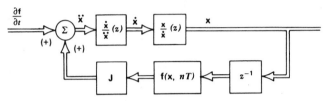

FIGURE 6-6. Block diagram of the numerical integration of the piecewise linear differential equation (6-6).

Of the two piecewise linear methods the author prefers the method shown in Figure 6-6 because it explicitly ensures that the equilibrium condition (final value) will be satisfied. More specifically, when equilibrium is reached

$$\frac{\partial \mathbf{f}}{\partial t} = 0, \qquad \text{for } \ddot{\mathbf{X}} = 0$$

then from (6-3)

$$\ddot{\mathbf{X}} = \mathbf{J}\mathbf{f}(\mathbf{X}, t) + \frac{\partial \mathbf{f}}{\partial t} \Rightarrow 0 = \mathbf{f}(\mathbf{X}, t)$$

while with (6-2)

$$\ddot{\mathbf{X}} = \mathbf{J}\dot{\mathbf{X}} + \frac{\partial \mathbf{f}}{\partial t} \Rightarrow 0 = \mathbf{J}\dot{\mathbf{x}}$$

which does not guarantee that $\mathbf{f}(\mathbf{X}, t) = 0$. In fact, from Figure 6-5 it is apparent that if numerical error were to enter into the last integral it would never be canceled by the closed-loop process around $\dot{\mathbf{X}}$. In short, the last integration is an open-loop integration that will wander to any final value depending only on the amount of numerical error generated in the last integration. Such is not the case for the process shown in Figure 6-6.

The mathematical flow for solving the nonlinear differential equation (6-3) is shown in Figure 6-7.

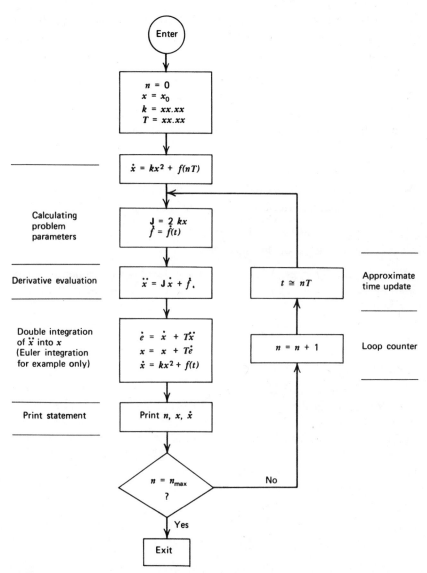

FIGURE 6-7. A mathematical flow for illustrating the numerical integration of (6-5). Note that although $\dot{x}$ is calculated in the first numerical integration $(\dot{e})$, we print out and close the feedback loop using the calculation of $\dot{x}$ based on x and t.

By now you must be wondering why (6-2) and (6-3) and the mathematical flow of Figure 6-7 show the explicit calculation of **J**. Why use the differential equation

$$\ddot{x} = \mathbf{J}\big(kx^2 + f(t)\big) + \dot{f}\,(t) \qquad (6\text{-}7)$$

instead of the algebraically simplified version of (6-5)? In this case the algebraically simplified equation would be of the form

$$\ddot{x} = 2k^2x^3 + 2kxf(t) + \dot{f}\,(t) \qquad (6\text{-}8)$$

The answer is that the intention throughout this section is to emphasize the fact that two separate effects are being controlled in this method:

1. The generation and use of the Jacobian.
2. The use and control of the final value.

When Figure 6-7 is examined, we see the Jacobian prominently in the equation. Also, when equilibrium is established ($\dot{f} = 0$ and $\ddot{x} = 0$), it is clear that

$$x = \sqrt{\frac{-f(t)}{k}}\,, \quad \text{for } f = \text{constant}, k < 0$$

as it should be.

There is another reason for writing this equation in the form of (6-3). For many problems it is also the **fast** numerical evaluation form of the equation. Differential equations written in the form of (6-3) often require the fewest number of arithmetic and memory operations for derivative evaluation. For example if we implemented (6-8) on a limited-capability minicomputer, personal computer, or programmable pocket calculator, we would (at worst) program the evaluation somewhat as follows:

$$\ddot{x} = 2 \times k \times k \times x \times x \times x \text{ STO CLR } 2 \times x \times f \times k + \dot{f} \text{ RCL } + ,^{*}$$

8 multiply, 2 add, 2 memory = 12 arithmetic operations

while (6-2) would (at worst) be programmed as

$$\ddot{x} = k \times x \text{ STO } \times x + f \text{ RCL } \times 2 \times \dot{f} + ,^{*}$$

4 multiply, 2 add, 2 memory = 8 arithmetic operations

---

*Assumes reverse-polish machine language.

Although the difference between 12 and 8 operations may not seem like much of a penalty for this example, it does amount to 50% more operations than are necessary. In fact, when one takes into account that roughly 14 microseconds are required to perform an add and 27 microseconds for a multiply in a typical IBM PC/AT, the time difference in the arithmetic can amount to 44% more time than is really necessary.

If efficiency is not at a premium, (6-8) is of course just as satisfactory as (6-2).

6.2   THE CLOSED-FORM SOLUTION OF $\ddot{X} = Jf + \partial f/\partial t$

To develop a piecewise linear difference equation to simulate a general nonlinear process described by

$$\dot{X} = f(X, t)$$

we need to solve the piecewise linear differential equation

$$\ddot{X} = J\dot{X} + \frac{\partial f}{\partial t}$$

in closed form. To do this we must assume a known form of $\dot{f}$. In this case we will assume a zero-order hold reconstructs $\dot{f}$ into a sequence of stairsteps and we will seek the response of the system

$$\ddot{X} = J\dot{X}, \qquad \text{for} \quad J = \text{constant}$$

to the stairstep forcing function. The approach we use to derive analytically the difference equation for the system is shown in Figure 6-8.

FIGURE 6-8.   The block diagram of the digital simulation of $x = f(x, t)$.

First we solve the homogeneous equation

$$\ddot{X} - J\dot{X} = 0$$

to develop the state transition matrix Φ. Assume a solution of the form

$$\dot{X} = e^{At}$$

On substitution we find

$$(A - J) = 0$$

$$\therefore A = J$$

The solution to the homogeneous equation becomes

$$\dot{X} = e^{Jt}C$$

When $t = 0$

$$\dot{X} = \dot{X}_0 = C \quad \text{and} \quad J = J_0$$

Thus

$$\dot{X} = e^{J_0 t}\dot{X}_0$$

and

$$\Phi = e^{Jt}$$

$$\Phi_0 = e^{J_0 t}$$

The particular solution for the nonhomogeneous equation becomes

$$\dot{X} = \Phi_0\dot{X}_0 + \int_0^t \Phi(t - \tau)\left(\frac{\partial f}{\partial t}\right)_0 d\tau$$

where $\dfrac{\partial f}{\partial t}$ is constant over the integration step. Evaluating the integral, we find

$$\dot{X} = e^{J_0 t}\dot{X}_0 + J_0^{-1}(I - e^{-J_0 t})\left(\frac{\partial f}{\partial t}\right)_0$$

which is integrated again to derive the final form of the difference equation as

$$X = X_0 + \int_0^t \dot{X}(t) \, dt$$

which is

$$\mathbf{X} = \mathbf{X}_0 + \mathbf{J}_0^{-1}(e^{\mathbf{J}_0 t} - I)\dot{\mathbf{X}}_0 + \mathbf{J}_0^{-2}(e^{\mathbf{J}_0 t} - t\mathbf{J}_0 - I)\left(\frac{\partial \mathbf{f}}{\partial t}\right)_0$$

It follows, then, that

$$\boxed{\mathbf{X}_n = \mathbf{X}_{n-1} + \mathbf{J}_{n-1}^{-1}(e^{\mathbf{J}_{n-1}T} - I)\dot{\mathbf{X}}_{n-1} + \mathbf{J}_{n-1}^{-2}(e^{\mathbf{J}_{n-1}T} - T\mathbf{J}_{n-1} - I)\left(\frac{\partial \mathbf{f}}{\partial t}\right)_{n-1}}$$

or, for reasons discussed later,

$$\boxed{\mathbf{X}_n = \mathbf{X}_{n-1} + \mathbf{J}_{n-1}^{-1}(e^{\mathbf{J}_{n-1}T} - I)\mathbf{f}_{n-1} + \mathbf{J}_{n-1}^{-2}(e^{\mathbf{J}_{n-1}T} - T\mathbf{J}_{n-1} - I)\left(\frac{\partial \mathbf{f}}{\partial t}\right)_{n-1}}$$

$$(6\text{-}9)$$

since

$$\dot{\mathbf{X}}_{n-1} = \mathbf{f}_{n-1}$$

Example

For the simple one-dimensional problem

$$\dot{x} = kx^2 + f(t), \qquad \text{for} \quad f(t) = 0$$

$$\mathbf{J}_{n-1} = 2kx_{n-1}, \qquad \text{for} \quad \mathbf{J}_{n-1}^{-1} = \frac{1}{2kx_{n-1}}$$

Then the simulating difference equation is

$$x_n = x_{n-1} + \frac{1}{2kx_{n-1}}(e^{2kx_{n-1}T} - 1)(kx_{n-1}^2)$$

which simplifies to

$$x_n = \frac{x_{n-1}}{2}(1 + e^{2kx_{n-1}T})$$

This example illustrates an important limitation of the piecewise linear difference equation method. The calculation of the steps ensures that each incremental step is taken in accordance with the local stability characteristics of the nonlinear differential equation but the final value is computed in an open-loop manner by accumulating the incremental steps. In this sense these difference equations are not too useful for simulation unless an error control technique is employed. Interestingly, there are a few situations where error control methods are used as a standard practice. They are the numerical integration of rotational equations of motion.

The equations of motion of a rotating body are used in the design of virtually all transportation systems, from automobiles to submarines to aircraft carriers to spacecraft. For these cases the popular techniques for simulating rotational motion include:·

- Euler equations.
- Quaternion equations.
- Direction cosine equations.

Of these, both the quaternion and direction cosine methods employ error correction techniques. These techniques hinge on evaluating the orthogonality of the coordinate system implied by the orthogonal components of rotation (except in the nonorthogonal Euler equations). When the orthogonality test is not satisfied, small corrections are made to the coordinate system to re-orthogonalize it. In this type of situation the coordinate system orthogonalization process never permits the errors in computing the steady state to build up to a noticeable amount.

6.3   THE BOWLES LL ALGORITHM

Roland Bowles of NASA-Langley developed an equation that is identical to (6-9) for simulating nonlinear systems with piecewise linear difference equations. He used the method [called the LL (local linearization) algorithm] with much success in simulating the rotational motion of high-performance aircraft. Bowles published his work in 1973.* This document reports his significant breakthrough in the fast simulation of rotational motion. He used perturbation analysis to develop the difference equation.

The steps proceed as follows. Given

$$\dot{\mathbf{X}} = \mathbf{f}(\mathbf{X}, t)$$

$\mathbf{f}$ can be Taylor-series expanded (multidimensional) as

$$\mathbf{f}(\mathbf{X}, t) = \mathbf{f}(\mathbf{X}_n, nt) + \left(\frac{\partial \mathbf{f}}{\partial \mathbf{X}} \right)_n \delta\mathbf{X} + \left(\frac{\partial \mathbf{f}}{\partial t} \right)_n \delta t + \cdots$$

* Development and Application of a Local Linearization Algorithm for Integration of Quaternion Rate Equations in Real-Time Flight Simulation Problems," Barker, Bowles, and Williams, *NASA TN-D*-7347, December 1973.

where

$$\delta X = (X - X_n) \qquad \text{and} \qquad \delta t = (t - nT)$$

Thus

$$\dot{X} = f(X_n, nT) + \left(\frac{\partial f}{\partial X} \right)_n \delta X + \left(\frac{\partial f}{\partial t} \right)_n \delta t + \cdots$$

Note that since

$$\frac{d}{dt} (\delta X) = \dot{X}$$

we can also write

$$\frac{d}{dt} (\delta X) = J_n \, \delta X + f_n + \left(\frac{\partial f}{\partial t} \right)_n (t - nT)$$

which is a first-order differential equation. When J_n, f_n, and $(\partial f / \partial t)_n$ are held constant over T, this becomes a piecewise linear differential equation with constant coefficients. The solution results in

$$\delta X = \left\{ J_n^{-1}(e^{-J_n T} - I)f_n + (J_n^{-1})^2 (e^{J_n T} - I - TJ_n) \left(\frac{\partial f}{\partial t} \right)_n \right\}$$

Then one can write

$$X_{n+1} = X_n + \delta X$$

Comparison of this result with (6-9) shows that the results are identical although the thinking processes are somewhat different. Of course, the limitation discussed before also holds for the LL algorithm.

A final comment on the difference equation techniques presented here: if the simulation involves many state vectors, a significant difficulty can arise when the Jacobian must be inverted at each and every step. This is particularly true if the Jacobian is an ill-conditioned matrix. Of course, all these factors bear on the decision of whether to use piecewise linear difference equations to simulate nonlinear systems or numerically integrate the equations of motion.

CHAPTER 7

MODERN NUMERICAL INTEGRATION METHODS

In the classical development of numerical integration, weighted-average estimates of the integrand over an integration interval are usually based on polynomial approximation methods. When used to solve a complex system of equations (such as those found in real-time digital simulation, digital computer controlled systems, and other discrete information systems), these approximations introduce phase shift and amplitude distortion into the problem. The errors affect each system of equations differently, often compounding into inaccuracy and instability.

The numerical integrators developed here are based on variable "phase gain" digital filters. The weighted-average estimates of the integrand are based on averaging filters whose phase and amplitude characteristics can be varied, resulting in numerical integrators that have error-controlling parameters. These parameters can be selected to compensate directly for phase shift and amplitude distortion, whatever its source. It is found that introducing integrand-reconstruction distortion filtering leads to simple numerical integration formulas, which can be "tuned" to the system of equations being integrated. Specifically, numerical accuracy and stability are controlled by adjusting phase and amplitude of the integrator transfer function. When operating efficiently (i.e., near the Shannon sampled-data information limit), these integrators are easily tuned to be highly accurate and unusually stable. The "tunability" in both the time domain and frequency domain has no counterpart in classical numerical integration.

These numerical integrators reduce to certain classical integration formulas as the phase of the integrand is shifted. This leads to an interesting corollary that large classes of classical numerical integrators are actually the same integrator, differing only by the amount of integrand phase shift.

Adapted from J. M. Smith, "Recent Developments in Numerical Integration," *Journal of Dynamic Systems, Measurement, and Control*, March 1974. Published by the American Society of Mechanical Engineers. Used by permission.

7.1 NUMERICAL INTEGRATION FROM THE SAMPLED-DATA VIEWPOINT

In this chapter, numerical integration formulas are derived by:

1. Synthesizing a discrete approximation to continuous integration.
2. Writing the difference equation that describes the discrete system.

The difference equation is the numerical integration formula.

Methods for synthesizing discrete systems that approximate continuous systems are seen in Figure 7-1. Figure 7-1a shows a continuous process which is to be approximated by a discrete process. Figure 7-1b shows a discrete approximation of the continuous process, where the reconstructed signal (continuous) is compensated for reconstruction distortion. In Figure 7-1c the reconstruction compensation is applied to the discrete signal before the reconstruction occurs. Of the many approaches to approximating continuous systems with discrete systems, the methods shown in Figure 7-1 are particularly useful. To a large degree they separate information-related from stability-related considerations when selecting the reconstruction process and compensation filtering.

The reconstruction process can be selected from time-domain considerations and information content (such as sampling rate, quantization error, spectrum folding, and interpolation algorithms), whereas the reconstruction compensation process can be selected from frequency-domain and stability considerations (such as phase shift, amplitude spectra, pole and zero location, and root locus). This type of approximation method, which is based on both time- and frequency-domain considerations, is important because it results in a better approximation than methods based on either

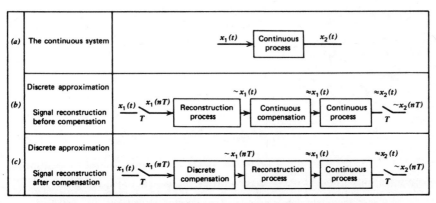

FIGURE 7-1.   Discrete methods of approximating continuous systems.

time-domain or frequency-domain considerations alone.

The zero-, first-, and second-order holds and the triangular hold will be used in the development of the compensated integrators. The amplitude spectra for these reconstruction processes are shown in Chapter 2. A glance at the frequency-domain characteristics of these holds shows that the higher the order of the reconstruction processes, the greater the distortion of the higher frequencies. Remember that reconstruction of the integrand with the zero-order reconstruction process can introduce as much as a half period of time delay in the reconstructed signal. This delay increases as the order of the reconstruction process increases.

7.2 A BRIEF REVIEW OF DISCRETE APPROXIMATIONS OF CONTINUOUS FUNCTIONS

Figure 7-2 shows a simple discrete approximation to continuous integration. Figure 7-2a is a block diagram of continuous integration. The discrete approximation of this process is shown in Figure 7-2b.

In this case a zero-order hold reconstruction is used to reconstruct the integrand. The zero-order hold reconstruction process is equivalent to reconstructing the integrand with a zero-order collating polynomial curve (Newton-Gregory approximation) fitted through the discrete values of the integrand.

The transfer function relating the z transforms of X and $\dot{X}$ is *

$$\frac{X(z)}{\dot{X}(z)} \cong Z\left(\frac{1 - e^{-sT}}{s}\right)\left(\frac{1}{s}\right)$$

$$\frac{X}{\dot{X}}(z) \cong \frac{z-1}{z} Z\left(\frac{1}{s^2}\right) = \frac{z-1}{z} Z(t) \qquad (7\text{-}1)$$

$$\frac{X}{\dot{X}}(z) \cong \frac{T}{z-1}$$

The difference equation that describes this discrete approximation of continuous integration is

$$X_n \cong X_{n-1} + T\dot{X}_{n-1} \qquad (7\text{-}2)$$

This is Euler's integration formula, which describes the process of sampling the continuous integration of a zero-order reconstructed integrand.

*Numerical integration only approximates analytic integration; therefore the "approximately equals" sign is used in the numerical integration formula.

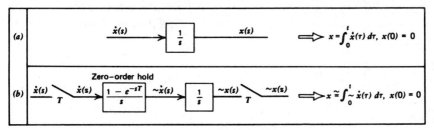

FIGURE 7-2. Zero-order hold integration.

Figure 7-3 shows the discrete equivalent of continuous integration when a first-order hold reconstruction process (Newton-Gregory first-order polynomial approximation) is used to reconstruct the integrand.

The difference equation that describes this process can be developed as follows:

$$\frac{X}{\dot{X}} \cong \left(\frac{z-1}{z}\right)^2 Z\left(\frac{1+Ts}{Ts^3}\right) = \left(\frac{z-1}{z}\right)^2 Z\left(\frac{1}{Ts^3} + \frac{1}{s^2}\right)$$

$$\frac{X}{\dot{X}} \cong \left(\frac{z-1}{z}\right)^2 Z\left(\frac{t^2}{2T} + t\right) = \left(\frac{z-1}{z}\right)^3$$

$$\left\{\frac{Tz(z+1)}{2(z-1)^3} + \frac{Tz}{(z-1)^2}\right\} \tag{7-3}$$

$$\frac{X}{\dot{X}} \cong \frac{T}{2}\left\{\frac{3z-1}{z(z-1)}\right\}$$

Inverting, we find the difference equation:

$$X_n \cong X_{n-1} + \frac{T}{2}\left(3\dot{X}_{n-1} - \dot{X}_{n-2}\right) \tag{7-4}$$

Here, we find that the first-order-hold reconstruction process results in Adams' second-order integration formula—again a well-known result. Fi-

First-order hold

$$\underset{T}{\overset{\dot{X}(s)}{\diagdown}} \quad \underset{T}{\overset{\dot{X}(z)}{\diagdown}} \boxed{\left(\frac{1-e^{-sT}}{s}\right)^2 \left(\frac{1+Ts}{T}\right)} \overset{\sim\dot{X}(s)}{\longrightarrow} \boxed{\frac{1}{s}} \overset{\sim X(s)}{\underset{T}{\diagdown}} \quad \overset{\sim X(z)}{\diagdown}$$

FIGURE 7-3. First-order hold integration.

nally, numerical integration based on the second-order-hold reconstruction, which is seen in Figure 7-4, results in the Adams-Bashforth explicit integrator.

$$X_n \cong X_{n-1} + \frac{T}{12}\left(23\dot{X}_{n-1} - 16\dot{X}_{n-2} + 5\dot{X}_{n-3}\right) \qquad (7\text{-}5)$$

FIGURE 7-4. Second-order hold integration.

Since higher-order reconstruction processes are related to (but not the same as) higher-order Newton-Gregory approximating polynomials, it seems reasonable to expect that other classical higher-order integrators would be found to correspond with higher-order reconstruction processes.

From a sampled-data system viewpoint, these integrators are characterized by their integrand reconstruction process. The fidelity of the integrand reconstruction is related to the accuracy and stability of the integrator. This again focuses our attention on the integrand reconstruction process, its characteristics and properties, a subject that has received considerable attention in the field of sampled-data control and information systems. Of particular interest are sampled-data control system stability-controlling techniques. They will be used here for controlling numerical instabilities. Also, certain of these sampled-data techniques will be used to control signal reconstruction distortion—a principal source of numerical error and instability in numerical integration.

7.3 TUNABLE NUMERICAL INTEGRATION

The sources of error in numerical integration are numerous. In lieu of predetermining the compensation for each individual source of error, variable phase-amplitude compensation filtering will be included in the development of difference equations used for numerical integration; then compensation can be analytically determined according to a total-system criterion or empirically by trial and error. Both methods will be discussed.

Three continuous phase-shifting filters are used in the derivation of the tunable-type integrators (T-integrators) and are tabulated in Table 7-1. These "lead" filters are truncated series expansions of the operator e^{+sT}.

Table 7-1. Continuous Compensation

Type of Compensation	Transfer Function	Derivation
Single-zero	$1 + \gamma Ts$	$e^{+\gamma Ts} = 1 + \gamma Ts + \dfrac{\gamma^2 T^2 s^2}{2} + \cdots \approx 1 + \gamma Ts$
Single-pole	$\dfrac{1}{1 - \gamma Ts}$	$e^{+\gamma Ts} = \dfrac{1}{e^{-\gamma Ts}} = \dfrac{1}{1 - \gamma Ts + \dfrac{\gamma^2 T^2 s^2}{2} \cdots} \approx \dfrac{1}{1 - \gamma Ts}$
Single-pole/zero	$\dfrac{2 + \gamma Ts}{2 - \gamma Ts}$	$e^{+\gamma Ts} = \dfrac{e^{+\gamma Ts/2}}{e^{-\gamma Ts/2}} = \dfrac{1 + \dfrac{\gamma Ts}{2} + \dfrac{\gamma^2 T^2 s^2}{8} + \cdots}{1 - \dfrac{\gamma Ts}{2} + \dfrac{\gamma^2 T^2 s^2}{8} - \cdots} \approx \dfrac{2 + \gamma Ts}{2 - \gamma Ts}$

The zero-order-hold integrator with the single-zero continuous phase-gain compensation is seen in Figure 7-5. The transfer function relating X and $\dot{X}$ is

$$\frac{X}{\dot{X}} \cong Z\left\{\left(\frac{1 - e^{-sT}}{s}\right)(e^{\gamma sT})\left(\frac{\lambda}{s}\right)\right\} \qquad (7\text{-}6)$$

$$\frac{X}{\dot{X}} \cong \lambda\left(\frac{z - 1}{z}\right) Z\left(\frac{e^{\gamma sT}}{s^2}\right) \qquad (7\text{-}7)$$

$$\frac{X}{\dot{X}} \cong \lambda\left(\frac{z - 1}{z}\right)\left\{\frac{Tz}{(z - 1)^2} + \frac{\gamma Tz}{z - 1}\right\} \qquad (7\text{-}8)$$

$$\frac{X}{\dot{X}} \cong T\lambda\left\{\frac{\gamma z + (1 - \gamma)}{z - 1}\right\} \qquad (7\text{-}9)$$

from which we find the numerical integration formula

$$X_n \cong X_{n-1} + \lambda T\left\{\gamma \dot{X}_n + (1 - \gamma)\dot{X}_{n-1}\right\} \qquad (7\text{-}10)$$

FIGURE 7-5.   Zero-order tunable integrator. T = integration time interval; λ = gain compensation parameters; γ = phase compensation parameter.

With single-pole and single-pole/zero continuous "lead-lag" filter compensation, we find the following numerical integration formulas, respectively,

$$X_n \cong (1 - e^{1/\gamma})X_{n-1} - e^{1/\gamma}X_{n-2} + \lambda T\Big[\big\{1 + \gamma(1 - e^{-1/\gamma})\big\}\dot{X}_{n-1}$$
$$- \big\{e^{1/\gamma} + \gamma(1 - e^{1/\gamma})\big\}\dot{X}_{n-2}\Big]$$

(7-11)

$$X_n \cong (1 - e^{2/\gamma})X_{n-1} - e^{2/\gamma}X_{n-2} + \lambda T\Big[\big\{1 + \gamma(1 - e^{-2/\gamma})\big\}\dot{X}_{n-1}$$
$$- \big\{e^{2/\gamma} + \gamma(1 - e^{2/\gamma})\big\}\dot{X}_{n-2}\Big]$$

(7-12)

We see that the zero-order hold with single-zero compensation leads to an integration formula whose coefficients are simple in form. Similarly, only when the single-zero compensation is used with the higher-order reconstruction holds are the coefficients of the resulting integration formula simple in form. These formulas are tabulated in Table 7-2.

Table 7-2. Continuous Compensation Integration Formulas

Reconstruction Process	Difference Equation
Zero-order hold	$X_n = X_{n-1} + \lambda T\{\gamma\dot{X}_n + (1 - \gamma)\dot{X}_{n-1}\}$
First-order hold	$X_n = X_{n-1} + \dfrac{\lambda T}{2}\{\gamma(\gamma + 2)\dot{X}_n - (2\gamma^2 + 2\gamma - 3)\dot{X}_{n-1} + (\gamma^2 - 1)\dot{X}_{n-2}\}$
Second-order hold	$X_n = X_{n-1} + \dfrac{\lambda T}{12}\{(2\gamma^3 + 9\gamma^2 + 12\gamma)\dot{X}_n - (6\gamma^3 + 21\gamma^2 + 12\gamma - 23)\dot{X}_{n-1}$ $+ (6\gamma^3 + 15\gamma^2 - 16)\dot{X}_{n-2} - (2\gamma^3 + 3\gamma^2 - 5)\dot{X}_{n-3}\}$
Triangular hold	$X_n = X_{n-1} + \dfrac{\lambda T}{2}\{\gamma^2\dot{X}_n + (1 + 2\gamma - 2\gamma^2)\dot{X}_{n-1} + (1 - 2\gamma + \gamma^2)\dot{X}_{n-2}\}$

Tunable integrators were also developed using discrete compensation. A simple type of discrete filter compensation was developed by deriving the discrete equivalent of the single-zero continuous compensation using a triangular-hold reconstruction process (Figure 7-6). The transfer function

FIGURE 7-6. A digital approximation of continuous compensation.

of this discrete process is

$$D(z) \cong \frac{\dot{X}}{\dot{X}} = \lambda z \left(\frac{z-1}{z} \right)^2 Z \left(\frac{1+\gamma Ts}{Ts} \right)$$

$$= \lambda \left(\frac{z-1}{z} \right)^2 z \left\{ \frac{z}{(z-1)^2} + \frac{\gamma z(z-1)}{(z-1)^2} \right\} \qquad (7\text{-}13)$$

$$D(z) \cong \frac{\dot{X}}{\dot{X}} = \lambda \{ \gamma z + (1-\gamma) \}$$

Discretely compensated numerical integrators are developed by inverting the transfer function

$$\frac{X}{\dot{X}}(z) \cong D(z) Z \left(\frac{H(s)}{s} \right)$$

where $D(z)$ is the transfer function of the discrete compensation and $H(s)$ is the transfer function of the reconstruction hold.

$$\frac{X}{\dot{X}}(z) \cong \lambda \{ \gamma z + (1-\gamma) \} \frac{z-1}{z} Z \left(\frac{1}{s^2} \right) \qquad (7\text{-}14)$$

$$\frac{X}{\dot{X}} \cong \lambda \{ \gamma z + (1-\gamma) \} \left\{ \frac{z-1}{z} \right\} \left\{ \frac{Tz}{(z-1)^2} \right\} \qquad (7\text{-}15)$$

which simplifies to

$$\frac{X}{\dot{X}} \cong \lambda T \left\{ \frac{\gamma z + (1-\gamma)}{z-1} \right\} \qquad (7\text{-}16)$$

which inverts into the difference equation

$$X_n \cong X_{n-1} + \lambda T \{ \gamma \dot{X}_n + (1-\gamma)\dot{X}_{n-1} \} \qquad (7\text{-}17)$$

Table 7-3.   Discrete Compensation Integration Formulas

Reconstruction Process	Difference Equation
Zero-order hold	$X_n + X_{n-1} + \lambda T\{\gamma \dot{X}_n + (1 - \gamma)\dot{X}_{n-1}\}$
First-order hold	$X_n = X_{n-1} + \dfrac{\lambda T}{2} \{3\gamma \dot{X}_n + (3 - 4\gamma)\dot{X}_{n-1} + (\gamma - 1)\dot{X}_{n-2}\}$
Second-order hold	$X_n = X_{n-1} + \dfrac{\lambda T}{12} \{23\gamma \dot{X}_n + (23 - 39\gamma)\dot{X}_{n-1}$ $+ (21\gamma - 16)\dot{X}_{n-2} + 5(1 - \gamma)\dot{X}_{n-3}\}$
Triangular hold	$X_n = X_{n-1} + \dfrac{\lambda T}{2} \{\gamma \dot{X}_n + \dot{X}_{n-1} + (1 - \gamma)\dot{X}_{n-2}\}$

Interestingly, this is the same formula that was developed by a single-zero continuous compensation of the zero-order-hold reconstruction. Table 7-3 lists the numerical integration formulas for the higher-order holds using this simple phase-amplitude discrete compensation.

7.4   FREQUENCY-DOMAIN UNIFICATION OF CLASSICAL DEVELOPMENTS

These numerical integration formulas have the interesting feature that they reduce to certain well-known classical integrators for certain values of phase shift and gain. For example, when $\lambda = 1$ and γ takes on integer multiples of one-half, the zero-order numerical integration formula

$$X_n \cong X_{n-1} + \lambda T \left\{ \gamma \dot{X}_n + (1 - \gamma)\dot{X}_{n-1} \right\} \qquad (7\text{-}18)$$

takes the form shown in Table 7-4.

A great many other classical numerical integrators can be found from this and the higher-order integration formulas for integer multiples of $\gamma = \frac{1}{3}, \frac{1}{4}, \frac{1}{5}, \ldots, 1/n$, where n is an integer. The list is far too large to present here. What is important is that the eight integration formulas of Tables 7-2 and 7-3 reduce to a great many of the classical formulas. Thus many of the widely varied classical numerical integration formulas, each of which is considered in some way to be different from the others, are actually the same integrator, differing only in the amount of phase shift of the integrand. Notice that these integrators are members of an infinite set of phase-related integrators that all stem from the same single integration

Table 7-4. Compensated Integrators Reducing to Certain Classical Integrators for Certain Values of λ and γ

Integration Equation	γ	Name
$X_n \cong X_{n-1} + T(2\dot{X}_{n-1} - \dot{X}_n)$	-1	—
$X_n \cong X_{n-1} + \dfrac{T}{2}(3\dot{X}_{n-1} - \dot{X}_n)$	$-\frac{1}{2}$	—
$X_n \cong X_{n-1} + T(\dot{X}_{n-1})$	0	Euler
$X_n \cong X_{n-1} + \dfrac{T}{2}(\dot{X}_n + \dot{X}_{n-1})$	$+\frac{1}{2}$	Trapezoidal
$X_n \cong X_{n-1} + T(\dot{X}_n)$	$+1$	Rectangular
$X_n \cong X_{n-1} + \dfrac{T}{2}(3\dot{X}_n - \dot{X}_{n-1})$	$+\frac{3}{2}$	Implicit Adams second - order
$X_n \cong X_{n-1} + T(2\dot{X}_n - \dot{X}_{n-1})$	$+2$	—

formula. In general, all of these new integrators differ from classical integrators by their general treatment of integrand phasing. Also, although perhaps of less significance, the phase-related integrators are all characterized by having coefficients that are functions, not numbers.

The symmetry of the form of the first-order integration formulas around the $\gamma = +\frac{1}{2}$ case (again see Table 7-4) arises from the fact that the zero-order-hold integrand reconstruction process introduces a half period of lag, which is compensated by a half period of lead when $\gamma = +\frac{1}{2}$. Note the uniform weight on both terms of the integration formula. It is clear that if there is no phase shift other than that introduced by the reconstruction process, trapezoidal integration would introduce no phase shift in the integral.

It is important to recognize that the compensated numerical integrators have phase shift as a parameter. This allows their use either as explicit or implicit integrators. This flexibility in integrator application is an important difference between applying compensated numerical integrators and other integration methods.

More specifically the T integrator

$$x_n = x_{n-1} + T\lambda\left[\gamma\dot{x}_n + (1 - \gamma)\dot{x}_{n-1}\right]$$

can be used explicitly by using only past values of $\dot{x}$ but compensating with a sample period of lead in γ. That is, we would use

$$\gamma' = \gamma + 1$$

as

$$x_n = x_{n-1} + T\lambda\left[(\gamma + 1)\dot{x}_{n-1} + \gamma\dot{x}_{n-2}\right]$$

or

$$x_n = x_{n-1} + T\lambda\left[\gamma'\dot{x}_{n-1} + (1 - \gamma')\dot{x}_{n-2}\right]$$

Those who are accustomed to using explicit numerical integrators in simulations will find it useful to remember that all of the T-integration formulas can be written in terms of the past values of the integrand by simply changing the indices in each of the integrand terms respectively from n to $n - 1$; from $n - 1$ to $n - 2$; from $n - 2$ to $n - 3$; and so on. To attain reasonable performance with the integrator, it is necessary to include a sample period of lead (to compensate for the lag just introduced):

1. By changing the integration formula as demonstrated above.
2. By numerically adding 1 to the value of γ.

7.5 APPLYING TUNABLE INTEGRATION

In this section the application of the zero-order integrator to simple problems will be emphasized. This will simplify the analysis and focus on the principles of applying the compensated integrators to simulation, control, and other information systems. The zero-order integrator can usually be tuned to be highly accurate and stable. The reason from the stability viewpoint is that, being first-order, it can be adjusted so as to introduce no more poles into the dynamic process than true continuous integration would provide. This is not the case for any higher-order integrators, including the Runge-Kutta integrators. Substituting higher-order numerical integrators (explicitly or implicitly) into a differential equation results in a difference equation with more poles than the differential equation from which it was derived. For large integration step sizes, these extra poles often impact the stability of the integrated equations of motion more than any other source of error.

From an accuracy viewpoint, the mean value theorem guarantees that zero-order integration can exactly integrate over a sample period provided the integrand can be sampled at precisely the right time. Zero-order T integration has the transport lead parameter γ which can be adjusted to permit this precise timing of the integrand sampling. For linear constant-coefficient systems, γ need only be adjusted once. For time-variable and/or nonlinear systems, γ must be tuned empirically or by variable phase algorithms (analogous to variable step size algorithms). Interestingly, variable phase integration operates with a fixed integration step size, but adjusts phase to achieve desired integration accuracy; a new development for precise real-time numerical integration applications.*

Where before we were forced to control unwanted and unexpected phase shift and the influence of extra poles with small integration step size and higher-order expansions of the integrand, the low-order tunable integrators allow us to compensate for these effects directly with compensation filtering.

7.6   ANALYTICAL PHASE/GAIN SELECTION

Many analytical criteria can be used for uniquely selecting λ and γ. For example, λ and γ can be selected so as to match the roots of a simulation difference equation to the roots of the system being simulated. Also, γ and λ can be selected so as to minimize the mean square difference between the response of the continuous system and the response of the approximating discrete system to a known forcing function. In many cases these and other criteria will lead to a satisfactory discrete system for approximating continuous systems whether for simulation, for use in digital control or for processing digital information. Interestingly, different methods of choosing λ and γ for complex problems rarely lead to the same λ and γ. This lack of generality (i.e., the uniqueness of synthesizing discrete systems that approximate continuous systems) is a well-known characteristic of discrete system synthesis. An example of phase and gain selection by root matching follows.

Consider the first-order system shown in Figure 7-7. The equations of motion that describe this process are

$$\dot{X} = F - kX, \quad X(0) = 0 \qquad (7\text{-}19)$$

where F is the system's forcing function. The discrete system that we can use to approximate this continuous system is shown in Figure 7-8.

*See Appendix C.

FIGURE 7-7. Linear first-order constant coefficient continuous system.

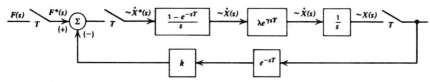

FIGURE 7-8. Linear first-order constant coefficient discrete system analogous to linear first-order constant coefficient continuous system.

The e^{-sT} in the feedback is characteristic of the explicit formulation of discrete systems where the forward loop must be computed before the feedback can be computed and the loop closed. This system is shown in z-domain notation in Figure 7-9.

The transfer function for the discrete process is

$$\frac{X(z)}{F(z)} = \frac{\lambda Tz\{\gamma z + (1 - \gamma)\}}{z^2 + (\lambda kT\gamma - 1)z + k\lambda T(1 - \gamma)} \qquad (7\text{-}20)$$

The characteristic poles of this second-order discrete system are

$$Z_{\text{pole}} = \frac{1 - kT\gamma\lambda}{2} \pm \frac{1}{2}\left\{(\lambda kT\gamma - 1)^2 - 4kT\lambda(1 - \gamma)\right\}^{1/2} \quad (7\text{-}21)$$

The single pole of the continuous process is

$$S_{\text{pole}} = -k \qquad (7\text{-}22)$$

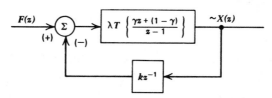

FIGURE 7-9. Discrete approximation in z-domain notation.

We can match the second-order discrete system closed-loop poles with the first-order continuous system closed-loop pole by first eliminating one of the discrete system second-order roots by setting $\gamma = 1$, and then setting λ so as to match the remaining discrete system pole with the continuous system pole. When $\gamma = 1$, the discrete system transfer function becomes

$$\frac{X(z)}{F(z)} = \frac{\lambda Tz}{z + (k\lambda T - 1)} \tag{7-23}$$

with a pole at

$$Z_{\text{pole}} = 1 - k\lambda T \tag{7-24}$$

To match the pole of the continuous system with that of the discrete system, λ is selected so that

$$Z_{\text{pole}} = e^{S_{\text{pole}}T} = e^{-kT} = 1 - k\lambda T \tag{7-25}$$

Solving for λ, we find

$$\lambda = \frac{1 - e^{-kT}}{kT} \tag{7-26}$$

Substituting γ and λ in the transfer function and simplifying gives

$$\frac{X(z)}{F(z)} = \frac{z(1 - e^{-kT})}{(z - e^{-kT})} \tag{7-27}$$

which inverts into the difference equation

$$X_n = e^{-kT}X_{n-1} + (1 - e^{-kT})F_n \tag{7-28}$$

We see then that selecting λ and γ by root matching results in integration that is *exact* for the homogeneous solution to the continuous system, *exact* for the step response, a good approximation for computing system response to arbitrary forcing functions, and incapable of going unstable no matter what the integration step size (since the magnitude of the difference equation transfer function pole is e^{-kT}, which is always less than 1 provided $k > 0$).

7.7 EMPIRICAL PHASE/GAIN SELECTION

Since the variable phase/gain integrator reduces to many of the well-known fixed interval numerical integrators, empirically selecting the lead and gain is nothing more than a trial-and-error approach to selecting an integrator that works for a given system of equations.

A tuning procedure for empirically selecting λ and γ is as follows:

1. Set $\gamma = \lambda = 1$.
2. Generate a check case at $W_s \gg W_i$ where W_s is the sampling frequency and W_i is the information frequency of interest.
3. Set $W_s \cong 10 W_i$, and select γ to best match the check case.
4. Select λ to better match the check case.
5. Iterate steps 3 and 4.

When using the zero-order integrator, setting $\lambda_i = \gamma_i = 1$ transforms the variable lead/gain integrators into rectangular integrators. Rectangular integration has the property of not introducing additional roots into the discrete system. Thus an nth-order continuous system is transformed into an nth-order discrete system. In this way, further gain adjustment can be interpreted as matching the roots of the discrete system to the roots of the continuous system. Finally, empirically "tuning" the integrator can be simplified in many cases by the following rule of thumb:

1. γ affects the transient response, but not the steady state.
2. $\lambda \neq 1$ can affect the steady state; so the steady state must be checked when γ is varied. When γ is varied, a "gain" is required on the forward loop input to compensate for γ's effect on the system's final value.

Where there is more than one check case to be matched, each integrator may have many values of λ and γ. Aircraft flight-training simulators are an example of simulations where different nominal flight conditions can require different values of lead and gain for each flight condition (e.g., flaps up or down, landing gear up or down, and high and low Mach number). The γ and λ for each condition are selected by repeating the four-step tuning procedure. These gains and phases are stored and used in the simulation when the appropriate condition has been reached (e.g., when a flap handle has been put in the *down* position, a gear handle is placed in the *up* position, or Mach > 0.5 etc.).

An example of empirical phase and gain selection for the second-order system shown in Figure 7-10 follows.

The equation that describes the motion of this system is

$$\ddot{X} = F - 2\zeta w_n \dot{X} - w_n^2 X, \tag{7-29}$$

$$\zeta = 0.3, \qquad X(0) = \dot{X}(0) = 0 \tag{7-30}$$

$$w_n = 1 \text{ hertz} \tag{7-31}$$

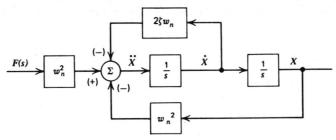

FIGURE 7-10.   Linear second-order constant coefficient continuous system.

For this example the check case is generated by first computing the unit step response, at a sample frequency 1000 times faster than the natural frequency of the system. Figure 7-11 shows the check case for unity gain and for $\gamma = +3$ and $\gamma = -3$, respectively. It is apparent that at this high frequency the effect of this small phase shift is negligible.

Figures 7-12a, 7-12b, and 7-12c show the effect of varying γ (for $\lambda = 1$) at a sampling frequency of 100 hertz. Figures 7-13a, 7-13b, and 7-13c show the effect of varying γ for a sampling frequency of 10 hertz. Notice that in all cases one sample period of lead ($\gamma = 1$, $\lambda = 1$) results in transient responses that fairly closely match the check case, even without gain

FIGURE 7-11.   Second-order system approximation unit step response when $T = 0.001$ second.

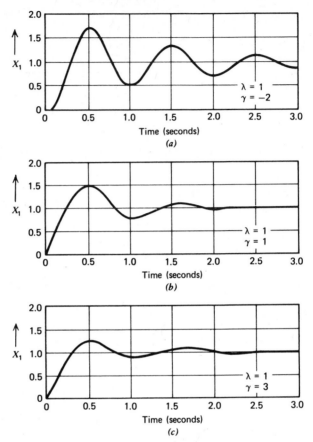

FIGURE 7-12. Second-order system approximation response when $T = 0.01$ second.

adjustment. It is easy to show that setting $\gamma = 1$ eliminates two roots in an otherwise fourth-order discrete system. In general, it is true that when simulating linear constant-coefficient systems, setting $\gamma = 1$ reduces the number of roots in the linear system. The gain adjustment can then be used to match the root locus of the discrete system with the root locus of the continuous system. This does not hold true for nonlinear equations.

An example of empirical λ and γ selection for a nonlinear system is shown in Figure 7-14. This problem has been used by Beisner to study Fowler's method, the Gurk integrators, and the Adams method for real-time simulation as a simple example of mixed closed-loop systems comprised of linear elements, hard nonlinearities, and integrators. This problem gives a simple comparison of any given method, or mixed methods,

FIGURE 7-13. Second-order system approximation unit step response when $T = 0.1$ second.

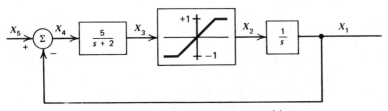

FIGURE 7-14. A nonlinear test problem.

and is sufficiently simple that its dynamics properties can be predetermined either on a machine or by manual analysis. The continuous system can be viewed as a second-order linear process with an embedded nonlinear rate limiter. When the rate is sufficiently low, that is, $|X_3| < 1$, this system acts as a stationary linear process whose transfer function is

$$\frac{X_1}{X_5} = \frac{K}{s^2 + 2s + K} \tag{7-32}$$

For step inputs whose magnitude M is sufficiently low (i.e., $|M| \lesssim 2\frac{1}{2}$), this system will reach its steady state when the output equals the input. The trajectory will match the response of a second-order system with a natural frequency and damping of

$$W_n = \sqrt{K}$$

$$\zeta = \frac{1}{\sqrt{K}}$$

This follows from the observation that the rate will limit when the magnitude of X_3 exceeds 1. The steady-state response of the first-order process $K/(s + 2)$ is $K/2$. It achieves 68% of this steady state in $\frac{1}{2}$ second. During this time, the feedback increases slowly and will not hold the rate X_3 off its limit of 1 if the magnitude of X_4 is greater than $2/K$. For this system when

$$K = 5$$

$$W_n = 2.236 \text{ radians/second} = 0.356 \text{ hertz}$$

$$\zeta = 0.447$$

and the unit steps on the order of 2.5 will result in a rate X_3 which is greater than 1, hence to its limit.

The discrete system that will be used to simulate this system is shown in Figure 7-15. In this discrete system, the process $K/(s + 2)$ is approximated by a sample and zero-order reconstruction with a half sample period of lead to compensate for the half sample period of lag introduced by the zero-order reconstruction process. The difference equation that describes this process is

$$X_{3_n} = e^{-2T}\dot{X}_{3_{n-1}} + \frac{K}{2}\left\{(1 - e^{-T})X_{4_n} + (e^{-T} - e^{-T/2})X_{4_{n-1}}\right\}$$

FIGURE 7-15. The discrete version of the system shown in Figure 7-16.

$$X_{4_n} = X_{5_n} - X_{1_{n-1}}$$

$$X_{3_n} = e^{-2T}X_{3_{n-1}} + \frac{5}{2}\left\{(1 - e^T)X_4 + (e^{-T} - e^{-T/2})X_{4_{n-1}}\right\}$$

$$
\begin{array}{l}
\phantom{X_{3_n} > 1}\quad \text{yes}\\
X_{3_n} > 1 \xrightarrow{} \\
 X_{2_n} = 1 \\
\text{yes}\\
X_{3_n} < -1 \\
X_{2_n} = X_{3_n} \rightarrow \\
X_{2_n} = -1
\end{array}
\left.\rule{0pt}{85pt}\right\} \quad \text{Saturation limit logic}
$$

$$X_{1_n} = X_{1_{n-1}} + aT\left\{lX_{2_n} + (1 - l)X_{2_{n-1}}\right\}$$

$$X_{1_{n-1}} = X_{1_n}$$

$$X_{2_{n-1}} = X_{2_n}$$

$$X_{3_{n-1}} = X_{3_n}$$

FIGURE 7-16.   Computer program for simulating the nonlinear test problem.

In this example the zero-order T integrator will be used to integrate X_2 with the equation

$$X_{1_n} = X_{1_{n-1}} + \lambda T\left\{lX_{2_n} + (1 - l)X_{2_{n-1}}\right\}$$

The program used in the simulation is shown in Figure 7-16. Note that the current estimate of X_4 uses the current value of X_5 and a past value of X_1. As mentioned previously, this arises from the fact that in digital data processing the forward loop must be calculated before the feedback loop can be closed. This introduces a physical delay in the data related *not* to the simulating difference equations but to the dynamics of information flow in a digital computer. This delay is also shown in the feedback loop of Figure 7-17.

For this example, a sampling period of $\frac{1}{2}$ second was used; the ratio of sampling frequency to natural frequency then was

$$\frac{W_s}{W_n} = \frac{2 \text{ sps*}}{0.356 \text{ hertz}} = 5.618$$

*sps = samples per second.

FIGURE 7-17.   Simulation results.

which is close to the Shannon limit for being able to reconstruct a continuous function for a sequence of sampled values.

The response of the discrete system to a step input of 2.5 is shown in Figure 7-17 for various values of γ. The check case was generated by setting the integration step size to 0.0001. An integration step size this small guarantees that, as γ is varied $+3$ to -3, the phase shift in the solution does not exceed ± 0.3 milliradians and the magnitude of the printout does not change more than 5×10^{-4} between runs. From Figure 7-17 we see that a reasonably acceptable fit of the sequence of solutions at large step size with the check case occurs when $\lambda \cong 1$ and $\gamma \cong 1$.

7.8   VARIABLE PHASE INTEGRATION

Variable phase integration is akin to variable step size integration in that a test is made to determine if two half-step integrations are significantly more accurate than a single step. If so, the phase is advanced slightly. The accuracy test is applied again and phase advance made if required. This process is continued until the accuracy test is satisfied. If, however, on the first step of phase-advanced integration the accuracy is degraded, the phase is retarded on the succeeding step(s) until the test is satisfied.

Once the γ which satisfies the accuracy test is identified, the original step size is assumed and the integration of the next step(s) is undertaken. The phase adjustment calculation is conducted on a "side loop" in milliseconds as compared with the integration that is proceeding (usually) in hundreds of milliseconds at a step. This permits controlled accuracy real-time numerical integration. Unlike variable step size integration, variable phase integration proceeds at the same step size (or even larger if the step size is permitted to increase when the accuracy exceeds that required for the problem).

The variable phase algorithm discussed here is the simplest version studied to date. Obviously there are many algorithms that will permit T integration to be self-adaptive. All of those with which the author is familiar are variations of this basic concept.

As a practical matter the phase and gain parameters can be used to compensate for systematic (not random roundoff) computing errors, no matter what their source. When developing large-scale digital or hybrid simulations or when developing digital control systems, parts of the system software are often developed by different groups, at different times, and (occasionally) at different places. When these parts are brought together and integrated into a whole system, the cumulative effects of small amounts of phase shift in many programs can lead to software system stability problems. In these situations the variable phase-gain integration formulas can be (and have been) used for integrating the equations of motion with the phase and amplitude parameters (λ and γ) selected empirically either to best fit a check case or from rough estimates of the amount of phase and amplitude distortion buildup in the simulation process.

7.9 PROPERTIES

Comparing Tables 7-2 and 7-3 we see that the discretely compensated integrators are simpler in form than the continuously compensated integrators. This sophistication lends itself to comparatively easy determination of the properties of the discretely compensated integrators, and for this reason they will be examined in more detail. The continuously compensated integrators are presented for the sake of completeness.

Previously it was implied that predetermining numerical error in any but the simplest of simulations of control systems is at best quite difficult. Of more practical interest in both digital control and digital simulation is the way in which error propagates through a system of equations. A useful measure of the error propagation characteristics of a numerical integrator (its smoothness when used in real-time digital controls or displays) is its response to noise, which is characterized by the variance of the "jump" from step to step in the numerical integration process. For both the discrete and continuously compensated numerical integrators, the "jump" from step to step is given by

$$\Delta X_n = (X_n - X_{n-1}) = \lambda T \left[\gamma \dot{X}_n + (1 - \gamma) \dot{X}_{n-1} \right] \qquad (7\text{-}33)$$

The variance in ΔX_n is given by the average of ΔX_n^2 as

$$\sigma_{\Delta X}^2 = E\left(\Delta X_n^2\right) = \lambda^2 T^2 E\left\{ \gamma^2 \dot{X}_n^2 + 2\gamma(1 - \gamma)\dot{X}_n \dot{X}_{n-1} + (1 - \gamma)^2 \dot{X}_{n-1}^2 \right\}$$

$$(7\text{-}34)$$

where E is the expectation operator.

For zero mean, uncorrelated and stationary random (or pseudorandom) sequences of $\dot{X}$,

$$E\left(\dot{X}_n \dot{X}_{n-1}\right) = 0 \qquad (7\text{-}35)$$

and

$$E\left(\dot{X}_n^2\right) = E\left(\dot{X}_{n-1}^2\right) = \sigma_{\dot{X}}^2 \qquad (7\text{-}36)$$

Thus the "white noise response" of the integrator is given by

$$\sigma_{\Delta X}^2 = \lambda^2 T^2 \left(2\gamma^2 - 2\gamma + 1\right)\sigma_{\dot{X}}^2 \qquad (7\text{-}37)$$

The value of γ which minimizes the variance propagation of this integrator is $\frac{1}{2}$ and the minimum variance transfer function for the integrator is

$$\frac{\sigma_{\Delta X}^2}{\sigma_{\dot{X}}^2} = \frac{\lambda^2 T^2}{2} \qquad (7\text{-}38)$$

Similar results can be developed for the other integrators. The variance propagation equations for both the continuous and discretely compensated integrators are given in Table 7-5.

The γ's which minimize variance propagation for these integrators are presented in Table 7-6, along with the minimum-variance transfer functions of the integrators. A plot of the normalized variance transfer functions as a function of the phase shift parameter γ for the discretely compensated integrators is shown in Figure 7-18.

Table 7-5. Integrator Error Propagation Equations

Reconstruction Process	Continuous Compensation	Discrete Compensation
Zero-order hold	$\sigma_{\Delta x}^2 = \lambda^2 T^2 (2\gamma^2 - 2\gamma + 1)\sigma_X^2$	$\sigma_{\Delta x}^2 = \lambda^2 T^{-2}(2\gamma^2 - 2\gamma + 1)\sigma_X^2$
First-order hold	$\sigma_{\Delta x}^2 = \dfrac{\lambda^2 T^2}{4}(6\gamma^4 + 12\gamma^3 - 6\gamma^2 - 12\gamma + 10)\sigma_X^2$	$\sigma_{\Delta x}^2 = \dfrac{\lambda^2 T^2}{4}(26\gamma^2 - 26\gamma + 10)\sigma_X^2$
Second-order hold	$\sigma_{\Delta x}^2 = \dfrac{\lambda^2 T^2}{144}(80\gamma^6 + 450\gamma^5 + 723\gamma^4 + 457\gamma^3 - 1189\gamma^2 - 522\gamma - 248)\sigma_X^2$	$\sigma_{\Delta x}^2 = \dfrac{\lambda^2 T^2}{144}(2516\gamma^2 - 2516\gamma + 810)\sigma_X^2$
Triangular hold	$\sigma_{\Delta x}^2 = \dfrac{\lambda^2 T^2}{4}(6\gamma^4 - 12\gamma^3 + 6\gamma^2 + 2)\sigma_X^2$	$\sigma_{\Delta x}^2 = \dfrac{\lambda^2 T^2}{4}(2\gamma^2 - 2\gamma + 2)\sigma_X^2$

Table 7-6. Minimum Variance Integration Characteristics

Reconstruction Process	γs for Minimum Variance		Minimum Variance Transfer Function	
	Discrete Compensation	Continuous Compensation	Discrete Compensation	Continuous Compensation
Zero-order hold	$\gamma = \frac{1}{2}$	$\gamma = \frac{1}{2}$	$\lambda^2 T^2/2$	$\lambda^2 T^2/2$
First-order hold	$\gamma = \frac{1}{2}$	$\gamma = 0.5714$	$7\lambda^2 T^2/8$	$\lambda^2 T^2$
Second-order hold	$\gamma = \frac{1}{2}$	$\gamma = 0.250$	$10\lambda^2 T^2/8$	$4\lambda^2 T^2$
Triangular hold	$\gamma = \frac{1}{2}$	$\gamma = 0\ \&\ 1$	$3\lambda^2 T^2/8$	$\lambda^2 T^2/2$

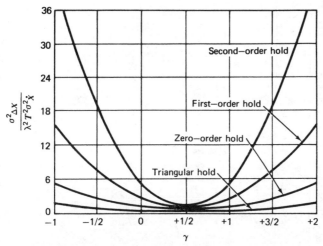

FIGURE 7-18. Normalized variance transfer function of the phase shift parameter γ for certain discretely compensated integrators.

The minimum variance discretely-compensated-integrators are tabulated in the second column of Table 7-7. Each of the integrators is an implicit integration algorithm that can be used implicitly or as a corrector in a predictor-corrector integration algorithm. The predictor is found by setting $\gamma = 0$. The predictor-corrector pairs are presented in Table 7-7.

Similar results can be developed for the continuously compensated integrators. Finally, it is found that the tunable integrators have the following general properties:

1. For continuously compensated integrators, the γ for minimum variance approaches zero from a maximum of $\frac{1}{2}$ as the order of the reconstruction process increases.

Table 7-7. Discretely Compensated Minimum Variance Integrators

Reconstruction Process	Corrector Formulas (Minimum Variance γ)	Predictor Formulas ($\gamma = 0$)
Zero-order hold	$X_n = X_{n-1} + \frac{\lambda T}{2}(\dot{X}_n + \dot{X}_{n-1})$	$X_n = X_{n-1} + \lambda T \dot{X}_{n-1}$
First-order hold	$X_n = X_{n-1} + \frac{\lambda T}{4}$ $(3\dot{X}_n + 2\dot{X}_{n-1} + \dot{X}_{n-2})$	$X_n = X_{n-1} + \frac{\lambda T}{2}$ $(3\dot{X}_{n-1} - \dot{X}_{n-2})$
Second-order hold	$X_n = X_{n-1} + \frac{\lambda T}{12}$ $(6\dot{X}_n + 13\dot{X}_{n-1} - 12\dot{X}_{n-2} + 5\dot{X}_{n-3})$ or $X_n = X_{n-1} + \frac{\lambda T}{24}$ $(12\dot{X}_n + 25\dot{X}_{n-1} - 25\dot{X}_{n-1} + 12\dot{X}_{n-3})$	$X_n = X_{n-1} + \frac{\lambda T}{12}$ $(23\dot{X}_{n-1} - 16\dot{X}_{n-2} + 5\dot{X}_{n-3})$
Triangular hold	$X_n = X_{n-1} + \frac{\lambda T}{4}$ $(\dot{X}_n + 2\dot{X}_{n-1} + \dot{X}_{n-2})$	$X_n = X_{n-1} + \frac{\lambda T}{2}(\dot{X}_{n-1} + \dot{X}_{n-2})$

2. For discretely compensated integrators, the γ for minimum variance is $\frac{1}{2}$ and is independent of the reconstruction process.

3. Variance propagation sensitivity to phase shift increases as the order of the reconstruction process increases.

4. The minimum variance increases as the order of the reconstruction process increases.

7.10 SPECTRAL CHARACTERISTICS

While variance propagation analysis provides insight into accuracy and error sensitivity on an amplitude basis, no phase information can be inferred from the integration of a random process. Frequency response analysis gives both the phase and amplitude characteristics of these integrators. The spectral characteristics of these integrators provide insight into their practical application.

An approach to determining the frequency response of these integrators is, first, to develop the Z-domain transfer function for the integrator difference equation; second, transform from the Z plane to the W plane using the algebraic transformation

$$Z = \frac{1 + W}{1 - W} \tag{7-39}$$

and then to transform from the W domain to the frequency domain through the intermediate algebraic and trigonometric transformations

$$W = jv \tag{7-40}$$

and

$$v = \tan\left(\frac{\omega T}{2} \right) \tag{7-41}$$

This procedure leads to amplitude and phase information over the closed interval $(\omega \leqslant \omega_s/2)$, where ω_s is the sampling frequency. Following this procedure, the amplitude spectra and phase shift associated with the zero-order-hold integrator are developed as follows. The transfer function for the zero-order-hold integrator is

$$\frac{X}{\lambda T \dot{X}} (z) = \frac{\gamma z + (1 - \gamma)}{z - 1} \tag{7-42}$$

Substituting

$$z = \frac{1 + W}{1 - W} \tag{7-43}$$

we find

$$\frac{X}{\lambda T \dot{X}}(W) = \frac{1 + (2\gamma - 1)W}{2W} \tag{7-44}$$

Substituting

$$W = j \tan\left(\frac{\omega T}{2}\right) \tag{7-45}$$

we find

$$\frac{X}{\lambda T \dot{X}}(\omega) = \frac{(2\gamma - 1)\tan(\pi\omega/\omega_s) - j}{\tan(\pi\omega/\omega_s)} \tag{7-46}$$

From which we can write

$$\left(\frac{X}{\lambda T \dot{X}}\right)^2 = \frac{\left\{(\gamma - \frac{1}{2})2 \tan(\pi\omega/\omega_s)\right\}^2 - 1}{\left\{2 \tan(\pi\omega/\omega_s)\right\}^2} \tag{7-47}$$

and

$$\phi = \tan^{-1}\left\{(\gamma - \tfrac{1}{2})2 \tan(\pi\omega/\omega_s)\right\} - 90° \tag{7-48}$$

It is apparent that the spectral characteristic for this integrator is greatly different than that for continuous integration where

$$\left(\frac{X}{\dot{X}}\right)^2 = \frac{1}{\omega^2}, \quad \text{and} \quad \phi = -90° \tag{7-49}$$

Note that a good approximation to continuous integration is achieved when $\gamma = \frac{1}{2}$, $\lambda = 1$. Then

$$\lim_{\omega \to 0}\left(\frac{X}{\lambda T \dot{X}}\right)^2 = \lim_{\omega \to 0}\left\{4 \tan^2(\pi\omega/\omega_s)\right\}^{-1} \cong \frac{1}{T^2\omega^2} \tag{7-50}$$

$$\lim_{\omega \to 0}(\phi) = -90° \tag{7-51}$$

Also notice that the amplitude spectrum is symmetrical about $\gamma = \frac{1}{2}$ (7-47), while phase shift is antisymmetrical (7-48). Furthermore, $(A(\omega))^2$ depends on both γ and λ, while phase depends only on γ. This difference between phase and amplitude frequency response suggests an empirical procedure for selecting γ and λ when T integration is used in complex nonlinear closed-loop systems:

1. First select γ to eliminate phase errors.
2. Then select λ to minimize amplitude errors.

Equation 7-48 shows that when $\gamma = \frac{1}{2}$, this integrator (used in its implicit form) will only have amplitude spectrum distortion and the gain parameter λ can be selected to minimize this distortion. Thus if the amplitude spectrum of the process being simulated is known, the variance between the amplitude spectrum of the continuous process and that of its discrete approximation can be minimized as a function of λ. The λ and γ can also be selected empirically or analytically as discussed in Section 7-3. Finally, it is generally true that since λ "scales" the integrator output, it can affect the steady-state solution of a system of equations if the steady-state integrator input is not zero. In these situations, λ must always be made equal to 1.

The spectral analysis of the higher-order integrators can be developed in a similar manner.* It is found that

1. All these integrators approach continuous integration as $\omega \to 0$ and $\lambda = 1$.
2. For the discretely compensated integrators, the phase shift depends only on γ, while $(A(\omega))^2$ depends on both λ and γ.
3. Phase errors are the major source of inaccuracy when the integration step size is large compared with the natural period of the system of equations being integrated.
4. Amplitude errors are the major source of inaccuracy when the integration step size is small compared to the natural period of the system of equations being integrated.

7.11   STABILITY CHARACTERISTICS

There are two viewpoints to consider when examining the stability of a numerical integrator; the intrinsic stability of the integrator itself and the

*Marc L. Sabin, "Bode Magnitude and Phase-Angle Characteristics of the Tunable Integrators," Vol. 6, Part 1, *Proceedings of the Sixth Annual Pittsburgh Modeling and Simulation Conference*, April 24–25, 1975.

influence the integrator has on the stability of the process being controlled or simulated.

The intrinsic stability of an integrator, from a control and simulation viewpoint, is characterized by its stability both as an integrator and a differentiator. The root of the zero-order tunable integrator is $+1$ and, as such, is neutrally stable. As a differentiator, however, the magnitude of the z pole is given by the expression

$$|Z_{pole}| = \left| \frac{\gamma - 1}{\gamma} \right| \tag{7-52}$$

which is less than or equal to 1 for all $\gamma \geq \frac{1}{2}$. We conclude that the first-order integrator is stable for all $\gamma \geq \frac{1}{2}$. Furthermore, it is found that as γ increases beyond $\frac{1}{2}$, more accurate integration is achieved up to a critical value of γ beyond which the integrator's accuracy is degraded. Note that trapezoidal integration ($\gamma = \frac{1}{2}$) is neutrally stable both as an integrator and a differentiator.

The two roots of the triangular and first-order discretely compensated integrators are found to be 0 and $+1$ and, like the zero-order integrator, are stable integrators. The magnitudes of the poles of these integrators, when used as differentiators, are

$$|Z_{pole}| = \left| -\frac{1}{2\gamma} \pm \frac{1}{2\gamma} \{1 - 4\gamma(1 - \gamma)\}^{1/2} \right| \tag{7-53}$$

and

$$|Z_{pole}| = \left| \frac{(4\gamma - 3)}{6\gamma} \pm \frac{(4\gamma - 3)}{6\gamma} \{(3 - 4\gamma)^2 - 12\gamma(\gamma - 1)\}^{1/2} \right| \tag{7-54}$$

respectively. They are both less than or equal to 1 for all $\gamma \geq \frac{1}{2}$. The same result is also found to be true for the second-order discretely compensated integrator. It is concluded, then, that while the compensated integrator may be stable for all γ, only $\gamma \geq \frac{1}{2}$ assures the user that the integrator is an intrinsically stable element in the computing process.

The usual procedure for examining an integrator's impact on the numerical stability of a system of equations being integrated is to substitute the integrator (either explicitly or implicitly) into the differential equations being integrated so as to form a difference equation. This difference equation has as its parameters the coefficients in the differential equation and the integration step size. The stability of the difference equations is examined and stability charts are prepared showing the combinations of differential equation coefficients and integration step sizes where the integration will be numerically stable. The T integrators presented in Tables 7-2 and 7-3 do not require this kind of analysis. These integrators have stability-controlling parameters that can be selected to make the integration process not only stable but also highly accurate. Suffice it to say that when the coefficient in the integration formula includes phase shift and gain parameters as well as integration step size, the integration of a system of equations can be made to be both stable and accurate.

CHAPTER 8

CLASSICAL NUMERICAL INTEGRATION METHODS

This chapter deals with classical numerical integration methods. The numerical integration method presented in Chapter 7 is relatively new. It is a flexible and powerful integration method. Little work has been done in comparing it with classical methods because of the difficulty of equating a method such as T integration (which has flexibility designed into it) with classical methods that are not tuned to the problem they are solving. The classical methods are included for completeness and because a number of them are widely accepted for solving difference equations and for digital simulation.

The derivation of these methods is not presented here and can be found in such excellent books as Hamming's *Numerical Methods for Scientists and Engineers.*

As mentioned in Chapter 7 there are many numerical integration methods. Those that can be adapted to simulation are presented here. The criterion for selecting an integration algorithm usually involves consideration of accuracy, speed, stability, and simplicity. Useful nth-order numerical integrators can introduce as much as $n/2$ periods of lag, which is undesirable from the stability viewpoint. This is particularly true if the simulation is large (many equations), is real time, and involves man-in-the-loop training. Such simulations are often characterized by cycle times (integration step sizes) of 0.05 to 0.1 second. For example, a fourth-order integration formula that involves estimating the rate based on the last four sample periods can introduce as much as two sample periods of lag, or between 0.1 and 0.2 second, in closing feedback loops. The simulation of a closed-loop system with a 1-hertz natural frequency and with this much delay can result in a phase shift of 16 to 32 degrees. From the standpoint of either manual or simulated automatic control, this is not only undesirable but unacceptable. Most control systems operate with a phase shift of less than 3 degrees.

On the other hand, from the trajectory analyst's viewpoint, trajectory errors for classical integrators are usually of the order

$$\sim T^{n+1}\left(\frac{d^{n+1}f}{dt^{n+1}}\right)$$

where n is the order of the integration formula. For small T, classical integration error analysis indicates that higher-order integrators are desirable for precision integration. The questions one must answer when considering the use of classical numerical integrators include the following:

1. Which methods are more useful for quadrature (definite integration) and which are more useful for indefinite integration of differential equations?

2. Which methods are applicable to real-time simulation?

3. Which methods are applicable to nonreal-time simulations?

4. What are the stability properties associated with a given numerical integrator (i.e., the intrinsic stability when used in the simulation of a system)?

5. What are the accuracy properties of each method from both the truncation and variance propagation viewpoints?

6. What time delay (integrand averaging lag) can be expected by the use of a particular integrator? This parameter, when multiplied by the highest frequency of interest in the integrand, is a rough measure of the phase shift associated with an integrator and thus is a measure of the degree to which the integration formula will affect closing of feedback loops in closed-loop systems simulation. A rule of thumb is to control closed-loop simulation phase shift to a degree or so. This gives a means for estimating the integration step size that will be required to simulate a continuous process.

We will be basically concerned with two types of integration—the definite and indefinite integrals. The definite integral is given by

$$y(b) = y(a) + \int_a^b f(x)\, dx \tag{8-1}$$

while the indefinite integral is defined by

$$y(x) = y(a) + \int_a^x f(t)\, dt \tag{8-2}$$

Some take the position that the definite integral computes a single number which is the area under the curve of a bounded function and that the indefinite integral performs an antiderivative operation on the integrand, thus generating a sequence of numbers that are values of the antiderivative function. In this book this distinction is unimportant, since the predict-correct concept of numerically integrating differential equations can be considered as generating sequences of alternating direct and indirect integration. In whatever manner the reader elects to conceptualize numerical integration and its subtleties, it is worthwhile to study both concepts. Thus we will study definite integrals from the standpoint of quadrature (computing the area under a curve) and indefinite integrals from the standpoint of integrating differential equations.

The definite integral will be considered first.

8.1   DEFINITE INTEGRATION

Computing the area under an arbitrary curve is usually based on the concept of analytic substitution, that is, substituting a known function whose definite integral is easily evaluated for the (usually known but too difficult to analytically integrate) arbitrary function to be integrated. The integration is actually performed on the substitute function and attributed to the integral of the arbitrary function to the degree that it approximates the latter. In classical mathematics, the substitute functions to be integrated are usually polynomials which are analytically integrated and, insofar as the polynomial approximates the continuous function, the integral is attributed to the integral of the arbitrary function. When the integrand is a polynomial of degree n and the approximating function is also a polynomial of degree n, the formula can be made exact by appropriately selecting the coefficients in the integration formula.

The process of *analytic substitution* or of other means of approximating definite and indefinite integrals is so fascinating that almost all numerical analysts find new ways to rederive many of the classical formulas and a few more besides. While the temptation is great to present the most sophisticated integration methods, the focus here will be on classical developments that are straightforward and easy to apply. The reader should be aware, however, of the tremendous quantity of good numerical integration mathematics developed in the last 20 years as a result of calculations on the digital computer and the use of numerical analysis in solving high-technology problems. Structures, communications systems, control systems, design of aircraft, and the design of chemical plants are a few of the areas where the simulation of systems with very different eigenvalues and the numerical integration of functions that are almost neutrally stable (at large integration step sizes) have produced new integration concepts. Structural dynamicists have developed special numerical integration formulas for integrating their "stiff differential equations." Controls analysts have produced such formulas based solely on frequency-domain considerations. And special single-step real-time numerical integration formulas have been developed by simulation scientists.

While problems such as these may be encountered, the focus will be on classical formulas that have fairly general and broad applications to the more analytically tractable functions. Furthermore, a vast body of literature on these classical methods is available for further reference.

Trapezoidal Integration

If we approximate the function $f(x)$ on a bounded interval $a \leqslant x \leqslant b$ by a line through the end points, we can write the equation for the approximating function over the interval as

$$y(x) = f(a) + \left[\frac{f(b) - f(a)}{b - a} \right](x - a)$$

$$y(x) = \frac{(b - x)f(a) + (x - a)f(b)}{b - a} \tag{8-3}$$

Integrating (8-3) we find

$$\int_a^b y(x)\, dx = \left(\frac{f(b) + f(a)}{2} \right)(b - a) \tag{8-4}$$

Equation 8-4 computes the area under the straight-line interpolation between the two end points. This is called trapezoidal integration because the area is enclosed by a trapezoid formed by lines connecting the end points, the abscissa, and the lines connecting the end points to the abscissa. If the interval is large, the trapezoidal approximation can lead to large numerical integration error. The resolution of this error is the repeated application of the trapezoidal rule on smaller intervals of the dependent variable. When this is done for equally spaced intervals, Δx, trapezoidal integration takes the form

$$\int_a^b f(x)\, dx = \Delta x \left(\frac{f(a)}{2} + f(a + \Delta x) + f(a + 2\Delta x) + \cdots + \frac{f(b)}{2} \right) \tag{8-5}$$

While trapezoidal integration is not the simplest to derive or compute (Euler, modified Euler, and rectangular integration are simpler concepts), and its error formula does not give the least error for the fewest computations, it is straightforward to apply, is useful for example analysis, and is easily remembered. As we move to integration formulas involving mid-values and their derivatives and integration that estimates a roundoff and truncation error, or integration formulas that adjust phase shift and amplitude, simple visualization of the integration process is difficult and we rely more and more on abstract rationale for its development to assure that the numerical integration formula is applicable to the problem. Ultimately, analytical integration is compared with the approximate numerical integration to evaluate the difference between several methods of integration for a particular problem. Clearly, this is an overkill for back-of-the-envelope engineering analysis intended simply to compute the area under the curve of a discrete function. If trapezoidal integration is sufficiently accurate and the number of intervals needed to obtain the desired accuracy is not prohibitive, it can be very useful.

8.2   ERROR IN TRAPEZOIDAL INTEGRATION

We do not propose here to explore the derivation of integration formulas or error formulas, but rather to tabulate those commonly used, and to put them in a form that is useful for simulation. It is instructive, however, to examine the error of a simple integration formula as a means for understanding the error equations given for the more sophisticated integration formulas. Following Hamming, we examine the truncation error in the trapezoidal integration algorithm by substituting a Taylor series expansion into the integration formula. By comparing both sides of the results we can then determine the error associated with the analytic substitution process in the numerical integration. Specifically, if we write the integrand in its Taylor series expanded form as

$$f(x) = f(a) + (x - a)f'(a) + \frac{(x - a)^2}{2!} f''(a) + \cdots \qquad (8\text{-}6)$$

and substitute this into both sides of the trapezoidal integration formula, we find that the left side becomes

$$\frac{(b - a)}{1!} f(a) + \frac{(b - a)^2}{2!} f'(a) + \frac{(b - a)^3}{3!} f''(a) + \cdots \qquad (8\text{-}7)$$

while the right side becomes

$$\frac{\Delta x}{2}\left[f(a) + (b - a)f'(a) + \frac{(b - a)^2}{2} f''(a) + \cdots + f(b) \right] + \epsilon \quad (8\text{-}8)$$

where $\Delta x = (b - a)$. After canceling like terms on both sides of the equation, we can derive the truncation error formula:

$$\epsilon + \frac{(b - a)^3}{4} f''(a) + \cdots = \frac{(b - a)^3}{3!} f''(a) \quad (8\text{-}9)$$

$$\epsilon = \left(\frac{1}{3!} - \frac{1}{4} \right)(b - a)^3 f''(a) - \frac{(b - a)^4}{5} f'''(a) - \cdots \quad (8\text{-}10)$$

If we assume that the largest part of the error term is given by the first term in its series expansion,* we can write

$$\epsilon \approx - \frac{(b - a)^3 f''(a)}{12} \quad (8\text{-}11)$$

or more generally

$$\epsilon \approx - \frac{(b - a)^3 f''(\theta)}{12} , \quad \text{for} \quad a \leqslant \theta \leqslant b \quad (8\text{-}12)$$

If the function under consideration and/or the integration interval being used has contributions to the error formula that are large in the higher-order terms, this error formula of course does not apply. It will apply, however, to many practical engineering problems and thus (8-12) is gener-ally quoted as the error associated with trapezoidal integration.

The specific error formula for trapezoidal integration is not as important here as is the method by which it is derived. In this particular example we used the Taylor series expansion for the integrand in order to derive an error term related to the effect of Taylor series truncation. An alternative would be to use a Fourier series representation of the function to de-termine the truncation in the frequency domain. Another approximating polynomial could be the Chebyshev polynomial approximation of $f(x)$ which gives another type of truncated polynomial approximation error formula. While the interpretation of the results of each error formula is

---

* This is not a proper assumption for efficient, fast-running integration formulas such as T integration, because the object is to make the interval $(b - a)$ as large as possible.

different, the magnitude of the error is not; the error is a characteristic of the integration formula, not the approximating polynomial used in the error formula evaluation.

Figure 8-1 shows that, for concave-up functions, trapezoidal integration will always be slightly more than the integration it is trying to approximate, while for concave-down functions it will be slightly less. It seems reasonable to expect that, when integrating "wavy" functions, the intervals should be set up so that at a minimum the eyeball approximation of the errors on one interval may have a chance to cancel the errors on the other interval. The error formula for simple trapezoidal integration can be extended to the composite formula by similar reasoning, and the error formula is

$$\epsilon \approx - \frac{(b-a)\Delta x^2}{12} f''(\theta), \qquad \text{for} \quad a \leqslant \theta \leqslant b \qquad (8\text{-}13)$$

One approach to a meaningful evaluation of error formulas such as (8-12) and (8-13) is to determine the second derivative of the function under consideration, compute numerically the sum of the minimum and maximum errors, and divide by 2 to obtain the average error of the integration over the interval. Another approach is to take the worst-case error. A great number of other alternatives also exist. What is the criterion

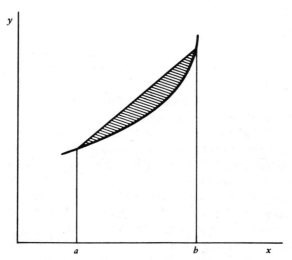

FIGURE 8-1. Truncation error in trapezoidal integration. Source: J. M. Smith, *Scientific Analysis on the Pocket Calculator*, Wiley, 1975. Used by permission of the publisher.

for numerically evaluating the error? Unfortunately there is no easy answer. From an engineering viewpoint, the error defined by (8-9) has more meaning than those most often presented in numerical analysis books. The process of deriving the error formula is the more fundamental issue in that the engineer or scientist can compute his own error formula when considering his specific problem.

The student or first-time numerical analyst is cautioned to be wary of error formulas in general and to be prepared to derive his or her own for a particular problem. An estimate of the error in a numerical approximation over an analytical calculation must be made, but its interpretation is not straightforward and the result cannot be casually given from questionable error equations. Error analysis is an art in itself.

8.3 MIDPOINT INTEGRATION

Midpoint integration uses the midvalue of an interval and the derivative of the integrand evaluated at the midvalue to define the slope at the midpoint of the interval to form a trapezoid whose area under the curve approximates the area under the curve of the integrand.

The Hamming midpoint integration formula is particularly straightforward and is a convenient introduction to a general approach to deriving polynomial approximations for analytic substitution. We are to derive an integration formula of the form

$$\int_a^b f(x)\, dx = w_1 f\left(\frac{a+b}{2}\right) + w_2 f'\left(\frac{a+b}{2}\right) \tag{8-14}$$

Hamming's weighting coefficients can be easily derived by first requiring that this formula be exact for $f(x) = 1$. This gives

$$b - a = w_1 \tag{8-15}$$

We also require that this formula be exact for $f(x) = x$, which leads to

$$\frac{b^2 - a^2}{2} = w_1\left(\frac{a+b}{2}\right) + w_2 \tag{8-16}$$

We can determine the two Hamming coefficients by solving these equations simultaneously, and we get

$$w_2 = \left(\frac{b^2 - a^2}{2}\right) - \frac{(b-a)(a+b)}{2} = \left(\frac{b^2 - a^2}{2}\right) - \left(\frac{b^2 - a^2}{2}\right) = 0$$

$$w_1 = b - a \tag{8-17}$$

We therefore find the midvalue integration formula to be

$$\int_a^b f(x)dx = (b - a)f\left(\frac{a + b}{2}\right)$$ (8-18)

Midpoint integration developed in this manner results in rectangular integration. That is, the area formed by the rectangle sampled at the midvalue is identically equal to the area under the tangent line at the midvalue of the interval. At first, it might seem paradoxical that rectangular integration might be as good as trapezoidal integration, that is, that formulas based on a single point of f could be as accurate as a two-point trapezoidal formula. In fact, rectangular integration can be made as precise as desired if the sample point on a bounded interval can be varied until the mean value theorem of calculus is satisfied (see Appendix C). *Once again,* rectangular integration can be made as precise as the true integral provided the point at which the function is sampled on the interval can be determined, so that the rectangle formed by the sampled value and the lines connecting the end points of the function to the interval and the abscissa itself have the same area as that under the function bounded on the interval. This fact is reflected in (8-18).

Again, to find the truncation error term, we can use the Taylor series

$$f(x) = f(a) + \frac{(x - a)}{1!} f'(a) + \frac{(x - a)^2}{2!} f''(a) + \cdots$$ (8-19)

where, upon substituting in both sides of (8-18), we find

$$\epsilon + \frac{(b - a)^3}{8} f''(a) + \cdots = \frac{(b - a)^3}{6} f''(a)$$ (8-20)

which is simplified to the form

$$\epsilon \approx \frac{(b - a)^3 f''(a)}{20}$$ (8-21)

More generally, for $a < \theta < b$

$$\epsilon \approx \frac{(b - a)^3 f''(\theta)}{20}$$

Comparing (8-21) and (8-12) we see that midpoint rectangular integration is more accurate than trapezoidal integration even though the rectangular integration is based on knowing the function at only one point while the trapezoidal rule requires knowledge of the function at two points.

Extending the midpoint integration formula, we find the composite midpoint integration formula to be

$$\int_a^b f(x)\, dx = \Delta x\left[f\left(a + \frac{\Delta x}{2}\right) + f\left(a + \frac{3\Delta x}{2}\right) + f\left(a + \frac{5\Delta x}{2}\right)\right.$$
$$\left. + \cdots + f\left(b - \frac{n\Delta x}{2}\right)\right] + \epsilon$$

where its error formula is given by

$$\epsilon \approx \frac{(b-a)\Delta x^2}{24} f''(\theta), \qquad \text{for} \quad a \leqslant \theta \leqslant b \qquad (8\text{-}22)$$

Note also that extended trapezoidal integration can be modified to include end points outside the interval $[a, b]$. The modified trapezoidal rule is given by the formula

$$\int_a^b f(x)\, dx = \Delta x\left[\frac{f(a)}{2} + f(a + \Delta x) + f(a + 2\Delta x) + \cdots + \frac{f(b)}{2}\right]$$
$$+ \frac{\Delta x}{24}\left[-f(a - \Delta x) + f(a + \Delta x) + f(b - \Delta x) - f(b + \Delta x)\right]$$
$$(8\text{-}23)$$

where the error associated with modified trapezoidal integration is given by

$$\epsilon = \frac{11(b-a)\Delta x^4}{720} f''''(\theta), \qquad \text{for} \quad (a + \Delta x) \leqslant \theta \leqslant (b + \Delta x) \quad (8\text{-}24)$$

Other Popular Definite Integration Formulas

Simpson's rule, perhaps the most commonly used integration formula, is given by

$$\int_0^{2\Delta x} f(x)\, dx = \frac{\Delta x}{3}(f_0 + 4f_1 + f_2) \qquad (8\text{-}25)$$

Its associated error formula is given by

$$\epsilon = -\frac{\Delta x^5}{90} f''''(\theta), \qquad \text{for} \quad 0 \leqslant \theta \leqslant 2\Delta x$$

Simpson's rule has the nice property that it will exactly integrate cubics even though it samples only three points of the integrand and in addition has very small error terms when Δx is less than $\frac{1}{2}$.

Simpson's rule can also be extended (on an even number of intervals) according to the formula

$$\int_{x_0}^{x_{2n}} f(x)\, dx = \frac{\Delta x}{3}\,(f_0 + 4f_1 + 2f_2 + 4f_3 + 2f_4 + \cdots + f_{2n}) \quad (8\text{-}26)$$

and it has an error formula given by

$$\epsilon = \frac{n\Delta x^5}{90}\, f''''(\theta), \qquad \text{for} \quad x_0 \leqslant \theta \leqslant (x_0 + 2n\,\Delta x) \quad (8\text{-}27)$$

Perhaps the simplest extended integration formula is the Euler-Maclaurin formula:

$$\int_{x_0}^{x_n} f(x)\, dx = \Delta x\left(\frac{f_0}{2} + f_1 + f_2 + f_3 + \cdots + \frac{f_n}{2} \right)$$

$$- \left(\frac{B_2\,\Delta x^2}{2!} \right)(f_n' - f_0') - \cdots$$

$$- \left(\frac{B_{2k}\,\Delta x^{2k}}{(2k)!} \right)(f_n^{(2k-1)} - f_0^{(2k-1)}) + \epsilon_{2k} \quad (8\text{-}28)$$

It has the error formula

$$\epsilon_{2k} = \left\{ \frac{\theta_n B_{2k+2}\,\Delta x^{(2k+3)}}{(2k+2)!} \right\}\left\{ \max_{x_0 < x < x_n} |f(x)^{2k+2}| \right\}, \qquad \text{for} \quad -1 \leqslant \theta \leqslant 1$$

$$(8\text{-}29)$$

Here B_{2k} is a Bernoulli number.

The three-eighths rule for definite integration is given by the formula

$$\int_{x_0}^{x_3} f(x)\, dx = \frac{3\Delta x}{8}\,(f_0 + 3f_1 + 3f_2 + f_3) \quad (8\text{-}30)$$

Its associated error formula is

$$\epsilon = - \frac{3\Delta x^5}{80}\, f''''(\theta), \qquad \text{for} \quad x_0 \leqslant \theta \leqslant x_3 \quad (8\text{-}31)$$

Table 8-1. Bode's Definite Integration Formulas for Integrating Functions Whose End Points Are Known

Integration Formulas	Error Formulas
$\int_{x_0}^{x_4} f(x)\,dx = \dfrac{2\Delta x}{45}(7f_0 + 32f_1 + 12f_2 + 32f_3 + 7f_4)$	$-\dfrac{8\Delta x^7 f^{VI}(\theta)}{945}$
$\int_{x_0}^{x_5} f(x)\,dx = \dfrac{5\Delta x}{288}(19f_0 + 75f_1 + 50f_2 + 50f_3 + 75f_4 + 19f_5)$	$-\dfrac{275\Delta x^7 f^{VI}(\theta)}{12096}$
$\int_{x_0}^{x_6} f(x)\,dx = \dfrac{\Delta x}{140}(41f_0 + 216f_1 + 27f_2 + 272f_3 + 27f_4 + 216f_5 + 41f_6)$	$-\dfrac{9\Delta x^9 f^{VIII}(\theta)}{1400}$
$\int_{x_0}^{x_7} f(x)\,dx = \dfrac{7\Delta x}{17280}(751f_0 + 3577f_1 + 1323f_2 + 2989f_3 + 2989f_4$ $\qquad + 1323f_5 + 3577f_6 + 751f_7)$	$-\dfrac{8183\,\Delta x^9 f^{VIII}(\theta)}{518400}$
$\int_{x_0}^{x_8} f(x)\,dx = \dfrac{4\Delta x}{14175}(989f_0 + 5888f_1 - 928f_2 + 10496f_3 - 4540f_4$ $\qquad + 10496f_5 - 928f_6 + 5888f_7 + 989f_8)$	$-\dfrac{2368\,\Delta x^{11} f^{X}(\theta)}{467775}$

Table 8-2. Newton-Cotes Definite Integration Formulas for Integrating Functions Whose End Points Are Undefined or Unknown or Are Singular Points

Integration Formulas	Error Formulas
$\int_{x_0}^{x_3} f(x)\,dx = \dfrac{3\Delta x}{2}(f_1 + f_2)$	$\dfrac{\Delta x^3}{4} f^{II}(\theta)$
$\int_{x_0}^{x_4} f(x)\,dx = \dfrac{4\Delta x}{3}(2f_1 - f_2 + 2f_3)$	$\dfrac{14\Delta x^5}{45} f^{IV}(\theta)$
$\int_{x_0}^{x_5} f(x)\,dx = \dfrac{5\Delta x}{24}(11f_1 + f_2 + f_3 + 11f_4)$	$\dfrac{95\Delta x^5}{144} f^{IV}(\theta)$
$\int_{x_0}^{x_6} f(x)\,dx = \dfrac{6\Delta x}{20}(11f_1 - 14f_2 + 26f_3$ $\qquad - 14f_4 + 11f_5)$	$\dfrac{41\Delta x^7}{140} f^{VI}(\theta)$
$\int_{x_0}^{x_7} f(x)\,dx = \dfrac{7\Delta x}{1440}(611f_1 - 453f_2 + 562f_3$ $\qquad + 562f_4 - 453f_5 + 611f_6)$	$\dfrac{5257\,\Delta x^7}{8640} f^{VI}(\theta)$
$\int_{x_0}^{x_8} f(x)\,dx = \dfrac{8\Delta x}{945}(460f_1 - 954f_2 + 2196f - 2459f_4$ $\qquad + 2196f_5 - 954f_6 + 460f_7)$	$\dfrac{3956\,\Delta x^9}{14175} f^{VIII}(\theta)$

Two types of formulas are used for quadrature when many sample points of the integrand are known. They are Bode's definite integral formulas and the Newton-Cotes formulas of the open type. Bode's rules for quadrature are shown in Table 8-1, and the Newton-Cotes formulas are tabulated in Table 8-2.

The high-order formulas, such as the Newton-Cotes formulas and Bode's formulas, can have some very undesirable properties for large n. For some analytic and discrete functions, the sequence of the integrals of the interpolating polynomials does not converge toward the integral of the function. Additionally, the coefficients in these integration formulas are large and of alternating sign which undesirably propagates roundoff error. It is primarily for these reasons that the Newton-Cotes formulas are rarely used for high values of n. For lower values of n they can be simplified to some of the other well-known formulas, such as the previously discussed trapezoidal formula and Simpson's rule. Although Bode's rule gets around the alternating signs associated with the Newton-Cotes formulas, it too has convergence problems for certain occasionally encountered functions. Suffice it to say that extended trapezoidal integration with end effect modification provides reasonable accuracy, does not propagate roundoff error, and is consistent with an acceptable amount of work associated with computing the integral of any function. It is recommended for engineering analysis where small absolute error is not required.

8.4 ELEMENTARY CONCEPTS IN INDEFINITE NUMERICAL INTEGRATION

Indefinite numerical integration is the numerical method used to solve differential equations. For example: If we are given the equation

$$\frac{dy}{dx} = f(x, y) \tag{8-32}$$

we would usually solve this equation by indefinite integration as

$$y = y_0 + \int_{x_0}^{x} f(t, y)\, dt \tag{8-33}$$

It is apparent from (8-33) that the solution of the differential equation depends on itself to evaluate the integral. This is the chief problem in indefinite integration, that is, indefinite integrals are in an implicit form.

Note that an explicit indefinite integral takes the form

$$y = y_0 \int_{x_0}^{x} f(t)\, dt \tag{8-34}$$

which is a special case of the differential equation

$$\frac{dy}{dx} = f(x) \tag{8-35}$$

Clearly, this type of numerical integration can be performed analytically and is of no concern here.

The simplest indefinite numerical integration algorithm is Euler's integration formula

$$y_{n+1} = y_n + \Delta x \left(\frac{dy}{dx} \right)_n \qquad (8\text{-}36)$$

Here we see that a new estimate (y_{n+1}) of y is based on the old estimate (y_n) and its derivative $(dy/dx)_n$, which is usually calculated directly from the differential equation once the estimate of y is made. Since the new estimate of y is based on the old estimate of y' and the old value of y, it is an "open-loop" process—the new value of y is based on an extrapolation of previously known data and thus is subject to extrapolation errors. The process of determining new values of y is really a simple extension of determining the *direction field* associated with a solution of a differential equation. In general, the approach is to start at some initial condition (that is, x_0, y_0), and calculate the slope using the differential equation giving

$$y'_0 = f(x_0, y_0)$$

We then move an interval h in the direction of the slope to a second point, which we now regard as the new initial point, and repeat the process iteratively. If small enough steps are taken we can reasonably hope that the sequence of solution values given by this procedure will lie close to the solution of the differential equation. In general, all of the elements of solving differential equations using indefinite numerical integration are here. A table of the values of x, y, y', and Δy must be computed at each step in the numerical integration process. Also, the problem must be defined by specifying not only the differential equation and its initial conditions, but also the interval over which it is desired to solve the equation. It is then possible to select a convenient integration interval and an integration formula that is accurate for that interval. For example,

$$\frac{dy}{dx} = e^{-y} - x^2$$

with initial conditions $y = 0$, $x = 0$. When integrated with Euler's integration formula

$$y_n - y_{n-1} + (\Delta x) y'_{n-1}$$

requires a specification of the interval Δx. The simplest approach is to

Table 8-3. Solution of $dy/dx = e^{-y} - x^2$

	Exact Solution	Euler Integrated Solution			
x	y	$\Delta x = 0.05$	$\Delta x = 0.10$	$\Delta x = 0.2$	$\Delta x = 0.3$
0.0	0.0				
0.1	0.09498	0.09694	0.09900	—	—
0.2	0.17977	0.18261	0.18557	0.19200	—
0.3	0.25389	0.25672	0.25964	—	0.27300
0.4	0.31667	0.31872	0.32077	0.32506	—
0.5	0.36731	0.36786	0.36833	—	—
0.6	0.40488	0.40329	0.40152	0.39756	0.39333
0.7	0.42839	0.42407	0.41942	—	—
0.8	0.43686	0.42923	0.42119	0.40395	—
0.9	0.42929	0.41782	0.40582	—	0.35277
1.0	0.40477	0.38895	0.37264	0.33749	—

experimentally determine the Δx that will accurately (as judged by the analyst) integrate the differential equation. Consider solutions of this differential equation with $x = 0.05$, 0.1, 0.2, and 0.3. The results are tabulated in Table 8-3. A comparison of the numerically integrated solutions with the exact solution shows that the sensitivity of the solution's accuracy depends strongly on the integration step size. This is true, in general, for all numerical integrators when the integration step size is even a reasonable fraction of the "response time"* of the differential equation.

A disadvantage of the Euler method is that it introduces systematic phase-shift or lag (extrapolation) errors at each step. The procedure can be modified (modified Euler integration) to give better results, that is, greater accuracy for essentially the same method and the same amount of work or the same accuracy but with less work.

8.5 THE MODIFIED EULER INDEFINITE INTEGRATION METHOD

An alternative to introducing lag into the calculation is to arrange the sampling so that the integrand is sampled not at the end point of the interval over which the integration is taking place but at the midpoint. This

---

* Approximately the time required for the transition from one equilibrium condition to another— only strictly applicable to differential equations whose independent variable is time; however, the concept is applicable more generally.

is similar to the development of the midpoint trapezoidal formula developed in Section 8.3. The task is to perform the integral

$$\int_{x_{n-1}}^{x_{n+1}} y'(x)\, dx \tag{8-37}$$

using the midpoint formula (see Section 8.3). We wish to predict the next value of y based on present and past values of the independent variable. The midvalue prediction leads to

$$p_{n+1} = y_{n-1} + 2(\Delta x) y_n' \tag{8-38}$$

Using this predicted value we can now compute the slope at the predicted solution point by way of the differential equation

$$p_{n+1}' = f(x_{n+1}, p_{n+1}) \tag{8-39}$$

and then apply the trapezoidal rule developed previously to update the estimate of the predicted solution point:

$$y_{n+1} = y_n + \frac{h}{2}(p_{n+1}' + y_n') \tag{8-40}$$

The correction is called the corrected value of y_{n+1}. It is apparent that we are using the average of the slopes at the two end points of the interval of integration as the average slope in the interval.

In summary, this method has three steps:

Step 1.   Predict the value of y_{n+1} given the formula

$$p_{n+1} = y_{n-1} + 2(\Delta x) y_n' \tag{8-41}$$

Step 2.   Compute the derivative at the predicted value, using the differential equation that describes the system:

$$p_{n+1}' = f(x_{n+1}, p_{n+1}) \tag{8-42}$$

Step 3.   Make a second estimate of the value of y_{n+1}, using trapezoidal integration

$$y_{n+1} = y_n + \frac{\Delta x}{2}(y_n' + y_{n+1}') \tag{8-43}$$

This process of prediction and correction has led to the naming of this type of integration as the predict-correct concept of numerical integration. A number of predict-correct algorithms are tabulated at the end of this chapter; they can be used for indefinite integration of differential equations.

8.6 STARTING VALUES

In our previous analysis we assumed that we had values for the dependent and independent variables at the starting or initial point. However, the algorithm requires not only starting values, but also earlier values. The previous values can be obtained in two ways. They can be computed on the computer or they can be analytically hand calculated. Both methods are presented here.

The hand calculation method is based on the use of the Taylor series expansion of the function

$$y(x + \Delta x) = y(x) + \Delta x y'(x) + \frac{\Delta x^2}{2} y''(x) + \cdots \qquad (8\text{-}44)$$

The derivatives to be evaluated in the Taylor series expansion can be found from the differential equation by repeated differentiation. The number of terms depends on the step size and the accuracy desired. These are all matters that can be easily evaluated, and the number of terms required can be empirically determined by continuing to take them until the desired accuracy is achieved.

The method for machine calculation is based on repeated use of the corrector formula. If we are given the initial point (x_0, y_0), we can estimate the earlier point (x_{-1}, y_{-1}) by way of the unmodified Euler integration and working backward as follows:

$$x_{-1} = x_0 - \Delta x$$

$$y_{-1} = y_0 - \Delta x y'_0 \qquad \text{(first estimate of } y_{-1}) \qquad (8\text{-}45)$$

We can use the estimate of the previous values of y combined with the differential equation to evaluate the derivative of the previous value of y. The trapezoidal corrector formula can then be repeated to iteratively correct the previous estimate until it achieves the accuracy desired for the calculation. The system of equations for the correction process becomes

$$y'_{-1} = f(x_{-1}, y_{-1}) \qquad \text{(first estimate of } y'_{-1})$$

$$y_{-1} = y_0 - \frac{\Delta x}{2}(y'_0 + y'_{-1}) \qquad \text{(second estimate of } y_{-1}) \quad (8\text{-}46)$$

$$y'_{-1} = f(x_{-1}, y_{-1}) \qquad \text{(second estimate of } y'_{-1})$$

$$\vdots \qquad \vdots$$

If, after a few iterations, the previous value of y does not stabilize, the integration step size can be halved, the previous value of $y_{n-1/2}$ computed, and the process repeated to compute y_{n-1}. An alternative is to use the value of $y_{n-1/2}$ to estimate the value of $y_{n+1/2}$, and repeat the process to take a half step forward to y_{n+1}. These values are then used as the starting values for the predict-correct integration algorithm.

8.7   ERROR ESTIMATES AND MODIFYING THE PREDICT-CORRECT PROCESS

The predictor formula just discussed is a midpoint integration formula that has the error equation

$$\epsilon_p = \frac{\Delta x^3}{3} y^{\text{III}}(\theta) \qquad (8\text{-}47)$$

The corrector formula given in Section 8.2 has the error formula

$$\epsilon_c = -\frac{\Delta x^3}{12} y^{\text{III}}(\theta) \qquad (8\text{-}48)$$

Since these error formulas are of opposite sign, the difference between the predicted value and the corrected value gives

$$y_p - y_c \approx (y_{\text{exact}} - \epsilon_p) - (y_{\text{exact}} - \epsilon_c) \qquad (8\text{-}49)$$

Thus at any given step the difference between the predicted value and the corrected value is

$$-\frac{5}{12} \Delta x^3 y^{\text{III}}(\theta) \qquad (8\text{-}50)$$

Furthermore, we see from (8-49) that approximately four-fifths of the difference results from the predictor component and one-fifth from the corrector component. It is a natural extension of the predict-correct technique, then, to modify the integration process slightly as we proceed. When we predict with the equation

$$p_{n+1} = y_{n-1} + 2\Delta x y_n \qquad (8\text{-}51)$$

we might immediately modify the value of this prediction, using the previous value of the predict-correct difference and the formula

$$m_{n+1} = p_{n+1} \frac{-4}{5}(p_n - c_n) \qquad (8\text{-}52)$$

Then we use the differential equation to compute the modified derivative:

$$m'_{n+1} = f(x_{n+1}, m_{n+1}) \qquad (8\text{-}53)$$

which is then corrected by way of

$$c_{n+1} = y_n + \frac{\Delta x}{2}(m'_{n+1} + y'_n) \qquad (8\text{-}54)$$

leading to the final value of y_{n+1}:

$$y_{n+1} = c_{n+1} + \tfrac{1}{5}(p_{n+1} - c_{n+1}) \qquad (8\text{-}55)$$

Clearly, this procedure of predicting, modifying, correcting, and modifying again is about the extent to which we can go in solving differential equations by hand calculation. More advanced methods become too cumbersome.

8.8 OTHER USEFUL INDEFINITE NUMERICAL INTEGRATION FORMULAS

There are a number of commonly used predict-correct algorithms that are suitable for solution of ordinary differential equations. The two most popular point slope formulas are the Euler predictor and midvalue predictor. They are given by

$$y_{n+1} = y_n + (\Delta x)y'_n, \qquad \text{for} \quad \epsilon \sim \Delta x^2$$

$$y_{n+1} = y_{n-1} + 2(\Delta x)y'_n, \qquad \text{for} \quad \epsilon \sim \Delta x^3$$

and are usually used in conjunction with the trapezoidal corrector formula

$$y_{n+1} = y_n + \frac{\Delta x}{2}(y'_{n+1} + y'_n), \quad \text{for} \quad \epsilon \sim \Delta x^3$$

Another popular and extensively used predict-correct method is the Adams method. The fourth-order Adams' predictor and corrector formulas are given by:

$$y_{n+1} = y_n + \frac{\Delta x}{24}(55y'_n - 59y'_{n-1} + 37y'_{n-2} - 9y'_{n-3}), \quad \text{for} \quad \epsilon \sim \Delta x^5$$

$$y_{n+1} = y_n + \frac{\Delta x}{24}(9y'_{n+1} + 19y'_n - 5y'_{n-1} + y'_{n-2}), \quad \text{for} \quad \epsilon \sim \Delta x^5$$

The numerical stability of these methods and the roundoff error associated with the alternating sign of the coefficients may lead to difficulties.

Runge-Kutta Methods

The Runge-Kutta methods are based on implicitly developing increasingly higher orders of Taylor series expansions of a function through combinations of the derivatives of a function numerically evaluated on certain intervals of the independent variable. Since the Runge-Kutta methods are yet another variant using the Taylor series expansion method and thus are limited in the sense that, if the integrand is not Taylor series expandable or if the integrand is to be evaluated across a discontinuity, the location of the discontinuity must be determined and the solution is computed up to the discontinuity and then restarted at the discontinuity.

The second-order Runge-Kutta method (Heun's method) is given by

$$y_{n+1} = y_n + \tfrac{1}{2}(k_1 + k_2), \quad \text{for} \quad \epsilon \sim \Delta x^3 \qquad (8\text{-}56)$$

where

$$k_1 = \Delta x f(x_n, y_n)$$

$$k_2 = \Delta x f(x_n + \Delta x, y_n + k_1)$$

The Runge-Kutta methods use Euler integration at each step. Thus to evaluate (8-56), it is necessary to compute both k_1 and k_2. To compute k_2, the predicted value of y ($y_n + k_1$) must be evaluated. It is apparent that this is equivalent to Euler's method. Thus the procedure consists of first using Euler's method to compute the first estimate of y_{n+1}, which is then used along with $x_n + \Delta x$ to compute the value of the derivative at $x(n + \Delta x)$ to get k_2. Then (8-56) is formed, using k_1 and k_2.

Another form of second-order Runge-Kutta equation is

$$y_{n+1} = y_n + k_2, \quad \text{for} \quad \epsilon \sim \Delta x^3$$

$$k_1 = \Delta x f(x_n, y_n) \tag{8-57}$$

$$k_2 = \Delta x f\left(x_n + \frac{\Delta x}{2}, y_n + \frac{k_1}{2}\right)$$

In this form, k_1 is employed to make a half step from x_n to $x_n + \Delta x/2$, where y_n is evaluated as $y_n + k_1/2$. Then the derivative at this midvalue, defined by $x_n + \Delta x/2$ is computed and used to estimate the midvalue rate from which k_2 is calculated. Then (8-57) is numerically evaluated using only k_2. Again, Euler integration must be used first to make the first half step, and the first full step is taken by means of the midvalue estimates of the rate on the interval.

Another Runge-Kutta method is also given in two forms. One is

$$y_{n+1} = y_n + \frac{k_1}{6} + \frac{4k_2}{6} + \frac{k_3}{6}, \quad \text{for} \quad \epsilon \sim \Delta x^4$$

$$k_1 = \Delta x f(x_n, y_n)$$

$$k_2 = \Delta x f\left(x + \frac{\Delta x}{2}, y_n + \frac{k_1}{2}\right)$$

$$k_3 = \Delta x f(x_n + \Delta x, y_n + 2k_2 - k_1)$$

This is the most popular and convenient form of third-order Runge-Kutta integration.

Another form of third-order Runge-Kutta is

$$y_{n+1} = y_n + \frac{k_1}{4} + \frac{3}{4}k_3, \quad \text{for} \quad \epsilon \sim \Delta x^4$$

$$k_1 = \Delta x f(x_n, y_n)$$

$$k_2 = \Delta x f\left(x_n + \frac{\Delta x}{3}, y_n + \frac{k_1}{3}\right)$$

$$k_3 = \Delta x f\left(x_n + \frac{2\Delta x}{3}, y_n + \frac{2k_2}{3}\right)$$

The two most popular forms of the Runge-Kutta fourth-order numerical integration are

$$y_{n+1} = y_n + \frac{k_1}{6} + \frac{k_2}{3} + \frac{k_3}{3} + \frac{k_4}{6}, \qquad \text{for} \quad \epsilon \sim \Delta x^5$$

$$k_1 = \Delta x f(x_n, y_n)$$

$$k_2 = \Delta x f\left(x_n + \frac{\Delta x}{2}, y_n + \frac{k_1}{2}\right)$$

$$k_3 = \Delta x f\left(x_n + \frac{\Delta x}{2}, y_n + \frac{k_2}{2}\right)$$

$$k_4 = \Delta x f(x_n + \Delta x, y_n + k_3)$$

and

$$y_{n+1} = y_n + \frac{k_1}{8} + \frac{3k_2}{8} + \frac{3k_3}{8} + \frac{k_4}{8}, \qquad \text{for} \quad \epsilon \sim \Delta x^5$$

$$k_1 = \Delta x f(x_n, y_n)$$

$$k_2 = \Delta x f\left(x_n + \frac{\Delta x}{3}, y_n + \frac{k_1}{3}\right)$$

$$k_3 = \Delta x f\left(x_n + \frac{2\Delta x}{3}, y_n + k_2 - \frac{k_1}{3}\right)$$

$$k_4 = \Delta x f(x_n + \Delta x, y_n + k_3 - k_2 + k_1)$$

The accuracy of this fourth-order integrator is related to the remainder formula, which gives an error term that is proportional to Δx^5. Hamming points to a valid criticism of Runge-Kutta methods — that they throw away all old information and begin each step anew. One would hardly expect this to be an efficient method of integration. However, it is self-starting, and as such seems to be easier to apply in general circumstances.

Finally, all Taylor series expansion methods are based on truncated Taylor series that have well-defined functions:

$$f(t + T) = f(t) + Tf'(t) + \frac{T^2}{2} f''(t) + \frac{T^3}{6} f'''(t) + \cdots$$

$$\mathcal{L}\{f(t + T)\} = \left(1 + Ts + \frac{T^2 s^2}{2!} + \frac{T^3 s^3}{3!} + \cdots\right) f(s)$$

whose frequency-domain amplitude response is limited to that of the truncated polynomial in s. Ultimately, then, the Runge-Kutta methods, as well as any finite difference calculus method that is based on truncated Taylor series expansions, are limited in the frequency domain to the characteristics of the truncated Taylor series transfer function. The spectral characteristics of the Runge-Kutta integrators are fixed by the number of terms retained in the Taylor series expansion. Furthermore, when discontinuities in the state variable occur, the Runge-Kutta algorithms, which are usually based on halving the integration interval until a single-step versus half-step comparison reduces the integration step size, are inefficient. Additionally, since Runge-Kutta does not have remainder formulas* from which to develop error terms, it is impossible to estimate the error at each step in the same manner as with the predict-correct algorithms. This is a fundamental weakness in the Runge-Kutta method, which can lead to inefficient error-controlled algorithms. Still, even with these qualifiers, the ease of programming and applying Runge-Kutta integration on large computers makes it an attractive formula. It has nice self-starting properties and operates quite autonomously, although perhaps quite inefficiently. When simulating or using numerical integration for data processing on minicomputers, the author recommends the examination of other methods, in particular the tunable integration method of Chapter 7 and the predict-correct algorithms of this chapter.

In all of the methods presented in this section, it is assumed that the differential equation is of the first order and generally written in the form $y' = f(x, y)$, since an nth-order differential equation can be written in terms of n first-order differential equations. These methods are applicable to systems of equations or to higher-order equations.

Special Integration Methods

A number of methods are available for specific use with higher-order differential equations and in those cases special predict-correct algorithms can be developed. While, for general-purpose computing, these are not very useful for numerical evaluation of the solution of the differential equation, they simplify the number of calculations involved in numerical evaluation. For example, Milne's predict-correct algorithms for first-order differential equations take the forms

$$
\begin{matrix} P \\ C \end{matrix} \Bigg\} \begin{cases} y_{n+1} = y_{n-3} + \dfrac{4\Delta x}{3} \left(2y'_n - y'_{n-1} + 2y'_{n-2}\right) \\ y_{n+1} = y_{n-1} + \dfrac{\Delta x}{3} \left(y'_{n-1} + 4y'_n + y'_{n+1}\right) \end{cases} \quad \text{for} \quad \epsilon \sim \Delta x^5
$$

---

* Except as used in the recently developed Fehlberg Runge-Kutta type of integrators.

$$P \atop C \Bigg\} \begin{cases} y_{n+1} = y_{n-5} + \dfrac{3\Delta x}{10} (11y'_n - 14y'_{n-1} + 26y'_{n-2} - 14y'_{n-3} + 11y'_{n-4}) \\[2ex] y_{n+1} = y_{n-3} + \dfrac{2\Delta x}{45} (7y'_{n+1} + 32y'_n + 12y'_{n-1} + 32y'_{n-2} + 7y'_{n-3}) \end{cases}$$

$$\text{for} \quad \epsilon \sim \Delta x^7$$

The equivalent accuracy Milne predict-correct formulas for second- and third-order differential equations are written as follows:

$$P \atop C \Bigg\} \begin{cases} y_{n+1} = y_{n-2} + 3(y_n - y_{n-1}) + \Delta x^2 (y''_n - y''_{n-1}) \\[2ex] y_{n+1} = y_n + \dfrac{\Delta x}{2} (y'_{n+1} + y'_n) - \dfrac{\Delta x^2}{12} (y''_{n+1} - y''_n) \end{cases} \quad \text{for} \quad \epsilon \sim \Delta x^5$$

$$P \atop C \Bigg\} \begin{cases} y_{n+1} = y_{n-2} + 3(y_n - y_{n-1}) + \dfrac{\Delta x^3}{2} (y'''_n - y'''_{n-1}) \\[2ex] y_{n+1} = y_n + \dfrac{\Delta x}{2} (y'_{n+1} + y'_n) - \dfrac{\Delta x^2}{10} (y''_{n+1} - y''_n) \end{cases} \quad \text{for} \quad \epsilon \sim \Delta x^7$$

$$+ \frac{\Delta x^3}{120} (y'''_{n+1} + y'''_n)$$

For systems of differential equations of the form

$$y' = f(x, y, z), \qquad z' = g(x, y, z)$$

second-order Runge-Kutta can be written as

$$\begin{cases} y_{n+1} = y_n + \dfrac{k_1}{2} + \dfrac{k_2}{2} \\[2ex] z_{n+1} = z_n + \dfrac{l_1}{2} + \dfrac{l_2}{2} \end{cases} \quad \text{for} \quad \epsilon \sim \Delta x^3$$

$$k_1 = \Delta x f(x_n, y_n, z_n)$$

$$l_1 = \Delta x g(x_n, y_n, z_n)$$

$$k_2 = \Delta x f(x_n + \Delta x, y_n + k_1, z_n + l_1)$$

$$l_2 = \Delta x g(x_n + \Delta x, y_n + k_1, z_n + l_1)$$

Fourth-order Runge-Kutta for this system of equations takes the form

$$y_{n+1} = y_n + \frac{k_1 + 2k_2 + 2k_3 + k_4}{6}$$

$$z_{(n+1)} = z_n + \frac{l_1 + 2l_2 + 2l_3 + l_4}{6}$$

$$k_1 = \Delta x f(x_n, y_n, z_n)$$

$$l_1 = \Delta x g(x_n, y_n, z_n)$$

$$k_2 = \Delta x f\left(x_n + \frac{\Delta x}{2}, \ y_n + \frac{k_1}{2}, \ z_n + \frac{l_1}{2}\right)$$

$$l_2 = \Delta x g\left(x_n + \frac{\Delta x}{2}, \ y_n + \frac{k_1}{2}, \ z_n + \frac{l_1}{2}\right)$$

$$k_3 = \Delta x f\left(x_n + \frac{\Delta x}{2}, \ y_n + \frac{k_2}{2}, \ z_n + \frac{l_2}{2}\right)$$

$$l_3 = \Delta x f\left(x_n + \frac{\Delta x}{2}, \ y_n + \frac{k_2}{2}, \ z_n + \frac{l_2}{2}\right)$$

$$k_4 = \Delta x f(x_n + \Delta x, \ y_n + k_3, \ z_n + l_3)$$

$$l_4 = \Delta x f(x_n + \Delta x, \ y_n + k_3, \ z_n + l_3)$$

Another special form of second-order differential equation is

$$y'' = f(x, y, y')$$

Milne's predict-correct method for these types of second-order equations is

$$y'_{n+1} = y'_{n-3} + \frac{4\Delta x}{3}(2y''_{n-2} - y''_{n-1} + 2y''_n)$$

$$\text{for} \quad \epsilon \sim \Delta x^5$$

$$y'_{n+1} = y'_{n-1} + \frac{\Delta x}{3}(y''_{n-1} + 4y''_n + y''_{n+1})$$

and the single-step self-starting Runge-Kutta method takes the form

$$y_{n+1} = y_n + \Delta x y'_n + \frac{\Delta x}{6} (k_1 + k_2 + k_3)$$

$$\qquad \text{for} \quad \epsilon \sim \Delta x^5$$

$$y'_{n+1} = y'_n + \frac{1}{6} (k_1 + 2k_2 + 2k_3 + k_4)$$

$$k_1 = \Delta x f(x_n, y_n, y'_n)$$

$$k_2 = \Delta x f\left(x_n + \frac{\Delta x}{2}, y_n + \frac{\Delta x}{2} y'_n + \frac{\Delta x k_1}{8}, y'_n + \frac{k_1}{2} \right)$$

$$k_3 = \Delta x f\left(x_n + \frac{\Delta x}{2}, y_n + \frac{\Delta x y'_n}{2} + \frac{\Delta x k_1}{8}, y'_n + \frac{k_2}{2} \right)$$

$$k_4 = \Delta x f\left(x_n + \Delta x, y_n + \Delta x y'_n + \frac{\Delta x k_3}{2}, y'_n + k_3 \right)$$

For second-order differential equations of the form

$$y'' = f(x, y)$$

Milne's method takes the forms

$$y_{n+1} = y_n + y_{n-2} - y_{n-3} + \frac{\Delta x^2}{4} (5y''_n + 2y''_{n-1} + 5y''_{n-2})$$

$$\qquad \text{for} \quad \epsilon \sim \Delta x^6$$

$$y_{n+1} = 2y_n - y_{n-2} + \frac{\Delta x^2}{12} (y''_{n+1} + 10y''_n + y''_{n-1})$$

The Runge-Kutta method appears as

$$y_{n+1} = y_n + \Delta x \left[y'_n + \left(\frac{k_1 + 2k_2}{6} \right) \right]$$

$$y'_{n+1} = y'_n + \frac{k_1}{6} + \frac{2k_2}{3} + \frac{k_3}{6}, \qquad \text{for} \quad \epsilon \sim \Delta x^4$$

$$k_1 = \Delta x f(x_n, y_n)$$

$$k_2 = \Delta x f\left(x_n + \frac{\Delta x}{2}, y_n + \frac{\Delta x}{2} y'_n + \frac{\Delta x}{8} k_1 \right)$$

$$k_3 = \Delta x f\left(x_n + \Delta x, y_n + \Delta x y'_n + \frac{\Delta x}{2} k_2 \right)$$

In the second-order forms, the Runge-Kutta algorithms involve the numerical evaluation of rates by Euler integration of the second-order differential equation. For small machines with limited memory, these alternate forms of numerically evaluating indefinite integrals are particularly useful because they dispense with computing the two first-order differential equations that would be required to make up the second-order equation for use with the more general first-order indefinite integration formulas.

Some General Observations on Predict-Correct Methods

A great deal of work has gone into the development of predict-correct methods. Hamming, Milne, Adams, Bashforth, and others have examined and recommended predict-correct procedures. The author's experience in predict-correct methods leads him to make the following recommendations:

1. When using the single-step algorithms for real-time simulation on small word size machines, carefully test the propagation of roundoff error due to the difference of small numbers. While the modifiers generally reduce the error in the numerical integration, occasionally by a factor of 10, they can on minicomputers amplify roundoff error. The author has personally experienced one case where the modifier reduced the accuracy of the integration on a long run.

2. When numerical instabilities are encountered in real-time simulation using the predict-correct algorithms with modifiers, the stability of the integration process may be improved by eliminating the modifiers.

3. In real-time simulation (where integration step size is fixed and thus the modifiers cannot be used to change the integration step size), mixing the order of accuracy levels can improve the overall computing accuracy.

4. As with any numerical integration method based on the integration of interpolation or extrapolation polynomials, these methods are sensitive to discontinuities in the integrand. The occurrence of large differences in the modifiers in any given integration step can be indicative of a discontinuity. In these circumstances, the integration algorithm itself can be modified so as not to change integration step size until a large modifier error is observed for n sample periods. Another approach is to permit the integration step size to change, provided there is no sharp change in the rate at which the modifier indicates the accuracy of the integration process.

5. The predict-correct methods discussed here require starting values. Runge-Kutta is presently widely used to compute each step of the integration process, but it is often overlooked that the method requires four evaluations of the derivative for every step forward, whereas the predict-correct methods usually require two evaluations of the derivative per step. Both methods achieve about the same degree of accuracy.

PART IV

SIMULATING CONTINUOUS RANDOM PROCESSES ON A DIGITAL COMPUTER

CHAPTER 9

AN INTRODUCTION TO CONTINUOUS STATIONARY RANDOM PROCESSES

9.1 MATHEMATICAL MODELING RANDOM PROCESSES

The previous sections of this book dealt with determining the response of systems to known forcing functions and initial conditions. In this section we deal with computing the response of a system to random and pseudorandom forcing functions.

Pseudorandom phenomena is phenomena which, though perfectly orderly and predictable, is very complex. Such phenomena is often analyzed using statistical methods. Under these circumstances we refer to such phenomena as pseudorandom. Examples include pseudorandom number generators in digital computers, complex wave motion on the ocean, fluid and gas flows in transition from order to chaos, and so on. In fact, recent studies of order in chaos indicate that certain phenomena previously thought to be random is in fact pseudorandom. More is said on this in Chapter 10.

Calculating a deterministic time history of a systems response to truly random forcing functions is impossible. Instead, relationships that relate the group properties of the input (input statistics) to group properties of the output (output statistics) are developed. They are the important relationships commonly used in design and performance evaluation for systems that must operate in the presence of noise and uncertainty.

If you are asked to describe the forcing function

$$f(t) = A \sin(\omega t + \phi)$$

you might say it is an oscillation and then specify its amplitude, frequency, and phase of $f(t)$. Knowing the frequency response characteristics of the system to be driven, you can judge whether $f(t)$ may result in a resonance

FIGURE 9-1.   A typical random forcing function.

or instability in the system. With only a little analysis, you can pin down the systems response fairly precisely. This is not so with random inputs to a system, which are not so easily characterized (see Fig. 9-1).

9.2   THE MEAN VALUE

A random forcing function is usually characterized first by its mean value (see Fig. 9-2).

$$\mu_f = \overline{f(t)} = \lim_{T \to \infty} \frac{1}{T} \int_0^T f(t)\, dt$$

This is a measure of the average amplitude of the random forcing

FIGURE 9-2.   The mean value calculation starting at time zero. Note: μ settled in $t \approx \tau$.

function which is particularly useful when one is studying the long-term properties of a systems response to noise (see Fig. 9-2). The average value, however, tells nothing of the size of the fluctuations that the system will see. The standard deviation gives a statistical measure of the size of the fluctuations in a random forcing function.

9.3   THE STANDARD DEVIATION

The most frequently used measure of the magnitude (size) of random fluctuations is the square of the variance (standard deviation).

$$\sigma^2 = \overline{\left(f(t) - \overline{f(t)} \right)^2} = \lim_{T \to \infty} \frac{1}{T} \int_0^T \left(f(t) - \overline{f(t)} \right)^2 dt$$

See Figure 9-3.

By themselves, the mean and standard deviation tell us about random forcing functions from an amplitude point of view but give no information on the rapidity with which the variations take place or the frequency with which certain amplitude fluctuations can be expected to occur; for that type of information we will use the autocorrelation function and the power spectral density.

FIGURE 9-3.   The standard deviation calculation starting at time zero. Note: σ settled in $t \approx \tau / 2$.

9.4   THE AUTOCORRELATION FUNCTION

In the time domain, analysts traditionally use the autocorrelation function to quantify a measure of the time over which fluctuations occur (are correlated) in a given random variable. The cross-correlation function is used to quantify the time interval between when fluctuations of a random input to a system result in fluctuations of the output (are cross-correlated). Of course, cross correlation can apply between any two random variables as a means of testing the degree to which the variables are correlated. The autocorrelation is defined as

$$R(\tau) = \lim_{T \to \infty} \frac{1}{T} \int_0^T f(t) f(t - \tau) \, dt$$

(see Figure 9-4) and the cross-correlation function as

$$R_{12}(\tau) = \lim_{T \to \infty} \frac{1}{T} \int_0^T f_1(t) f_2(t - \tau) \, dt$$

See Figure 9-5.

Theoretically speaking, perfectly random noise is uncorrelated for all τ except $\tau = 0$; consequently, $R(\tau)$ is a delta function whose weight is mean squared value of the noise as

$$R(\tau) = \sigma^2 \delta(0)$$

This is an ideal concept of noise. It is useful in understanding the degree to

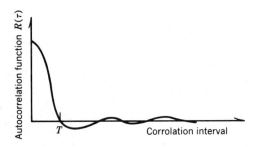

FIGURE 9-4.   A typical autocorrelation for a random variable $f(t)$. Notes: (1) Values of $f(t)$ separated in time by T are said to be uncorrelated. (2) Pure "white" noise is defined by specifying its autocorrelation function to be a delta function at $\tau = 0$.

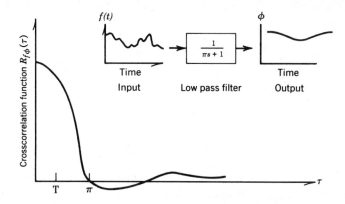

FIGURE 9-5. A typical crosscorrelation function relating the output of a low-pass filter of time constant π to a random forcing function whose autocorrelation function crosses zero at $\tau = T$. Note: A highly uncorrelated input can be correlated with the output of the system it is driving.

which real noise matches the ideal concept of noise. The closer the autocorrelation function approaches a delta function, the closer real noise approaches the ideal concept of noise.

9.5 THE POWER SPECTRAL DENSITY

To quantify the frequency with which fluctuations of a certain amplitude are likely to occur, one can examine the autocorrelation and cross-correlation functions in the frequency domain by Fourier transforming these time dependent functions. The Fourier transform of the autocorrelation function is called the power spectral density (see Figure 9-6) and that of the cross-correlation function is called the cross-spectral density.

Until the time of the Fast Fourier Transform, analysis of random processes typically proceeded from time domain records of the random signal to auto or cross correlation functions which were then Fourier transformed. With the advent of the Fast Fourier Transform, it is more typical now to bypass the autocorrelation function and measure the power spectrum directly.

FIGURE 9-6.   A typical power spectral density for (1) white noise (a theoretical concept) and (2) a low-pass filtered random variable characterized as white noise.

The power spectral density, as defined in the time domain, can be in either of two forms.

$$\Phi(\omega) = \lim_{T \to \infty} \lim_{\Delta\omega \to 0} \left\{ \frac{(1/T)\int_0^T f^2(t)\, dt}{\Delta\omega} \right\} = \frac{d\sigma^2}{d\omega} \qquad (9\text{-}1)$$

Note that

$$\sigma^2 = \int_0^\infty \Phi(\omega)\, d\omega$$

and

$$\Phi(\omega) = \frac{1}{2\pi} \int_0^\infty R(\tau) \cos(\omega\tau)\, d\tau^* \qquad (9\text{-}2)$$

Note also that for pure noise, the autocorrelation function is a delta function; thus the power spectral density is a constant. Additionally, for a constant power spectral density, the mean squared variance is unbounded. Real noise sources which have well-defined mean squared values have power spectral densities whose area under the curve of Φ is finite; thus their power spectral densities are not constant. We might expect, however, that

---

*The factor $\dfrac{1}{2\pi}$ is associated with the Fourier transformation of the autocorrelation function because of the way the power spectral density is defined in equation (9-1). In some of the literature, the factor $\dfrac{1}{2\pi}$ is associated with the inverse Fourier transformation of the power spectral density.

noise generators which simulate real noise might be developed by starting with a noise source whose power spectrum is constant *over the frequencies of interest* and then "shaping" the noise with filters whose power spectrum matches the power spectrum to be simulated. Such is the case as we shall see in Chapter 10.

For linear constant coefficient systems, the output PSD/PSD is related to the input by the relations

$$\frac{\Phi_\phi(\omega)}{\Phi_i(\omega)} = |G(j\omega)|^2$$

and

$$\sigma_\phi^2 = \int_0^\infty \Phi_0 \, d\omega = \int_0^\infty |G(j\omega)|^2 \Phi_i(\omega) \, d\omega$$

where $G(j\omega)$ is the transfer function relating the output to input for a linear constant coefficient system $G(s)$.

It is important to remember that while the integrals associated with statistical analysis look formidable, especially when the transfer function for real systems is inserted into the integrand, these integrals can often be accurately estimated using numerical integration.

While statistical information, such as the mean value, standard deviation, autocorrelation function, and the power spectral density, tell us a great deal about random processes (and quantify this information in a useful way from a design point of view), no information is given about the likelihood that a random variable will take on certain values. This is the role of the probability density functions.

9.6 PROBABILITY DENSITY FUNCTIONS

In the design of automatic landing systems, for example, it is important to know the average touchdown position and associated standard deviation. It is also important to be able to quantify the probability that the landing will occur beyond the boundaries of the runway. The functions that specify how the probability of occurrence of a random variable varies as a function of the random variable itself, is called the probability density function.

In the case of a continuously varying random variable

$$x(t)$$

we can define the probability that $x(t)$ resides in the interval $(x_1, x_1 + \Delta x)$ as

$$\text{Probability } (x_1 < x < (x_1 + \Delta x)) = P(x, \Delta x) = \lim_{T \to \infty} \left(\frac{\Sigma \Delta t_i}{T} \right)$$

where Δt_i are the intervals of the time when

$$x_1 < x < (x_1 + \Delta x)$$

and where T is the length of the time record. Note that as

$$\Delta x \to 0, \qquad P(x, \Delta x) \to \Delta P \to 0$$

but the ratio of ΔP to Δx does not, thus

$$\lim_{\Delta x \to 0} \left(\frac{\Delta P}{\Delta x} \right) = \frac{dP}{dx} = P_D(x) \triangleq \text{Probability density function}$$

Note that by the way we defined $P(x, \Delta x)$ we have transformed a description of a random variable $x(t)$ in the time domain (time history) to a description of the random variable in a probability domain. Instead of asking the question, what is the value of $x(t)$ at any given time (an unanswerable question for a random variable), we now answer the question what is the probability that a stationary random variable x will lie in an interval (x_1, x_2)? The answer, of course is

$$P = \int_{x_1}^{x_2} P_D(x) \, dx$$

See Figure 9-7.

Note that

$$P(x) = \int_{-\infty}^{\infty} P_D(x) = 1$$

and $P_D(x)$ is a positively valued function (otherwise $P(x)$ could decline over intervals of x which is not physically possible).

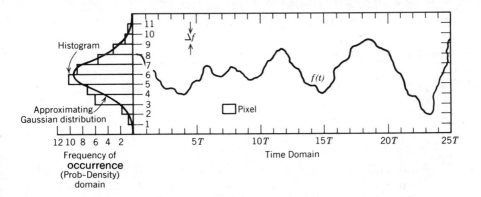

FIGURE 9-7. Typical probability density function associated with the random variable $f(t)$. *Note*: $\text{prob}(2 < x < 5) \simeq \dfrac{2 + 6 + 7}{1 + 2 + 6 + 7 + 10 + 9 + 6 + 4 + 2}$ $= \dfrac{15}{47} \simeq \int_{2}^{5} P_D(f)\, dt$. Frequency of occurrence = number of times $f(t)$ was found in a pixel bounded by f and $f + \Delta f$ and nT and $(n + 1)T$. A plot of the frequency of occurrence on the ordinate of the time history is called a histogram. For a truly stationary random variable, the limit to which the histogram (stairstep) function approaches as $\Delta f \to 0$ is the Gaussian probability density function. The probability that f will be found in an interval (f_1, f_2) is given by

$$\text{prob}(f_1 < f < f_2) = \int_{f_1}^{f_2} P_D(f)\, df.$$

Now what's important here is that *any function $G(x)^*$* which is always positive, and which satisfies the relationship

$$\int_{-\infty}^{\infty} G(x) = 1$$

can serve as a probability density function.

---

*Typically, analysts study discrete random variables and then derive or curve fit suitable continuous functions, such as $G(x)$ to histograms of the measured data as a means of studying the properties of random processes and/or simplifying the numerically evaluation of probabilities associated with discrete random events.

9.7 EXAMPLES OF USEFUL PROBABILITY DENSITY FUNCTIONS

As you are probably aware (no pun intended), the field of statistics has led to a number of such functions being defined for a number of problems which have been studied:

> When studying the distribution of hits on a target (the probability that hits will occur within rings around the target center) the Poisson probability density function is very useful.
>
> When studying the probability that a gambler's roll* of a pair of dice will result in a given sum, the binomial probability density function is useful.
>
> When studying the effects of medication on a small sample of patients and extrapolating the results to a large population, the Student-t distribution is sometimes used.
>
> When studying the combined effect of a large number of random phenomena such as local wind direction and velocity over a period of a few minutes, or when studying the distribution of hits on a target on each of the axes of an x-y coordinate system, or when measuring a random variable such as the voltage from a temperature sensor or the direction of the return from an airborne radar signal, the Gaussian probability density function (distribution) is often very useful. (See Figure 9-8)

The list of useful probability density functions is almost as long as the list of great statisticians. For our work here we will only consider those random variables whose real probability density functions can be usefully approximated (modeled) with a Gaussian distribution or a uniform distribution. There is a wide body of experience with such random variables and the simulation of such random processes.

---

*Interestingly, this nice model can be used to roughly guess the outcome of investments by using one die to represent possible revenues and the other die to represent possible costs. The six faces of each die allow the relative frequency of the outcomes to be roughly modeled. For example, if an investor's judgment is that the nominal revenues (NR) are four times more likely to occur than either the greatest revenues (GR) or the least revenue (LR), the revenue die would have four faces marked NR, one face marked GR and another marked LR. Similarly, if he judged the nominal, least, and greatest costs to be equally as likely to occur, he would mark two faces NC, another two faces GC, and the remaining two faces LC. Then, to judge the gross profits of the investment, he can roll the dice many times, sum the results on each roll, and plot the frequency of occurrence of the gross profits and estimate the mean and standard deviation (risk level) of the profits from the investment.

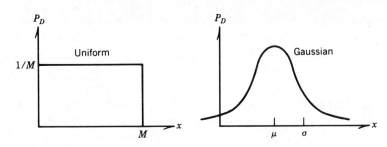

FIGURE 9-8.   Uniform and Gaussian distributions.

$(a) \ P_D = \begin{cases} 0 \text{ for } M < x < 0 \\ 1 \ / \ M \text{ for } 0 \le x \le M. \end{cases}$ $(b) \ P_D = \dfrac{1}{\sqrt{2\pi}\,\sigma} e^{-(x-\mu)^2/2\sigma2}.$

9.8   THE FUNDAMENTALS OF RANDOM PROCESS SIMULATION

How to put all this information together in a simulation is our challenge now. The approach is quite simple and very easy to apply once a few fundamentals are known and remembered:

FUNDAMENTAL 1.   In digital simulation work, virtually all useful distributions can be developed from a uniform distribution. Many involve nonlinear curve fitting techniques (more on this in Chapter 10), but one important one does not, the Gaussian distribution.

FUNDAMENTAL 2.   In digital simulations, a Gaussianly distributed stationary random variable can be generated by low-pass digital filtering (averaging) a uniformly distributed random variable with a linear constant coefficient low-pass digital filter (averager).*

FUNDAMENTAL 3.   Most commercially available noise generators and random number generators that are sampled at a frequency ω_s are characterized by having a fairly constant power spectral density over a specified frequency range. In the case of the random number generator, the range is typically $0 < \omega < (\omega_s)/7$.

*An implementation of the Central Limit Theorem of Statistics.

FUNDAMENTAL 4.   In digital simulation work, the power spectral density of a stationary continuous random variable is usually "shaped" with linear constant coefficient digital filters. The digital filters can be derived using the discrete analog method of Chapter 4.

FUNDAMENTAL 5.   Changing a stationary, uniformly distributed random variable with a constant power spectral density to a Gaussianly distributed random variable with a "shaped" power spectrum can usually be done with simple linear constant coefficient digital filters.

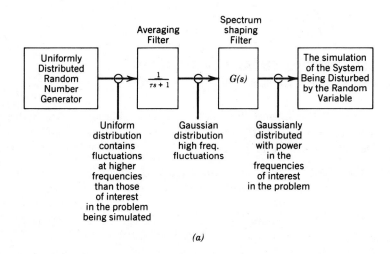

(a)

The Discrete Analog Simulation

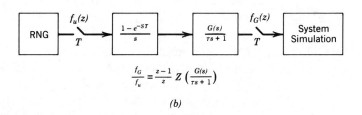

$$\frac{f_G}{f_u} = \frac{z-1}{z} Z\left(\frac{G(s)}{\tau s + 1}\right)$$

(b)

FIGURE 9-9.   (a) Simulating stationary random processes (b) The discrete analog simulation.

FUNDAMENTAL 6. Simulating a continuous random variable on a digital computer is done with a random number generator which outputs uniformly distributed random numbers with a frequency at least seven to ten times the highest frequency of interest in the simulation problem.

FUNDAMENTAL 7. Spectrum shaping and averaging the output of a random number generator to generate Gaussianly distributed noise can be done quickly with the discrete analog simulation technique presented in Chapter 4.

The details of the application of these fundamentals to the digital simulation of random processes are covered in Chapter 10 and visualized here in Figure 9-9.

CHAPTER 10

GENERATING CHAOS, RANDOM NUMBERS, AND SIMULATING RANDOM PROCESSES

10.1 INTRODUCTION

In this chapter we are interested in the digital simulation of stationary noise. The approach here is to understand how continuous stationary random noise is developed and modeled for simulation and then to transform the continuous model to a discrete model for digital simulation using the discrete analogy method as described in Chapter 4.

A stationary process is one whose statistical properties do not change with time. In practice many random variables may be considered stationary for only limited durations of time: atmospheric turbulence would be an example. Wind and turbulence may be mathematically represented as stationary within a reasonable degree of approximation if the variation in their statistical properties is small during the time or location of interest in the simulation.

difficult and is not discussed here. However, simple nonstationary disturbances (such as a noise signal having statistical properties that are invariant except for a slowly but uniformly increasing intensity) might be handled piecewise as stationary approximations of nonstationary disturbances.

There are a number of different approaches to generating random variables for simulation:

In real-time simulations the actual signal, if available and occurring concurrently, may be used in the simulation.

A recording of the actual random variable may be used. Here the playback rate need not be the same as the recording rate, consequently, the simulation may be run in scaled time.

A simulated random variable may be generated in analog form and then sampled and used in the digital simulation.

The random variable may be generated digitally from a sequence of random measurements of the actual random variable of interest or from a table of random numbers suitably scaled to model the random variable being simulated.

A pseudorandom (chaotic) process is developed and *designed* to match the power spectral density and probability density of the signal to be simulated.

A pseudorandom (chaotic) process is developed and *designed* to match the power spectral density and probability density of the signal to be simulated. We will be concerned with this approach primarily as it is the more common technique.

10.2 GENERATING DIGITAL PSEUDORANDOM VARIABLES

There are two well-developed and thoroughly studied methods for generating pseudorandom numbers. The most commonly used method is the modulo arithmetic "scrambler." This method employs a simple mathematical concept to scramble or shuffle a set of numbers, analogous to the way a gambler shuffles and mixes cards in a deck or a taffy puller mixes ribbons of candy.

One of the oldest but least commonly used methods is nonlinear functional iteration. This method, in its simplest terms, is a simple way to develop highly complex functional relationships between numbers in a sequence. When analyzed from a statistical point of view, the numbers appear uncorrelated and, consequently, are said to be pseudorandom.

Over the last two decades, studies of nonlinear functional iteration has been a mathematical curiosity which recently has led to some remarkable insights into the relationship between order and chaos in nature. Because of these remarkable developments, and because the general principles of pseudorandom number generation are easily illustrated with functional iteration, it will be discussed first.

Functional iteration is a process where the dependent variable of a function is iteratively assigned to be the independent variable of the function such as

$$x_n = f(x_{n-1}) \tag{1}$$

What results is a sequence of pseudorandom numbers $\{x_n\}$ which have complex behavior. Simply stated, this method generates the next pseudorandom number by performing a *functional* transformation on the current pseudorandom number. On a pocket calculator the process is implemented by simply stroking a function key repeatedly, using the result of each key stroke as the input for the next function evaluation.

If we denote the function as f, and the initial value of f is x_0, then the sequence of pseudorandom numbers, $x_0, x_1, x_2, \cdots, x_n$, are evaluated as

$$x_1 = f(x_0)$$

$$x_2 = f(x_1) = f(f(x_0))$$

$$\vdots$$

$$x_n = f(x_{n-1}) = f(\cdots f(f(x_0)) \cdots) \triangleq f^n(x_0)$$

where n is the number of times f is repeatedly evaluated (iterated).

Not all functions produce pseudorandom numbers. Those that seem to work best are nonlinear functions that result in increasingly complex functional iterates. For example, the function

$$f = \lambda x(1 - x)$$

is one of many quadratic forms that produce pseudorandom numbers for certain values of λ and x_0. When used as a pseudorandom number generator, it is programmed in the form

$$x_{n+1} = \lambda x_n (1 - x_n) \tag{2}$$

In terms of the initial value, x_0, this recursion formula generates the following sequence of numbers

$$x_1 = \lambda x_0 (1 - x_0)$$

$$x_2 = \lambda^2 x_0 \left[1 - (1 + \lambda) x_0 + 2\lambda x_0^2 - \lambda x_0^3 \right]$$

$$x_3 = \lambda^3 x_0 [\text{Complex 7th order polynomial in } x_0]$$

$$x_4 = \lambda^4 x_0 [\text{Complex 15th order polynomial in } x_0]$$

It is apparent that even after only a few iterations, the simple nonlinear function $\lambda x(1 - x)$ generates a number that is related to the *seed number* (initial value) in a very complex (pseudorandom) way. In this sense, we say x_n is weakly correlated with x_0 and thus we say it is pseudorandom.

Notice that the selection of λ and x_0 can lead to perfectly orderly, noncomplex results. For example, when either

$$\lambda = x_0 = 0 \quad \text{or} \quad \lambda = x_0 = 1$$

$$x_1 = x_2 = x_3 = \cdots = x_n \cdots = 0$$

If, however, we select $\lambda = 2$ and $x_0 = \frac{1}{4}$, then our number generator, (2), produces the following sequence of numbers

$$x_0 = \tfrac{1}{4}$$

$$x_1 = \tfrac{12}{32}$$

$$x_2 = \tfrac{15}{32}$$

$$x_3 = \tfrac{15}{32}\left(\tfrac{17}{16}\right)$$

$$\vdots$$

Note how quickly the sequence moves into the vicinity of $\frac{1}{2}$ and seems to be converging there. In fact, if for $x_0 = \frac{1}{2}$ and $\lambda = 2$ we find

$$x_0 = \tfrac{1}{2} = x_1 = x_2 = x_3 = \cdots = x_n = \cdots$$

In this sense, we say x has a stable point at

$$x = \tfrac{1}{2}$$

It can be shown that for $\lambda = \gamma$ and $0 < x < 1$

$$\lim_{n \to \infty} (x_n) = 1/\gamma$$

Said slightly differently, all sequences of x_n starting on the interval $(0, 1)$

converge to $1/\gamma$ for $\lambda = \gamma$. In a sense, they are *attracted* to the stable point no matter what the initial conditions.*

Now, what is *remarkable* is that at $\lambda = 3$ the single stable point goes *bistable*, and the number generator produces numbers that seek two stable points to which the sequence x_n converges. At $\lambda = 3.2$, a stable oscillation sets up between the two fixed points 0.5130446 and 0.7994555. Set up the following BASIC program and you will see this process occur:

BASIC

```
100 LET X = .2
110 INPUT "L"; L
120 LET X = L*X*(1 − X)
130 PRINT X
140 N = N + 1
150 If N = 100 THEN 170
160 GO TO 120
170 END
```

Here you will see that (2) quickly converges to generating only two numbers. At $L = 3.45$, you will see the number generator settle down and generate for a repeating sequence of numbers corresponding to the stable points:

0.8749972
0.3828199
0.8269408
0.5008841

In fact, what is occurring is that as λ increases to 3.5700, our number generator moves from a simple initial condition to a set of stable points with repeating cycles of length 2^n. Interestingly, for certain λ, these numbers occur in such a way that they exhibit the properties of randomness (they are highly uncorrelated). We say, then, that they are pseudorandom. The mathematicians who study certain subtleties of Equation (2) say that at $\lambda = 3$ the period doubling region begins, at $\lambda = 3.5700$ the chaotic region begins, at $\lambda = 3.6786$ the first odd period begins, at $\lambda = 3.8234$ cycles with every integer period begins, and for $\lambda = 4.0000$, the chaotic region ends and all solutions of Equation (1) are attracted to ∞.

---

*This is an important observation from a physical point of view. This observation says that the final value(s) and the complexity of the final states of existence of physical processes described by (1) are often independent of the initial conditions.

Figure 10-1 gives the locus of stable points for (2) illustrating

1. The period doubling phenomena.
2. The rapidity of the onset of chaos as a function of λ.
3. The distribution of stable points as a function of λ.

Equation (2) has been used as a random number generator as early as 1947 by Ulam and von Neumann. In their work, they used the value $\lambda = 4$ and found that for initial values on the interval $0 < x_0 < 1$ equation (1) produced a pseudorandom sequence of numbers with a density function

$$P_D \propto [x(1 - x)]^{1/2}; \quad 0 < x < 1$$

Of course, since that time, numerous other nonlinear functions that, on iteration, produce chaos have been studied but none have been widely used as pseudorandom number generators because breakthroughs in binary multiplicative, pseudorandom sequence generators made hardware implementation of modulo arithmetic scramblers so much easier and faster to implement on digital computers.

If the reader chooses to employ (2) or other nonlinear iterative pseudo-

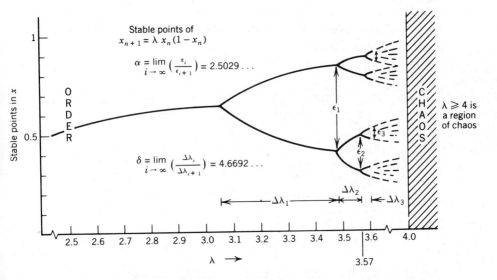

FIGURE 10-1. Period doubling route to chaos. Note: α and δ are new universal constants discovered by Feigenbaum. For details see *Universal Behavior in Nonlinear Systems; Universality in Chaos*, 1984, Adam Hilger Limited, publishers, pages 49 – 84.

If the reader chooses to employ (2) or other nonlinear iterative pseudo-random number generators (which follow period doubling as a path to chaos) as a means of developing pseudorandom numbers, then the author suggests verifying Feigenbaum's* recent discovery that the value of λ at which the stable points bifurcate are related by the simple linear formula

$$4.6692016 = \lim_{k \to \infty} \left(\frac{\lambda_{k+1} - \lambda_k}{\lambda_k - \lambda_{k-1}} \right)$$

as a means of learning about order in chaos.

10.3 MODULO ARITHEMATIC SCRAMBLERS

The modern pseudorandom number generators use *shift registers* to generate relatively uncorrelated binary numbers in a "logical" way electronically (see Figure 10-2). These schemes are fast compared with software generated algorithms and they are a convenient way to implement modulo arithmetic scramblers. The reader may remember that in modulo arithmetic, one counts numbers on the circumference of a circle instead of on the endless line of real numbers (see Figure 10-3). While modulo arithmetic is usually taught as an arithmetic of remainders (for example, 3 is the remainder of $13 \div 10$; thus we say 13 modulo(10) = 3), the notion of counting on a circle's circumference visualizes the shuffling or scrambling quality of the random number generator.

FIGURE 10-2.   A simple shift register sequence generator.

Universal Behavior in Nonlinear Systems, M. J. Feigenbaum, ed. Physica TD (1983), pp. 16–38, North Holland Publishing Company.

Figure 10-3 illustrates how an algorithm such as

$$x_n = 13x_{n-1} \ (\text{Mod } 10)$$

can generate a shuffled (scrambled) sequence of numbers. If $x_0 = 1$, then this algorithm outputs the following simple sequence of numbers:

n	$13x_{n-1} \ (\text{Mod } 10)$
0	1
1	3
2	9
3	7
4	1
5	3
6	9
7	7
8	

Note that the sequence repeats itself. Also note that for a modulus 10 counting scheme, if the starting value is 1 and the multiplier is 15, then the sequency of numbers is $1, 5, 5, 5, 5, \ldots$. As with the iterative nonlinear noise

FIGURE 10-3. Counting in modulo 10 arithmetic. 3 Mod(10) = 3; 8 Mod (10) = 8; 11 Mod(10) = 1; 21 Mod(10) = 1 ... N Mod(10) = FIV < 10 for (N − 10i) i_2 1, 2, 3, ... (FIV = first integer value.)

generator, the multiplier, the starting value, and the modulus number are very important to select properly to get an extended sequence of pseudorandom numbers. Much study has gone into this matter. Random number generators provided in most scientific software packages are carefully designed to generate a uniform distribution of random decimal numbers for use in scientific simulations. One such algorithm for use in digital computers, which does not have short cycles or lock up, is:

$$x_{n+1} = (8t - 3)x_n \ (\text{Mod } 2^S); \qquad x_0 = 1$$

where 2^S is at least four times the number of pseudorandom numbers necessary for simulation, and $(8t - 3)$ is an odd integer near the size of the modulus. (Some have suggested $\sim 2^{3/2}$.) To generate 10,000 pseudorandom numbers, 2^S should be approximately 40,000. $S = 15$ satisfies this nicely and the modulus is then 32,768. $(8k - 3)$ then should be selected on the order of $2^8 = 256$. Thus the algorithm to generate approximately 10,000 pseudorandom variables is

$$x_{n+1} = 256x_n \ (\text{Mod } 32,768); \qquad x_0 = 1$$

This algorithm can be programmed in machine language to execute it quickly with register shifts of eight places for the multiplication by 256 and 15 places for the division by the modulus. Such an algorithm has the nice properties that

1. The length of the useful period is known (Modulus/4).
2. The distribution of the numbers is uniform from 1 to 32,768.
3. The autocorrelation is beyond $\tau = 0$ very small.
4. The sequence of runs are balanced and equal.

10-4   STATISTICAL NATURE OF RANDOM NUMBER GENERATOR OUTPUTS

Before considering means by which the output of the digital random-number generator may be scaled to represent a random variable being simulated, the statistical nature of the pseudorandom variable produced by using the modulo arithmetic process will be developed. These random number generators produce an approximately uniform probability density of integers ranging from $x = 1$ to $x = m$. That is,

$$f(x) = \begin{cases} \dfrac{1}{m} & \text{for } 0 < x \le m \\ 0 & \text{for } x \le 0 \text{ or } x > m \end{cases}$$

Following Chapter 9, the mean value of any random variable is computed from its probability density as follows:

$$\bar{x} = \int_{-\infty}^{\infty} xf(x)\, dx$$

Thus,

$$\bar{x} = \int_0^m x\frac{1}{m}\, dx = \frac{m}{2}$$

The mean-squared value is determined by the relation

$$\overline{x^2} = \int_{-\infty}^{\infty} x^2 f(t)\, dx$$

Thus

$$\overline{x^2} = \int_0^m x^2 \frac{1}{m}\, dx = \frac{m^2}{3}$$

The mean deviation is defined as the mean-square value of the variance around the mean value which is evaluated as follows:

$$\sigma_x^2 = \int_{-\infty}^{\infty} [x - \bar{x}]^2 f(x)\, dx$$

It is easily shown that

$$\sigma_x^2 = \overline{x^2} - x^{-2}$$

Hence the random signal produced by these random number generators has a mean deviation of

$$\sigma_x^2 = \frac{m^2}{3} - \left(\frac{m}{2}\right)^2 = \frac{m^2}{12}$$

To produce purely random numbers which are symmetrically located about zero, the mean value is determined and subtracted from the number generated. The numbers that remain will be designated as $x(t)$; they are generated sequentially at intervals of time Δt.

Since the number generated at the beginning of an interval Δt applies throughout the interval, the number generator is said to produce a pseudo-random variable which is equivalent to a stepwise continuous function as shown in Figure 10-4.

The autocorrelation function for $x(t)$ and corresponding power-spectral density can now be determined.

Since each number generated, x_n, is virtually statistically independent, the autocorrelation function is easily determined and is of the form shown in Figure 10-5.

Remembering now that the power spectral density is defined mathematically as the Fourier transform of the autocorrelation function as

$$\Phi_x(\omega) = \int_{-\infty}^{\infty} R_x(\tau)e^{-j\omega\tau}\,d\tau$$

the corresponding power-spectral density of $x(t)$ can be derived by Fourier transforming the triangular autocorrelation function. What results is a power-spectral density of the form

$$\Phi_x(\omega) = \sigma_x^2\,\Delta t\left\{\frac{1 - \cos(\omega\,\Delta t)}{\left(\frac{1}{2}\right)(\omega\,\Delta t)^2}\right\}$$

$$= \frac{m^2\,\Delta t}{6}\left\{\frac{1 - \cos(\omega\,\Delta t)}{(\omega\,\Delta t)^2}\right\}$$

When graphed, this spectral density appears as in Figure 10-6. If the iteration interval is sufficiently small (i.e., $\omega\,\Delta T \ll 1$),

$$\Phi_x \simeq \frac{m^2\,\Delta t}{12}\left[1 - \frac{(\omega\,\Delta t)^2}{12}\right]$$

If $\omega\,\Delta T$, for the range of frequencies involved in the simulation problem, is small so that the simulation dynamics are confined to the flat part of the noise spectrum curve, then the pseudorandom variable may be considered white noise with a constant spectrum of

$$\Phi = \frac{m^2\,\Delta t}{12}^{*} \qquad\qquad (2)$$

*Note that on the flat part of the noise spectrum

$$\sigma^2 = \frac{1}{2\pi}\int_{-\infty}^{\infty}\Phi\,d\omega = \frac{m^2\,\Delta t\,\Delta\omega}{(2\pi)(12)} = \frac{m^2}{12}$$

as we would expect.

FIGURE 10-4. Pseudorandom time series. $a = x_0 - m/2$; $b = x_1 - m/2$; $c = x_2 - m/2$; $d = x_3 - m/2$.

FIGURE 10-5. The autocorrelation function of the time series shown in Figure 10-4.

FIGURE 10-6. The power spectral density of the time series shown in Figure 10-4.

It is on this basis that shaping filters can then be designed to simulate the actual power-spectral density desired to represent the random variables in the simulation.

10-5 SHAPING THE POWER-SPECTRAL DENSITY

First a brief refresher on the practical concepts of power spectral density. While the probability density function describes the amplitude characteristics of the random variable, the manner in which the variable varies in the frequency domain must be specified: that is the role of the power-spectral density, $\Phi(\omega)$. The modern fast Fourier transformation makes direct measurement of the power spectrum quick and easy and is usually the way a noise source is defined.

The power-spectral density of the random variable $x(t)$, $\Phi_x(\omega)$ describes the frequency content of the random variable associated with the Fourier transform of $R_x(\tau)$. (The word 'power' appears in the description because the square of many physical variables is proportional to the power in the process). Power spectral density can be visualized physically: Suppose that $x(t)$ is applied to a band-pass filter that has a pass range from the frequency ω to $\omega + \Delta\omega$. Within this range, the transmission is assumed to be unity, outside of it, zero. The output of this filter, described as x_f, would contain only the frequency components of x that lie within this frequency range. This output is then squared and averaged (averaging over a long time). What results is a signal $\overline{(x_f)}^2$. Figure 10-7 illustrates this procedure. The time constant of the averaging filter must be such that $\omega T \gg 1$ where ω is the lower band limit of the filter.

The quantity obtained when $(x_f)^2$ is divided by the filter bandwidth, $\Delta\omega$, is an approximation of $\Phi_x(\omega)$ for the value of ω employed in the filter. As $\Delta\omega$ is made smaller, this ratio approaches a constant value. In the limit, as $\Delta\omega \to 0$ it becomes $\Phi_x(\omega)$ as

$$\Phi_x(\omega) \triangleq \lim_{\Delta\omega \to 0} \left(\frac{\overline{x_f^2}}{\Delta\omega} \right)$$

If this process were applied to all ω then we would say the power spectrum is defined for all ω.

The autocorrelation function $R_x(\tau)$ is the inverse Fourier transform of $\Phi_x(\omega)$, that is,

FIGURE 10-7. Visualizing the calculation of power spectral density.

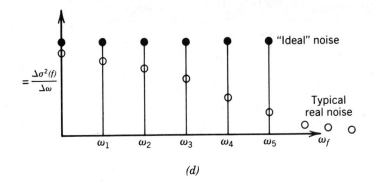

$$= \frac{\Delta \sigma^2 (f)}{\Delta \omega}$$

(d)

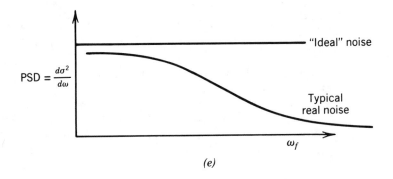

$$PSD = \frac{d\sigma^2}{d\omega}$$

(e)

Practical implementation

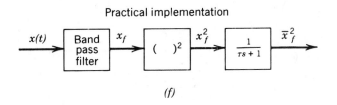

(f)

FIGURE 10-7. (*Continued*).

$$R_x(\tau) = \frac{1}{2\pi} \int_{-\infty}^{\infty} \Phi_x(\omega) e^{j\omega\tau} \, d\omega$$

and conversely,

$$\Phi_x(\omega) = \int_{-\infty}^{\infty} R_x(\tau) e^{-j\omega\tau} \, d\tau$$

Since the output of a random number generator is stationary, then the autocorrelation function can also be determined from the relation

$$R_x(\tau) = \int_{0}^{\infty} x(t)x(t - \tau) \, d\tau$$

The form of noise power-spectral density used most frequently is that of white noise, where

$$\Phi_x(\omega) = \Phi_x \qquad \text{(constant for all } \omega\text{)}$$

The power spectrum for white noise is illustrated in Figure 10-8. White noise is a strictly theoretical concept. What usually is meant by white noise (as in commercially available analog or digital white-noise generators), is that the power-density spectrum remains essentially constant within the frequency range of interest. The power-spectral density for real noise generators, of course, approaches zero as ω approaches $\pm\infty$. (It should be noted that although it is a mathematical convenience to consider ω as possessing both positive and negative values, as is done when employing the Fourier transform of deterministic functions, the power-spectral density of real random variables are even functions of ω only).

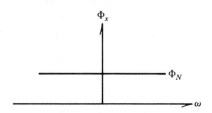

FIGURE 10-8. A constant power spectral density implies a delta function autocorrelation, which is a strictly theoretical concept. Real noise is said to be almost white or white in the frequencies of interest when its power spectrum is flat on an interval of ω.

Now, the design of power-spectral density shaping filters is quite simple. Let $x_1(t)$ be the random input to a linear filter and $x_2(t)$ its random output. Let the transfer function relating them be designated as $G_{21}(s)$, that is, if

$$x_2(s) = G_{21}(s)x_1(s)$$

then it is also true that

$$\Phi_{x_2} = G_{21}(j\omega)G_{21}(-j\omega)\Phi_{x_1}$$

or

$$\Phi_{x_2} = |G_{21}(j\omega)|^2 \Phi_{x_1}$$

Now suppose we were to use an analog computer random noise generator with a power-spectral density of Φ_N to drive a low-pass filter as shown in Figure 10-9.

The power spectral density of x_2 is developed as follows:

$$\Phi_{x_2} = \left[\frac{k/\tau}{j\omega + (1/\tau)}\right]\left[\frac{k/\tau}{-j\omega + (1/\tau)}\right]\Phi_N$$

$$\Phi_{x_2} = \frac{k^2(1/\tau)^2}{(1/\tau)^2 + \omega^2}\Phi_N$$

This power spectral density is sketched in Figure 10-10. Remember that σ_x^2 is the mean squared value of the random variable $x(t)$. One property of any spectral density function is that the area it encloses, when plotted versus ω, is the mean-square value of the function. Specifically,*

$$\sigma_x^2 = \frac{1}{2\pi}\int_{-\infty}^{\infty}\Phi_x(\omega)\,d\omega$$

It is easy to show, then, that

$$\sigma_{x_2}^2 \cong \frac{12k^2}{4\pi\tau}\Phi_N$$

*Note-For complicated integrands consider using numerical integration.

FIGURE 10-9. Shaping the power spectral density with a low-pass filter. Note: The PSD of $x_1(s) = \Phi_N$, a constant.

Now, if the noise generator power spectral density is flat over the interval $5/\tau$, then the power spectral density can be approximated with the formula

$$\Phi_N \simeq \frac{m^2 \, \Delta t}{12} \tag{2}$$

and the mean variance of the output of the filter is approximately

$$\sigma_{2x}^2 \simeq \frac{k^2 m^2}{4\pi} \left(\frac{\Delta t}{\tau} \right)$$

The same general principles are employed for the purpose of shaping the spectral density of random disturbances when they appear in digital form as are used for those appearing in analog form. The necessary modifying-filter transfer function, $G(s)$ is determined. From this the digital counterpart is established most easily by means of a discrete analog as covered in Chapter 4 (see Figure 10-11).

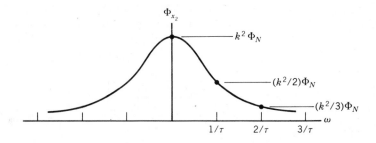

FIGURE 10-10. A commonly used noise power spectrum arrived at by low-pass filtering white noise.

FIGURE 10-11.   The digital equivalent of Figure 10-9.

Here we find the transfer function of the digital filter can be written in recursion form as

$$\frac{x_2(z)}{x_1(z)} = Z\left(\frac{1 - e^{-sT}}{s}\right)\left(\frac{k}{\tau s + 1}\right)$$

$$= \frac{(1 - e^{-T/\tau})}{(z - e^{-T/\tau})}$$

Thus,

$$x_{2_{n+1}} = e^{-T/\tau}x_{2_n} + k(1 - e^{-T/\tau})x_{1_n}$$

This digital filter recursion formula is used to shape the power spectrum of the pseudorandom number generator.

10-6 MEASURING THE POWER SPECTRAL DENSITY EXPERIMENTALLY

It is a good practice to experimentally verify the power spectrum of a noise generator before actually employing it in the simulation. The power-spectral density of a noise generator can then be measured experimentally as sketched in Figure 10-12. In this setup $\tau_2 \gg \tau_1$. In steady state, one can

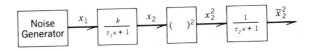

FIGURE 10-12.   A simple experimental method for checking the power spectral density of a random noise generator.

FIGURE 10-13. The power spectral density calculation where the slope is a constant.

make a plot of $\overline{x_2^2}$ vs. $1/\tau_1$ as shown in Figure 10-13. The slope of the curve is approximately the power spectral density of the noise generator over the frequency band where the power spectrum is flat. Again, the discrete analog method of Chapter 4 is useful in deriving the difference equations to use in this process.

The pseudorandom numbers that flow from the discrete analog of the low-pass filter are Gaussianly distributed. The central limit theorem* of statistics holds in this situation because the low-pass filter serves as an avenger and that transforms the output of a pseudorandom number generator whose distribution is uniform to a filtered pseudorandom number generator whose output is Gaussian.

10-7 TRANSFORMING PROBABILITY DENSITY FUNCTIONS

In the case where a non-Gaussian distribution of numbers is desired, it is necessary to modify the output of the filter with a function that maps the random variable x into another random variable y as shown in Figure 10-14. While there are analytical techniques available for some distributions, it is important to understand how to generate functions such as $q(x_2)$ graphically for piecewise linear or polynomial approximation methods.

The approach to generating functions such as q is sketched in Figure 10-15. Interestingly, the function that maps x into y, when x is uniformly distributed on the interval $(0, 1)$, is the inverse cumulative probability

---

*Central Limit Theorem—The sum of an infinite set of continuous, non-Gaussianly distributed numbers is Gaussianly distributed.

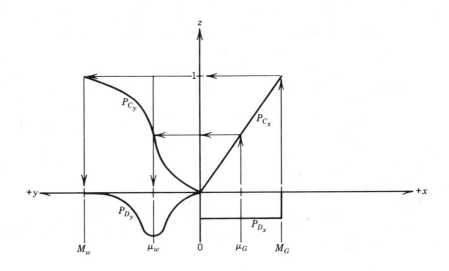

FIGURE 10-14. Transforming a Gaussian distribution into a non-Gaussian distribution requires a function $g(x_2)$.

FIGURE 10-15. Understanding distribution transformation functions. The problem: Given $P_{D_x}(x)$ Find $g(x)$ such that $y = g(x)$ has the probability density function P_{D_y}. The solution: For both P_D's $z = P_{C_x}(x)$; $z = P_{C_y}(y)$ Solve for y and substitute $y = P_{C_y}^{-1}(z) = \underbrace{P_{C_y}^{-1}(P_{C_x}(x))}_{g(x)}$.

function P_C^{-1} of the random variable y whose desired probability density function is P_D. From Figure 10-15, we see that

$$y = g(x_2) = P_{C_y}^{-1}\left(P_{c_{x_2}}(x_2)\right)$$

For example: Suppose P_{D_x} is uniform on the interval $(0, M)$ and P_{D_y} is uniform on the interval $(0, N)$, then

$$P_{C_x} = \frac{1}{M}x, \qquad 0 \le x \le M$$

$$P_{C_y} = \frac{1}{N}y, \qquad 0 \le y \le N$$

then, since P_{C_x} and P_{C_y} share the same ordinate z

$$y = N(z) = N\left(\frac{1}{M}x\right) = \frac{N}{M}(x), \qquad 0 \le x \le M$$

$$\therefore g = \frac{N}{M}x$$

Suppose P_{D_x} is the Gaussianly distributed with zero mean and P_{D_z} is uniformly distributed between $y = -a$ and $y = b$, then

$$P_{D_x} = \frac{1}{\sqrt{2\pi\sigma_x}}e^{-1/2(x/\sigma_x)^2}$$

$$P_{D_y} = \begin{cases} \dfrac{1}{a+b}; & -a < y < b \\ 0; & -a \ge y \ge b \end{cases}$$

then it can be shown that

$$g = \frac{b-a}{2} + (a+b)\,\mathrm{erf}\left(\frac{x}{\sigma_x}\right)$$

here, $g(x)$ is sketched in Figure 10-16.

FIGURE 10-16. The analytic function that transforms a Gaussianly distributed random variable in x into a uniformly distributed random variable in y.

PART V

SIMULATION VERIFICATION

CHAPTER 11

PRACTICAL FAULT DETECTION
AND ISOLATION TECHNIQUES
FOR SIMULATOR VERIFICATION

11.1 INTRODUCTION

Here we will deal with a subject that is more of an art than a science. Perhaps for this reason it is not dealt with in many other books on digital simulation or control system design. It is a subject of considerable importance in the development and checkout of real-time operator training simulations because the results of faulty simulator operation can have serious negative training consequences when the operator takes control of the system.

Specifically, the subject of this chapter arises from questions such as: How do we detect faults in a flight simulator used to train airline flight crews to handle emergency situations in aircraft that can carry up to 600 people into life-threatening situations? How do you isolate faults in the design of a plant simulator used to train nuclear power plant operators on emergency reactor shut-down procedures? In the case of scaled time simulators, the question might be: How do we check out the scaled-time simulation used in the design of a $100M power plant whose critical tolerances are a few thousandths of an inch over a 1500°F temperature range, or a personal computer simulation of a bouncing ball with "spin" that is used in a high school physics course training software package that is used to train many thousands of children each year?

11.2 DETECTING SOFTWARE PROGRAMMING ERRORS

Faulty simulation can arise in either the hardware or software of a simulation. Both manifest themselves in the observables of the simulation and thus can be detected by placing *error detectors* on key observables in the simulation. The more common faults in the development of a simulation, or control system for that matter, are programming errors. Here we are concerned with both an error in programming the equations of motion or equations of state as well as an error in programming data table entry. Data tables, equations of motion, information equations, and the logical equations for control make up most simulation software packages. Subtle errors in any of these can render a simulation result invalid over regions of the observables, state vectors, dependent and independent variables, and/or phase space. A simple sign reversal of the feedback in a complex multiloop control system simulation or high-order system of matrix/vector equations can lead to the simulation system dynamics which are quite *unlike* the system being simulated.

A simple method for finding numerical errors used by Newton and many of the early numerical analysts is available for detecting errors in simulation. The author finds this method to be very useful, though it is little discussed for finding modern simulation errors. The method can be used to find errors in programming differential equations of motion, integration of differential equations, data tables, and logical equations associated with the flow of information in a simulation and/or system (switching trees and operating modes).

A classical method for finding errors in data was to make a table of *finite differences* and look for discontinuities. For example, consider the function $y = x^2$. For values of $x = 0, 1, 2, 3, 4, 5$, we know $y = 0, 1, 4, 9, 16, 25, \ldots$. Suppose, however, an error from some unknown source resulted in y being computed to be $y = 0, 1, 4, 9, 17, 25, \ldots$. Early numerical analysts had learned the error propagates in "data tables" as shown in Table 11-1. The errors are significantly magnified and grow rapidly in the generation of ascending differences in the data table. In the case of $y = x^2$, we see the unit error propagation as shown in Table 11-2.

Note the characteristics $(+), (-), (+), (-)$ pattern of error propagation. The early analysts noted that the errors were weighted by binomial coefficients and thus errors could be corrected as well as detected. For example, knowing that the 4th difference of a quadratic function at each step of the independent variable should be zero. If it was not zero it was 6ϵ, the error could be calculated and the data table corrected. In Table 11-2, we see the 4th difference to be 6; thus the error is $+1$ so the data table can be adjusted to show at $x = 4$, $y = 17 - \epsilon = 16$.

Table 11.1. Error Propagation in Difference Tables

y	$\Delta y = y_n - y_{n-1}$	$\Delta^2 y$	$\Delta^3 y$	$\Delta^4 y$
y_0				
	0			
y_0		0		
	0		0	
y_0		0		$+\epsilon$
	0		$+\epsilon$	
y_0		$+\epsilon$		-4ϵ
	$+\epsilon$		-3ϵ	
$y_0 + \epsilon$		-2ϵ		$+6\epsilon$
	$-\epsilon$		$+3\epsilon$	
y_0		$+\epsilon$		-4ϵ
	0		$-\epsilon$	
y_0		0		$+\epsilon$
	0		0	
y_0		0		
	0			
y_0				

Table 11.2. Unit Error Propagation in the Difference Table in the Function $y = x^2$

x	y	Δy	$\Delta^2 y$	$\Delta^3 y$	$\Delta^4 y$
0	0				
		1			
1	1		2		
		3		0	
2	4		2		1
		5		1	
3	9		3		-4
		8		-3	
4	17		0		$+6$
		8		$+3$	
5	25		3		-4
		11		-1	
6	36		2		$+1$
		13		0	
7	49		2		
		15			
8	64				

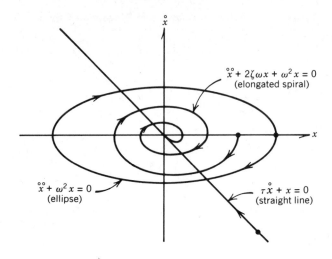

FIGURE 11-1. Typical phase plane trajectories for first and second order systems. τ — decay time constant, ω — natural frequency of oscillation, and ζ — damping factor.

This concept would be difficult to implement in a simulation as used in traditional numerical analysis, but a variation on the concept is to note that finite differences are the numerators in numerical differentiators; thus the first difference is approximately proportional to the first derivative of a function, the second difference is proportional to the second derivative, and so on. In numerical form, the *plot* of a variable against its first difference is similar to a phase plane of the variable (see Figure 11-1). For stable systems, the phase planes are bounded, thus a plot of the first difference of a variable against the variable itself is bounded for stable systems. The approach, then, is to make such phase plane plots for the observables in a simulation and look for (+), (−), (+), zig-zag JUMP DISCONTINUITIES (JD's) as a means of detecting errors.

The method, then, is to make two phase-plane plots ("state vs. rate" and "rate vs. acceleration") for *all* the primary parameters or state vectors or observables in the simulation. Then carefully evaluate these plots for zig-zag discontinuities (see Figures 11-2 and 11-3).

For fixed interval time step type simulations, the rates and accelerations are approximated using simple finite differences. The phase planes can be developed on a CRT display or with a plotter and analyzed as follows:

Step 1. A nominal condition check case is run immediately after the

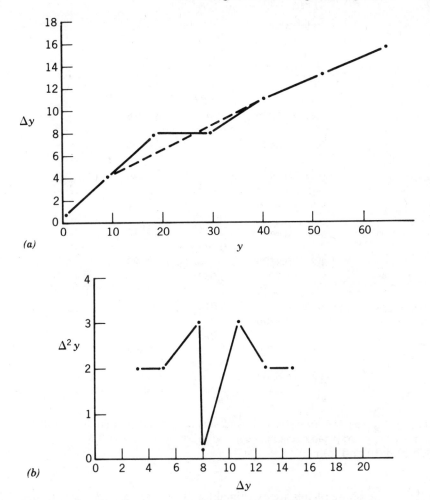

(a)

(b)

FIGURE 11-2. Error detection by observing jump discontinuities in phase planes of the function $y = x^2$ and as described in Table 11-2.

software is programmed and *before* extensive subroutine checkout is complete and *before* comparison with real-world test data. (Remember, the objective is to find programming errors, not verify simulation fidelity).

Step 2. During the run, phase planes are drawn for all key variables and their derivatives. (In certain simulations, the author has monitored more than 50 variables.)

Data Table

t	x $\sin(\omega t)$	Δx	$\Delta^2 x$
0	0		
		0.1986	
0.2	0.1986		−0.0078
		0.1908	
0.4	0.3894		−0.0156
		0.1752	
0.6	0.5646		−0.0224
		0.1528	
0.8	0.7174		+0.0713
		0.2241	
1.0	0.9415		−0.2336
		−0.0095	
1.2	0.9320		+0.0629
		0.0534	
1.4	0.9854		−0.0394
		0.0142	
1.6	0.9996		−0.0400
		−0.0258	
1.8	0.9738		−0.0387
		−0.0654	
2.0	0.9093		

(a)

FIGURE 11-3(a).   Error detection by observing jump discontinuities in phase planes of a 1 rad / sec oscillator (second order system): $\epsilon = 0.1$ at $t = 1$ sec. (See also (b) and (c).)

Step 3.   The phase planes are examined for JD's. They are very easy to see. Once JD's were identified, the time at which the discontinuity occurred is found by rerunning the simulation with a *level detector* on the finite difference of interest; when the level is exceeded, the software "time-tags" the phase-plane discontinuity. The trajectory equations and the logic and data tables can be investigated and tested at, and in the neighborhood of, the time the JD occurred.

This simple technique is a very fast way of finding errors, whatever their source (e.g., data table input errors, programming errors, logic errors, aliasing errors, etc.).

Step 4.   It is only after the software and hardware implementation errors are corrected that simulation should be tested for trajectories that verify the

(b)

(c)

FIGURE 11-3 (*Continued*).

fidelity of the simulation by comparing the simulator's performance with real-world test data or from mathematical modeling and analytical data.

Using the phase plane finite difference error detection method has led to some very practical considerations that saved time and simulator development costs. There are four types of phase plane error found in real-time simulators:

TYPE A ERROR. An error that is observable by the person being trained and will result in negative training. An example would be a substantial delay in the feedback of attitude information on the cockpit flight director in an aircraft flight simulator used to train airline pilots in emergency procedures. Such a delay will mistrain pilots on what to expect from the plane in response to a pilot's control inputs.

TYPE B ERROR. An error that is not observable by the "student" but will lead to negative training. An example would be errors in the aerodynamic data tables in an aircraft simulation. The effect is that the simulated aircraft flies unlike the real aircraft.

TYPE C ERROR. Is observable by the student but will not lead to negative training. An error in a fuel quantity gauge is an example of type C error in an aircraft flight control simulator.

TYPE D ERROR. Is not observable and will not have led to negative training. A simple, hard to find (not necessarily small) error in one of hundreds of aero-thermodynamic data points used in modeling the operation of high-performance jet engines. Such errors often result in a brief, unexpected jump or "blip" in the simulated engine performance.

It is the author's opinion that type A and type B errors should be fixed before training begins. Provided the simulation engineer does not believe the error would result in a loss in confidence in the simulation, the decision can be made to proceed with training with type C errors and inform the students of the errors. The type C error can be corrected as soon as practical. Type D errors can be cleared up as part of routine operational maintenance. The approach to error detection and correction as developed here is quick and easy to employ and can save time and money in simulator development. This approach has been criticized as not being mathematically robust. While the arguments are heuristic, from a mathematical point of view, for justifying the use of this method, they are really rationalizations of a method that works great in many types of simulation checkout. So, keep it in mind and use it, either as an experiment, or as a means to detect, isolate, and correct faults during simulator verification.

11.3 ERROR SIZE

By using the phase plane finite difference error detection technique, errors of 1% to 4% were regularly detected in data tables. Large errors on the order of 10% are unusually easy to spot. This can be understood by examining the phase plane vectors.

Phase-Plane Vector at
Time mT
$\begin{cases} x(nT) = x_n + \epsilon & \text{(where ϵ is the} \\ \Delta x\,(nT) = x_n + \epsilon - x_{n-1} & \text{error in question)} \end{cases}$

Phase-Plane Vector at
Time $(n + 1)T$
$\begin{cases} x((n + 1)T) = x_{n+1} \\ \Delta x\,((n + 1)T) = x_{n+1} - (x_n + \epsilon) \end{cases}$

Note that when $x_{n+1} \simeq x_n \simeq x_{n-1}$

$$x_n = x_n + \epsilon$$

$$\Delta x_n = \epsilon$$

$$x_{n+1} = x_{n+1}$$

$$\Delta x_{n+1} = -\epsilon$$

The plot of the two vectors is shown in Figure 11-4.

We can see that the phase-plane "jumps" at roughly twice the error magnitude. A 2% error results in a 4% jump in a phase-plane trajectory. Second derivatives jump four times the error magnitude. Generally, phase planes of "state-trajectories" are useful for detecting large errors while phase planes of "rate-trajectories" are useful for detecting small errors. In general, phase plane plots of higher order derivatives can be made to detect smaller and smaller simulation errors. For smoothly varying (analytic) type processes, the relationship is typically

$$|\text{Error Detected}| \propto \frac{1}{\text{The factorial of the highest order derivative in the phase plane plots of the variable of interest}}$$

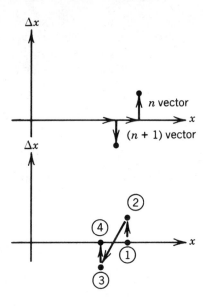

FIGURE 11-4.   Zig-zag error detector. Note: While X moves smoothly from n to $m + 1$, Δx jumps from $+\epsilon$ to $-\epsilon$. Note characteristic zig zag in phase plane is easy to spot because of z shape.

11.4   COUNTERINTUITIVE BEHAVIOR DETECTION

When subsystem simulation equations are developed by another organization or firm and provided to a system design firm, the system designers have to trust that the equations are correct and that the real subsystem is modeled by the simulation equations. Further, just by studying the equations, it is often difficult for the systems designer to develop much of an appreciation for the dynamics of a subsystem and its effect on the overall system being designed or controlled. Most will agree, however, that a good intuitive grasp and "feel" for a subsystem's performance, dynamic response, and operation will improve an integrated system design.

Since some would hold that both the practices of system design and system simulation are as much an art as a science, then *monitoring* for what your intuition and common sense tell you to expect in the system's operating behavior can serve as an aid for finding unknown-unknown

(UNK-UNK)* errors. In simulation, counterintuitive behavior detectors simply compare cause and effect in a simulation with what a design engineer would reasonably expect to happen, based on common sense about the *system being simulated*.

Example

In the design of an aircraft flight control system, it would be reasonable to expect (intuition says) that a right rudder displacement would result in the prompt development of a slewing of an aircraft (yaw rate) to the right. Actually, aircraft that have a very tall vertical fin and a short fuselage and short wing span develop a slight roll movement to the left at the initial onset of right rudder displacement. This motion in turn requires left-aileron-down deflection to counter the roll. This in turn causes an unbalanced drag on the left wing which results in a slew (yaw rate) to the left, opposite the direction of the rudder. This is an example of counterintuitive behavior in a complex system.† Here is a case where the aerodynamic configuration would lead to control system considerations which might be considered *counterintuitive* at the outset.

In this example, a way to bring one's engineering intuition into alignment with the aircraft being controlled (and/or to identify faults in the simulation equations) is by searching for counterintuitive behavior of the controlled system. This requires the development of a *counterintuitive behavior detector*: a software module which can be straightforward and easy to develop. An approach that has been used on a number of flight type simulators is as follows:

Step 1.   Take the time to prepare a list of the intuitive behavior characteristics that are expected of the aircraft, say for example, when under automatic control. The list should include a description of what one would expect to see most of the time when monitoring the observables (print-outs of the simulation variables normally available to the engineer) on which intuitive behavior is expected to be observed by the simulation designer. The example here is that, "Given a right rudder command, one would

---

*UNK-UNK's are errors that you don't know you don't know. Contrast this type of error with a known unknown error. If you know you don't know the source of a fault, you can do something about it. If you don't know you don't know of a fault which may be present, then you can't do anything about it. In this case, counterintuitive behavior detectors are useful in finding the UNK-UNK's.

†Knowing about such behavior leads aircraft control system designers to compensate for adverse yaw by coupling roll and yaw commands in various control modes.

expect to detect *prompt* right turn motion of the aircraft." Another example might be that given added power, one would expect to observe the aircraft promptly accelerate, coupled with a slight pitch up of the nose if the engine is below the Cg of the aircraft. Still another example might be that short-period attitude motion should have less damping with the Cg aft than with the Cg forward. The list of measures of the intuitive behavior of the motion of an aircraft or any system is fairly quickly brought together when the list is developed with a group of engineers involved in the design of the system.

Step 2.   Reduce as many of these intuitive motion tests (counterintuitive fault detectors) as possible to simple tests. For example, when the yaw damper (automatic control) is on and the aircraft is yawing (slewing) left for whatever reasons, the rudder should be displaced right to serve as the cause for the aircraft to come under control. The binary test is as follows: *If* the product of rudder deflection and yaw rate is positive, *then* counterintuitive motion of the controlled aircraft is observed. When such behavior is detected:

- The simulation should be immediately checked with phase plane plots to identify programming errors.
- The counterintuitive phenomena should be studied until such time as the designer's intuition is changed, based on a better understanding of the system.

The product of rudder displacement and yaw rate should never be positive when the aircraft is under control.

Step 3.   Program the counterintuitive behavior detection logic as a subroutine of the simulation. Develop this software module so that it operates when computing time is available to determine if counterintuitive events have occurred. For real-time simulation, this way may require storing the parameters until the CPU has sufficient time to process the data without interrupting real-time simulation. It is important to build time-tag capability into these types of monitors so that when counterintuitive behavior is detected, it can be time-tagged and analysis can begin at or near the time at which the event was observed.

Step 4.   When a careful analysis indicates counterintuitive behavior is detected, a group meeting can be convened to isolate (*a*) whether one's intuition is wrong, (*b*) whether the simulation is wrong, (*c*) whether the math model is in error and does not match what one would intuitively expect from the flight vehicle, or (d) whether the system design needs revision.

The use of counterintuitive behavior detection is also useful as a means of getting a team of designers on top of a brand new simulation and design problem quickly. When managing a simulation or system design, a manager can even develop a module with his or her own "technical monitor" and require that his or her group "report in" when the monitor detects some unusual behavior in the simulated design problem.

It is the author's experience that the time spent trying to understand the intuitive behavior of a system, predict it, and then test for it, is invaluable when it comes to solving design and simulation problems. Developing intuitive performance monitors is also a management technique for developing talented teams of engineers who intuitively understand the system's performance so well that they can efficiently detect and correct design errors.

The benefits of step 1 to a system design and simulation are unexcelled by any other method which have been employed by the author. It is found that engineers who have a good intuitive physical feel for the plant to be controlled often develop special control modes and control techniques that are best suited to the plant in a manner which is not mathematically tractable. It is found that simulation engineers who have a good intuitive physical feel for the system being simulated often develop special numerical methods, data spaces, and parallel processing modes to simulate the system with high fidelity and high speed. The counterintuitive error detection technique may be employed when investigating any simulation which has encountered difficulties in test checkout and verification.

11.5   MONITORING PHYSICAL LAWS AND MATHEMATICAL IDENTITIES

Simulation development errors can manifest themselves in many ways. Errors in the data tables of mass properties or in inertia tensors can result in mechanical motion unlike the system being simulated. Errors in mass transport and/or heat transfer coefficients can result in thermal characteristics of the simulated system which are unlike the system being simulated. When such errors only occur in certain regions of a data base or problem state space, the effects of the errors can appear intermittently and not continuously. Further, since the data bases and initial conditions for many types of simulation change frequently, what can be done to quickly reverify a simulation in which you already have a high degree of confidence?

A technique which is proven to be useful is to monitor the dynamics of the simulation to verify that the basic laws of physics, chemistry, and mathematics are not being violated. A simple example is shown in Figure 11-5. Note that x and y are integrated along separate paths. It is tacitly assumed that the integration is done ideally. In fact, when this simulation is implemented on a digital computer, the integration is done numerically, and x and y will generally have some numerical error:

$$x_{sim} = x + \epsilon_x$$

$$y_{sim} = y + \epsilon_y$$

Further, these errors reflect themselves in an *inconsistency* in the simulation. If the simulation were consistent, then the position of the block in the x, y cartisian coordinator should be identical to its position in polar coordinator where

$$x_{sim} = R_{sim}\cos(\theta); \qquad \theta \text{ is known exactly in this example.}$$

$$y_{sim} = R_{sim}\sin(\theta)$$

$$R_{sim} = \left(x_{sim}^2 + y_{sim}^2\right)^{1/2}$$

Since

$$x + \epsilon_x \neq \left(x^2 + y^2 + 2x\epsilon_x + 2y\epsilon_y + \epsilon_x^2 + \epsilon_y^2\right)^{1/2}\cos(\theta)$$

and

$$y + \epsilon_y \neq \left(x^2 + y^2 + 2x\epsilon_x + 2y\epsilon_y + \epsilon_x^2 + \epsilon_y^2\right)^{1/2}\sin(\theta)$$

we say that in this sense the simulation is inconsistent. Not only is the simulation in error, in that ϵ_x and ϵ_y exist, there is a further inconsistency in that the block's position in the orthogonal coordinates, $x - y$, are not identical to the same coordinates if computed in the orthogonal $R - \theta$ coordinate system. In effect, the simulated position of the block is not *constrained* to stay on the inclined plane. Now, a graphics display of the simulated position would actually show the error by showing the block either penetrating the inclined plane or rising off of it.

In this sense, then, testing to verify that the simulated results do not violate the physical reality of the system being simulated, is a way to monitor and verify the simulation. Interestingly, when such a monitor or

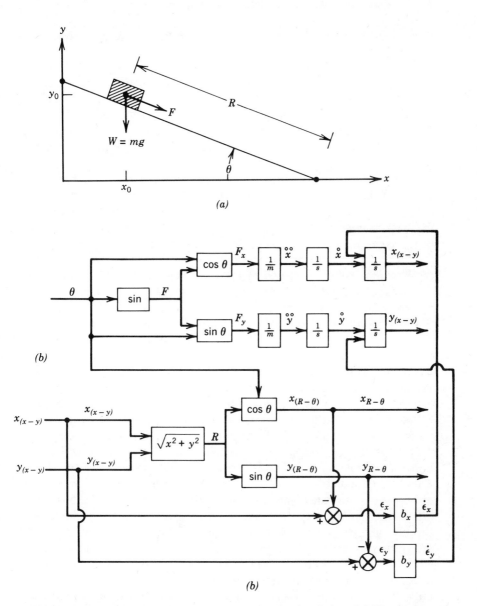

FIGURE 11-5. Monitoring the physics of a simple simulation. (*a*) The system — A block on an inclined plane. Assumption — No friction or other dissipative forces. ω = weight of block, m = mass of block, g = gravitational acceleration at Earth's surface. Inputs — θ allowed to vary; input by simulation operator. Output — Position in x, y coordinates. Math model is shown in (*b*), (*c*), and (*d*).

365

test shows there is an error or a difference, it is frequently possible to CORRECT the situation.

To correct this simple simulation, it is necessary to compute x and y based on a calculation of R and the input θ. See Figure 11-5(b). The difference between $x_{(x-y)}$ and $x_{(R-\theta)}$ is a measure of the inconsistency of the simulation resulting from the error introduced in the numerical integration of $\ddot{x}$. In this sense, such errors can sometimes be corrected using "rate-feedback." Rate feedback is a simple concept where the difference in the position of a state vector, between "where it is" versus "where it should be (relative to some reference)" is used as a feedback to that which generates the motion in a system. The sign of the feedback is reversed so that the induced motion will move to cancel the error. The magnitude of the feedback is controlled by a proportionality constant and is usually established experimentally or based on some analytic criteria. In the case of our simulation, this "consistency correction feedback" loop is shown in 11-5(c). Note that the only time $\mathring{\epsilon}_x$ and $\mathring{\epsilon}_y$ go to zero is when ϵ_x and ϵ_y are zero. (In this sense, we say the error is nulled with a rate feedback loop.) Typically $b_x = b_y = 1/100T$, where T is the integration step size.

While the inconsistency can be removed, it is important to observe that the numerical integration error itself *is not* eliminated. It is often said that the error is eliminated using such techniques, but it is easy to argue from the error equations that in fact, it is not. What is important about this example is that it shows even simple problems with known error sources can result in simulated behavior that is inconsistent with the physical system in ways that are often observable and in ways that are inconsistent with the way the real system behaves.

During the early development of simulations of vehicles with three-dimensional rotational and translational motion, it became well known that Euler's differential equations for describing rotational motion in non-orthogonal coordinates, when used alone, are not useful in digitally simulating the motion of a rotational system when the motion is large in angle and the changes in orientation are frequent. The reason is that numerical integration of Euler's differential equations can lead to numerical errors which can result in apparent divergent motion of the system being simulated. When studying the dynamics of systems which rotate, it is usually important to separate physical effects such as precession, nutation, aniso-elastic torquing, and so on, on the system being simulated. When numerical integration error enters into such problems, it can manifest itself as pseudo-precession, pseudo-nutation, or simply as rotational motion as viewed from a non-orthogonal coordinate system.

In the early seventies, a number of approaches were used to circumvent such problems. Some simulations represented rotational motion using differential equations written in orthogonal coordinates. The two most popular techniques involve the use of direction cosines or/and quaternions. In both of these cases, it was possible to DETECT the effect that errors had on the orthogonality of the coordinate system. The approach was to numerically integrate the differential equations and then test to see if the resultant angular motion satisfied an orthogonal condition.

It is well known that in classical mechanics three angles are all that are required to define the orientation of the angular velocity vector of a rotating system. Further, by the fact that θ_i are measured from the three orthogonal coordinates x, y, z, (see fig. 11-6) it is easily shown that the θ_i should satisfy the trig identity

$$\cos^2\theta_1 + \cos^2\theta_2 + \cos^2\theta_3 = 1$$

When the numerical integration of $\dot\theta_1$, $\dot\theta_2$, and $\dot\theta_3$ resulted in non-orthogonalization of the reference, it was possible to adjust θ_1, θ_2, and θ_3 to eliminate the further consequences of observing $\bar\omega$ in a nonorthogonal coordinate system. While the orthogonality problem was solved, it was done at the expense of adjustments in θ_1, θ_2, and θ_3 that were not *real* motions of $\bar\omega$. Similarly, in our simple example, adjustments in the simulated position of the block (see Fig. 11-5), for the sake of satisfying the physical constraints in the problem are done by inducing motion in the system that is not a result of the natural forces on the system being simulated. Of

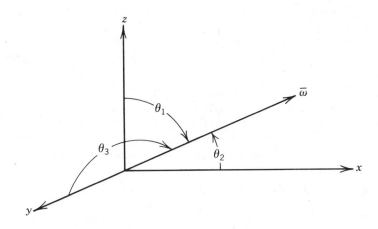

FIGURE 11-6. Direction cosines associated with $\bar\omega$.

course, the motions are never large, so the procedure is usually justified on the basis that in certain cases, consistency and orthogonality are more important than absolute accuracy.

Energy and power are often useful ways to monitor simulator performance. For mechanical systems which are conservative, energy is conserved and it only changes in form. In our simple example (see Figure 11-5), the change in kinetic energy of the block is independent of the trajectory taken by the block—it must equal the change in potential energy as:

$$mg\left(y_{0_{\text{sim}}} - y_{\text{sim}}\right) - \tfrac{1}{2}m\left(\dot{x}_{\text{sim}}^2 + \dot{y}_{\text{sim}}^2\right) = 0$$

If this test is not satisfied, it means that error has crept into the system and is manifesting itself as a violation of the conservation of energy.

While systems are rarely conservative in their motion (perhaps spacecraft maneuvering simulations are notable exceptions), it is frequently possible to eliminate dissipation forces or entropy increasing phenomena in a *simulation* and operate the system as a purely conservative system. When such modifications are made to the simulation, the total energy should increase as the time integral of the applied power. It is often easy to detect when the total of the various forms of mechanical, electrical, and thermal energy do not total to the time integral of the power supplied by the engines in the simulation (whether mechanical, electrical, thermal, chemical, etc.). Remember, when the simulation is "conservative" the energy change is independent of the path taken, so the test should be applied over many different simulated paths as a means of checking out many data bases and other sources or programming errors.

When the dissipative processes are then reintroduced into the system, a useful measure of the physics of the simulation is the time it takes for the simulated system to dissipate a known amount of energy when no power is applied to the system. This is a fairly sensitive measure of how well the simulation compares with the system to be simulated.

Finally, with the power reapplied to the system, it is possible to measure the ratio of changes in the total energy to changes in the applied power to measure the energy dissipation/absorption "time-constant" of the system. When such a measure is employed as a system monitor, it usually requires that a matrix of time-constants be developed for the various simulated conditions and/or regions in which the simulation is to operate. For example, flight simulators used to train airline pilots must function properly with the landing gear up and down, flaps and spoilers up and down, and with various engines not operating. In each condition (18 for 3-engine aircraft such as DC-10, L1011, Boeing 757, etc.), the time constant is different and must be determined in order for this type of monitor to work.

Summary: A number of ways to monitor and verify the performance of a simulator have been discussed. In all cases, the intent is to encourage the simulation engineer to build and make them a permanent part of the simulation. Once the monitor detects errors or problems with the simulation, the source can be quickly identified if the monitor appropriately tags the error so that the simulation can be initialized in the region of the simulation state space where the error was detected.

PART VI

FAST FUNCTION
EVALUATION TECHNIQUES

CHAPTER 12

NESTED PARENTHETICAL FORMS AND CHEBYSHEV ECONOMIZATION

This chapter presents certain elementary techniques for improving the efficiency of numerically evaluating functions. The methods are simple and easy to use and remember. They have broad application and should be helpful to the beginning simulation designer. These methods are well known to most systems software specialists. Many engineers have not been exposed to these techniques, so they are covered here for those not familiar with fast function evaluation.

12.1 NESTED PARENTHETICAL FORMS

Many functions of interest to engineers can be written in a power series that can be generated by using Taylor's theorem, Maclaurin's theorem, Chebyshev polynomials, and so on. Additionally, an empirical data set can be fit with power series. When so written, they take the form

$$f(x) = a_0 + a_1 x + a_2 x^2 + a_3 x^3 + \cdots + a_n x^n + \cdots \qquad (12\text{-}1)$$

Evaluating this series in standard form typically involves the following operations to evaluate the nth partial sum of $f(x)$:

(1)   Compute x and store in X
(2)   Store x in Y
(3)   Multiply
(4)   Multiply
        $\vdots$

$(n + 2)$ Multiply
$(n + 3)$ Call a_n
$(n + 4)$ Multiply
$(n + 5)$ Call previous partial sum of $f(x)$
$(n + 6)$ Store new partial sum of $f(x)$

The total number of operations involved is approximately

$$\frac{n^2}{2} - 12n$$

By rewriting (12-1) using nested parentheses we get

$$a_0 + x\left(a_1 + x\left(a_2 + x\left(a_3 + \cdots + x(a_{n-2} + x(a_{n-1} + a_n x)) \cdots \right)\right)\right)$$

The number of operations is reduced because the series is organized in the natural language of the computer and requires no redundant multiplication. The typical set of operations to evaluate the partial sum of $f(x)$ in nested parenthetical form is

(1)   Compute x and store in X
(2)   Recall a_n
(3)   Multiply
(4)   Recall a_{n-1}
(5)   Add
(6)   Recall X
(7)   Multiply
           $\vdots$

The total number of operations involved is approximately

$$7n$$

Comparing the two approaches, we see that the number of operations required to compute the series in standard form increases as the square of the number of terms in the series, whereas the number of operations needed to evaluate the series in nested parenthetical form is proportional to the number of terms in the series. In general, nested parenthetical forms are processed faster than standard forms. Note also that it is unnecessary and in fact wasteful to use computer storage for intermediate calculations when evaluating series in nested parenthetical forms. The more familiar series of these forms are referenced in Table 12-1.

Table 12-1. Familiar Series Expansions Written in Nested Parenthetical Forms

$$\ln(1 + x) \cong x\left(1 - \frac{x}{2}\left(1 - \frac{2x}{3}\left(1 - \frac{3x}{4}\left(1 - \frac{4x}{5}\right)\right)\right)\right), \qquad \text{for } |x| < 1$$

$$\ln(x) \cong y\left(1 + \frac{y}{2}\left(1 + \frac{2y}{3}\left(1 + \frac{3y}{4}\left(1 + \frac{4y}{5}\right)\right)\right)\right), \qquad \text{for } y = \frac{x-1}{x}, \text{ Re } x > \tfrac{1}{2}$$

$$\ln(x) \cong y\left(1 - \frac{y}{2}\left(1 - \frac{2y}{3}\left(1 - \frac{3y}{4}\right)\right)\right), \qquad \text{for } y = (x - 1), |x - 1| < 1$$

$$\ln\left(\frac{x+1}{x-1}\right) \cong \frac{2}{x}\left(1 + \frac{1}{3x^2}\left(1 + \frac{3}{5x^2}\left(1 + \frac{5}{7x^2}\left(1 + \frac{7}{9x^2}\right)\right)\right)\right), \qquad \text{for } |x| > 1$$

$$e^x \cong 1 - x\left(1 + \frac{x}{2}\left(1 + \frac{2x}{6}\left(1 + \frac{6x}{24}\left(1 + \frac{24x}{120}\left(1 + \frac{120}{720}x\right)\right)\right)\right)\right)$$

$$\sin(x) \cong x\left(1 - \frac{x^2}{6}\left(1 - \frac{6x^2}{120}\left(1 - \frac{120x^2}{5040}\left(1 - \frac{5040}{362880}x^2\right)\right)\right)\right)$$

$$\cos(x) \cong \left(1 - \frac{x^2}{2}\left(1 - \frac{2x^2}{24}\left(1 - \frac{24x^2}{720}\left(1 - \frac{720}{40320}x^2\right)\right)\right)\right)$$

$$\tan(x) \cong x\left(1 + \frac{x^2}{3}\left(1 + \frac{6x^2}{10}\left(1 + \frac{255}{630}x^2\right)\right)\right)$$

$$\cotan(x) \cong \frac{1}{x} - \frac{x}{3}\left(1 + \frac{3x^2}{45}\left(1 + \frac{90}{945}x^2\right)\right)$$

$$\arcsin(x) \cong x\left(1 + \frac{x^2}{6}\left(1 + \frac{18x^2}{40}\left(1 + \frac{600}{1008}x^2\right)\right)\right), \qquad \text{for } |x| \leqslant 1$$

$$\arctan(x) \cong x\left(1 - \frac{x^2}{3}\left(1 - \frac{3x^2}{5}\left(1 - \frac{5x^2}{7}\right)\right)\right), \qquad \text{for } x^2 < 1$$

$$\arctan(x) \cong \frac{\pi}{2} - \frac{1}{x}\left(1 - \frac{1}{3x^2}\left(1 - \frac{3}{5x^2}\right)\right), \qquad \text{for } |x| > 1$$

These formulas were selected on the basis of the reasonableness of their intervals of convergence.

Another approach to evaluating these scientific functions is to use a curve-fit polynomial over the broad range of the argument. These polynomials will permit precise evaluation of the logarithmic, exponential, and transcendental functions. Table 12-2 sets out such curve-fit polynomials for the more familiar functions.

Table 12-2. Polynomial Approximations of Many Functions

(1) $\text{Log}_{10}(x) = t\left(a_1 + t^2\left(a_3 + t^2\left(a_5 + t^2\left(a_7 + a_9^2\right)\right)\right)\right) + \epsilon(x)$

Here

$$t = (x - 1)(x + 1)^{-1}$$

and

$$|\epsilon(x)| < 10^{-7} \quad \text{where} \quad 10^{-1/2} \leqslant x \leqslant 13^{+1/2}$$

for

$$a_1 = 0.868591718 \quad a_7 = 0.094376476$$
$$a_3 = 0.289335524 \quad a_9 = 0.191337714$$
$$a_5 = 0.177522071$$

(2) $\text{Log}_{10}(x) = t(a_1 + a_3 t^2) + \epsilon(x)$
where $t = (x - 1)(x + 1)^{-1}$, $a_1 = 0.86304$, and $a_3 = 0.36415$.
Then

$$|\epsilon(x)| < 10^{-4} \quad \text{where} \quad 10^{-1/2} \leqslant x \leqslant 10^{+1/2}$$

(3) $\text{Ln}(1 + x) = x\left(a_1 + x\left(a_2 + x\left(a_3 + x(a_4 + a_5 x)\right)\right)\right) + \epsilon(x)$

Here

$$a_1 = 0.99949556 \quad a_4 = -0.13606275$$
$$a_2 = -0.49190896 \quad a_5 = 0.03215845$$
$$a_3 = 0.28947478$$

Then

$$|\epsilon(x)| < 10^{-5} \quad \text{where} \quad 0 \leqslant x \leqslant 1$$

(4) $\text{Ln}(1 + x) = x\left(a_1 + x\left(a_2 + x\left(a_3 + x\left(a_4 + x\left(a_5 + x\left(a_6 + x(a_7 + a_8 x)\right)\right)\right)\right)\right)\right)$
$ + \epsilon(x)$

Here

$$a_1 = 0.9999964239 \quad a_5 = 0.167654071$$
$$a_2 = -0.4998741238 \quad a_6 = -0.0953293897$$
$$a_3 = 0.3317990258 \quad a_7 = 0.0360884937$$
$$a_4 = 0.2407338084 \quad a_8 = 0.0064535442$$

and

$$|\epsilon(x)| < 3 \times 10^{-8} \quad \text{where} \quad 0 \leqslant x \leqslant 1$$

Table 12-2 (*Continued*)

(5) $e^{-x} = 1 + x(a_1 + a_2x) + \epsilon(x)$
where
$$a_1 = -0.9664 \quad \text{and} \quad a_2 = 0.3536$$
Then
$$|\epsilon(x)| < 3 \times 10^{-3} \quad \text{where} \quad 0 < x < \ln 2$$

(6) $e^{-x} = 1 + x\big(a_1 + x(a_2 + x(a_3 + a_4x))\big)$
where
$$a_1 = -0.9998684 \quad a_3 = -0.1595332$$
$$a_2 = 0.4982926 \quad a_4 = 0.0293641$$
Then
$$|\epsilon(x)| < 5 \times 10^{-5} \quad \text{where} \quad 0 < x < \ln 2$$

(7) $\text{Sin}(x) = x\big(1 + x^2(a_2 + a_4x^2)\big) + x\epsilon(x)$
where
$$a_2 = -0.16605 \quad \text{and} \quad a_4 = 0.00761$$
Then
$$|\epsilon(x)| < 2 \times 10^{-4} \quad \text{where} \quad 0 < x < \frac{\pi}{2}$$

(8) $\text{Sin}(x) = x\Big(1 + x^2\big(a_2 + x^2(a_4 + x^2(a_6 + x^2(a_8 + a_{10}x^2)))\big)\Big) + x\epsilon(x)$
where
$$a_2 = -0.1666666664 \quad a_8 = 0.0000027526$$
$$a_4 = 0.0083333315 \quad a_{10} = -0.0000000239$$
$$a_6 = -0.001984090$$
Then
$$|\epsilon(x)| < 2 \times 10^{-9} \quad \text{where} \quad 0 < x < \frac{\pi}{2}$$

(9) $\text{Cos}(x) = 1 + x^2(a_2 + a_4x^2) + \epsilon(x)$
where
$$a_2 = -0.49670$$
$$a_4 = 0.03705$$
Then
$$|\epsilon(x)| < 9 \times 10^{-4} \quad \text{where} \quad 0 < x < \frac{\pi}{2}$$

(10) $\text{Cos}(x) = 1 + x^2\big(a_2 + x^2(a_4 + x^2(a_6 + x^2(a_8 + a_{10}x^2)))\big) + \epsilon(x)$
where
$$a_2 = -0.4999999963 \quad a_8 = 0.0000247609$$
$$a_4 = 0.0416666418 \quad a_{10} = -0.000000605$$
$$a_6 = -0.001388839$$

Table 12-2 (*Continued*)

Then
$$|\epsilon(x)| < 2 \times 10^{-9} \qquad \text{where} \qquad 0 < x < \frac{\pi}{2}$$

(11) $\text{Tan}(x) = x\left(1 + x^2(a_2 + a_4x^2)\right) + x\epsilon(x)$

where
$$a_2 = 0.31755$$
$$a_4 = 0.20330$$

Then
$$|\epsilon(x)| < 10^{-3} \qquad \text{where} \qquad 0 < x < \frac{\pi}{4}$$

(12) $\text{Tan}(x) = x\left(1 + x^2\left(a_2 + x^2\left(a_4 + x^2\left(a_6 + x^2\left(a_8 + x^2(a_{10} + a_{12}x^2)\right)\right)\right)\right)\right)$
$$+ x\epsilon(x)$$

where
$$\begin{array}{ll} a_2 = 0.3333314036 & a_8 = 0.0245650893 \\ a_4 = 0.1333923995 & a_{10} = 0.0029005250 \\ a_6 = 0.0533740603 & a_{12} = 0.0095168091 \end{array}$$

Then
$$|\epsilon(x)| < 2 \times 10^{-3} \qquad \text{where} \qquad 0 < x < \frac{\pi}{4}$$

(13) $\text{Cotan}(x) = \frac{1}{x}\left(1 + x^2(a_2 + a_4x^2)\right) + \frac{\epsilon(x)}{x}$

where
$$a_2 = -0.332867$$
$$a_4 = -0.024369$$

Then
$$|\epsilon(x)| \leqslant 3 \times 10^{-5} \qquad \text{where} \qquad 0 \leqslant x \leqslant \frac{\pi}{4}$$

(14) $\text{Cotan}(x) = \frac{1}{x}\left(1 + x^2\left(a_2 + x^2\left(a_4 + x^2\left(a_6 + x^2(a_8 + a_{10}x^2)\right)\right)\right)\right) + \frac{\epsilon(x)}{x}$

where
$$\begin{array}{ll} a_2 = -0.3333333412 & a_8 = -0.0002078504 \\ a_4 = -0.0222220287 & a_{10} = -0.0000262619 \\ a_6 = 0.0021177168 \end{array}$$

Then
$$|\epsilon(x)| \leqslant 4 \times 10^{-10} \qquad \text{where} \qquad 0 \leqslant x \leqslant \frac{\pi}{4}$$

(15) $\text{Arcsin}(x) = \frac{\pi}{2} - (1 - x)^{1/2}\left(a_0 + x(a_1 + x(a_2 + a_3x))\right) + \epsilon(x)$

where
$$\begin{array}{ll} a_0 = 1.5707288 & a_2 = 0.0742610 \\ a_1 = -0.2121144 & a_3 = -0.0187293 \end{array}$$

Table 12-2   (*Continued*)

Then

$$|\epsilon(x)| \leqslant 5 \times 10^{-5} \qquad \text{where} \qquad 0 \leqslant x \leqslant 1$$

(16) $\text{Arctan}(x) = x\left(a_1 + x^2\left(a_3 + x^2\left(a_5 + x^2\left(a_7 + a_9x^2\right)\right)\right)\right) + \epsilon(x)$

where

$$a_1 = 0.9998660 \qquad a_7 = -0.0851330$$
$$a_3 = -0.3302995 \qquad a_9 = 0.0208351$$
$$a_5 = 0.1801410$$

Then

$$|\epsilon(x)| \leqslant 10^{-5} \qquad \text{where} \qquad -1 \leqslant x \leqslant 1$$

Functions may be put into forms that are easily computed by the following procedures:

PROCEDURE 1

(*a*) Either find or generate a table of values for the function of interest to the accuracy of interest.

(*b*) Prepare an interpolating polynomial that passes through selected points of interest in the table but spans the range of interest in the argument.

(*c*) Identify the maximum error of the polynomial approximation on the interval of interest.

(*d*) If the accuracy is satisfactory, write the polynomial in nested parenthetical form and use it for approximate evaluation of the function.

If a table is not available and there is not sufficient time to generate one, use procedure 2.

PROCEDURE 2

(*a*) Prepare a series approximation of the function centered on the interval of interest.

(*b*) Use a Chebyshev economization scheme (see Section 12.2) to reduce the order of the polynomial.

(*c*) Test the polynomial for accuracy over the argument's interval of interest.

(*d*) If the polynomial is not sufficiently accurate, include more terms in the original approximating polynomial before Chebyshev economization and use the Chebyshev procedure to test the polynomial again.

(*e*) When the polynomial is sufficiently accurate, write it in nested parenthetical form and use it to evaluate the function.

The question of how accurate a function evaluation should be is a touchy subject. Often engineers specify the accuracy by requiring the function to be good to one part in 10^3. Other engineers say the percentage error in the function evaluation must be good to one part in 10^3. What is the difference? To evaluate e^{-x} when $x = 3$ using the first criterion requires 12 terms of a Taylor series expansion of e^{-x} around zero. The latter criterion requires only 8. Why? The answer is simply that the first error criterion is an absolute error criterion:

$$\text{absolute error} = \text{true} - \text{approximate}$$

The latter criterion is a relative error criterion:

$$\text{relative error} = \frac{\text{true} - \text{approximate}}{\text{true}} = \frac{\text{absolute error}}{\text{true}}$$

Since the absolute error in the true value is generally smaller than the true value itself, the denominator will usually be larger than the numerator and thus the relative error criterion is satisfied at a smaller absolute error than the absolute error criterion alone.

Another point is this: most engineers work problems in percentages (or by relative error). Although highly scientific simulations may require high absolute accuracy, it is usually found that engineering simulations only require a few percent relative accuracy and thus fewer terms are required in the evaluation of functions with truncated infinite series.

12.2   CHEBYSHEV POLYNOMIALS

In this section we are concerned with the derivation of polynomials that can be used for analytic substitution, rather than with simulation per se. Such derivation is pertinent in simulation because there are many series expansions of many advanced functions that converge slowly and thus are too inefficient for **fast** simulation. These series can be modified however to converge more quickly using the Chebyshev economization technique or rational polynomial approximation methods. The polynomial approximations of truncated series expansions of functions have the advantage that they can be written in nested parenthetical form and efficiently (quickly) evaluated with high precision. The objective here is to improve the convergence of series approximations of given functions.

Chebyshev polynomials can be used in a unique process, commonly called economization, to transform a truncated power series expansion of a function into a more quickly converging polynomial. They can transform tables of infinite series of questionable numerical analysis value into fast converging series (of which the error is well known) by use of the Chebyshev approximation theorem. These polynomials should then be written in nested parenthetical form for fast function evaluation. In short Chebyshev polynomials can make tables of infinite series representation of advanced mathematical functions (of which there are a great many) eminently practical for fast function evaluation. Because the process of economization is easy to perform and makes immediately available to the analyst large tables of infinite series, this section is dedicated to the marvelous properties of Chebyshev polynomials and their application to conditioning series for improved convergence.

Chebyshev polynomials have five important mathematical properties:

1. They are orthogonal polynomials, with a suitable weighting function, whether defined on a continuous interval or a discrete set of points.

2. They are equal-ripple functions, that is, they alternate between maxima and minima all of the same size.

3. The zeros of successive Chebyshev polynomials interlace each other.

4. All Chebyshev polynomials satisfy a three-term recurrence relation.

5. They are easy to compute and convert to and from a power series form.

These properties together generate a minimax approximating function (i.e., one that minimizes the maximum error in its approximation). This is quite different from, for example, least-squares approximation where the sum of the squares of the errors is minimized. In least-squares approximations the average square error is minimized; the maximum error itself can be quite large. In Chebyshev approximation, the average error can often be large but the maximum error is minimized.

Chebyshev Polynomials Defined

Chebyshev polynomials are simply defined by the relations

$$T_0(x) = 1 \tag{12-2}$$

$$T_n(x) = \cos(n\theta) \tag{12-3}$$

$$\cos \theta = x \tag{12-4}$$

It is apparent from (9-3) that these polynomials are orthogonal (with a

It is apparent from (12-3) that these polynomials are orthogonal (with a suitable weighting factor), since cosine is an orthogonal function and $\cos(n\theta)$ is a polynomial of degree n in $\cos\theta$.

Noting the trigonometric identity

$$\cos(n+1)\theta + \cos(n-1)\theta = 2\cos\theta\cos n\theta$$

we can write immediately that

$$T_{n+1} + T_{n-1} = 2xT_n$$

$$\therefore T_{n+1} = 2xT_n - T_{n-1} \tag{12-5}$$

Using this recurrence relation for the Chebyshev polynomials we can easily generate the successive polynomials as follows: Since

$$T_0 = 1$$

and

$$T_1 = x$$

in (12-5) we find

$$T_2 = 2xT_1 - T_0 = 2x^2 - 1$$

Then starting with

$$T_1 = x$$

and

$$T_2 = 2x^2 - 1$$

and again using the recurrence formula (12-5), we find

$$T_3 = 2xT_2 - T_1 = 4x^3 - 3x$$

Continuing in a similar manner we can form the table of Chebyshev polynomials:

$$T_0 = 1$$
$$T_1 = x$$
$$T_2 = 2x^2 - 1$$
$$T_3 = 4x^3 - 3x$$
$$T_4 = 8x^4 - 8x^2 + 1$$
$$T_5 = 16x^5 - 20x^3 + 5x$$
$$T_6 = 32x^6 - 48x^4 + 18x^2 - 1$$
$$T_7 = 64x^7 - 112x^5 + 56x^3 - 7x$$
$$T_8 = 128x^8 - 256x^6 + 160x^4 - 32x^2 + 1$$

Note that we can also form a table for powers of x in terms of Chebyshev polynomials by solving for the powers of x from this table:

$$1 = T_0$$

$$x = T_1$$

$$x^2 = \frac{T_0 + T_2}{2}$$

$$x^3 = \frac{3T_1 + T_3}{4}$$

$$x^4 = \frac{3T_0 + 4T_2 + T_4}{8}$$

$$x^5 = \frac{10T_1 + 5T_3 + T_5}{16}$$

$$x^6 = \frac{10T_0 + 15T_2 + 6T_4 + T_6}{32}$$

$$x^7 = \frac{35T_1 + 21T_3 + 7T_5 + T_7}{64}$$

$$x^8 = \frac{35T_0 + 56T_2 + 28T_4 + 8T_6 + T_8}{128}$$

An important aspect of the Chebyshev polynomials is that Chebyshev proved that of all polynomials of degree n having a leading coefficient of 1, the Chebyshev polynomials (when divided by 2^{n-1}) have the least extreme value in the interval

$$-1 \leqslant x \leqslant +1$$

There are no other polynomials of degree n, whose leading coefficient is 1, that will have a smaller extreme value than

$$\max \left| \frac{T_n(x)}{2^{n-1}} \right| = \frac{1}{2^{n-1}}$$

in the interval

$$-1 \leqslant x \leqslant +1$$

This is an important finding because it says that if we approximate a function on the interval $|x| \leqslant 1$ with Chebyshev polynomials that are truncated at n terms, the maximum error in the approximation is

$$\frac{1}{2^{n-1}}$$

The objective then is to find an expansion for function $f(x)$ in terms of Chebyshev polynomials as

$$f(x) = \sum_{n=0}^{n} a_n T_n(x)$$

An approach to approximating $f(x)$ with Chebyshev polynomials (credited primarily to Lanczos) is powerful and simple to use and has the nice property that it will usually improve the convergence of any truncated series expansion of a function $f(x)$. This is:

1. Write a truncated series of polynomial approximations of $f(x)$ in nested form.

2. Rewrite the polynomial expansion in terms of Chebyshev polynomials.

3. Truncate the new series one or two more terms.

4. Rewrite the Chebyshev polynomials in terms of polynomials in x.

5. Rewrite this polynomial in nested parenthetical form for convenient numerical evaluation.

For example if we write a truncated power series representation of a function in the form

$$f(x) = \sum_{n=0}^{m} a_n x^n \qquad (12\text{-}6)$$

and rewrite (12-6) in nested parenthetical form

$$f(x) = a_0 + x\big(a_1 + x(a_2 + \cdots + x(a_{m-1} + a_m x) \cdots)\big)$$

we can convert this to a series of Chebyshev polynomials by starting at the inner parentheses and rewriting it in the form

$$a_{m-1} + a_m x = a_{m-1} T_0 + a_m T_1 \qquad (12\text{-}7)$$

Assuming that at the nth parenthetical nest

$$a_0 T_0 + a_1 T_1 + \cdots + a_n T_n \qquad (12\text{-}8)$$

we can multiply this by x and add to it the next coefficient in the power series a_{m-n-1} to get the $(n + 1)$st nest. Then, by using the relationships

$$xT_0 = T_1$$

$$xT_n = \frac{T_{n+1} + T_{n-1}}{2} \tag{12-9}$$

the power series in the nth parentheses is transformed in the $(n + 1)$st power series in Chebyshev polynomials as

$$\frac{x_n T_n}{2} + \frac{a_{n-1} T_{n-1}}{2} + \cdots + \left(\frac{a_1 + a_3}{2} \right) T_2$$

$$+ \left(a_0 + \frac{a_2}{2} \right) T_1 + \left(a_{m-n-1} + \frac{a_1}{2} \right) T_0 \tag{12-10}$$

The process for generating the coefficients at any given stage in the development of the Chebyshev polynomial expansion of $f(x)$ can be visualized in Figure 12-1. Here the coefficients at a given stage are used to generate the coefficients in the next stage according to the diagram.

In this approach, the coefficient associated with the mth term of the original series

$$a_m x^m$$

becomes, in the Chebyshev polynomial expansion,

$$\frac{a_m}{2^{m-1}} T_m(x)$$

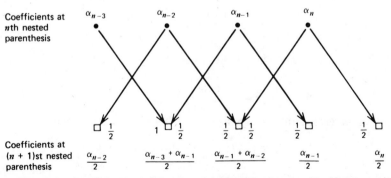

FIGURE 12-1. Process for generating coefficients for the Chebyshev expansion of $f(t)$. Source: J. M. Smith, *Scientific Analysis on the Pocket Calculator*, Wiley, 1975. Used by permission of the publisher.

Thus, if we were to truncate the Chebyshev polynomial expansion of $f(x)$ beginning with the mth term, the error would be on the order of a_m/z^{m-1} instead of a_m as it would be in the original polynomial approximation (see Table 12-3). In this sense, then, we say that the Chebyshev expansion converges more quickly than the original expansion.

Stated in another way, if the original approximation of the function was accurate to some error, the Chebyshev polynomial approximation will usually be almost as accurate (to the same error) with fewer terms. Additional terms can therefore be dropped from the reexpressed polynomial. This is called the economization process.

The procedure followed in (12-7) through (12-9) shows the general approach to generating Chebyshev polynomial approximations of $f(x)$ for n terms. The table of powers of x in terms of the Chebyshev polynomials, presented earlier and partly repeated here for convenience, is useful for direct substitution of powers of x for its equivalent Chebyshev polynomial

$$1 = T_0$$

$$x = T_1$$

$$x^2 = \frac{T_0 + T_2}{2}$$

$$x^3 = \frac{3T_1 + T_3}{4}$$

$$x^4 = \frac{3T_0 + 4T_2 + T_4}{8}$$

$$x^5 = \frac{10T_1 + 5T_3 + T_5}{16}$$

In this way, a power series of the form

$$f(x) = a_0 + a_1 x + a_2 x^2 + \cdots + a_m x^m$$

can be converted into an expansion in Chebyshev polynomials

$$f(x) = b_0 + b_1 T_1 + b_2 T_2 + \cdots + b_m T_m$$

In order for this process to be accurate, the series must be written in a form where the evaluation of $f(x)$ takes place for x on the interval $-1 \leqslant x \leqslant +1$. Once the expansion is written in terms of Chebyshev

Table 12-3.   **Expansions of** $f_N(x) = \sum\limits_{n=0}^{N} a_n x^n$ **In Chebyshev Polynomials**

Expansion in powers of x	Chebyshev expansion
$f_0 = a_0$	$a_0 T_0$
$f_1 = a_0 + a_1 x$	$a_0 T_0 + a_1 T_1$
$f_2 = a_0 + a_1 x + a_2 x^2$	$\left(a_0 + \dfrac{a_2}{2}\right) T_0 + a_1 T_1 + \left(\dfrac{a_2}{2}\right) T_2$
$f_3 = a_0 + a_1 x + a_2 x^2$ $+ a_3 x^3$	$\left(a_0 + \dfrac{a_2}{2}\right) T_0 + \left(a_1 + \dfrac{3a_3}{4}\right) T_1 + \left(\dfrac{a_2}{2}\right) T_2 + \left(\dfrac{a_3}{4}\right) T_3$
$f_4 = a_0 + a_1 x + a_2 x^2$ $+ a_3 x^3 + a_4 x^4$	$\left(a_0 + \dfrac{a_2}{2} + \dfrac{3a_4}{8}\right) T_0 + \left(a_1 + \dfrac{3a_3}{4}\right) T_1 + \tfrac{1}{2}(a_2 + a_4) T_2$ $+ \left(\dfrac{a_3}{4}\right) T_3 + \left(\dfrac{a_4}{8}\right) T_4$
$f_5 = a_0 + a_1 x + a_2 x^2$ $+ a_3 x^3 + a_4 x^4 + a_5 x^5$	$\left(a_0 + \dfrac{a_2}{2} + \dfrac{3a_4}{8}\right) T_0 + \left(a_1 + \dfrac{3a_3}{4} + \dfrac{10a_5}{16}\right) T_1$ $+ \left(\dfrac{a_2 + a_4}{2}\right) T_2 + \left(\dfrac{a_3}{4} + \dfrac{5a_5}{16}\right) T_3 + \left(\dfrac{a_4}{8}\right) T_4 + \left(\dfrac{a_5}{16}\right) T_5$

polynomials, they can be replaced by polynomials in x from the table previously presented and repeated here for convenience

$$T_0 = 1$$

$$T_1 = x$$

$$T_2 = 2x^2 - 1$$

$$T_3 = 4x^3 - 3x$$

$$T_4 = 8x^4 - 8x^2 + 1$$

$$T_5 = 16x^5 - 20x^3 + 5x$$

and then algebraically simplified and written in nested parenthetical form for quick evaluation.

Hamming works the easy-to-follow example

$$y = \ln(1 + x) \cong x - \frac{x^2}{2} + \frac{x^3}{3} \tag{12-11}$$

to illustrate the method of economization. By direct substitution for powers of x, we can rewrite this power series expansion in terms of the Chebyshev polynomials as

$$y \cong T_1 - \left(\frac{T_0 + T_2}{4}\right) + \left(\frac{3T_1 + T_3}{12}\right)$$

$$y \cong -\frac{T_0}{4} + \left(1 + \frac{3}{12}\right)T_1 - \frac{T_2}{4} + \frac{T_3}{12} \qquad (12\text{-}12)$$

$$y \cong -\frac{T_0}{4} + \frac{15T_1}{12} - \frac{T_2}{4} + \frac{T_3}{12}$$

Dropping the last term in the power series (12-11) results in dropping 0.25 from the numerical evaluation of y (when $x = 1$); while a roughly equivalent error is produced in the power series (12-12) by dropping the last two terms. At most the error will be

$$\epsilon = \tfrac{1}{12} - \tfrac{1}{4} = -0.1666 \cdots$$

We know this because the magnitude of the value of the Chebyshev polynomials is less than or equal to 1 for all x on the interval $0 \leqslant x \leqslant 1$. Thus we can write

$$y = \ln(1 + x) \cong -\frac{T_0}{4} + \frac{15T_1}{12} - \frac{T_2}{4} \qquad (12\text{-}13)$$

with somewhat better accuracy than given by (12-11). This, then, is the process of economization. Using the definitions of the Chebyshev polynomials we can rewrite (12-13) in the form

$$y = \ln(1 + x) \cong -\frac{1}{4} + \frac{15x}{12} - \frac{2x^2}{4} + \frac{1}{4} = x(1.25 - 0.5x)$$

The numerical comparison of the economized second-order polynomial and the (noneconomized) second-order polynomial is given in Table 12-4. The economized quadratic equation has a smaller average error (-0.0646) than the noneconomized quadratic equation (0.0795) as well as having the smallest maximum error (0.1 at $x = 0.5$) on the interval

$$0 \leqslant x \leqslant 1$$

Table 12-4.   Comparison of Economized and Noneconomized Quadratics

x	Exact $y = \ln(1 + x)$	Economized $y \cong x(1.25 - 0.5x)$		Noneconomized $y \cong x - 0.5x^2$	
		y	Error	y	Error
0.1	0.09531018	0.1200	− 0.0246	0.0950	0.0003
0.3	0.26236426	0.3300	− 0.0676	0.2550	0.0074
0.6	0.47000363	0.5700	− 0.0999	0.4200	0.0500
0.9	0.64185389	0.7200	− 0.0781	0.4950	0.1469
1.0	0.69314718	0.7500	− 0.0569	0.5000	0.1931

Recapping function evaluation techniques, we have found that by writing polynomials in nested parenthetical form we can achieve fifth- and sixth-order polynomial accuracy with the same number of numerical operations required for the third-order unnested polynomial evaluation. This provides more accuracy for a given number of operations. We have further found that the Chebyshev economization process can provide high-order polynomial accuracy with low-order polynomials, even further reducing the number of numerical operations. We also have found that by using a relative error criterion we can reduce the number of terms required in the polynomial. Thus fifth-order polynomial relative accuracy obtained with Chebyshev polynomials can be equivalent to the absolute accuracy of seventh- or eighth-order noneconomized polynomial expansions. Then when the Chebyshev polynomial is written in nested parenthetical form, it provides this accuracy with operations that would normally be required for up to eighth- or ninth-order polynomial expansions. Thus the nested parenthetical evaluation of Chebyshev polynomial approximation whose error is specified in terms of relative error has the effect of reducing the workload from that associated with a ninth-order polynomial approximation of $f(x)$ to that of a second- or third-order polynomial approximation of $f(x)$. This can result in an order-of-magnitude reduction in numerical operations.

In general the approach to evaluating advanced mathematical functions is as follows:

1. Write the function in a polynomial form truncated on the basis of relative error.

2. Rewrite the expression so that the interval on which $f(x)$ is to be evaluated is between $-1 \leqslant x \leqslant +1$.

3. Economize the series using Chebyshev polynomials.

4. Rewrite the Chebyshev approximation to the function in nested parenthetical form.

5. Use it for numerical evaluation.

Numerical Evaluation of Chebyshev Polynomials

It is useful to know that the recurrence formula (restated here) for generating Chebyshev polynomials

$$T_n(x) = 2xT_{n-1}(x) - T_{n-2}(x)$$

can be used to numerically evaluate Chebyshev polynomials. The starting values for the recurrence formula can be computed with

$$T_0 = 1$$

$$T_1 = x$$

In this way, the Chebyshev polynomial expansion of a function once written need not necessarily be written in powers of x but can be numerically evaluated directly. For example, the equation

$$y = \ln(1 + x) \cong -\frac{T_0}{4} + \frac{15}{12} T_1 - \frac{T_2}{4} + \frac{T_3}{12} \qquad (12\text{-}14)$$

is the Chebyshev approximation to $\ln(1 + x)$ which was developed previously. Using the recursion formula and the fact that $T_0 = 1$ and $T_1 = x$, we can now numerically evaluate (12-14) by first evaluating the numerical values for the five Chebyshev polynomials as, for example, when $x = 0.3$:

$$T_0 = 1$$

$$T_1 = 0.3$$

$$T_2 = (2)(0.3)T_1 - T_0 = 2 \times 0.3 \times 0.3 - 1 = -0.82$$

$$T_3 = (2)(0.3)T_2 - T_1 = -2 \times 0.3 \times 0.82 - 0.3 = 0.792$$

These can then be substituted in the power series expansion to evaluate numerically the series

$$y = \ln(1.3) \cong -\frac{1}{4} + \frac{15}{12} \times 0.3 - \frac{1}{4}(-0.82) + \frac{1}{12}(-0.792) = 0.2640$$

$$y = \ln(1.3) \equiv 0.26236426$$

This procedure allows convenient numerical evaluation of Chebyshev polynomials of high order (e.g., 20). Although writing the nested parenthetical form of the Chebyshev polynomial expansion of a function is possible, its form is cumbersome and the user can be tripped up if he or she forgets which parentheses are currently being treated in the numerical evaluation process. The alternative of first computing the numerical values of the Chebyshev polynomials and then substituting those into the polynomial expansion equation is more straightforward, since it does not directly involve the evaluation of high-order polynomials.

Example

Economize the Maclaurin series expansion of e^x:

$$e^x = 1 + x + \frac{x^2}{2} + \frac{x^3}{6} + \frac{x^4}{24} + \frac{x^5}{120} + \frac{x^6}{720} + \cdots$$

Since

$$1 = T_0$$

$$x = T_1$$

$$x^2 = \tfrac{1}{2}(T_0 + T_2)$$

$$x^3 = \tfrac{1}{4}(3T_1 + T_3)$$

$$x^4 = \tfrac{1}{8}(3T_0 + 4T_2 + T_4)$$

$$x^5 = \tfrac{1}{16}(10T_1 + 5T_3 + T_5)$$

$$x^6 = \tfrac{1}{32}(10T_0 + 15T_2 + 6T_4 + T_6)$$

we can rewrite e^x as

$$e^x = T_0 + T_1 + \tfrac{1}{4}(T_0 + T_2) + \tfrac{1}{24}(3T_1 + T_3) + \tfrac{1}{192}(3T_0 + 4T_2 + T_4)$$

$$+ \tfrac{1}{1920}(10T_1 + 5T_3 + \cdots) + \tfrac{1}{23040}(10T_0 + 15T_2 + \cdots) + \cdots$$

$$e^x = 1.2661T_0 + 1.1302T_1 + 0.2715T_2 + 0.0443T_3 + \cdots$$

$$e^x = 1.2661 + 1.1303x + 0.2715(2x^2 - 1) + 0.0444(4x^3 - 3x) + \cdots$$

$$e^x \cong 0.9946 + 0.9974x + 0.5430x^2 + 0.1771x^3 + \cdots$$

Table 12.5. Comparison of Maclaurin and Economized Chebyshev Polynomials

x	e^x	Maclaurin	Chebyshev	Error M	Error C
1.0	2.7183	2.6667	2.7120	0.0516	0.0063
0.8	2.2255	2.2053	2.2307	0.0202	− 0.0052
0.6	1.8221	1.8160	1.8267	0.0061	− 0.0046
0.4	1.4918	1.4907	1.4917	0.0011	0.0001
0.2	1.2214	1.2213	1.2172	0.0001	0.0042
0.0	1.0000	1.0000	0.9946	0.0000	0.0054

Note that the terms involving T_0, T_1, T_2, and T_3 were carried from substitutions of polynomials for up to six terms in the Maclaurin series. Thus we carry the effect of the sixth term on the first and succeeding terms —the effect that makes the economization work.

Comparison of the Chebyshev and Maclaurian approximations (four terms each) is shown in Table 12-5. Note that the Chebyshev error is a maximum at $x = 0$ and the Maclaurian error is a minimum. This is because of the osculating nature of the Maclaurian approximation at the origin as compared with the minimax nature of the Chebyshev approximation on the interval (0, 1). This is illustrated in Figure 12-2.

Example

Approximate $\sin x$ with Chebyshev polynomials by the method of economization.

In this simple example we use the Maclaurin approximation of $\sin x$, again because it is an approximation centered on the interval $-1 \leqslant x \leqslant +1$. We see that

$$\sin x \cong x - \frac{x^3}{6} + \frac{x^5}{120}$$

Then

$$\sin x \cong T_1 - \tfrac{1}{24}(3T_1 + T_3) + \tfrac{1}{1920}(10T_1 + 5T_3 + T_5)$$

$$\sin x \cong \tfrac{169}{192} T_1 - \tfrac{5}{128} T_3 + \tfrac{1}{1920} T_5$$

The higher powers of x from the Maclaurin series would make further

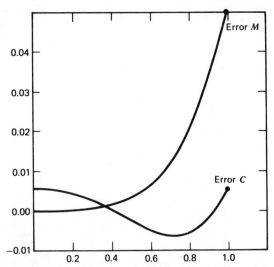

FIGURE 12-2. Error in Chebyshev economization of a Maclaurin series expansion of e^x. Source: J. M. Smith, *Scientific Analysis on the Pocket Calculator*, Wiley, 1975. Used by permission of the publisher.

contributions to the T_1, T_3, and T_5 coefficients. The contributions are small, however, especially for the early T_x terms. The x^5 term, in particular, changes the T_1 coefficient by less than 1% and the x^7 term alters it by less than 0.01%.

Economizing the Chebyshev approximation (dropping the T_5 term), we find

$$\sin x \cong \tfrac{169}{192} T_1 - \tfrac{5}{128} T_3$$

On substituting

$$T_1 = x$$

$$T_3 = 4x^3 - 3x$$

we find

$$\sin x \cong 0.9974x - 0.1562x^3 = x(0.9974 - 0.1562x^2)$$

The errors for the Maclaurin approximation of $\sin x$ and the economized Chebyshev approximation are compared in Figure 12-3.

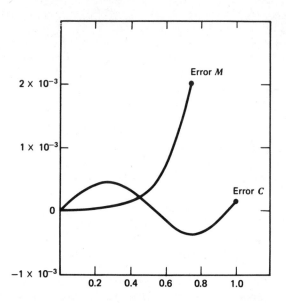

FIGURE 12-3. A comparison between the error that results from a Maclaurin approximation and an economized Chebyshev approximation of sin x. Source: J. M. Smith, *Scientific Analysis on the Pocket Calculator*, Wiley, 1975. Used by permission of the publisher.

APPENDIX A

SUBSTITUTION METHODS FOR SIMULATING TRANSFER FUNCTIONS

The substitution method for simulating transfer functions derives difference equations as follows:

1. By substituting an $f(z)$ for s^{-1} in the transfer function of the system to be simulated.

2. By inverting the resulting z-domain transfer functions into a difference equation.

Tustin's well-known substitution method leads to fairly stable, though not necessarily accurate, difference equations for simulating a continuous process. Tustin developed the $f(z)$ for his method as follows:

$$z = e^{-sT}$$

$$\therefore s = \frac{1}{T} \ln(z) \cong \frac{2}{T} \left(\frac{z-1}{z+1} \right)$$

by truncating the Laurent series expansion of $\ln(z)$. Thus

$$s^{-1} \cong \frac{T}{2} \left(\frac{z+1}{z-1} \right)$$

and

$$s^{-n} \cong \left(\frac{T}{2} \right)^n \left(\frac{z+1}{z-1} \right)^n = f^n(z)$$

Example

Use Tustin's method to develop the difference equation to simulate the first-order system

$$\frac{y}{x} = \frac{1}{\tau s + 1}$$

Following the method:

$$\frac{y}{x} = \frac{1/s}{\tau + 1/s} = \frac{\dfrac{T}{2}\left(\dfrac{z+1}{z-1}\right)}{\tau + \dfrac{T}{2}\left(\dfrac{z+1}{z-1}\right)}$$

$$= \frac{T/2(z+1)}{\tau(z-1) + T/2(z+1)} = \frac{\dfrac{T}{2\tau}(z+1)}{\left(1 + \dfrac{T}{2\tau}\right)z + \left(\dfrac{T}{2\tau} - 1\right)}$$

$$= \frac{T/2\tau(1 + z^{-1})}{(1 + T/2\tau) - (1 - T/2\tau)z^{-1}} = \frac{\left(\dfrac{T/2\tau}{1 + T/2\tau}\right)(1 + z^{-1})}{1 - \left(\dfrac{1 - T/2\tau}{1 + T/2\tau}\right)z^{-1}}$$

Thus

$$y = \left(\frac{1 - T/2\tau}{1 + T/2\tau}\right)z^{-1}y + \left(\frac{T/2\tau}{1 + T/2\tau}\right)(1 + z^{-1})x$$

Inverting by inspection we find

$$y_n = \left(\frac{1 - T/2\tau}{1 + T/2\tau}\right)y_{n-1} + \left(\frac{T/2\tau}{1 + T/2\tau}\right)(x_n + x_{n-1})$$

Now let us examine the properties of this difference equation. First note that

$$z_{\text{pole}} = \left(\frac{1 - T/2\tau}{1 + T/2\tau}\right)$$

and that

$$\lim_{T \to \infty} |z_{\text{pole}}| = 1$$

Thus the difference equation is stable no matter how large T becomes. This is a nice property of Tustin's method, which carries over to higher-order difference equations.

Next note that the "transition coefficient"

$$\frac{1 - T/2\tau}{1 + T/2\tau}$$

is the truncated series expansion of $e^{-T/\tau}$. This is easily seen as

$$e^{-T/\tau} = \frac{e^{-T/2\tau}}{e^{T/2\tau}} \approx \frac{1 - T/2\tau}{1 + T/2\tau}$$

This means that at each step of the difference equation the transition is only a good approximation of continuous motion when $T/2\tau \ll 1$. The rule of thumb used by the author is that for Tustin's method $T \cong \tau/15$. Said slightly differently, the sampling frequency must be at least 15 times the highest frequency of interest in the system being simulated. Many who use Tustin's method use lower sampling frequencies. The author's experience is that although the difference equation remains stable the magnitude of the absolute error in the transition is on the order of 10^{-3} to 10^{-4} for $\omega_s = 15\omega_n$ where ω_s is the sampling frequency and ω_n is the natural frequency of the system being simulated. Of course, these numbers vary from system to system so they should not be taken literally. They are only intended to give the author's heuristic rationale for using small step size with Tustin's method.

The alert reader will have noticed that the transfer function for s^{-1} in Tustin's method is nothing more than the transfer function for trapezoidal integration

$$x_n = x_{n-1} + \frac{T}{2}(\dot{x}_n + \dot{x}_{n-1})$$

which is an implicit numerical integrator. The fact that Tustin's method is based on the use of an implicit integration algorithm gives further justification for its success as a good substitution method.

It is obvious that with the knowledge that Tustin's method is simply the use of implicit trapezoidal integration to integrate the differential equations of motion, it can be extended to certain nonlinear differential equations.

Obviously the extension of the substitution method to other numerical integrators is straightforward. All one must do is to take the z transform of the integrator and develop the integrator transfer function. Then this function can be substituted for each s^{-1} in the transfer function of the system being simulated.

Example

$$x_n = x_{n-1} + T\dot{x}_n$$

has the z transform

$$(1 - z^{-1})x = T\dot{x}$$

$$\therefore \frac{x}{\dot{x}} = \frac{Tz}{z - 1}$$

which when used to simulate

$$\frac{y}{x} = \frac{s^{-1}}{\tau + s^{-1}}$$

leads to

$$\frac{y}{x}(z) = \frac{Tz}{\tau(z - 1) + T} = \frac{T/\tau}{1 - z^{-1} + (T/\tau)z^{-1}}$$

$$= \frac{T/\tau}{1 - (1 - T/\tau)z^{-1}}$$

which inverts into the difference equation

$$y_n = (1 - T/\tau)y_{n-1} + (T/\tau)x_n$$

The T integrator can be used for substitution. Its transfer function is

$$\left\{ \frac{\lambda T[\gamma z + (1 - \gamma)]}{z - 1} \right\}^n \approx s^{-n}$$

Then λ and γ can be used to tune the integrator to the equations of motion of the system being simulated, as discussed in Chapter 7.

There is a fairly extensive literature on the substitution method. Some of the often-used substitution algorithms are shown in Table A-1.

Table A-1. Integrators Commonly Used in Applying the Substitution Method

$1/S^k$	Method	Operator	Method	Operator
$\dfrac{1}{S}$	Tustin	$\dfrac{T}{2}\dfrac{z+1}{z-1}$	Exact z transform	$\dfrac{Tz}{z-1}$
	Madwed-Truxal	$\dfrac{T}{2}\dfrac{z+1}{z-1}$	z form	$\dfrac{T}{2}\dfrac{z+1}{z-1}$
$\dfrac{1}{S^2}$	Tustin	$\dfrac{T^2}{4}\dfrac{z^2+2z+1}{(z-1)^2}$	Exact z transform	$\dfrac{T^2 z}{(z-1)^2}$
	Madwed-Truxal	$\dfrac{T^2}{6}\dfrac{z^2+4z+1}{(z-1)^2}$	z form	$\dfrac{T^2}{12}\dfrac{z^2+10z+1}{(z-1)^3}$
$\dfrac{1}{S^3}$	Tustin	$\dfrac{T^3}{8}\dfrac{z^3+3z^2+3z+1}{(z-1)^3}$	Exact z transform	$\dfrac{T^3}{2}\dfrac{z(z+1)}{(z-1)^3}$
	Madwed-Truxal	$\dfrac{T^3}{24}\dfrac{z^3+11z^2+11z+1}{(z-1)^3}$	z form	$\dfrac{T^3}{2}\dfrac{z(z+1)}{(z-1)^3}$
$\dfrac{1}{S^4}$	Tustin	$\dfrac{T^4}{16}\dfrac{z^4+4z^3+6z^2+4z+1}{(z-1)^4}$	Exact z transform	$\dfrac{T^4}{6}\dfrac{z(z^2+4z+1)}{(z-1)^4}$
	Madwed-Truxal	$\dfrac{T^4}{120}\dfrac{z^4+26z^3+66z^2+26z+1}{(z-1)^4}$	z form	$\dfrac{T^4}{6}\dfrac{z(z^2+4z+1)}{(z-1)^4}$

Using adaptable integrator improves selection process $\dfrac{1}{s^n} = \left\{ \dfrac{\lambda T[\gamma z + (1-\gamma)]}{z-1} \right\}^n$

APPENDIX B

JURY'S TABLE OF Z TRANSFORMS

From Eliahu I. Jury, *Theory and Application of the Z-Transform Method*, Wiley, New York, 1964. Reproduced by permission.

TABLE I. z-TRANSFORM PAIRS

Number	Discrete Time-Function $f(n)$, $n \geq 0$	z-Transform $\mathscr{F}(z) = \mathfrak{z}[f(n)]$, $\|z\| > R$ $= \sum\limits_{n=0}^{\infty} f(n)z^{-n}$
1	$u(n) = \begin{cases} 1, & \text{for } n \geq 0 \\ 0, & \text{otherwise} \end{cases}$	$\dfrac{z}{z-1}$
2	$e^{-\alpha n}$	$\dfrac{z}{z - e^{-\alpha}}$
3	n	$\dfrac{z}{(z-1)^2}$
4	n^2	$\dfrac{z(z+1)}{(z-1)^3}$
5	n^3	$\dfrac{z(z^2 + 4z + 1)}{(z-1)^4}$
6	n^4	$\dfrac{z(z^3 + 11z^2 + 11z + 1)}{(z-1)^5}$
7	n^5	$\dfrac{z(z^4 + 26z^3 + 66z^2 + 26z + 1)}{(z-1)^6}$
8	n^{k*}	$(-1)^k D^k\left(\dfrac{z}{z-1}\right)$; $D = z\dfrac{d}{dz}$

* Table IV represents entries for k up to 10.

TABLE 1 (Continued)

Number	Discrete Time-Function $f(n)$, $n \geq 0$	z-Transform $\mathscr{F}(z) = \mathscr{z}[f(n)], |z| > R$ $= \sum_{n=0}^{\infty} f(n)z^{-n}$
32	$\dfrac{1}{n}, \quad n > 0$	$\ln \dfrac{z}{z-1}$
33	$\dfrac{1 - e^{-\alpha n}}{n}$	$\alpha + \ln \dfrac{z - e^{-\alpha}}{z-1}, \quad \alpha > 0$
34	$\dfrac{\sin \alpha n}{n}$	$\alpha + \tan^{-1} \dfrac{\sin \alpha}{z - \cos \alpha}, \quad \alpha > 0$
35	$\dfrac{\cos \alpha n}{n}, \quad n > 0$	$\ln \dfrac{z}{\sqrt{z^2 - 2z \cos \alpha + 1}}$
36	$\dfrac{(n+1)(n+2)\ldots(n+k-1)}{(k-1)!}$	$\left(1 - \dfrac{1}{z}\right)^{-k}, \quad k = 2,3,\ldots$
37	$\displaystyle\sum_{m=1}^{n} \dfrac{1}{m}$	$\dfrac{z}{z-1} \ln \dfrac{z}{z-1}$
38	$\displaystyle\sum_{m=0}^{n-1} \dfrac{1}{m!}$	$\dfrac{e^{1/z}}{z-1}$
39	$\dfrac{(-1)^{(n-p)/2}}{2^n \left(\dfrac{n-p}{2}\right)! \left(\dfrac{n+p}{2}\right)!},$ for $n \geq p$ and $n - p = $ even $= 0,$ for $n < p$ or $n - p = $ odd	$J_p(z^{-1})$

40

$$\sum_{\substack{n|k \\ =0}} \binom{\alpha}{n|k} b^{n|k}, \qquad \begin{aligned} &n = mk, \quad (m = 0,1,2,\ldots) \\ &n \neq mk \end{aligned} \qquad\qquad \left(\dfrac{z^k + b}{z^k}\right)^{\alpha}$$

41

$$a^n P_n(x) = \dfrac{a^n}{2^n n!}\left(\dfrac{d}{dx}\right)^n (x^2 - 1)^n \qquad\qquad \dfrac{z}{\sqrt{z^2 - 2xaz + a^2}}$$

42

$$a^n T_n(x) = a^n \cos(n\cos^{-1} x) \qquad\qquad \dfrac{z(z - ax)}{z^2 - 2xaz + a^2}$$

43

$$\dfrac{L_n(x)}{n!} = \sum_{r=0}^{\infty}\binom{n}{r}\dfrac{(-x)^r}{r!} \qquad\qquad \dfrac{z}{z-1}\,e^{-x/(z-1)}$$

44

$$\dfrac{H_n(x)}{n!} = \sum_{k=0}^{[n/2]}\dfrac{(-1)^{n-k}x^{n-2k}}{k!\,(n-2k)!\,2^k} \qquad\qquad e^{-z/z - 1/2z^2}$$

45

$$a^n P_n^m(x) = a^n(1 - x^2)^{m/2}\left(\dfrac{d}{dx}\right)^m P_n(x), \qquad m = \text{integer} \qquad\qquad \dfrac{(2m)!}{2^m m!}\dfrac{z^{m+1}(1 - x^2)^{m/2}a^m}{(z^2 - 2xaz + a^2)^{m+1/2}}$$

46

$$\dfrac{L_n^m(x)}{n!} = \left(\dfrac{d}{dx}\right)^m \dfrac{L_n(x)}{n!}, \qquad m = \text{integer} \qquad\qquad \dfrac{(-1)^m z}{(z-1)^{m+1}}\,e^{-z/(z-1)}$$

47

$$-\dfrac{1}{n}\,\mathscr{z}^{-1}\left[z\dfrac{\mathscr{F}'(z)}{\mathscr{F}(z)} - z\dfrac{\mathscr{G}'(z)}{\mathscr{G}(z)}\right], \text{where } \mathscr{F}(z) \text{ and } \mathscr{G}(z) \text{ are rational} \qquad\qquad \ln\dfrac{\mathscr{F}(z)}{\mathscr{G}(z)}$$

polynomials in z of the same order

48

$$\dfrac{1}{m(m+1)(m+2)\ldots(m+n)} \qquad\qquad (m-1)!\,z^m\left[e^{1/z} - \sum_{k=0}^{m-1}\dfrac{1}{k!\,z^k}\right]$$

49

$$\dfrac{\sin(\alpha n)}{n!} \qquad\qquad e^{\cos\alpha/z}\cdot\sin\left(\dfrac{\sin\alpha}{z}\right)$$

TABLE I (*Continued*)

Number	Discrete Time-Function $f(n), n \geq 0$	z-Transform $\mathscr{F}(z) = \mathscr{I}[f(n)], |z| > R$ $= \sum_{n=0}^{\infty} f(n)z^{-n}$
9	$u(n-k)$	$\dfrac{z^{-k+1}}{z-1}$
10	$e^{-\alpha n}f(n)$	$\mathscr{F}(e^{\alpha}z)$
11	$n^{(2)} = n(n-1)$	$2\dfrac{z}{(z-1)^3}$
12	$n^{(3)} = n(1-1)(n-2)$	$3!\dfrac{z}{(z-1)^4}$
13	$n^{(k)} = n(n-1)(n-2)\ldots(n-k+1)$	$k!\dfrac{z}{(z-1)^{k+1}}$
14	$n^{[k]}f(n), n^{[k]} = n(n+1)(n+2)\ldots(n+k-1)$	$(-1)^k z^k \dfrac{d^k}{dz^k}[\mathscr{F}(z)]$
15	$(-1)^k n(n-1)(n-2)\ldots(n-k+1)f_{n-k+1}\dagger$	$z\mathscr{F}^{(k)}(z),\ \mathscr{F}^{(k)}(z) = \dfrac{d^k}{dz^k}\mathscr{F}(z)$
16	$-(n-1)f_{n-1}$	$\mathscr{F}^{(1)}(z)$
17	$(-1)^k(n-1)(n-2)\ldots(n-k)f_{n-k}$	$\mathscr{F}^{(k)}(z)$
18	$nf(n)$	$-z\mathscr{F}^{(1)}(z)$
19	$n^2 f(n)$	$z^2\mathscr{F}^{(2)}(z) + z\mathscr{F}^{(1)}(z)$
20	$n^3 f(n)$	$-z^3\mathscr{F}^{(3)}(z) - 3z^2\mathscr{F}^{(2)}(z) - z\mathscr{F}^{(1)}(z)$

21	$\dfrac{c^n}{n!}$	$e^{c/z}$
22	$\dfrac{(\ln c)^n}{n!}$	$c^{1/z}$
23	$\dbinom{k}{n} c^n a^{k-n}$, $\quad \dbinom{k}{n} = \dfrac{k!}{(k-n)!\,n!}$, $\quad n \le k$	$\dfrac{(az+c)^k}{z^k}$
24	$\dbinom{n+k}{k} c^n$	$\dfrac{z^{k+1}}{(z-c)^{k+1}}$
25	$\dfrac{c^n}{n!}$, $\quad (n = 1,3,5,7,\ldots)$	$\sinh\left(\dfrac{c}{z}\right)$
26	$\dfrac{c^n}{n!}$, $\quad (n = 0,2,4,6,\ldots)$	$\cosh\left(\dfrac{c}{z}\right)$
27	$\sin(\alpha n)$	$\dfrac{z \sin \alpha}{z^2 - 2z\cos\alpha + 1}$
28	$\cos(\alpha n)$	$\dfrac{z(z - \cos\alpha)}{z^2 - 2z\cos\alpha + 1}$
29	$\sin(\alpha n + \psi)$	$\dfrac{z^2 \sin\psi + z\sin(\alpha - \psi)}{z^2 - 2z\cos\alpha + 1}$
30	$\cosh(\alpha n)$	$\dfrac{z(z - \cosh\alpha)}{z^2 - 2z\cosh\alpha + 1}$
31	$\sinh(\alpha n)$	$\dfrac{z\sinh\alpha}{z^2 - 2z\cosh\alpha + 1}$

† It may be noted that f_n is the same as $f(n)$.

TABLE I (*Continued*)

Number	*Discrete Time-Function* $f(n), n \geq 0$	*z-Transform* $\mathscr{F}(z) = \mathfrak{z}[f(n)], |z| > R$ $= \sum_{n=0}^{\infty} f(n)z^{-n}$
50	$\dfrac{\cos(\alpha n)}{n!}$	$e^{\cos \alpha/z} \cdot \cos\left(\dfrac{\sin \alpha}{z}\right)$
51	$\displaystyle\sum_{k=0}^{n} f_k g_{n-k}$	$\mathscr{F}(z)\mathscr{G}(z)$
52	$\displaystyle\sum_{k=0}^{n} k f_k g_{n-k}$	$-\mathscr{F}^{(1)}(z)\mathscr{G}(z), \quad \mathscr{F}^{(1)}(z) = \dfrac{d\mathscr{F}(z)}{dz}$
53	$\displaystyle\sum_{k=0}^{n} k^2 f_k g_{n-k}$	$\mathscr{F}^{(2)}(z)\mathscr{G}(z)$
54	$\dfrac{\alpha^n + (-\alpha)^n}{2\alpha^2}$	$\dfrac{1}{z^2 - \alpha^2}$
55	$\dfrac{\alpha^n - \beta^n}{\alpha - \beta}$	$\dfrac{z}{(z - \alpha)(z - \beta)}$
56	$(n + k)^{(k)}$	$k! \, z^k \dfrac{z}{(z - 1)^{k+1}}$
57	$(n - k)^{(k)}$	$k! \, z^{-k} \dfrac{z}{(z - 1)^{k+1}}$
58	$\dfrac{(n \mp k)^{(m)}}{m!} e^{\alpha(n-k)}$	$\dfrac{z^{1 \mp k} e^{m\alpha}}{(z - e^{\alpha})^{m+1}}$

59    $\dfrac{1}{n}\sin\dfrac{\pi}{2}n$ $\dfrac{\pi}{2}+\tan^{-1}\dfrac{1}{z}$

60    $\dfrac{\cos\alpha(2n-1)}{2n-1}$ $\dfrac{1}{4\sqrt{z}}\ln\dfrac{z+2\sqrt{z}\cos\alpha+1}{z-2\sqrt{z}\cos\alpha+1}$

61    $\dfrac{\gamma^n}{(\gamma-1)^2}+\dfrac{n}{1-\gamma}-\dfrac{1}{(1-\gamma)^2}$ $\dfrac{z}{(z-\gamma)(z-1)^2}$

62    $\dfrac{\gamma+a_0}{(\gamma-1)^2}\gamma^n+\dfrac{1+a_0}{1-\gamma}n+\left(\dfrac{1}{1-\gamma}-\dfrac{a_0+1}{(1-\gamma)^2}\right)$ $\dfrac{z(z+a_0)}{(z-\gamma)(z-1)^2}$

63    $a^n\cos\pi n$ $\dfrac{z}{z+a}$

64    $e^{-\alpha n}\cos an$ $\dfrac{z(z-e^{-\alpha}\cos a)}{z^2-2ze^{-\alpha}\cos a+e^{-2\alpha}}$

65    $e^{-\alpha n}\sinh(an+\psi)$ $\dfrac{z^2\sinh\psi+ze^{-\alpha}\sinh(a-\psi)}{z^2-2ze^{-\alpha}\cosh a+e^{-2\alpha}}$

66    $\dfrac{\gamma^n}{(\chi-\alpha)^2+\beta^2}+\dfrac{(\alpha^2+\beta^2)^{n/2}\sin(n\theta+\psi)}{\beta[(\alpha-\gamma)^2+\beta^2]^{1/2}}$

     $\theta=\tan^{-1}\dfrac{\beta}{\alpha}$

     $\psi=\tan^{-1}\dfrac{\beta}{\alpha-\gamma}$ $\dfrac{z}{(z-\gamma)[(z-\alpha)^2+\beta^2]}$

67    $\dfrac{n\gamma^{n-1}}{(\gamma-1)^3}-\dfrac{3\gamma^n}{(\gamma-1)^4}+\dfrac{1}{2}\left[\dfrac{n(n-1)}{(1-\gamma)^2}-\dfrac{4n}{(1-\gamma)^3}+\dfrac{6}{(1-\gamma)^4}\right]$ $\dfrac{z}{(z-\gamma)^2(z-1)^3}$

68    $\displaystyle\sum_{\nu=0}^{k}(-1)^\nu\binom{k}{\nu}\dfrac{(n+k-\nu)^{(k)}}{k!}e^{\alpha(n-\nu)}$ $\dfrac{z(z-1)^k}{(z-e^\alpha)^{k+1}}$

TABLE I (Continued)

Number	Discrete Time-Function $f(n), n \geq 0$	z-Transform $\mathscr{F}(z) = \mathscr{J}[f(n)], \|z\| > R = \sum_{n=0}^{\infty} f(n)z^{-n}$
69	$\dfrac{f(n)}{n}$	$\displaystyle\int_z^\infty p^{-1}\mathscr{F}(p)\,dp + \lim_{n\to 0}\frac{f(n)}{n}$
70	$\dfrac{f_{n+2}}{n+1}, \quad \begin{array}{l} f_0 = 0 \\ f_1 = 0 \end{array}$	$\displaystyle z\int_z^\infty \mathscr{F}(p)\,dp$
71	$\dfrac{1+a_0}{(1-\gamma)[(1-\alpha)^2+\beta^2]} + \dfrac{(\gamma+a_0)\gamma^n}{(\gamma-1)[(\gamma-\alpha)^2+\beta^2]}$ $+ \dfrac{[\alpha^2+\beta^2]^{n/2}[(a_0+\alpha)^2+\beta^2]^{1/2}}{\beta[(\alpha-1)^2+\beta^2]^{1/2}[(\alpha-\gamma)^2+\beta^2]^{1/2}}\sin(n\theta +\,\psi + \lambda),$ $\psi = \psi_1 + \psi_2, \quad \psi_1 = -\tan^{-1}\dfrac{\beta}{\alpha-1}, \quad \theta = \tan^{-1}\dfrac{\beta}{\alpha}$ $\lambda = \tan^{-1}\dfrac{\beta}{a_0+\alpha}, \quad \psi_2 = -\tan^{-1}\dfrac{\beta}{\alpha-\gamma}$	$\dfrac{z(z+a_0)}{(z-1)(z-\gamma)[(z-\alpha)^2+\beta^2]}$
72	$(n+1)e^{\alpha n} - 2ne^{\alpha(n+1)} + e^{\alpha(n-2)}(n-1)$	$\left(\dfrac{z-1}{z-e^\alpha}\right)^2$
73	$(-1)^n \dfrac{\cos \alpha n}{n}, \quad n > 0$	$\ln\dfrac{z}{\sqrt{z^2+2z\cos\alpha+1}}$
74	$\dfrac{(n+k)!}{n!}f_{n+k}, \quad f_n = 0, \text{ for } 0 \leqslant n < k$	$(-1)^k z^{2k}\dfrac{d^k}{dz^k}[\mathscr{F}(z)]$

75	$\dfrac{f(n)}{n+h},\quad h>0$	$z^h \displaystyle\int_z^\infty p^{-(1+h)}\,\mathscr{F}(p)\,dp$
76	$-na^n \cos\dfrac{\pi}{2}n$	$\dfrac{2a^2z^2}{(z^2+a^2)^2}$
77	$na^n \dfrac{1+\cos\pi n}{2}$	$\dfrac{2a^2z^2}{(z^2-a^2)^2}$
78	$a^n \sin\dfrac{\pi}{4}n \cdot \dfrac{1+\cos\pi n}{2}$	$\dfrac{a^2z^2}{z^4+a^4}$
79	$a^n\left(\dfrac{1+\cos\pi n}{2}-\cos\dfrac{\pi}{2}n\right)$	$\dfrac{2a^2z^2}{z^4-a^4}$
80	$\dfrac{P_n(x)}{n!}$	$e^{xz^{-1}}J_0(\sqrt{1-x^2z^{-1}})$
81	$\dfrac{P_n^{(m)}(x)}{(n+m)!},\quad m>0,\quad P_n^m=0,\quad \text{for } n<m$	$(-1)^m e^{xz^{-1}} J_m(\sqrt{1-x^2z^{-1}})$
82	$\dfrac{1}{(n+\alpha)^\beta},\quad \alpha>0,\ \mathrm{Re}\,\beta>0$	$\Phi(z^{-1},\alpha,\beta),\quad$ where $\Phi(1,\beta,\alpha)=\zeta(\beta,\alpha)$ = generalized Rieman-Zeta function
83	$a^n\left(\dfrac{1+\cos\pi n}{2}+\cos\dfrac{\pi}{2}n\right)$	$\dfrac{2z^4}{z^4-a^4}$
84	$\dfrac{c^n}{n},\quad (n=1,2,3,4,\ldots)$	$\ln z - \ln(z-c)$
85	$\dfrac{c^n}{n},\quad n=2,4,6,8,\ldots$	$\ln z - \tfrac12 \ln(z^2-c^2)$

TABLE I (Continued)

Number	Discrete Time-Function $f(n), n \geq 0$	z-Transform $\mathscr{F}(z) = \mathscr{z}[f(n)], \|z\| > R$ $= \sum_{n=0}^{\infty} f(n)z^{-n}$
86	$n^2 c^n$	$\dfrac{cz(z+c)}{(z-c)^3}$
87	$n^3 c^n$	$\dfrac{cz(z^2+4cz+c^2)}{(z-c)^4}$
88	$n^k c^n$	$-\dfrac{d\mathscr{F}(z/c)}{dz}$, $\quad \mathscr{F}(z) = \mathscr{z}[n^{k-1}]$
89	$-\cos\dfrac{\pi}{2}n \displaystyle\sum_{i=0}^{(n-2)/4}\binom{n/2}{2i+1}a^{n-2-4i}(a^4-b^4)^i$	$\dfrac{z^2}{z^4+2a^2z^2+b^4}$
90	$n^k f(n), \quad k>0$ and integer	$-z\dfrac{d}{dz}\mathscr{F}_1(z)$, $\;\mathscr{F}_1(z) = \mathscr{z}[n^{k-1}f(n)]$
91	$\dfrac{(n-1)(n-2)(n-3)\ldots(n-k+1)}{(k-1)!}a^{n-k}$	$\dfrac{1}{(z-a)^k}$
92	$\dfrac{k(k-1)(k-2)\ldots(k-n+1)}{n!}$	$\left(1+\dfrac{1}{z}\right)^k$
93	$na^n\cos bn$	$\dfrac{[(z/a)^3 + z/a]\cos b - 2(z/a)^2}{[(z/a)^2 - 2(z/a)\cos b + 1]^2}$
94	$na^n\sin bn$	$\dfrac{(z/a)^3\sin b - (z/a)\sin b}{[(z/a)^2 - 2(z/a)\cos b + 1]^2}$

95	$\dfrac{na^n}{(n+1)(n+2)}$	$\dfrac{z(a-2z)}{a^2}\ln\left(1-\dfrac{a}{z}\right)-\dfrac{2}{a}z$
96	$\dfrac{(-a)^n}{(n+1)(2n+1)}$	$2\sqrt{z/a}\,\tan^{-1}\sqrt{a/z}-\dfrac{z}{a}\ln\left(1+\dfrac{a}{z}\right)$
97	$\dfrac{a^n\sin\alpha n}{n+1}$	$\dfrac{z\cos\alpha}{a}\tan^{-1}\dfrac{a\sin\alpha}{z-a\cos\alpha}$ $+\dfrac{z\sin\alpha}{2a}\ln\dfrac{z^2-2az\cos\alpha+a^2}{z^2}$
98	$\dfrac{a^n\cos(\pi/2)\,n\sin\alpha(n+1)}{n+1}$	$\dfrac{z}{4a}\ln\dfrac{z^2+2az\sin\alpha+a^2}{z^2-2az\sin\alpha+a^2}$
99	$\dfrac{1}{(2n)!}$	$\cosh(z^{-1/2})$
100	$\dbinom{-\frac{1}{2}}{n}(-a)^n$	$\sqrt{z/(z-a)}$
101	$\dbinom{-\frac{1}{2}}{\frac{n}{2}}a^n\cos\dfrac{\pi}{2}n$	$\dfrac{z}{\sqrt{z^2-a^2}}$
102	$\dfrac{B_n(x)}{n!}$ $B_n(x)\triangleq$ Bernoulli polynomials	$\dfrac{e^{x/z}}{z(e^{1/z}-1)}$
103	$W_n(x)\triangleq$ Tchebycheff polynomials of the second kind	$\dfrac{z^2}{z^2-2xz+1}$
104	$\left|\sin\dfrac{n\pi}{m}\right|,\quad m=1,2,\ldots$	$\dfrac{z\sin\pi/m}{z^2-2z\cos\pi/m+1}\dfrac{1+z^{-m}}{1-z^{-m}}$
105	$Q_n(x)=\sin(n\cos^{-1}x)$	$\dfrac{z}{z^2-2xz+1}$

APPENDIX C

ZERO-ORDER *T*-INTEGRATION AND
ITS RELATION TO
THE MEAN VALUE THEOREM*

A zero-order T integrator is a simple rectangular numerical integrator that can be tuned to the problem it is trying to solve. This integrator is synthesized in such a way that it has frequency-response characteristics WHICH CAN BE VARIED. Thus the T integrator can be tailored to integrate accurately and efficiently in many different applications. All T integrators have stability, accuracy, and noise-controlling parameters that can be varied.

When the zero-order T integrator is tuned to integrate linear constant coefficient systems, these parameters can be chosen to permit EXACT numerical integration; furthermore, the parameters are invariant with time. When zero-order T integration is used to numerically integrate nonlinear and/or time-varying systems, T integration can often be made more precise than high-order numerical integrators. The question is, "Why can zero-order T integration be made so accurate?" This appendix presents an answer to this question. As it happens, zero-order T integration can be derived directly from the mean value theorem of integral calculus. The mean value theorem (simply stated) is based on proof that there is a rectangular integrator that will EXACTLY integrate an arbitrary continuous function on a bounded interval. We will find zero-order T integration to be a numerical integration concept with the means (its parameters) for finding the exact integral.

*J. M. Smith, "Zero-Order T-Integration and Its Relation to the Mean Value Theorem," Vol. 6, Part 1, *Proceedings of the Sixth Annual Pittsburgh Modeling and Simulation Conference*, April 24–25, 1975. Used by permission.

THE MEAN VALUE THEOREM OF INTEGRAL CALCULUS

Let f' be continuous on the bounded interval $[a, b]$. Then there is some number θ such that for $a \leqslant \theta \leqslant b$

$$\int_a^b f' \, dt = (b - a) f'(\theta) \qquad \text{(C-1)}$$

We will refer to (C-1) as the mean value equation. From the standpoint of numerical integration, the left side of the equation is the integral we would ideally like to compute with rectangular numerical integration on the right side. A corollary of the mean value theorem is that rectangular integration can be made to exactly integrate an arbitrary integrand over an interval $[a, b]$ if θ can be found. One of the better discussions that the author has found of the use of the mean value theorem for the estimation of integrals is by Courant.* The mean value theorem is illustrated in Figure C-1 for the case where f is a simple ramp function. In this case the θ that satisfies the mean value equation is the midvalue of the interval $[a, b]$.

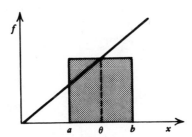

FIGURE C-1.   Mean value theorem: $(b - a)f'(\theta) = \int_a^b f'(x) \, dx$.

Four alternative forms of the mean value theorem suggest themselves for estimating indefinite integrals. Let f' be continuous on the bounded interval $[a, b]$. Then there exist numbers λ and γ such that

Alternate 1

$$\int_{nt}^{(n+1)T} f'(t) \, dt = Tf'(nT + \gamma T)$$

*R. Courant, *Differential and Integral Calculus*, Wiley Interscience, Vol. 1, 2nd Ed., 1937, 1959 reprint, pp. 126–8.

Alternate 2

$$\int_{nt}^{(n+1)T} f'(t)\, dt = T\lambda f'(nT)$$

Alternate 3

$$\int_{nt}^{(n+1)T} f'(t)\, dt = T\Gamma f'(nT + \xi T) \qquad \text{Explicit form}$$

Alternate 4

$$\int_{nt}^{(n+1)T} f'(t)\, dt = T\lambda f'\big[(n+1)T + \gamma T\big] \qquad \text{Implicit form}$$

Three of these alternatives are illustrated in Figure C-2. The first is to advance the integrand in time by an amount γT. Time shifting the integrand effectively permits the integrand to be sampled at times other than nT. The second is to scale (with the parameter λ) the present value of the integrand such that the area of the rectangle formed by "$\lambda f(nT)$" and the base "T" satisfy the mean value equation. The third and fourth alternatives are to both scale and time shift the integrand. What is required, then, is to find combinations of λ and γ that satisfy the mean value equation. The only difference between alternatives 3 and 4 is that the time shift in alternative 3 is relative (referenced) to the present value while the time shift in alternative 4 is relative (referenced) to the future value.

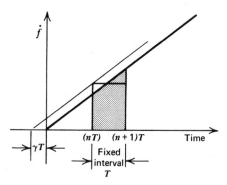

FIGURE C-2. Alternative mean value theorems.

$$\left.\begin{array}{l} T[\dot{f}(nT + \gamma T)] \\ T[\lambda \dot{f}(nT)] \\ T[\lambda \dot{f}(nT + \gamma T)] \end{array}\right\} = \int_{nT}^{(n+1)T} \dot{f}(t)\, dt$$

T-INTEGRATION FORMULA DERIVATION

The derivation of a numerical integration formula based on the mean value theorem involves the synthesis of a rectangular integrator that will satisfy the mean value equation. The approach is as follows:

1. Synthesize a block diagram of the mean value theorem.
2. Derive the integration formula using *Z*-transform techniques.

Block diagrams of continuous integration and the four mean value theorems are shown in Figure C-3. Also shown in the figure is a summary of the development of the transfer function of the *T* integrator derived by taking the *Z* transform of the combined transfer functions of:

1. The zero-order hold reconstruction process.
2. The scaling and phase shift "phase and gain filter" process.
3. The continuous integration process itself.

Inverting the transfer function for the zero-order *T* integrator, we find the implicit numerical integration formula

$$x_n = x_{n-1} + \lambda T \left[\gamma \dot{x}_n + (1 - \gamma) \dot{x}_{n-1} \right] \qquad (C\text{-}2)$$

This integration formula is the discrete approximation of the mean value theorem where λ and γ are to be found so as to satisfy the mean value equation. First, we note that this is an implicit integration formula in that x_n is a function of $\dot{x}_n$ and for many systems $\dot{x}_n$ is a function of x_n. Indefinite integration does not permit $\dot{x}_n$ to be evaluated exactly but $\dot{x}_n$ can be estimated either through extrapolation or other means of approximation. A simple expedient for adapting this integrator to explicit integration (x_n is a function of $\dot{x}_{n-1}$ and other past values of the rate) is to rewrite

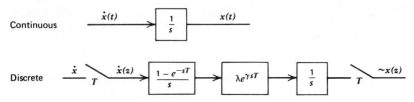

FIGURE C-3.   *T*-integration derivation

$$\frac{x(z)}{\dot{x}(z)} = \mathbf{Z} \left(\frac{1 - e^{-sT}}{s} \right) (\lambda e^{\gamma sT}) \left(\frac{1}{s} \right) = \lambda \left\{ \frac{\gamma Tz + (1 - \gamma)T}{z - 1} \right\}.$$

(C-2) in the form

$$x_n = x_{n-1} + \Gamma T\big[(\gamma + 1)\dot{x}_{n-1} + \gamma \dot{x}_{n-2}\big]$$

Here Γ is a scaling constant that, in general, will be different from λ. A sample period of transport lead is included in the time shift of the integrand to compensate for the fact that $\dot{x}_{n-1}$ is used in place of $\dot{x}_n$. Effectively, this puts an e^{-sT} in the forward loop of the block diagram of the mean value theorem alternative 4 which, by definition, is the block diagram of the mean value theorem alternative 3.

SELECTING THE VALUES OF THE PARAMETERS λ AND γ

One approach to selecting λ or Γ and γ is to use a Runge-Kutta or other high-confidence, high-order classical integrator to integrate the differential equations on the first step and then compute γ assuming $\lambda = 1$ or compute λ assuming $\gamma = 1$. This process of using an integrator that is well known to initialize the λ or γ or both (alternating between γ and λ) can be done repeatedly during a simulation run (say on every 100th step). *In this sense the T integrator is adaptively tuned to be as accurate as a high-order integrator and then allowed to run with no error control for a short while.*

If the zero-order T integrators are substituted into the nonlinear differential equation $x = F(x, t)$, a set of difference equations can be derived where λ's and λ's are parameters in the difference equation. Assume the difference equations to be programmed on a digital computer. Assume for the sake of discussion that a Runge-Kutta fourth-order integrator is used to numerically integrate the system of differential equations to generate one or more check cases. Then the phases and gains can be selected empirically by:

1. Choosing an integration sampling rate for the difference equation that is on the order of 7 to 10 times the highest frequency of interest in the dynamic process.

2. Setting $\lambda = 1$.

3. Empirically adjusting γ until the response computed by the difference equation best "matches"* the response computed by the numerically integrated differential equation.

4. Selecting λ while holding γ fixed to fine tune the equation.[†]

*Any number of criteria can be used.

[†]Care must be taken to ensure that λs are not acting as "system gains." Check-case comparison is the only safe way the author knows to safeguard against this possibility. Generally $\lambda = 1$.

This empirical technique is quick and accurate for simulating linear constant coefficient processes in that the tuning parameters remain invariant with time. For nonlinear processes, they generally vary with time; however, often an "average" set of parameters can be determined where, from an engineering point of view, the integration process works well over a broad dynamic range of the state variables of interest. These techniques are useful when simulating system elements that do not change too much from run to run in a simulation or control process (e.g., a digital filter built into a computer-controlled system or the simulation of that digital filter in a simulation of the control system). However, for engineering design simulation where the design parameters are being varied from run to run, the technique works well for linear systems but must be checked from time to time by setting the integration step size very small and running a check case to see if the dynamics of the simulated system changed appreciably.

The tuning parameters can be determined analytically. For example, the tuning parameters can be selected (for linear systems) by matching (equating) the characteristic roots of the discrete simulation equations* with the roots of the continuous system equations.

For systems that have more than one integrator, it is generally found that there are an infinite number of combinations of λ and γ for each of the integrators that can tune the integrators to the system of equations being solved. Certain integrators, however, have more effect on the transient response than others. As expected, the phase and gain parameters associated with those integrators will dominate the dynamics of the solution.

Tuning the integrators in a simulation or control system is quickly accomplished empirically by tuning the low-frequency loops (outer loops) first and proceeding into the inner loops or high-frequency loops last. The process is iterative but in the author's experience working with systems of 10 to 20th order involves only 1 to $1\frac{1}{2}$ hours to tune manually a simulation to four or five check points.

Empirically tuning the integrators to the system being simulated or controlled is similar to empirically fine tuning control systems once they have been designed. Most control systems have a means of adjustment that permits them to be tuned to the variances in the individual systems they are trying to control. Tuning simulations is a parallel to this process where the T integrator is used in a broad spectrum of applications but tuned for each specific application. All that is required to tune a simulation is the criterion. Whether engineering judgment or some analytical criterion is

---

*The discrete system of equations is derived by substituting the T-integrator Z-transformation transfer function for $1/s$ in the linear systems Laplace transformation-transfer function and then inverting the resulting systems Z-domain transfer function into a difference equation.

used, the tuning parameters can be adjusted in a manner analogous to adjusting "trim-pots" in an analog simulation. In fact, when the integrator was used on the Apollo program, the tuning parameters associated with the *T* integrators were input to the digital computer through A/D converters from potentiometers on an analog computer.

In most cases, it is necessary to tune a simulator for many different conditions. Check cases can be generated by using a very small integration step size with λ or $\Gamma = 1$ and $\gamma = 0$. Once the check case is prepared, the same simulator is tuned to operate in fast time (real-time if the process is a control system or man-in-the-loop simulator) by setting the integration step size to $1/7\omega_i$,* and then the tuning parameters are adjusted to match the conditions of interest. If the parameters vary with a key dynamic variable, they are curve-fit to that variable. For example, if γ varies with Mach number, three tuned conditions permit $\gamma = a_0 + a_1 M + a_2 M^2$ to be determined and used to keep the simulator "in tune" as M varies. A similar procedure has been used on airline flight simulators where tuning parameters were changed discretely as the landing gear was raised or lowered and as the flaps were raised and lowered.

In many simulations, the objective is to match the dynamic characteristics of the simulator to the dynamic characteristics of the process being simulated. In this case, tuning the integrator to the system of equations being solved, so as to permit this "dynamics matching," is a process that was formerly done by substituting one integrator for another until a particular numerical integrator was found to work well. With *T* integration, it is a matter of adjusting the time shift and gain parameters which implicitly change the type of integration formula being used so as to better satisfy the mean value equation.

ACCURACY CONTROL WHEN THE INTEGRATION STEP SIZE IS FIXED

An approach to fixed interval accuracy control is to fix the integration step size and vary γ until integration with a single step with the *T* integrator matches the desired number of places achieved with a double step of *T* integration over the same interval. The heuristic argument that supports this type of adaptive *T* integration is to envision the output of the zero-order reconstruction as being a stairstep function. The objective is to center the stairstep approximation of the continuous integrand on the continuous integrand. If the stairstep function is "on the average" centered

---

*ω_i is the highest frequency of interest in the simulation—in hertz.

on the continuous integrand, then halving the integration step size or refining the quantization of the stairstep function will not substantially change the accuracy of.the integration process. If the stair step approximation to the continuous integrand is not fairly well centered on the true continuous integrand, halving the integration step size will substantially change the accuracy. Thus, by halving the integration step size and comparing the accuracy to n places with a single-step integration over the same interval (holding γ fixed), one can determine whether γ needs to be adjusted. If it does, the only problem is an ambiguity on the first calculation as to whether the stairstep integrand approximation leads or trails the true continuous integrand. Thus, a trial step of γ is made to determine whether the accuracy improves or degrades as the step is made. If the accuracy improves, it means the change in γ was in the right direction. If the accuracy degrades the change in γ was in the wrong direction and a double-back step is required to change γ in the right direction. Once the proper γ is found, the simulation is allowed to continue with large single steps for a while. Then γ is readjusted again. Of course the tests are done in a high-speed test loop while the large steps are taken at the fixed step size.

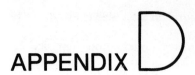
THE RELATIONSHIPS BETWEEN COMPUTER PROGRAMS, DIFFERENCE EQUATIONS, AND SIMULATION NUMERICAL STABILITY

Computer programs implement difference equations. Difference equations can be analyzed for stability and error propagation. It follows that computer programs can be so analyzed. When a computer program is developed intuitively without developing its companion difference equations, it is difficult to know the limits of a simulations fidelity, except by trial and error.

Let us see how a computer program can be understood and improved with only a little analysis. Consider the system shown in Figure D-1.

FIGURE D-1. A simple closed loop continuous process. Here x is a dependent variable — position, $\overset{\circ}{x}$ is its derivative in time, t is an independent variable — time, and f is a forcing function.

If we approximate $1/s$ with a numerical integrator, such as the Euler integrator

$$x_{n+1} = x_n + T\overset{\circ}{x}_n$$

we might develop the following computer program to implement and simulate the system.

```
000     LET T = T₀ ⎫
010     LET n = 0  ⎪
020     LET x1 = x₀ ⎬ INITIALIZATION
030     LET τ = τ₀  ⎪
040     LET f = f(0) ⎭
050     LET xD = (f − x1) / τ
060     TITLE: POSITION, VELOCITY, # of PASSES, TIME
070     PRINT: x1, xD, n, n * T
080     IF n > 100 THEN END
090     LET x1 = x1 + T * xD
100     LET n = n + 1
110     LET f = f(n * T)
120     GO TO 050
```

This computer program has the **Z** domain block diagram as shown in Figure D-2:

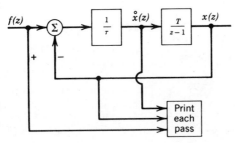

FIGURE D-2. A discrete process for simulating the system which is identical with the computer program 000 through 120.

Now compare the transfer function and describing equation for Figures D-1 and D-2

	Figure D-1	Figure D-2
Transfer function	$\dfrac{x(s)}{f(s)} = \dfrac{1}{\tau s + 1}$	$\dfrac{x(z)}{f(z)} = \dfrac{T/\tau}{z - (1 - T/\tau)}$
Describing equation	$\tau \dot{x} + x = f$	$x_{n+1} = (1 - T/\tau)x_n + (T/\tau)f_n$

Note that the difference equation for x_{n+1} produces identical numbers as the computer program for numerical integration. In fact, step 090 could be replaced with

$$090 \text{ LET } x1 = (1 - T/\tau)*x1 + (T/t)*f$$

and identical results would be achieved. If a complex high-order numerical integrator such as a Runga-Kutta sixth-order integrator, it would have been more efficient to use the difference equation instead of four iterative single steps.

Note that both the computer program and the continuous system are first-order systems with a single pole. The continuous system is stable for all $\tau \geq 0$. Not so with the computer program; it is stable only when

$$\left| \left(1 - \frac{T}{\tau} \right) \right| \leq 1$$

or when

$$0 \leq \frac{T}{\tau} \leq 2$$

further, the simulation is of highest fidelity when $T/\tau \ll 1$. In fact, for $T/\tau \geq 1$, the behavior of the computer program is quite unlike the behavior of the continuous process.

Finally, note that

$$e^{-T/\tau} = 1 - \frac{T/\tau}{1!} + \frac{(T/\tau)^2}{2!} + \frac{(T/\tau)^3}{3!} - \cdots \approx \left(1 - \frac{T}{\tau} \right) \quad \text{for small } T/\tau$$

and

$$1 - e^{-T/\tau} \approx \frac{T}{\tau}.$$

We can see that the difference equation and the computer program are approximations of the discrete system

$$\frac{x(z)}{f(z)} = \frac{1 - e^{-T/\tau}}{z - e^{-T/\tau}}$$

which is stable and accurate for all $T/\tau \geq 0$. Said differently, replacing the numerical integrator in step 090 in the computer program with the following code:

$$090 \text{ LET } x1 = e^{-T/\tau}x1 + (1 - e^{-T/\tau})f$$

will compute the exact response of the continuous system when $f = 0$ and will simulate the motion of the system's response to a non-zero forcing function f in an intrinsically stable manner. No step size T can make this difference equation go unstable. Only if τ is negative will this difference equation go unstable. It is required by Shannon's Theorem in information science that T be at most half the period of the highest frequency of interest in Fourier series approximation of f. Practical simulation experience shows that T must be at least $1/7$ to $1/10$ the period of the highest frequency of interest in f. If f is sinusoidal at frequency ω_n, then T should be on the order of

$$T \leq \frac{2\pi}{7\omega_n}$$

We see, then, that we have separated the numerical stability consideration from the accuracy (fidelity) with which we can faithfully reproduce the systems forcing function. From a theoretical point of view, this is the reason why the dynamics matching numerical methods developed in this book are so much easier to use, and produce so much better results, than classical numerical methods.

INDEX